Exploring the Spectrum of Autism and Pervasive Developmental Disorders

Intervention Strategies

Carolyn Murray-Slutsky, M.S., OTR
Betty A. Paris, PT

Therapy
Skill Builders®

A Harcourt Health Sciences Company

Reproducing Pages From This Book

As described below, some of the pages in this book may be reproduced for administrative and/or instructional use, not for resale. To protect your book, make a photocopy of each reproducible page. Then use that copy as a master for photocopying.

Library of Congress Cataloging-in-Publication Data

Murray-Slutsky, Carolyn, 1953–
    Exploring the spectrum of autism and pervasive developmental disorders
: intervention strategies / Carolyn Murray-Slutsky, Betty Paris.
        p. cm.
Includes bibliographical references and index.
    ISBN 0–7616–5500–X (pbk.)
1. Autism in children. 2. Developmental disabilities. I. Paris, Betty, 1952–   II. Title.
    RJ506.A9 M87 2000
    618.92'8982—dc21

                                                                00–008445

We dedicate this book to individuals with autism and the professionals who treat them.

Contents

CHAPTER 4
Behavioral Issues: Creating an Environment for Optimal Functioning 38

CHAPTER 5
Behavioral Issues: Treatment Strategies That Facilitate Positive Outcomes 46

CHAPTER 6
Behavioral Issues: Intervention Strategies 59

CHAPTER 7
Sensory Integration Theory and Treatment 80

CHAPTER 8 _____
Neuro-Developmental Theory and Its Integration Into Treatment 99

CHAPTER 9 _____
Sensory Modulation 107

CHAPTER 10 _____
Intervention Strategies for Sensory Modulation Disorders 125

CHAPTER 11
The Somatosensory System and Tactile Discrimination Disorders

CHAPTER 16 _____
Augmentative and Alternative Communication . .354

CHAPTER 17

The Importance of Play in Learning and Development 370

Figures

Tables

About the Authors

Carolyn Murray-Slutsky and **Betty Paris** are co-owners and directors of M P Rehabilitative Services, Inc., a multidisciplinary pediatric private practice located in North Miami Beach and Davie, Florida. With more than 30 therapists, the firm provides outpatient, home, and school therapy for Broward, Dade, and Palm Beach counties. They also contract with the Broward County School System, University of Miami Early Intervention Programs, Children's Home Society, and other programs.

Carolyn Murray-Slutsky received the M.S. degree in Occupational Therapy from Boston University. She received the B.S. degree in Education with a major in Special Education and teaching certificates in Educable Mental Retardation, Learning Disabilities, and Behavior Disorders from Ohio University, Athens. She is certified in the Sensory Integration and Praxis Test from Sensory Integration International. From the Neuro-Development Treatment Association, she holds the following certificates for advanced training: NDT in Pediatrics, NDT in the Treatment of Babies, and NDT for the Treatment of Adult Hemiplegia and Brain Injured.

Ms. Murray-Slutsky received the Manager of the Year award while serving as Director of Rehabilitation; and she received the 1999 Award of Excellence from the Florida Occupational Therapy Association for longstanding and significant contributions to her profession. Her professional affiliations include the American Congress of Rehabilitative Medicine, American Hippotherapy Association, American Occupational Therapy Association, Autism Society of America, Autism Society of Florida, Broward/Dade Occupational Therapy Forums, Center for Autism and Related Disorders, Florida Occupational Therapy Association, North American Riding for the Handicapped Association, Neuro-Developmental Treatment Association, and Sensory Integration International.

Betty Paris received the B.S. degree in Physical Therapy from Florida International University. She is certified in Sensory Integration and Praxis Test, NDT in Pediatrics, and NDT in the Treatment of Babies. Her professional affiliations include the American Physical Therapy Association, Florida Physical Therapy Association, Dade/Broward Physical Therapy Director's Forum, Neuro-Developmental Treatment Association, and Sensory Integration International. She has served on the advisory boards of several physical therapy programs.

Since graduating in 1977, both Carolyn Murray-Slutsky and Betty Paris have held administrative positions in various acute care and outpatient settings, and currently present workshops and seminars on a variety of topics throughout the United States. They are actively involved in community-based education, advocates for legislation and education for children with autism, and serve as consultants for universities, educators, therapists, and parent groups.

Contributors

Mary M. Murray, Ed.S.
Early Intervention Program Administrator
Lucas County Board of Mental Retardation and Developmental Disabilities
Toledo, Ohio

Robin Parker, M.S., CCC
Speech-Language Pathologist
Nova Southeastern University
Programs in Communication Sciences and Disorders
Davie, Florida

Carole Zangari, Ph.D., CCC-SLP
Coordinator of Research
Nova Southeastern University
Programs in Communication Sciences and Disorders
Fort Lauderdale, Florida

Preface

A psychologist arrived at the school to evaluate Jason's functional performance at school and make recommendations regarding his academic and behavioral needs. Three years previously, Jason had been diagnosed with severe autism and enrolled in a self-contained, low-functioning classroom for students with autism. Now he was enrolled in a regular first grade classroom. The psychologist observed the children for 15 minutes and could not identify Jason from his peers. He was amazed when the teacher identified Jason. The psychologist completed his assessment and declared that Jason was a happy, well-adjusted youngster who was functioning at or above age level. After consulting with the teacher, the psychologist arrived at the conclusion that no recommendations were needed; Jason was one of the top performers in the classroom.

Jason has progressed from being labeled as severely autistic with foretold needs for institutionalization, to being a well-adjusted, high-functioning, happy individual who is capable of being an integral participant in school and community events, learning and developing along with his peers. He is one of many children who have made dramatic transformations in their cognitive, social, communicative, behavioral, and academic functioning as a result of the techniques outlined in this manual.

Children with autistic spectrum disorders demonstrate a variety of confusing behaviors and mannerisms. When looking at these children holistically and examining the interrelationship between their behaviors, sensory processing, motor control, speech-language, and functional skills, we may start to untangle the confusion and better understand what we see. It is only after we understand what we are seeing that we can develop an intervention strategy.

This book is designed to provide such a holistic view of autistic spectrum disorders. We will identify common problems encountered and discuss intervention strategies for occupational, physical, and speech-language therapists. The contents of this book are intended for entry level and advanced professionals who either use sensory integrative (SI) and neuro-developmental treatment (NDT) techniques in their setting or are interested in learning more about these strategies.

Information presented in the book uses a "layering" method; that is, a concept is introduced in general terms, then gradual layers of explanation are given until the concept is explained in its full detail. As the chapters progress, the individual concepts gradually build upon one other.

While the book is written for occupational, physical, and speech-language therapists, parents and other professionals also can glean valuable information about autistic spectrum disorders and appropriate intervention strategies.

Treatment techniques outlined throughout this book are designed to change the child's central processing. The techniques are based on SI and NDT concepts and on speech-language and behavioral intervention strategies. These techniques are meant to be implemented or supervised by occupational, physical, and speech-language therapists who have training in both SI and NDT treatment concepts in addition to their basic training in biomechanics, movement sciences, anatomical and physiological precepts, and the development of functional skills.

Intervention strategies for the child with autistic spectrum disorders requires an integrated, holistic approach. Because we believe this, the information in this book is not divided among professions. Role delineation must be based on the therapists' skill and training, the child's needs, the setting in which the therapists work, and subsequent restrictions placed upon them. Overlap between professions should be expected. For example, in a child with a tactile discrimination disorder who displayed gross motor, fine motor, and oral motor problems and who is treated by a single specialist (such as an occupational therapist with training in both NDT and SI), the therapist would be qualified to treat the underlying problems. However, if the work setting and financial parameters allow, the child might best be served by being treated by a physical therapist for gross motor deficiencies; a speech therapist for oral motor and language and communication-related problems; and an occupational therapist for sensorimotor, fine motor, and oral motor problems.

The intervention strategies and philosophies presented within this book have evolved since the early 1980s when we took our sensory integration certification courses, the eight-week neuro-developmental training course, and the four-week NDT baby course. These provided the basis from which we researched and developed our work. We modified it based on the results we have seen in the clinic.

These treatment strategies and philosophies were further researched as we presented them in various training workshops over the past ten years:

> *Integrating NDT and SI*, a hands-on treatment techniques workshop, forced us to tease out and explain specific treatment techniques and how they could be varied and made more aggressive through integrating NDT into SI (or vice versa).
>
> *Pediatric Splinting Techniques*, a hands-on treatment workshop, forced us to look at the development, structure, and function of the hand and foot. We studied how motor control develops, the factors in development that can alter normal development, and intervention strategies to remediate abnormal motor development.
>
> *Autism, PDD, and Related Disorders*, a workshop addressing intervention strategies for occupational therapists, forced us to analyze children with these disorders, isolate the factors that attributed to the highest improvement and success rates, and research the rationale and neurological principles underlying them. It allowed us to talk to practitioners nationally and work with them to answer many questions.

This book is based on our successes in the clinic and the confirmation we have received from parents, physicians, neurologists, teachers, and behavioralists who reported the differences they have seen in the children following these techniques. The book also incorporates feedback from occupational, physical, and speech therapists who have attended our workshops or have been trained in our clinic.

This is not a cookbook. There are no recipes for the treatment of autistic spectrum disorders. However, when a therapist uses sound clinical judgment in guiding the problem analysis and intervention strategies, astonishing progress can be made.

Acknowledgments

We would like to express our gratitude to all the people who helped to make this book possible; especially:

—The parents of the children we treat. Your unending energy and drive to help your children has been an inspiring and compelling force behind us. You have allowed us into your lives, educated and enlightened us regarding your trials and tribulations, successes and failures, and have let us share your lives through this book. Thank you for trusting us with your children's lives, for your encouragement to write this book, and for believing that we do make a difference.

—The children that we treat. We are honored that you give us your trust, allow us into your world, and share with us glimpses of the world as you see and experience it. Thank you also for allowing us to help you experience *our* world, to share with you the pleasures we feel and see, and to celebrate your triumphs.

—The practitioners and professionals in the field. We thank the therapists who have worked for us and with us for the past twenty years, as well as all of the participants in our workshops. You have spurred our drive to find the answers through your questions asked, your genuine interest in helping your clients, your sharing of information from all over the world, and desire to work with us to analyze the problems. Your questions have helped us to identify the problems facing us, forced us to research the answers, crystalized our theories and beliefs, and defined our treatment techniques. Your feedback on the effectiveness of our techniques and philosophies, of how quickly you saw changes, and your encouragement to put those theories and beliefs in print has been a driving force behind this book. Thank you, and all the teachers, educational specialists, behavioralists, neurologists, and physicians who saw the difference in our intervention strategies and the functional, objective improvements in our children and encouraged us to continue teaching others.

—Southpaw Enterprises® for the support and promotion of sensory integration. Thank you for your dedication to our profession and our clients.

—The American Occupational Therapy Association for believing in us and giving us the opportunity to teach therapists throughout the United States.

—Our own families. Thank you for tolerating our never-ending quest for knowledge and our search for the answers.

Thanks also:

—To Herman, for your endless admiration and belief in us as individuals and as professionals. It is your strong drive, your belief that we are making important changes in the lives of the children and families we treat, and your endless help and support that enabled us to complete this and so many other projects.

—To Steve, for your strength, understanding, tolerance, and encouragement over the years. Thank you for your technical assistance in this and other endeavors, and your commitment to our family.

—To David, Stephanie, and Jerry, for your unfaltering love and assistance with the typing, photographs, and always, your help at the clinic.

—To Mom and Dad, for always being there for us, for your constant assistance, and for instilling your life values and fostering, nurturing, and sharing your beliefs and ours.

Without your sacrifices, support, assistance, and—most of all—love, this book would not have been possible.

CHAPTER 1

What Is Autism? How Is It Diagnosed?

Betty Paris

Autism is a behaviorally based disorder described in The American Psychiatric Association's 1994 publication, *The Diagnostic and Statistical Manual of Mental Disorders, Fourth Edition* (DSM—IV). It is a spectrum disorder with wide variances in expression, ranging from the very severely involved to those who appear only mildly affected or nearly normal. Many conditions or syndromes fall under the spectrum. Some conditions have characteristics in common, and others have characteristics unique to only a particular disorder. In general, however, autism is characterized by impairments in social interactions; delays or impairments in both verbal and nonverbal communication; by repetitive or stereotyped patterns of behavior, interest, and activities; and by a lack of or abnormal symbolic or imaginative play. Autism can exist with any other condition. It crosses all racial, ethnic, and social boundaries. It occurs four times more often in boys than in girls.

Classic autism, defined as *early infantile autism* by Dr. Leo Kanner in 1943, is currently defined as a severely incapacitating lifelong developmental disability that typically appears during the first three years of life (Autism Society of America, Home Page). Estimates of the numbers of cases of autism vary from source to source. Incidences ranging from 2 to 5 in 10,000 births (see References: Criteria for DSM—IV Classifications) to between 11 to 15 in 10,000 (Autism Society of America, Home Page) and up are not uncommon. The disparities in these numbers are not so well explained. We do know that autism was originally believed to be a psychiatric disorder, but now is viewed as a spectrum of disorders with similar symptomologies and neuropathological bases that stem from a variety of etiologies.

No two persons who have autism will behave in quite the same way. Children with autism may meet normal developmental milestones, then seem to stop. They may begin to speak, and then stop speaking; or they may fail to develop any communication strategies at all. Some have very good gross motor skills, while others have a limited number of movements that they perform repetitively. Still others may learn to read at a very early age, but be unable to initiate and sustain a conversation. This makes the diagnosis of autism more difficult.

Several autism-related disorders are grouped under the broad category of *pervasive developmental disorder* (PDD) within the DSM—IV. These include autism, PDDNOS (pervasive developmental disorder not otherwise specified), Asperger's syndrome, and Rett's syndrome. The diagnosis of autism is made when the child exhibits at least two of the characteristics listed under the DSM—IV criteria of impaired social interactions; one of the characteristics in social communication criteria; and one under the criteria of restricted, repetitive, and stereotyped patterns of behavior, interests, and activities. In addition, the disorder must be present prior to the age of three and cannot be better defined by other diagnoses. If a child has fewer than the required number of symptoms or criteria required for the diagnosis of autism, a diagnosis of PDDNOS may be made. Asperger's syndrome and Rett's syndrome are further delineated by the DSM—IV. For discussion of these disorders, see page 3.

Other tools may be used in diagnosis. These include the *Checklist for Autism in Toddlers* (CHAT) (Baron-Cohen et al. 1992), the *Childhood Autism Rating Scale* (CARS) developed at TEACCH (Treatment and Education of Autistic and Related Communication Handicapped Children, University of North Carolina) (Schopler et al. 1980), and the *Gilliam Autism Rating Scale* (GARS) (Gilliam 1995).

Finally, diagnosing autism can be complicated further by the fact that autism can coexist with any other conditions.

Criteria for Autistic Disorder

For a diagnosis of autistic disorder to be made, a total of six or more items are required from the following list. At least two from column A and one each from columns B and C are required. These symptoms, whether in part or all, must be present prior to age 3 and cannot be better accounted for by Rett's syndrome or Childhood Disintegrative Disorder.

Pervasive Developmental Disorder Not Otherwise Specified (PDDNOS)

This diagnosis is used when there is a severe and pervasive impairment in the development of reciprocal social interaction or verbal and nonverbal communications skills; or when stereotyped behavior, interests, and activities are present but do not meet the DSM—IV criteria for other disorders such as schizophrenia, schizotypal personality disorder, or avoidance personality disorder. This diagnosis is used when the presentations also do not meet the criteria for autistic disorder because of onset after the age of three years, atypical presentations or characteristics, or because the child has fewer than the specified number of symptoms for autistic disorder.

For specific diagnostic criteria on any of the disorders, see DSM—IV (American Psychiatric Association 1994). See also, *Autism Treatment Guide* (Gerlach 1996); and the *Merck Manual* (Merck and Co. 1996–97).

Asperger's Syndrome

This disorder was originally described by Hans Asperger, a Viennese pediatrician, and termed *autistic psychopathy*. Dr. Lorna Wing, the first person to use the term *Asperger's syndrome* (Wing 1981), attempted to explain the children who presented classic autistic features when very young, but later developed fluent speech and a desire to socialize. Wing described the primary clinical features of Asperger's syndrome as a lack of empathy; naivete; inappropriate, one-sided interaction; little or no ability to form friendships; pedantic, repetitive speech; poor nonverbal communication; intense absorption in certain subjects; and clumsy and ill-coordinated movements and odd postures.

Subsequent descriptions include coordination deficits, monotonic voice quality, repetitive speech patterns, depression, difficulty tolerating change, a liking of routine and ritualistic behaviors, and the inability to relate to people normally. Most of the individuals exhibiting these characteristics have IQ scores in the normal range. According to the DSM—IV, a diagnosis of Asperger's syndrome can be made when two criteria from column A and one from column B (see Table 1.1) are present. The disorder must cause significant impairment in social, occupational, or other important areas of function, and must not demonstrate delays in the development of verbal skills. The child with Asperger's uses single words by 2 years and phrases by 3 years of age.

Cognitive, self-help skills and adaptive behaviors other than in social interactions also develop at normal rates. The diagnosis cannot be given if the criteria are met for any other specific Pervasive Developmental Disorder or for Schizophrenia.

Rett's Syndrome

Rett's syndrome differs from autistic disorder in its characteristic sex ratios and pattern of deficits. It is seen only in girls (whereas autism is seen in girls, but is four times more prevalent in boys).

There is a characteristic pattern of head-growth deceleration. The symptoms include a loss of speech, loss of previously acquired voluntary use of the hands, presence of hand-wringing movements, and eating problems secondary to facial weakness. There is a severe and progressive dementia. Seizures usually develop between 2 and 4 years of age. There are periods of apnea and diffuse perspiration. A spastic quadriparesis or paraparesis evolves. Pathology studies reveal diffuse cerebral atrophy with neuronal cell loss and degeneration of axons in the peripheral nerves (see References, Pediatric Database).

TABLE 1.1   Criteria for autistic disorder

A	B	C
Abnormal or impaired social interactions	Impairments in social communication	Restricted, repetitive, and stereotyped patterns of behavior, interest, and activities
A lack of eye contact	Delays or lack of development of spoken language. There must be no attempt to compensate with alternative modes of communication	An abnormal preoccupation with one or more stereotyped and restricted patterns of interest (abnormal in intensity or focus)
Flat or masked facial expression Abnormal or atypical body postures Lack of the use of gestures to regulate social interaction		
Failure to develop peer relationships	In verbal children, impairment in the ability to initiate or sustain conversation with others	Inflexible adherence to specific, nonfunctional routines or rituals
Lack of sharing interests or achievements with other people (by showing, pointing out objects of interest to other people)	Stereotyped/reciprocal use of language or peculiar language	Stereotyped and repetitive motor mannerisms
Lack of social or emotional reciprocation; a lack of social play; preference of solitary activities; asocial behavior	Lack of variety in make-believe play or social imitation	Persistent preoccupation with parts of objects

Adapted with permission from the *Diagnostic and Statistical Manual of Mental Disorders, Fourth Edition (DSM—IV)*, Criteria for Autistic Disorder. Copyright © 1994 American Psychiatric Association.

Other Disorders With Autistic-Like Symptoms

Childhood Disintegrative Disorder (Heller's Syndrome)

Childhood disintegrative disorder (also known as Heller's syndrome) is a condition characterized by deterioration over several months of cognitive, social, and language functioning from previously normal functioning. Frequently lost are social skills, bowel and bladder control, expressive or receptive language, motor skills, and play skills. Children with this condition exhibit a failure to develop peer relationships, impairment of nonverbal behavior, and an inability to initiate or sustain a conversation. The disorder occurs usually between the third and fourth years of life. It has been linked to neurological conditions such as seizures and tuberous sclerosis.

Fragile-X Syndrome (Martin-Bell Syndrome)

Fragile-X syndrome (also known as Martin-Bell syndrome) is a genetic condition in which blood tests reveal a constriction on the long arm of the X chromosome. It affects 1 in 1,000 males and 1 in 2,000 females. Most have mild to moderate mental retardation, repetitive motor behaviors, hypersensitivity to sound, impairments in verbal and nonverbal communication, and cognitive processing problems. Delay in speech and language development often is the first indicator of a problem. This includes jargon or unintelligible syllables strung together, perseveration (the inappropriate repetition of words or phrases), or echoing of words (echolalia). Children with this condition are noted to have poor sensory perception and integration of information, and behavioral problems such as hyperactivity. Their physical features may include a long, narrow face and prominent ears.

Landau-Kleffner Syndrome

Children with this diagnosis develop normally for the first 3 to 7 years and then experience a rapid loss of language skills. These children often are misdiagnosed as being deaf. EEG readings during sleep are used to determine whether or not an individual has Landau-Kleffner syndrome. Behaviors include attention deficits, insensitivity to pain, echolalia speech patterns, and impaired motor skills.

Mobius Syndrome

This is a rare genetic disorder characterized by facial paralysis. It is caused by the absence of or failure of cranial nerves VI and VII to develop. Involvement of the Abducen's or cranial nerve VI affects eye movements and often leads problems with vision due to inability to control eye movements. Strabismus (crossed eyes) is common, as is eye sensitivity. Involvement of cranial nerve VII affects the facial nerve, and speech difficulties will evolve. Symptoms include inability to suck, excessive drooling, lack of facial expression, inability to smile, and high or cleft palate. There may be problems in feeding, swallowing, and choking. Other deformities affect the tongue, jaw, and limbs (for example, club foot deformity or webbed digits). Mental retardation may be present. Behavioral problems like those associated with autism also are seen.

Sotos Syndrome (Cerebral Gigantism)

Sotos syndrome (also known as cerebral gigantism) causes accelerated growth during the first five years, an enlargement of the skull, facial abnormalities, and often mental retardation. It is a known genetic condition accompanied by high, arched palate, poor suck, and delays in motor cognitive and social development. Muscle tone is low. Autistic symptoms include echolalia, head banging, aggression, obsessions, adherence to routines, twirling, and spinning, and impaired social interaction skills. Speech is markedly impaired; but in the early years, receptive language tends to be more advanced than expressive language. Physical features include head circumference documented above the 98th percentile, with tall, narrow skull, wide-set, downward-slanting eyes, a flat-bridged nose, thin hair, early eruption of teeth (as early as 3 months), pointed chin, prominent forehead, and a receding hairline. Children with Sotos syndrome are often larger and appear to be older than their peers, but act younger. Late in childhood, muscle tone tends to improve, as do speech patterns. These children develop borderline average intelligence with learning deficits, but develop at widely differing rates.

Tourette Syndrome

This disorder is characterized by involuntary tics such as eye blinking, shrugging, lip smacking, grunting, and cursing. Anxiety attacks and a short attention span are often present. The symptoms generally appear before 18 years of age. The disorder crosses ethnic barriers and is three to four times more prevalent in boys than in girls.

Williams Syndrome

This is a rare disorder in which the features are often described as "elf-like." The nose is small and upturned, the distance between the nose and upper lip is elongated, the mouth appears wide with full lips, the area around the eyes is puffy, and the chin is small. Symptoms include developmental delays in language and gross motor skills, hypersensitivity to sounds, obsession, perseveration with objects, and rocking behavior.

Schizophrenia

At one time, professionals thought that infantile autism and childhood schizophrenia were two forms of the same disorder, but they no longer believe this is so. A differential diagnosis must rule out schizophrenia which, with childhood onset, develops after years of normal or near-normal development. Characteristic features of schizophrenia are an active phase of prominent delusions or hallucinations that last for at least one month. Disordered speech patterns are common, particularly in which the child strays from the topic.

What Causes Autistic Spectrum Disorders?

What was once considered a psychiatric disorder is now being looked at from a medical prospective. However, although much is known about autism-spectrum disorders, the etiologies of the syndrome of autism continue to perplex the practitioner because there has been no consistently identified cause or risk factor.

Twin and sibling studies have yielded some evidence for a genetic link. It was reported in the January 11, 1998, edition of the *Sunday Times* that British researchers have identified the location of a group of genes that are believed responsible for autism. Viral causes also have been investigated. Cytomegalovirus (Stubbs 1978; Stubbs et al. 1984; Markowitz 1983), rubella (Chess 1971; Chess 1977), and herpes simplex (Gillberg 1986; Greer et al. 1989) have been cited. (See also Ritvo et al. 1990.)

Serotonin activity has been cited as a possible factor, but elevated serotonin levels are not diagnostic of Autism. Magnetic Resonance Imaging (MRI) and Positron Emission Tomography (PET) studies have demonstrated evidence of abnormalities in the structure of the cerebellum in some cases, but no specific pattern has been consistently identified. Additionally, the high incidence of epilepsy and abnormal electroencephalograms (EEG), which are common even in the absence of a seizure disorder, are evidence of a neurological cause. Immune-mediated causes also are being investigated.

The answer simply may be that anything that can cause a structural or functional change or damage within the central nervous system also can potentially cause an autistic-spectrum disorder.

CHAPTER 2

Characteristics of Autism

Betty Paris

The parents of a young child come to the clinic seeking help. Their beautiful youngster was beginning to speak, but now he is showing delays in using and acquiring speech. He doesn't appear to be aware of or take an interest in the people and events around him. He always is rocking back and forth, whether sitting or standing. He flaps his hands and fingers and walks on his toes much of the time. He also has a peculiar and unrelenting preoccupation with spinning the wheels on his toy cars, and he can spend much of the day lining up the cars in fastidious fashion, growing upset and exhibiting tantrum behavior if someone interrupts the alignment. The parents describe their son as being a difficult child to raise. He cries over nothing, uses tantrums to get his way, and sometimes appears unaware when they speak to him. At other times he seems to crave being hugged to the point of being crushed. His parents worry over his lack of interest in other children. The parents are confused and frustrated, and they seek information and help.

The "qualitative impairments in social interaction," as described in the DSM—IV criteria used for diagnosis of autism, may appear different at various times in the child's development. For example, a failure to develop peer relationships may take different forms at different ages. Babies may appear aloof and detached; young children may demonstrate little or no recognition of others, never mind an interest in establishing friendships; and older children sometimes may seem devoid of emotion and socially detached.

Although the diagnosis of autism or autistic spectrum disorder usually is not made before the age of 18 to 24 months, mothers of young babies say they know that "something is not quite right" with their child. They report that their babies look to them only for the provision of nourishment or simply to meet their physical needs. Both the mothers and fathers report reaching for their children with love, and feeling rebuffed when the children do not reciprocate. The babies may not appear to recognize or respond to the voices of their parents. They may fail to cuddle, seeming to have an aversion to affection or physical contact. Parents feel burdened with the care of these children when they get none of the positive feedback normally attached to developing infants. Some infants cry incessantly, seeming inconsolable. No matter what the parents try, it all seems to fail; nothing they do is rewarded. Both the children and the parents suffer from sleep deprivation, irritability, and frustration. Bonding is tenuous at best.

As young children, these individuals cannot engage their peers; furthermore, they have no interest in doing so. They steadfastly avoid eye contact when approached. They do not join in playgroups with their peers, and often they are shunned or made the victims of the cruelties of other youngsters. They seem odd or out of place in social situations, incapable of expressing any emotional response to a peer's predicament. They often prefer adult exchanges, engaging the adult in a series of ritualized, one-sided questions, with no particular interest in the answers. They may have better success interacting with adults, because adults tend to be better at decoding their wants and needs than are their peers, despite the quality of the interactions.

Older children may exhibit an interest in friendship, but fail to understand the conventions of social interaction. They lack an understanding of social boundaries and a respect for personal space. They violate the etiquette of reciprocal interactions, frequently interrupting conversations with a question or statement that is unrelated to the topic. Often they are blunt in their observations and statements, offending or driving others away, totally unaware that they have done so. They may use others as *tools* to obtain something or to get a job done, but not for social relationships; or they may prefer solitary activities. They may have a strong need for routine and resort to inappropriate, angry outbursts when routines are broken.

Individuals with autism have many problems in not only speech and language, but in their nonverbal communication. Many children, although able to speak, may never develop the ability to communicate effectively either verbally or nonverbally. Mute children who are not autistic use gesture, facial expression, pictures, sign language, and any other means to get their point across. However, this is not true in children with autism. There appears in some to be a basic void in the inherent capacity to communicate.

Moreover, even in people with autism who have relatively normal language development, there are many conflicting and confusing presentations. They may repeat everything that is said, but never use their words to request things. They may constantly repeat a string of ritualized questions, and yet have great difficulty in initiating conversations and volunteering information. Often they lack pragmatic language, the language used in a social context. Their vocal pitch, intonation, rate, and rhythm may be abnormal, often monotonic or robotic. Grammatical structure often is immature and characterized by repetitive phrases that are not contiguous with the topic of discussion or even relevant to it. These individuals may not use personal pronouns such as *I* or *me*, but may refer to themselves by name. Other striking disparities in their performance may be present. It is not unusual for children with autism to learn to read very early, some by the age of three; exhibit complex math skills well above their age level; or have seemingly advanced expressive capabilities, but not be able to follow simple verbal commands or directions. They may use language (words) at a higher level of development than their comprehension. This may confuse adults and lead them to assume that a child's lack of compliance is willful disobedience and a behavioral issue.

Seemingly unreasonable patterns of behavior may stem from these individuals' need for rituals and other sensory-based characteristics. They have no tolerance for variations.

> Erin, a 5-year-old with autism, had an unwavering fascination and obsession with the heroine of her favorite movie, Aladdin. She would go nowhere unless she was allowed to wear her quilted, golden slippers. She carried her Jasmine purse filled with ten Jasmine figurines. Under her Jasmine-styled dress, she wore her Jasmine T-shirt, Jasmine shorts, and Jasmine underwear. Her mother had to wash the clothing items daily, because Erin would not tolerate wearing any other items. She wore the attire until it quite literally fell apart. The articles had to be replaced until she became obsessed with a new film and heroine.

Repetitive motor movements may include hand clapping, finger flicking, whole-body rocking, and jumping in place. Parents grow frustrated at attempting to extinguish these behaviors that seem to occur whenever the child is disengaged from structured activity. Even more distressing are the self-aggressive behaviors of head banging, self-slapping, hand biting, and scratching or pinching the skin until it is broken.

Children with autism have difficulty in transitioning between activities. Once engaged in an activity, they are unwilling to cease that activity to move onto another. They appear to view the interruption as a violation or intrusion, and often respond by having a tantrum, screaming out in frustration to voice their distress and refute the need for change. Some children become aggressive; they have learned that this is the only way they will be afforded a choice on the matter.

They may be fascinated or overfocused on parts of objects, as in the case of the youngster who spins the wheels on a toy rather than playing with the entire toy or the baby who plays with only one object on a crib toy that has seven or eight selections. Older children may display fascination with mechanical objects such as a tape players, video games, vacuum cleaners, tools, and computers.

Imaginative play often is absent or very impaired. If it does develop, it may occur only out of context or robotically. The child cannot vary play. For example, typical children, when given access to a swing made of a strap of rubber material suspended between two chains, need no prompting to vary the way they play on that swing. They might sit on the swing, straddle it, lie on their abdomens, or stand on it. They may propel the swing forward and back, side to side, or spin on it. In contrast, children with autism will sit on the swing and will not tolerate alterations in their orientation and direction of sitting, of the movement of the swing, of slowing or stopping, or of other play activities involving the swing.

These children are unable to engage in games of pretend. They function in the literal context and cannot conceive that there is an imagined toy or item there to play with. In part, this characteristic may be secondary to a lack of comprehension from a language standpoint. If the ability to label items is lacking, symbolic play is difficult. Object permanence—the knowledge that an item exists even when it can't be seen—also may be limited. Lacking the knowledge that an imagined item exists, the child can't very well use it in play. The concept of an imagined toy or context is simply too abstract.

In summary, people with autism are a study in dualism. They may appear hyperactive with short attention spans, and yet engage in all-consuming fascinations. They may be aggressive or self-injurious, yet crave human touch. They may suffer violent, prolonged temper tantrums that abruptly cease and are replaced with a quiet air of contentment or total detachment from surrounding people and things.

Those with autism have been referred to as *asocial* rather than antisocial. The fact is, they are capable of relating to others and enjoying successful interactions. They are angered and frustrated by unsuccessful interactions. They don't always understand how and why things went wrong, and often they lack the communicative skills to explain and negotiate a more appropriate outcome. They do make eye contact, albeit fleetingly. They do like physical contact if it is presented in the correct form and for the correct amount of time that they can tolerate. They demonstrate emotions; and, like others, they respond to people and things around them. They have likes and dislikes in their environments, activities, and the people they deal with. They simply don't know the conventional methods in which to interpret and respond; they tend to relate in atypical ways or demonstrate wide fluctuations in responses. Because *they* are unconventional, *we* are not always successful in interpreting their needs and wants or their reactions. And because we do not understand and cannot accurately interpret them, we may feel uncomfortable and inadequate around them.

A Need to Function

Although individual motivations and interests may vary, all people have a fundamental need to function within their environments. To function efficiently and successfully, we need to make sense of our world and the messages we receive from it. We also need to know how to relate to the people and things in it. This involves sensory perception and processing, the cognitive skills to plan and perform, and successful interactions with people and things.

Those with autism are hampered in their attempts to function on many different levels.

- Sensory impairments have an impact on their perceptions of the world around them.

- Their levels of attention and arousal are less than optimal, affecting their learning and performance levels.

- The way they learn and store information is different, and therefore their cognitive functioning is different.

- Motor functioning impairments affect their abilities to perform activities.

- They have a limited repertoire of coping skills, thus setting the stage for the development of undesirable or nonproductive behaviors.

Many other peculiar or puzzling behaviors and characteristics are the subject of much conjecture. Researchers and people working with children and adults with autism have proposed many different theories to explain these behaviors. Let's look at a few examples that may help explain those theories.

All smiles, Michael came into the clinic for therapy. He wanted to play in the net swing, an activity he had performed many times before with his therapist—but this time he wanted to do it himself. He tried to climb into the net, but tactile defensiveness made it difficult to tolerate the touch of the net on his bare shoulders. He carefully pulled at the net strings, able to tolerate pinching it rather than spreading the net with his hands and arms. He managed to stick his head and the tips of his shoulders into the net, but that didn't produce enough force for Michael to be able to swing. He quickly grew frustrated and lost interest.

Nothing seems to bother "Sweet Will," a 4-year-old with low muscle tone. He has been described as a "slow poke," always the last to get up from his seat and dragging behind in the lines in school. He constantly is being prodded to move along. He acts as if he has no idea of what is expected or anticipated, but is happy enough to go along. No matter how the school staff tries to keep him clean, Will always appears to be disheveled. His shoelaces become untied and he trips, his shorts are always twisted, he drools and his shirt is wet. Yet he never fusses, never complains—not even when stung by a bee!

Kim, 2½ years old, was continuously afraid in her surroundings. Everything and everyone posed a threat. She couldn't make sense of her world and didn't have the words or gestures to ask for help. When she was not clinging to her mother for comfort, she wandered aimlessly, unable to select or engage in any activity. Trying to win her over, the therapists gave her a toy with lights and whistles that moved in different directions. Kim was oblivious to the toy; she didn't appear to see or hear it. She acted as if the toy didn't exist.

Jeremy is a 7-year-old who is able to function in a highly structured classroom with a 3:1 student-to-teacher ratio. There are nine children in his classroom. One day, when some children were vocalizing and banging toys, Jeremy's teacher was working with him and his partner to perform discrete trials, a task they practice daily. Jeremy appeared to comply, and the teacher praised his successful attempts. Suddenly, Jeremy flew out of control, slapped the teacher, pushed over the room divider separating his cubicle from the next, and raced out of the room.

Sensory Processing Issues

When sensory information is received in various areas within the brain, it is matched against all other information stored from previous experiences. In normally functioning systems, the brain then computes whether to attend to the information and react, or to suppress the information and consider it not in need of a response. This occurs in both conscious and subconscious levels and enables us to decide whether to allocate attention to a person, task, or event.

Sensory registration is a process that occurs on a subconscious level within the brain. It enables us to recognize changes within our environment and turn to the stimulus or make some other type of observable reaction to it. This reaction is known as the *orienting* response. Because individuals with autism have impaired sensory systems, they fail to react or to register changes and things in their environment. Kim failed to register the toy in her environment. For her, it didn't exist. Will fails to register that he is drooling and makes no attempt to wipe his face. He doesn't notice that his shoelace is untied. He doesn't even feel the pain of an insect bite! Because he fails to register these occurrences, he makes no attempt to remedy them or to react.

Gold and Gold (1975) speculated that the lack of the orienting response is due to a failure of the basic ability to analyze incoming sensory input. They speculated that:

- Either the incoming sensory input is perceived as abnormal and insignificant, and therefore does not trigger a response; or

- The message to disregard the stimulus is sent. The areas of the brain responsible for alerting and attentional mechanisms are told to disregard the stimulus.

Ayres (1979) also discussed the lack of or inconsistent orienting response in children with autism. She referred such a child's "registration" function as capricious, citing that the brain may decide to register a sensory input one day, but not register something similar another day. If a child doesn't register something, how can he orient to it?

If the thermostat on an air-conditioning system is set too high, the system will not register enough of a change between the air temperature and the desired response level set. The net result is that the air-conditioning system does not respond. Similarly, in children with hyporesponsive systems, sensory stimuli such as tactile, auditory, proprioceptive, and vestibular input may not register unless they are magnified in intensity. Children, who cannot feel their touch on certain objects, may press too hard or break those objects. If they cannot perceive or register auditory input, they will appear not to hear or tune out. If they cannot perceive the information that their muscles and joints are sending to their brains, they may not know where their arms or legs are in space or how to use them in a coordinated fashion. Their arm or leg placements may be awkward, their ability to sit in a chair impaired, and they will appear to be uncoordinated or clumsy. If they do not register changes in their vestibular system, their balance will be unreliable and their movements restricted. Both Kim and Will are examples of children with hyporesponsive systems. Kim failed to register and react to her environment. She was unable to select a toy or activity from the milieu of the clinic, and she didn't know what to do. Fearing movement of any kind, she clung to her mother for support and reassurance, relying on her mother to cope with the environment for her. Will's hyporesponsivity is inherent in his slowpoke approach. He is poorly aware of his body and how to move it. He fails to register when his clothing is askew. His movements are clumsy and uncoordinated.

Hyporesponsive children also may present as overactive children. Because their systems fail to respond to various sensory stimuli, they charge ahead, crashing into objects, remaining in constant motion because they lack the balance to stay in one place and seeking interactions within the environment that will register. These children play too hard with toys and peers, and often they break things or hurt other children when their play is too rough.

Ayres (1979) also described the hyperresponsive system in which the system may overreact to stimuli. She described intolerance of movement (the result of a hyperreactive response to vestibular input), tactile defensiveness (the result of overreaction to tactile stimuli), and auditory hypersensitivity as examples of hyperresponsive systems. Later, Ayres and Tickle (1980) developed the theory that the children, who have inconsistent responses to sensory input, actually may have a modulation disorder in which response to sensory input may be hyporesponsive at times and then quickly revert to hyperresponsiveness. Knickerbocker (1980) proposed that the oral defensiveness often seen in these children may be another example of a sensory system that is not only hyperresponsive to oral input, but lacking in the ability to modulate the sensory input bombarding it. Michael's tactile defensiveness hampers his ability to function. He cannot tolerate touching the net swing or having it touch his head, arms, or body. Therefore, he doesn't swing. Jeremy has a modulation disorder. He is unable to regulate his system within the noisy classroom in order to perform. The auditory stimulation, coupled with the demands from the various teachers and children in his classroom, gradually summate or mount to the point where he explodes, tearing out of his cubicle, slapping the teacher, and running from the room in an effort to escape his surroundings. Once calmed, he is able to return and try again.

Lovaas and colleagues (1971) addressed one possible explanation for the overfocusing seen in this population. He proposed that these children may fail to manage multiple stimuli in their environment, rather than fail within a particular system. When children with autism are presented with multiple stimuli, they tend to overfocus on one mode of sensory input rather than integrate all of the presenting stimuli. Overfocusing on objects also might explain the lack of orienting to other stimuli. In a system unable to manage multiple stimuli, might overfocusing be a coping strategy to effectively block out overwhelming amounts of stimulation? If the stimuli are effectively blocked, registration may occur on an unconscious level, but an observable reaction or orienting response to the stimuli will be lacking.

Both Becker (1980) and Ayres (1979) felt that there may be a failure to determine what stimulus is important. This process takes place at multiple levels within the area of the brain known as the limbic system, depending upon the complexity and type of the stimulus. Normal limbic-system processing enables us to give appropriate attention and orientation to the presenting stimulus, and enables us *not* to orient to irrelevant stimuli. Could this be Kim's problem? She did not appear to see or hear the toy; yet, we know from her reactions at other times that she has no visual or hearing problems. What would make her fail to register the toy in her environment? Will, too, doesn't appear to determine which stimulus is important. Although compliant, he requires assistance to realize that his shoelaces are untied and this will cause him to trip. Does he fail to feel that his nose is running, or is it simply not important to him?

Rimland (1965) theorized that the lack of responses to environmental input seen in children with autism was due to a deficit in perceptual capacity. He proposed that the problems may lie in the reticular formation, an area of the brain known to be involved with the ability to prepare for a response in advance of a presenting stimulus.

 ## Attention and Arousal

A calm-alert state is a *window* in which our ability to function is maximized. In this state, we have a balance between the ability to attend to a stimulus or a task, and the level of arousal within our brains and bodies to prepare us to respond. We all need a certain amount of stress or stimulation to bring our levels of attention and arousal to optimum levels. If we lack that level of stimulation, our systems are sluggish and hyporesponsive. We may not register easily, we have difficulty allocating our attention to the task, and we do not process information and assimilate it well. On the contrary, if our systems are overaroused or overstimulated, we are not able to process well. We may be hyperresponsive and overregistering to multiple stimuli, have difficulty filtering out pertinent from nonpertinent information, and not process information or assimilate it well. In the calm-alert state, we have sufficient levels of stimulation to be open to learning, processing, or functioning, yet not to the point at which stimulation begins to interfere.

Individuals with autism have smaller *windows*. They demonstrate levels of stress or arousal that may be either lower than optimal or high to the point of decompensation. Jeremy is a perfect example of a child with a very small window in which he functions within a calm alert state. His level of arousal and stress are easily escalated, and he rapidly decompensates and is unable to continue until the calm-alert state is regained.

Pribram and McGuinness (1975) addressed the underaroused state. They defined *arousal* as a basic physiological response to input; that is, the system asking, "What is it?" They defined *activation* as a tonal physiological readiness to respond; that is, the system asking, "What is to be done?" Finally, they defined *effort* as the coordination of arousal and activation. They proposed that the lack of arousal to sensory input in children with autism might be due to an inappropriate interaction between the areas of the brain involved with coordinating physiological readiness, namely the amygdala, basal ganglia, and the hippocampal region. As evidence of this theory, they cited these children's inability to demonstrate physiological readiness. Both Kim and Will have observable difficulties with arousal and activation. They fail to identify "what it is and what is to be done"; and therefore they lack the abilities to respond.

Ayres' theory of hyporesponsive systems in which the input needs to be of greater strength or intensity in order to register, and her description of hyperreactive states also help to explain the smaller *windows* of calm-alertness seen in people with autism. Kim and Will have hyporesponsive systems in which the intensity of the stimulus needs to be enhanced or magnified before they are able to register the change in their environment. Jeremy is an example of a child with a hyperreactive system.

Ornitz (1974) proposed the theory of faulty sensory modulation to explain how children can be both under- and overreactive to sensory input. He outlined the signs of poor sensory modulation as:

- A lack of orienting and attention to sensory stimuli,

- Inconsistent response to sensory input, and

- Increased sensitivity to sensory input, such as sensory defensiveness.

He observes that these children act as though they are in a constant state of "sensory deprivation" in that they demonstrate increased sensitivity of certain sensations coupled with tendencies or the apparent drive to seek other types of input.

Fluctuations between hypersensitivity to sensations, while seeming to be hypo- or underresponsive to others, are characteristics of a modulation disorder. These children will appear to crave the sensations that they appear underresponsive to. Jeremy appears to fit into this theory. He seems to crave heavy pressure and other vestibular input. He attempts to move heavy bookcases, and often places your hand over his and squeezes your hand, thereby increasing the pressure you exert on him. Conversely, he cannot tolerate light touch and will push away the teacher's hands when she attempts to rest them lightly on his hands to assist with a task. He attempts to block out noises and noise levels by humming constantly. He swings back and forth on the playground swing with a vengeance, and yet will not tolerate side-to-side or circular swinging.

Ayres and Tickle (1980) went one step further. They proposed that a child with a problem in registering and modulating sensory input will exhibit problems in learning, language, and purposeful interaction; and also will have difficulty with ideation or concept formation, initiation, motor planning, and organization of behaviors. Because learning, language, and purposeful interactions depend upon registering information, filtering extraneous input, and having an optimal state of arousal to attend to a task, a child with a sensory modulation disorder will be hampered in all of these areas.

Ideation is the ability to register something in the environment and to have some idea of its purpose or what to do with it. Concept formation includes the ability to formulate a sequential plan of thought or action. Motor planning is the ability to sequence and execute the motor acts to successfully complete an appropriate response. If a child is unable to register changes or things in the environment or to modulate his responses to those changes, his ability to formulate an idea or a plan of action and his motoric responses will be skewed. The information coming into a system suffering from a sensory modulation disorder is faulty information. If the child is fluctuating between hypo- and hyperresponsiveness to incoming sensory input, the information received will be disorganized and unreliable; and therefore, the child's outputs and behaviors also will be disorganized and unreliable. Inconsistencies are a hallmark of autism.

Many children with autism are in a state of either underarousal or overarousal. The underaroused child will miss much input and therefore fail to register and respond to it. The overaroused child is bombarded by a constant stream of unfiltered input and the intense stress posed by changing and unpredictable situations. The stress from this overwhelming stimulation may easily lead to sensory shutdown, overfocusing on a single form of input to the exclusion of others, flight from situations, disorganized and unproductive behavior, and lowered self-esteem. All of these behaviors are seen when children are not in their window of calm-alertness, are not open to learning, and are unable to function well. With this information, we can better understand autistic children's behaviors and difficulties.

Cognitive Issues and Functions

Neurobiologists have demonstrated alterations in neuronal circuitry and nerve cell size within limbic systems of the brains of individuals with autism. This area has been associated with emotional tone, processing of memory (needed for learning), and motivation. It houses the two major interhemispheric pathways for communication between the two sides of the brain and, therefore, the body. The limbic system exudes a major influence over incoming and outgoing stimuli. The alterations found in this area of the brain have been correlated with animal brain studies in which experimental lesions in the same areas have produced behaviors similar to those often seen in children with autism. These behaviors include purposeless hyperactivity, impaired social interaction, stereotyped motor behaviors, disordered responses to novel stimuli, and severe loss of recognition and associative visual and tactile memory.

Cerebellar abnormalities also have been found. The cerebellum receives sensory and motor information from the various areas of the brain. It adjusts the descending motor commands to ensure that they are smooth and appropriate and accomplish the task required. It also is an area of the brain that is important in learning and memorization of some motor skills. Animal and human studies imply that the cerebellum may have a role in the control of affective behavior and learning, and therefore, the lesions may result in disturbance of emotion, behavior, and learning in individuals with autism.

The third area in which abnormalities in brain structure have been cited is in the temporal lobe which is responsible for auditory sense, or the recognition of specific tones and intensities, and with memory functions.

How is Information Stored?

In the normally functioning system, there is a continuous stream of data entering from the senses. It is processed, filtered, and interpreted based on our past experience. *Data banks* or *folders* are formed within our memories that form our understanding of concepts.

Individuals with autism are often described as being very concrete in their thinking. In *Understanding the Nature of Autism*, Janzen (1996) describes how a typical child is able to automatically organize and integrate information from a new experience with relevant information from past experiences and form larger, more meaningful units or concepts. She cites an example of how typical children play with all types of balls-baseballs, beach balls, basketballs, and others. At some point, all of the information is integrated and the child recognizes that although they are of differing sizes, colors, and textures, they are all balls.

The individual with autism learns by memorization and cannot filter out extraneous information. All coexisting sensory information gets stored as well. Each experience with a ball may be stored in the child's memory as a separate folder. A single experience with a tennis ball may comprise a folder and include the texture of the ball, the place where the child played with it, the sequence or rules of the game played, and the sound of a bird singing while he played. The pertinent information about the tennis ball may never be merged into a collective of experiences with balls. In other folders, the child with autism may focus solely on the stitching on a baseball or the stripes on a beach ball and will miss the concept that all of these items fall into the same category. The child's data bank is filled with disorganized, cluttered folders. Generalizations tend to be all or none, and they may be very situation-specific.

> Zachary is a 5-year-old with sensorimotor difficulties. His therapist in school had worked with him on catching a tennis ball, and his therapist in the clinic had taught him to kick a beach ball. At first, Zachary could perform the desired task—either catching the tennis ball or kicking the beach ball—in the setting in which it was taught and under certain conditions that had to be replicated each time. After collaborating, his therapists and parents worked on both skills at school, home, and in the clinic. Now, when Zachary sees a tennis ball in any environment, he will give the ball to someone to throw to him; and similarly, in any environment, he will attempt to kick a beach ball. He has learned that tennis balls are caught and beach balls are kicked. He will not cooperate with trying to catch a beach ball. While he has learned by memorization and is able to generalize the functions or use of each type of ball to different environments, his learning has been very situation-specific. More work is required to generalize variety of play with each type of ball.

Speech and Language Deficits

Speech and language deficits are part of the core symptoms of autism. They vary depending upon the age of the child. Deficits can range from no speech at all, to complex speech with errors. Typical errors include staying on a particular topic too long, repeating parts of other conversations, exhibiting difficulty with eye contact while speaking, knowing when to use particular language (for example, a greeting, or slang), speaking in a monotonic voice, and changing topics rapidly.

> At 2 years of age, Sam had started to develop speech, and then stopped. His parents were concerned with this regression. He did not use words to request an item, but would lead a parent's hand to an object when he wanted it. He babbled often with a variety of sounds, but he had none of the words expected of a 2-year-old.

> Mark, 7-years-old, speaks in single words to three-word sentences. He also uses communication pictures to "speak." He plays with his brothers and a few friends in the neighborhood, enjoys

riding his bicycle and swimming, and has a very complex collection of model dinosaurs. He is able to match each model to its scientific name. Mark understands basic conversation and directions. Although he often makes requests and protests with either words or pictures, he does not ask questions or comment about new ideas or events.

Amy is a 13-year-old who is in a learning disabilities classroom. She is on grade level in math and reading. Although she is able to read well for facts, she has trouble with more abstract concepts. She speaks in long, complex sentences. Amy asks and answers questions in class. Her favorite topic is cartoon ads, and she attempts to bring many conversations to this topic. She becomes silly when talking about the cartoons. The children in the class have learned this and try to start her talking about cartoons in order to distract from the teacher's intended lesson plan.

Children with autism may develop expressive language far in advance of their expected age level. Often we see that although these children use terms that are advanced for their age, they use the words incorrectly or out of context. This is because they have deficits in word comprehension or receptive language. If verbal skills do develop, it is often devoid of descriptive and/or pragmatic language. Pragmatics is the language we use in everyday social contexts and to make our needs known. Lack of pragmatics prevents these children from being able to describe how or what they feel, make requests, ask questions to clarify a topic, or even realize that they have a question or a reaction.

Their language is often lacking in the use of personal pronouns, which are abstract forms of reference. Children with autism often refer to themselves by name—a more concrete form of reference that is easier for these children to understand. That is not to say that they don't understand and react to certain statements. However, we never can be certain that they comprehend the information in the way it was intended; and if they voice a reaction, it may not be phrased accurately.

These children's facial expressions often will not correlate with their verbal messages or their responses. They may smile when they say they are angry, or laugh when you reprimand them. When unreliable nonverbal communication (that is, facial expressions and emotional responses) is combined with difficulties in pragmatic expressive language, the stage is set for miscommunication, errors, misunderstanding, and wrongful assumptions from both the speaker and the listener. This may further hinder these children's attempts at peer interactions, because children are less adept at interpreting the accuracy of the communication than are adults.

How is Information Learned?

Children with autism learn, but not always what adults want to teach them. They learn by memorization, and they prefer concrete information. Many of these children prefer numbers, factual information, and historical data, all of which can be memorized and is unchanging under any circumstance. Many children steadfastly cling to this concrete information because it makes sense to them.

Rituals are built to structure conversations on their particular topic of interest. Because their processing systems don't enable them to develop uncluttered information or data banks on the entirety of a situation, rules may be learned incompletely, out of context, and with distortions. These children learn best in highly structured settings, devoid of extraneous tasks, visuals, and auditory stimulation that will clutter the information memorized or stored.

Individuals with autism lack social relatedness. Most people acquired the unspoken rules of social interaction by observing how others respond in different situations; for example, with facial grimaces, disapproving looks, or silent approvals. These observations start very early in life and continue as normal children develop. This knowledge—often termed *common sense*—is what we see lacking in individuals with autism. They seem to lack or have an impaired ability to relate to others and to discern implied meaning from body language, facial expression, or intonations. They fail to read situations, and they may not change their behavior by the situation's tone. Often they fail to register dangerous situations, and they may appear to be indifferent when facing impending doom. They must be taught in very concrete terms what is acceptable and what is unacceptable, what is important, and how to respond appropriately.

Delays in speech and language skills are included in their apparent lack of social relatedness. Children, who do not have autism but who have delays in speech, are very effective at compensating for their lack of language through gesture, body language, and facial expression. However, autism seems to affect the child's basic intuitive sense of *how* to communicate. The basic lack of a sense of communication combined with the impaired ability to discern implied information makes generalization of skills very difficult for these individuals. They can be taught splinter skills, but may lack the basic ability to interpret a particular situation and use an appropriate response because of the way in which their folders are stored in their data banks. Body language (such as motioning *over* with a broad sweep of your arms as a child climbs over a bolster, or holding up your hand to punctuate the command to stop) are methods that can be used to help in teaching these concepts. However, be careful not to assume that the child will automatically make the correct association. Validate the child's comprehension by analyzing his responses.

Because children with autism learn differently, they cannot be counted upon to understand, synthesize, and store new information reliably. Among other primary causes, this is due to language deficits. These children have impairments in both their receptive and expressive skills; and although word *use* may be advanced, word *comprehension* may be lacking. Verbal directions and information may be too abstract and difficult for the child to comprehend. Verbal children may have problems with word use, as evidenced by difficulties with initiation and use of pragmatics for requesting objects or assistance. These children can't pose questions for validation or clarification. Therefore, labeling of objects may be impaired, and information gained from descriptive language may be faulty or even meaningless.

This is compounded by the fact that information may be learned and stored in very situation-specific, cluttered contexts. These children may not comprehend what the adult perceives is the pertinent component of the experience, but may form an entirely unpredicted and erroneous conclusion.

Jake receives clinic-based therapy. His therapist always has the room and activities prepared when he arrives. However, one day she had to leave the building, and Jake arrived at the clinic moments before she returned. With no time to set up the environment or activities in advance, the therapist innocently said, "Jake, you choose the first activity." Jake immediately formulated a new rule: "I get to choose the first activity because I got here before you did." Then, on subsequent visits, he became upset when the therapist was in the clinic waiting for him. In his mind, that meant that he could not choose the first activity. If Jake had not been as verbally capable as he was, we would not have learned the rule that he had formulated for the situation and would not have been able to correct his perception.

Ashley's mother salted her dinner every night and then place the plate of food in front of her with the warning, "Be careful! It's hot!" Much to our surprise, we learned that Ashley believed the salt made her food hot!

Children often respond best when given visual cues, which are more concrete and meaningful to them. However, although visual prompts appear to be of some help, we also know that children with autism can't reliably interpret cues from other sources. Because pictures may be too abstract for very young children with autism, an object reference system will be necessary.

 # Motor Control and Its Impact on Functioning

Many autistic children also are impeded in their motor functioning. Many have an underlying hypotonia, or low muscle tone. Although many of these children attain developmental milestones—sitting, crawling, standing, and walking—the quality of their performances is poor, and therefore, their experiences also are poor.

Children with an underlying hypotonia have difficulty generating the kind of sustained, controlled efforts required for smooth transitions from one position to another, or the graded muscular control required for operation of their extremities in a graceful and efficient manner. Instead, they perform these tasks rapidly, never gaining the ability to slow down the movement or the ability to sustain postures without slouching.

Hallmark characteristics of hypotonia include a lack of pelvic control, as indicated by an increase in the lumbar lordosis or curvature of the spine; locking out or hyperextension of middle joints (that is, the elbows and knees); proximal muscle weakness throughout the shoulders, pelvis, and hips; and fixing patterns characterized by increased stiffness or postures.

An infant with weakness throughout the trunk will have difficulties in overcoming gravity. Use of compensatory movements and postures prevent the development of muscular control needed for optimal head and neck stability. Without head and neck stability, the infant lacks stability of the tongue for oral motor control and feeding and language skills. Lack of head control leads to a lack of midline orientation required for bilateral control at midline of the body.

Weakness within the trunk also hinders development in the muscles required for shoulder stability. A lack of proximal shoulder control impedes the child's ability to reach accurately, hold the arm away from the body for hand functions, and sustain weight and weight shifts over the arm for crawling and transition between postures. Decreased transitions lead to decreased elbow, wrist, and hand control; and limit development of the somatosensory system, which negatively affects development of body scheme and hand use.

This has an impact on posture, leading to the characteristic lordosis, forward-tipped shoulders, and a forward head. This affects balance, orientation in space, and visual perception. Furthermore, the weakness in the trunk exerts an impact on pelvic control required for sustaining balance in sitting, creeping, standing, and walking. Higher levels of coordination for running, jumping, riding a bicycle, and playing sports are sacrificed.

A lack of slow, sustained control in the pelvis and hips also leads to a lack of static balance; impaired ability to transition between postures; decreased coordination and strength in the knees, ankles, and feet; and decreased somatosensory development in the lower extremities. These children fail to develop the body scheme, coordination, and sense of self needed for function. Their upper and lower bodies often seem disconnected from each other, and their movements are awkward and clumsy.

From a sensory integrative theory base, children with hypotonic muscle tone also have abnormal sensory processing of tactile, proprioceptive-vestibular input that affects the development of body scheme and position awareness required for normal motor patterns. They tend not to register and process information from the joints and muscles that tells them where their bodies are and how they are moving.

Their early efforts at moving are impaired by poor strength and a lack of how to make their bodies move against gravity. They miss all the normal vestibular input gained as the typical child rolls, crawls, pivots, pulls to a standing position, and engages later in rough-and-tumble play. Consequently, many children with autism fail to develop an accurate internal compass system. Orientation in space and balance or equilibrium reactions are affected.

Some children with autism make themselves immobile out of fear. When there is an impairment of vestibular processing resulting in a functional impairment or lack of balance and equilibrium reactions, we may well see a sensory integrative dysfunction known as *postural insecurity*. The child is fearful of movement or is overly cautious, avoiding movement or positions because he lacks the balance and equilibrium reactions to move skillfully and safely.

In a second type of sensory integrative dysfunction known as *gravitational insecurity*, the child exhibits a fear reaction that seems incongruous with the type of threat posed. The child may be responding to abnormal vestibular-proprioceptive processing and impaired perceptions. The net result is that the child has a primal fear that will trigger either a flight response from the movement or a fight response—an aggressive behavior—to avoid any position or movement perceived as a threat. Therefore the child avoids precisely the type of movement and play experiences required for the development of balance, equilibrium, orientation in space, body scheme, and strength and motor control required for function.

The terms *motor apraxia* or *motor dyspraxia* have been used to describing the problems often seen in people with autism. Ayres (1979) described this as a sensory integrative disorder in which the brain cannot organize the tactile, vestibular, and proprioceptive sensations, and therefore cannot effectively motor plan. The child with dyspraxia, according to Ayres, has less of a sense of his body and what it can do. He doesn't manipulate toys, can't plan playing with them, and often is clumsy, accident-prone, and messy.

The Role of Play in Learning

Typical children learn through play. Early play experiences emphasize use of the whole body in environmental interactions. These total-body play experiences serve as primary ways to enhance the ability to organize sensations for use in creating more complex adaptive behaviors. As children become more organized in their ability to perform, learn to manipulate objects, and move through their environment, they acquire concepts such as direction, spatial relationships, and motor skills through the manipulation of their bodies and of objects within their environment. Later, they begin with imitative play, mimicking facial gestures, vocalizations, and motor sequences from the older children and adults with whom they interact. At about one year of age, children typically progress from playing with toys in a cause-effect manner, and begin to use symbolic play to replicate situations needed or encountered in real life. They will replicate brushing a doll's hair or washing its face, or pretend to feed it. They develop imaginary play in which they create new opportunities for problem solving and new physical challenges. They learn to label objects, and language develops. They learn the pragmatics necessary for questions; and they learn about descriptive language and the language needed for social interactions. As the concepts and relationships increase, the play sequences become longer and more complex. Children learn role delineation and social interaction; and they recognize and label their emotions and develop strategies to deal with those emotions.

The play experiences of children with autism are limited by decreased initiation, decreased eye contact, and lack of imitation; and perseveration (that is, the repetition of a motor act or vocalization and an inability to stop or change the behavior. This is neurological in nature and not a willful behavior). Their play is limited to actions that they have learned, but they lack the flexibility and creativity needed to master their environment, expand their capabilities, and generalize the data.

In summary, children with autism do not easily and readily learn to or from their play experiences. Often, their early play experiences are disorganized, unpredictable, and unsuccessful. They lack the opportunities to organize their sensations into creating more complex adaptive responses. They do not have the inherent ability to initiate creative play, and they cannot imitate others spontaneously. They do not acquire the basic concepts or motor skills developed by children in typical development. They fail to develop the idea of how to interact with objects and people in their environment, and therefore, they do not develop the neuronal modes necessary for analyzing new situations. They do not acquire language for labeling, requesting, or describing play. They cannot identify or explain their confusion, disorganization, or emotional reactions. They do not negotiate with peers because they lack the language and social skills to do so. Role delineation, social interaction, and emotional development suffer.

There are anatomical changes within the areas of the brain that analyze, combine, filter, and store information. The data banks of children with autism contain the spatial, temporal, and sensory components of their experiences, just as the data banks of normal-developing children. The difference may be that their data banks are based upon perceptions and conclusions that may be faulty; and therefore the components in their data banks also are faulty. Therefore, they are ill equipped to organize their perceptions and the resultant responses to those perceptions. They simply lack the basic ingredients for organizing themselves and for developing functional and reliable complex behaviors and concepts based upon the information in their data banks.

CHAPTER 3

Behavioral Issues
Analyzing the Behavior

Carolyn Murray-Slutsky and Betty Paris

Children with autism have a fundamental need to function within the environment. To be able to function, they quickly develop coping behaviors. Some of these behaviors are distressing, some are inappropriate, and most block their ability to learn and improve their functional skills.

Common behaviors include spinning objects or lining up toys, rocking rhythmically, covering their ears in response to noises, chewing or sucking on their clothing, and flapping their hands. The behaviors may extend into what we call *challenging behaviors*, such as hand biting, tantrums, head banging, and other abusive or difficult-to-manage behaviors. These behaviors interfere with the child's ability to attend, learn, and master new skills, or blend in with peers. Managing these behaviors often becomes a priority in therapy sessions and during everyday activities. To do that, we need to explore the many reasons that these behaviors occur and establish a philosophy for intervention.

Primary Causes and Secondary Reinforcers

These unique and challenging behaviors first develop to meet a need. That need may be sensory based, reflect a motor-control deficit, or serve as a form of communication for social or nonsocial purposes. Once the behavior occurs, it is reinforced by the success with which it is met. Often, it is these secondary rewards that contribute to the persistence of the behavior.

> Joey, 5-years-old, is nonverbal. He has sensorimotor difficulties that contribute to both fine motor and gross motor incoordination. Posturally insecure, Joey does not have good balance reactions. In the classroom, he often feels threatened by sitting in his chair and is fearful of falling out of his seat. Fine motor tasks also are threatening and offensive to him. He has neither the motor control for fine motor tasks nor the sensory awareness of his fingers to be successful. When a pencil is placed in his hand, he has no feeling of it and cannot manipulate or control it.

Joey's primary problems are sensorimotor based, combined with his decreased ability to communicate. Secondary behavioral problems developed. Whenever Joey was presented with a fine motor task or a situation that he perceived as threatening, he threw things, pushed everything off his desk, pushed his chair over backward, or pushed the table over. Every time he became destructive, attention was concentrated on blocking his behaviors, saving the supplies and equipment, and assuring the safety of those around him. Joey successfully avoided having to perform the threatening task and gained control over his environment. His destructive behavior was reinforced.

Remediation must be multifaceted to effectively correct these behavioral issues. We need to:

1. Increase sensorimotor skills

    As Joey's motoric and functional abilities improve, his need for avoidance behaviors should decrease.

2. Modify tasks for both success and sensory feedback

    Activities need to be graded to Joey's level or just slightly above. Tasks that are too difficult serve no purpose and will only perpetuate the problem. Joey needs not only to be able to accomplish the task physically, but believe he can accomplish it. Extensive encouragement and reinforcement are crucial. Activities need to be modified for enhanced sensory feedback that will reinforce Joey's body scheme and knowledge of where his hands and arms are.

3. Establish an effective system of communication

    Joey needs a method to communicate his fear or dislike of the task, frustration, or need to have control in the activity selection. In tasks that are not inherently motivating, he needs to know the benefits or rewards to be derived from completing the task. If the activity still is not desirable and control cannot be given to him, bartering or negotiating may be necessary. For example, you may choose the first activity and let Joey choose the next. In some situations, Joey may be allowed to choose the activity, but you will determine how the activity is to be completed (while sitting, standing, or on the arms; or otherwise modifying the instructions for more therapeutic value).

4. Extinguish the destructive behaviors

Joey needs to learn that the behaviors will no longer serve the purpose of letting him avoid the task or gain negative attention. To do this, two things must happen: Joey must complete the task successfully, and you must not draw attention to the undesirable behaviors. Intercede before the behaviors occur, providing assistance and reinforcing success. When the destructive behaviors do occur, block the behavior (without attending to it or reinforcing it by eye contact, verbal admonishments, or other forms of attention) while redirecting Joey to complete the task. Although task completion is critical, modifications in the number of repetitions required might be appropriate to assure success.

Alex appears to be a bright 3-year-old who is capable of learning new information quickly. He has speech and language delays characterized by both expressive and receptive language difficulties. In a social situation, Alex is lost. He does not know how to constructively initiate interaction or play with other children. He shows some repetitive speech and obsessive behaviors; specifically, he has a tendency to perseverate on the same subjects—lights and bathrooms—in every environment, and he overfocuses obsessively on minute details. He has both fine motor and gross motor difficulties and some sensory processing problems. He is posturally insecure and quickly becomes threatened and frightened on movable toys. He cannot stand on one foot, kick a stationary ball, or ride a tricycle. He constantly runs from place to place and has difficulty staying in his seat. Fine motor tasks are difficult for him. His fingers work as a unit, versus in isolation. When playing with manipulatives, he either pushes too hard or too lightly. He cannot effectively use tools or toys. He cannot dress or feed himself.

Alex's primary problems are speech and language delays coupled with decreased sensory processing (integration) and motor control difficulties that affect both gross and fine motor control. Many of his sensory-processing problems contribute to the perseverative and disorganized behaviors. Open, unstructured environments further exaggerate these problems. Alex uses challenging secondary behaviors to attract attention and avoid threatening activities. He has learned that *fleeing* behaviors are acceptable. The moment he anticipates a difficult task or becomes threatened, fearful, or frustrated, he runs. This running has been described as inattention and distractibility. However, the behavior consistently occurs when he wants to avoid a particular task or situation. When Alex is not permitted to run from the task, the behavior is blocked. The secondary behavior then is expressed in two other forms: Alex either acts silly and throws himself on the floor laughing, or seeks negative attention. Praise means nothing to him; but he constantly seeks the frown, scowl, or reprimand. On the playground, he seeks the same negative attention by pushing and shoving others.

Alex's secondary behaviors originated as an attempt to communicate. The task was too difficult for him, he could not perform it, and he did not have the skills needed for it. He was afraid to fail. He quickly learned that his fleeing behavior was excused as inattentiveness. It was effective in allowing him to avoid the task and obtain attention.

Remediation needs to be multifaceted to effectively correct Alex's behavioral issues. We need to:

1. Increase Alex's sensory processing and sensory integration of multisensory experiences

    Through improving his sensory processing and sensory integration of multisensory experiences, Alex will be more organized within his environment. Repetitive speech and obsessions on irrelevant details should diminish. He will be better able to focus on the salient aspects within his environment and will not become overwhelmed by multisensory experiences.

2. Alex must learn to connect the correct emotion with sensory experiences, his feelings, needs, and wants. Then he must use speech to describe them. The therapist must be sensitive to his responses and help him identify and verbalize the correct experience before he displays the fleeing behavior. Praise, positive reinforcement, and the success of receiving the verbalized request will help teach him the power of communication and the value of attaching meaning to the sensorimotor experience.

3. Increase Alex's expressive and receptive language skills while giving him the pragmatic skills he needs to effectively communicate

    Alex will need to learn functional communication skills and how to effectively interact and negotiate in his environment. Once he realizes the power of communication and learns the rules governing this power, we can expect a decrease in avoidance behaviors and an increase in verbally mediated interactions.

4. Modify or grade tasks for success while avoiding the threatening aspects

    Alex's behaviors originate as an attempt to avoid activities that are difficult or threatening for him. When tasks are graded to his level or just slightly above, Alex's avoidance response will not be triggered. Support and encouragement are vital. The appropriateness of the task, provision of the needed assistance and reinforcement, and stimulation and inherent motivation of the task itself become important considerations to assure success.

5. Improve Alex's motor control

    He needs to develop motor control and needed skills, not only to be able to perform the task successfully, but to move him ahead to more difficult tasks. While Alex learned the fleeing behaviors to avoid tasks, he did not have the postural control that helps him sustain his attention, sit still, and attend for long periods of time. Fleeing behaviors are not productive and cannot be excused. However, if we do not give Alex the skills he needs—motor, postural, and sensory-integrative skills—he may develop other nonproductive coping strategies. As Alex develops the motor and functional skills he needs, he will no longer need the challenging behaviors that are interfering with his learning and functioning. He will be free to use the productive strategies that he is being taught.

6. Replace the fleeing and silly behaviors with constructive, productive behaviors; and transfer the negative, attention-seeking behaviors to positive, praise-seeking ones

Alex needs to learn that these behaviors no longer function to avoid a task or draw attention to himself. Positive reinforcement must be given frequently, and to *only* the constructive behaviors. It is critical that no response or attention be given to his negative behaviors. Create situations in which positive behaviors can be praised and molded. Teach the power of communication through modeling appropriate responses to various situations. Fade the prompts and facilitate natural interactions.

 ## Analyzing Behaviors

When we thoroughly analyze a child's behaviors and understand the needs met or purposes served by those behaviors, we can develop a plan to find a more acceptable means of achieving the same purposes. The behaviors then should diminish. However, in many cases we also will need to work on systematically eliminating the undesirable behavior. It is important to identify the behavior, the precursors to the behavior, and the subtle signals that indicate the behavior is about to occur. Interceding before the behavior occurs is critical to eliminating the behavior.

Define Challenging Behaviors

To analyze the underlying causes, we must first clearly define the behavior and identify the situations in which it occurs. The situations will give us clues about the purpose served by the behavior.

It is important that behaviors be separated and not clustered together. We need to be specific. For example, Joey's aggressiveness needs to be specifically defined as "throwing things off the table, himself off the chair," and so on.

Are the Behaviors Linked?

Do the behaviors occur in a predictable sequence, or do they occur to the same situations or events? In Alex's case, the silliness, nonstop giggling, and throwing himself on the floor laughing always occurred in exactly the same situations as the fleeing or running away behaviors. If he could not run from the activity, he would block it out by throwing himself into extension and laughing.

Warning Signs

What are the warning signs that the behavior is about to occur? In most cases, a trained observer, therapist, or parent can predict the behavior. Restlessness, eye aversion or visual distractibility, a pause in actions, increased voice volume, grinding the teeth, increasing hand flapping, or hand posturing, and movements toward or away from an activity or object are a few warning signs that may predict the onset of the behavior. Reading these subtle signs and interceding before the behavior occurs is critical to eliminating the behavior.

What Promoted the Behavior?

We gain insight by knowing what event, activity, or situation occurred immediately before the challenging behavior. For example, before Joey's disruptive behavior, he

```
┌─────────────────────────────────────────────┐
│         Define challenging behaviors         │
└─────────────────────────────────────────────┘
                        │
┌─────────────────────────────────────────────┐
│            Are behaviors linked?             │
│ Do they occur in response to the same        │
│ situation?                                    │
│ Do they occur in a predictable pattern?       │
└─────────────────────────────────────────────┘
                        │
┌─────────────────────────────────────────────┐
│        Warning signs or predictors           │
│              of the behavior                  │
│              • Restlessness                   │
│              • Eye aversion                   │
│              • Distractibility                │
│              • Pause                          │
│              • Louder voice                   │
│              • Hand flapping                  │
└─────────────────────────────────────────────┘
                        │
┌─────────────────────────────────────────────┐
│          What activity or event              │
│          preceded the behavior?              │
│ What environmental factors had an impact on   │
│   the behavior? (See Table 5.1.)              │
│ What is the child reacting to?                │
└─────────────────────────────────────────────┘
              ╱                    ╲
┌──────────────────────┐  ┌──────────────────────┐
│    Primary cause     │  │     Secondary         │
│ *Obtain*             │  │    reinforcement      │
│ Communication        │  │   (consequences)      │
│ • Attention          │  │  • Attention          │
│ • Object, activity   │  │  • Avoid task         │
│ Internal/Systemic    │  │  • Habit              │
│ • Sensory            │  │  • Punishment         │
│ • Systemic/visceral  │  │  • Reprimand          │
│ *Avoid*              │  │  • Eye contact        │
│ Communication        │  │                       │
│ • Attention          │  │                       │
│ • Task, event        │  │                       │
│ Internal/Systemic    │  │                       │
│ • Sensory            │  │                       │
│    – Productive      │  │                       │
│    – Nonproductive   │  │                       │
└──────────────────────┘  └──────────────────────┘
```

FIGURE 3.1
Analyzing behaviors

was presented with a fine motor task. For another child, it may be attention given to another child, a parent's diverted attention, a loud noise or fire alarm, an interruption in a desired activity, or rising frustration.

Environmental factors can promote challenging behaviors. Unstructured tasks, noisy or cluttered environments, frequent changes in activities, excessive waiting times, crowded rooms, and unstimulating tasks tend to increase the probability. In Alex's case, unstructured environments further exaggerated his problems. See Table 4.1 for lists of environmental factors that make the behavior more or less likely to occur.

Analyze the child's reaction to ascertain how he interprets the experience. Is he reacting to what we see as the salient points, or is he responding to some other aspect of the activity or the environment? Children with autism often remember not only relevant data, but the sensory experiences that occurred at the same time. An irrelevant sound made by a therapist during a game may be the motivating factor rather than the game itself.

What the child sees as important in an event may be very different from what we see as important. For example, Alex has a tendency to perseverate on discussions about lights and bathrooms. Any time he enters a room, he comments about the lights. If he observes someone going into or coming out of the bathroom, he discusses his observations to the exclusion of the task at hand. This may appear as normal social conversation about children moving around in his environment; but in reality, it is a perseverative behavior that must be redirected and not reinforced.

Secondary Reinforcers

The consequences or actions that follow the behavior often provide insight into both the primary cause of the problem and the secondary reinforcers. In Joey's case, we learned that the secondary reinforcer to his behavior is the consequence he received; that is, strong negative attention and task avoidance. Joey's destructive behaviors were reinforced by these consequences, or secondary reinforcers.

Primary Cause

We now know when the challenging behavior occurs, the situations that make it more or less likely to occur, and the consequences and secondary reinforcers to the behaviors. Next, we need to analyze the primary cause of the behavior.

Behaviors often serve two purposes: the child is either trying to obtain something, or avoid or escape from something. Once we have identified the needs that the child is trying to meet, we can develop an intervention strategy that will not only give the child the skills he needs to function effectively (the primary need), but also will be able to modify the secondary reinforcers to eliminate the behavior.

Remediation must give these children the tools and skills to function optimally within the environment; teach them methods to effectively communicate; and eliminate the need to use challenging behaviors, rather than just eliminating the behaviors. If behaviors are extinguished but the underlying problems are not addressed, new behaviors will emerge to serve the same purpose. Our responsibility is to learn from the child what he is trying to seek or avoid from the behaviors (primary causes) and help him eliminate the problem.

To delve deeper into the causes of the behavior, we need to track whether the child is trying to *obtain* or *avoid* something or someone.

Obtaining Behaviors

When a behavior is displayed for the purpose of obtaining something, it usually falls into two categories:

- The behavior is social/communicative in nature; that is, the child is trying to obtain either attention or a need or want; or

- The behavior is internally/systemically driven to obtain sensorimotor input

Social/Communicative Obtaining Behaviors

When children have difficulty communicating, often they resort to nonverbal methods of getting their needs met. They may develop an elaborate system of communication that is understood only by people who are *in tune* with them, or they may use simple gestures or movements toward or away from an activity. Challenging behaviors are often a method of communication. By identifying what the child needs or wants, we are able to identify a comprehensive intervention program that addresses the child's underlying problems.

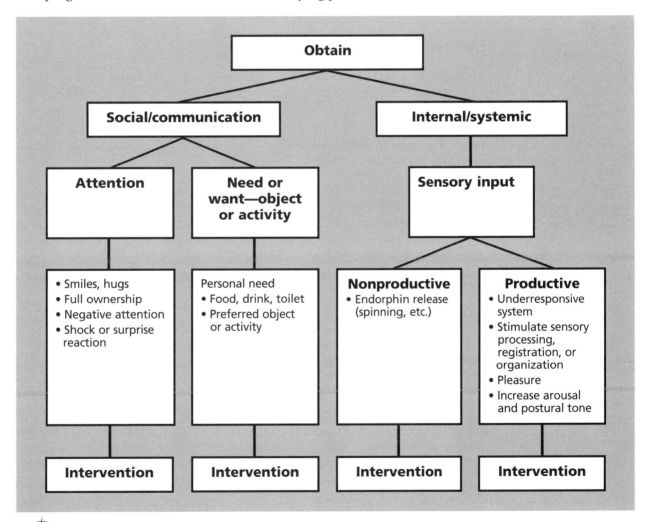

 **FIGURE 3.2**
Analyzing obtaining behaviors

Obtaining Attention

When a child uses challenging behaviors as a method of communicating, we need to analyze what activity preceded the behavior, our response to the child's behaviors (the secondary reinforcer), and the child's reactions. The child may be seeking attention from someone in the environment. This may be a smile, hug, or just attention to the child's activities. Many children also demand what is called *full ownership* of an individual; that is, full, undivided attention of the person caring for them or working with them. Parents, therapists, and teachers experience this when a child will not allow them to talk or interact with anyone else or displays disruptive behaviors to assure the adult's undivided attention.

Just as children can seek positive attention, they can equally seek negative attention or reactions from people around them. A frown, criticism, or reprimand voice can be a strong reward. Negative attention often is more strongly presented than praise. The strength of the delivery may be what the child responds to and seeks. A surprise or startled reaction often creates a pleasurable experience for children, and they may attempt to recapture it. It is important to determine whether the child is attempting to communicate with you, seek your attention, or get a reaction.

Obtaining a Need or Want/Object or Activity

What is the child attempting to communicate? Does he have a need or want? Is he trying to obtain food, water, or a drink? Is he voicing toileting needs or discomfort secondary to toileting needs? Is he using the behavior to express an emotion or a feeling? Does the behavior occur only when the child is happy or excited? When he is angry or frustrated? Is he trying to communicate with you about the activity that he is doing or you are asking him to do?

We know that children with autism prefer repetition of activities. It is difficult for them to change an activity, especially to one that is new and unfamiliar. Transition from one environment to another also is difficult. These children often register the sensory experience associated with the activity, and do not always register the salient aspects as we perceive them. It is important to identify what aspect of the activity or environment the child is trying to communicate about.

> When Sarah comes into the clinic, she enjoys swinging on the tire swing first. She looks forward to the activity and appears to find it relaxing and organizing. Today, Sarah gets on the tire swing; but within seconds, she throws herself on the floor screaming, banging her head on the floor, and lashing out at everyone in sight.

What happened today? Knowing more about Sarah helps us identify the problem. Sarah can propel the tire swing only if it is set at a certain height. Her motor planning skills are not sufficient to adapt to dramatic changes. When Sarah got on the swing, she couldn't effectively propel it. She expected a certain sensory feeling, but she couldn't elicit that feeling. She couldn't identify what was wrong with the swing, but she could identify and communicate that there was something wrong with how she felt, and she was frustrated.

It is important to know the person you are working with. Look at all factors within the environment that may be causing the response, and identify which factor may be directly linked to the behavior. In Sarah's case, the tire swing was attached incorrectly; it was too high, and she couldn't propel it. Her behaviors were a direct attempt to communicate an undesirable change in the activity and the environment that were based on her sensory perception. Sarah's method of communication needs to be improved, as do her self-awareness and general processing skills.

Internal/Systemic Obtaining Behaviors

When a child seeks something for internal or systemic reasons, it is normally of a sensory nature. Often the child is not cortically aware of this need, but seeks the input in order to serve an internal purpose. This purpose may either be of a nonproductive or a productive nature.

Nonproductive Sensory Behaviors

Nonproductive, sensory-seeking behaviors often are characterized as self-stimulation behaviors that involve an endorphin release. Examples of nonproductive endorphin-releasing behaviors include self-biting or head banging. Examples of more pleasurable nonproductive behaviors include rocking, self-spinning, or hand flapping.

Productive Sensory Behaviors

Productive, sensory-seeking behaviors are those in which the child consciously or unconsciously seeks to obtain sensory experiences that serve a purpose or meet a basic sensorimotor need. Usually the individual is underresponsive to sensory input and needs enhanced sensory input in order to improve the processing, registration, or organization of sensory information. Children inherently seek out information that helps them make sense of the world. Children who are underresponsive to touch or knowing where their arms and legs are moving (proprioception) may play hard with other children or prefer "crashing" games. This is productive in that it helps these children process their environments and better interpret information coming in from the environment. Children with low postural tone with low arousal levels (decreased proprioceptive and vestibular processing) may run around, appear hyperactive, jump up and down, and flap their hands. These behaviors may serve a sensory motor purpose of increasing these children's arousal levels and postural tone to help them function effectively within their environments. It also may provide a simultaneous pleasurable feeling.

While these behaviors are listed as productive, it is important to realize that they may not be considered desirable behaviors or socially acceptable. However, they do serve a productive, not necessarily a functional, purpose. The behavior also may be appropriate in one environment and not in another. When looking at intervention strategies, these factors becomes critical in effectively analyzing and designing a remediation program. Eliminating an undesirable behavior that serves a productive sensory need *without addressing that need* results in another behavior surfacing. In some occasions, the new behavior may be even more undesirable. Also, a productive behavior may be acceptable in one environment while totally unacceptable in another. A child who needs additional sensory input can productively receive it on the playground through climbing, running, crashing, and jumping. These sensory-seeking behaviors are both productive and

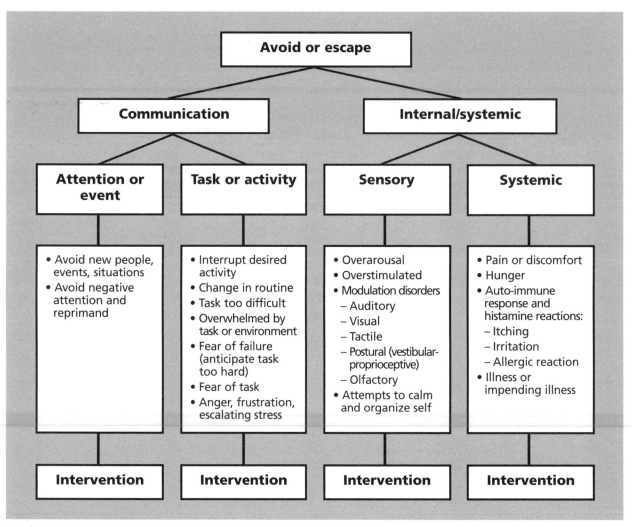

```
                        ┌─────────────────────┐
                        │    Avoid or escape   │
                        └─────────────────────┘
                 ┌──────────────┴──────────────┐
        ┌─────────────────┐          ┌─────────────────────┐
        │  Communication  │          │   Internal/systemic  │
        └─────────────────┘          └─────────────────────┘
        ┌───────┴───────┐            ┌───────────┴───────────┐
┌─────────────┐ ┌─────────────┐ ┌─────────────┐ ┌─────────────┐
│ Attention or│ │  Task or    │ │  Sensory    │ │  Systemic   │
│    event    │ │  activity   │ │             │ │             │
└─────────────┘ └─────────────┘ └─────────────┘ └─────────────┘
```

Attention or event	Task or activity	Sensory	Systemic

• Avoid new people, events, situations
• Avoid negative attention and reprimand
	• Interrupt desired activity
	• Change in routine
	• Task too difficult
	• Overwhelmed by task or environment
	• Fear of failure (anticipate task too hard)
	• Fear of task
	• Anger, frustration, escalating stress
		• Overarousal
		• Overstimulated
		• Modulation disorders
		  – Auditory
		  – Visual
		  – Tactile
		  – Postural (vestibular-proprioceptive)
		  – Olfactory
		• Attempts to calm and organize self
			• Pain or discomfort
			• Hunger
			• Auto-immune response and histamine reactions:
			  – Itching
			  – Irritation
			  – Allergic reaction
			• Illness or impending illness

Intervention	**Intervention**	**Intervention**	**Intervention**

FIGURE 3.3
Analyzing avoidance or escape behaviors

desirable. These same behaviors, while productive, are undesirable within a classroom situation, and a remediation program would be necessary.

Avoidance or Escape Behaviors

Children may display challenging behaviors in a conscious effort to avoid situations and activities, or in an unconscious attempt to escape from uncomfortable or unpleasant feelings. Avoidance of tasks, attention, or events falls under the general category of communication, while avoidance of sensory or systemic input are internal needs that fall under the category of internal/systemic reactions. Challenging behaviors occur when a child displays avoidance or escape behaviors rather than communicating. It is not uncommon for children to not know their needs, wants, and fears, or be able to relate them to their behaviors. Communication strategies become critical to increase these children's insights into their behaviors, provide constructive avenues for communication, and alleviate their underlying problems. By identifying the need that the child is trying to meet, we can develop an effective intervention strategy.

Task or Event Avoidance

Children avoid tasks for many reasons. The primary reason is that the child neither possesses the skills needed to complete a task successfully nor the ability to communicate this effectively. While the professional may believe the child is capable of functioning, the child may not believe that he possesses the skills, and will act accordingly. We must analyze the task, the environment, and the child's skills in order to determine the primary cause for the child's behavior. Then we must modify the environment and grade the task for success. The child's fear, frustration, and stress often are expressed in task avoidance and escape behaviors that can quickly develop into self-abusive or aggressive behaviors as the child's frustration mounts.

Children also avoid tasks that are boring and unstimulating and have no purpose or challenge. Professionals have a responsibility to find the just-right challenge (Koomar and Bundy 1991), in which the child is motivated and invested in the activity. Finding this level requires a comprehensive knowledge of the child's abilities. Underestimating the child's capabilities can be equally as harmful as overestimating them. Children often will rise to the occasion when people know their capabilities, place expectations slightly above that point, and simultaneously project to the children that you believe in their capabilities and will provide support and encouragement.

Children exhibiting decreased sensory awareness often find activities meaningless and unstimulating. In the case of Joey, who has decreased awareness of his fingers, hands, and arms, placing a pencil in his hands and asking him to draw is an unstimulating and meaningless task. Joey has no awareness of his hands, much less a pencil in them, and receives no sensory feedback from the task. (In Chapter 12, we will discuss intervention strategies for enhanced sensory feedback.)

A task also may be overstimulating. Tasks presented in an unstructured, disorganized, ungraded fashion can result in the child either shutting down or exhibiting avoidance and escape behaviors. This may occur even though the task is within the child's capabilities. The presentation of a task and the environment in which the task is performed can account for the child's varying functional levels with different professionals.

Because change is difficult for many children, transitions between activities and interruptions in their desired activity can lead to frustration and stress and result in behaviors that are less than optimal.

Attention Avoidance

Everyone has a basic need to be competent. Children often find safety and comfort in routine and consistency. Just as children avoid tasks and activities that are difficult or new to them, so may they avoid the attention of new people, events, or social situations. New situations may be viewed as threatening. They cannot control the events that occur, nor can they be sure that they will be able to function effectively. Social situations are known to be difficult for children with autism. They have difficulty grasping the *whole picture*, tend to focus on what appears to be irrelevant aspects of the environment, and have difficulty reading implied meaning and gestures associated with social situations. Some children are overwhelmed by the changes and stimulation presented within a new environment. Routine and consistency, something they crave, does not exist in new situations. The most comfortable response is to avoid new events and situations. They also avoid unfamiliar people. Avoidance of eye contact, physical contact, and general interaction can occur for many reasons—the voice quality, a perfume, the anticipated demands that the person may make, or simply that the child does not want to be bothered.

Internal/Systemic Responses

Sensory-Based Avoidance

Children who find themselves overaroused or overstimulated by sensory information, or as a response to modulation/regulatory disorders, often resort to challenging behaviors as a method of dampening or calming their nervous systems or blocking out sensory information. Auditory, visual, tactile, olfactory, and proprioceptive-vestibular (balance and posture) sensory systems are the most vulnerable. Some children's oversensitive nervous systems make them prone to easy overload.

Several problems may be seen with children who are susceptible to overstimulation, overarousal, or sensory-modulation difficulties. Each sensory modality (auditory, visual, olfactory, tactile; and postural, or vestibular/proprioceptive) may easily be registered and processed by the child as a single modality. However, when bombarded with multiple sensory information, the child may become overwhelmed and overstimulated. Processing of multiple sensory (polymodal) information can be particularly difficult; and the accumulation of information coming in from multiple-sensory experiences can trigger undesirable reactions.

In other cases, children may be particularly vulnerable to overarousal of information from one or two senses. Often there is a neurological association between these systems, such as the vestibular system and the auditory system. Tactile defensiveness (hypersensitivity to touch), gravitational insecurities (hypersensitivity to balance and movement), and auditory hypersensitivity are examples of modulation or regulatory disorders seen in specific sensory systems. These disorders may occur in isolation or in combination with other sensitivities. Sensory-based avoidance and escape responses will be discussed further in Chapters 9 and 10. Inconsistencies also may be noted; the child may be underresponsive to one system, such as vestibular, but oversensitive to, say, auditory information.

Often, children are not consciously aware that they are experiencing sensory overload. Each child will develop unique coping strategies. A child who is hypersensitive to sound may talk or chatter nonstop to block out other noises in the environment. A child who is hypersensitive to touch may obsessively control every aspect of the environment in order to manage the tactile information coming into his system. Children who are fearful of movement and balance activities may run away from threatening activities or become aggressive. Children develop unique and often challenging behaviors that help them feel better for the moment but may interfere with their long-term learning.

A nonverbal child may use head banging, biting, grinding the teeth, hiding under objects, or rocking as a method of calming himself when overstimulated. These methods all are a form of deep proprioceptive input that neurologically calms the nervous system. Slow, rhythmic movements, such as rocking or head banging, have been known to calm the system and provide a sense of organization through slow vestibular input. Head banging, biting and other self-injurious behaviors also may be used in an attempt to self-calm and self-sedate. These behaviors trigger the release of endorphins, pain inhibitors produced within the body. They are opiate-like substances that numb the system. These challenging behaviors need to be modified into more constructive, socially acceptable behaviors that give the child constructive methods of meeting sensory-based needs.

Systemic Avoidance

It takes years for normal children to learn how they feel inside and to be able to communicate these feelings to adults. In many situations, the child describes vague symptoms or discomforts and the parent struggles to learn what is causing the child to act distressed. The child is brought from doctor to doctor until either he starts to feel better or a problem and treatment is identified.

Children with autism experience similar feelings and discomforts. They may feel hot, fatigued, hungry, be in pain, or be generally irritable. Change may be more difficult for them to tolerate, and it may be actually uncomfortable. They may experience a change inside their bodies and be uncertain of what it is. This internal response may be as simple as hunger or more intense as pain or discomfort from an injury. Other possibilities include an illness or impending illness, an allergic reaction to food or to something they touched, or even a histamine reaction to an insect bite. Children experiencing sensory overload may learn techniques to block out the input or calm their systems; but with internal systemic reactions, often these children are ineffective in alleviating their discomfort. They may be cranky and inconsolable. Challenging behaviors may erupt out of frustration or the disorganization experienced within their systems.

CHAPTER 4

Behavioral Issues
Creating an Environment for Optimal Functioning

Carolyn Murray-Slutsky

After identifying the primary cause of the challenging behavior, we need to arrange the environment to enable the child to function to his maximum capabilities. Intervention needs to remediate the primary cause of the behavior, providing the child the optimal environment for functioning, while modifying the challenging behavior. Comprehensive intervention programs are necessary to improve the child's functional abilities while managing his behavior.

To create an environment that facilitates optimal functioning, we need look critically at both the environment and ourselves. What can we change that will assist the child to perform optimally and decrease the behaviors that are interfering? By analyzing the factors that contribute to an increase in the challenging behavior, we will develop insights into environmental factors that are adversely impacting the child's ability to function. Comparing the factors that make the behaviors less likely to occur to the factors that make the behaviors more likely to occur will help us prioritize environmental modifications. (See Table 4.1.)

We cannot accommodate all environmental changes that will contribute to the child's optimal functioning. However, changing only one or two aspects of your therapy approach, your teaching style, or your personal organization often contributes to the child's ability to process and interact more effectively within the environment.

TABLE 4.1   Environmental factors that impact behavior

Behaviors are more likely to occur when	Behaviors are less likely to occur when
In a large room	In a small room
Tasks are unstructured	Tasks are structured
Transitions are poorly planned	Transitions are planned in advance
Tasks are adult-directed	Tasks are child-directed
There is a high child-adult ratio	Child-adult ratio is 1:1
Others are in close proximity	Child has space; no one physically near
The child is stressed or frustrated	Assistance, support, and encouragement are provided
The environment is noisy, cluttered	The environment is quiet, free from distractions and clutter
People, activities, places change	People, activities, and the environment are familiar; there is repetition and routine
The child is bored, unstimulated	The child is engrossed in the task; activities are stimulating, interesting
Waiting time is excessive	Waiting time is minimized

The environmental factors identified are to be used as a general guide to assist your observation skills. No two children are the same. Environmental factors that diminish one child's challenging behavior may increase another child's behavior. Prepare an individualized list for each child and each challenging behavior.

 # Design the Environment

Predictability, structure, and *organization* are words that describe the environment in which children with autism thrive. These children have difficulty organizing themselves and recognizing which aspects of the environment are important. They feel relaxed, comfortable, and able to function when they are in environments that provide structure and organization. In the preparation phase of any treatment, assure that the environment is set up for optimal functioning. The guidelines set forth in Table 4.2 may help you in designing the optimal environment.

Defined Boundaries

Children with autism need external structure. The boundaries of a room are defined by their size. Small rooms have clear-cut, definable boundaries that help the child maintain a sense of organization and control. Large, open rooms often appear to have no boundaries, requiring greater internal organization and control from the child. Subdivide large rooms to provide boundaries. Arrange bookcases, portable partitions, and furniture to define the space and boundaries.

Children also need defined boundaries to help them organize their behavior. Establish rules and expectations for their behavior to help them define the boundaries within which they may function.

TABLE 4.2   Setting up the physical, sensory, and emotional environment

The environment	Preparation
Defined boundaries	Use small, enclosed rooms; or define boundaries by using portable partitions or bookcases. Set boundaries for expectations and behaviors.
Clutter-free environment	Eliminate extraneous distractions on the walls. Store supplies and equipment out of view when they are not in use. • Gather needed supplies in advance. Keep them close by, but out of sight, until needed. • Take out only the supplies needed at the time. • Put away all equipment when finished with each task. • When appropriate, make cleanup a part of every activity. • If it is inappropriate to spend time on cleanup, move used supplies out of the child's view, proceed to the next activity, and put them away later.
Sensory environment	Modifications may be needed based on the child's primary needs.
Emotional environment	Provide a nurturing, positive, and supportive environment.

Clutter-Free Environment

Children with autism commonly focus on aspects of their environment that are considered insignificant to others. By controlling the clutter in the environment, we can help these children develop their internal sense of organization, thereby helping them function optimally.

Keep walls free of extraneous distractions. If items are tacked on walls, be sure they are appropriate to what the children need to learn. Walls cluttered with pictures, words, designs, and other distracting information will require greater internal organization and higher sensory thresholds. Many of these children cannot suppress irrelevant visual information, and therefore, will have a very difficult time functioning in a visually distracting environment.

Set up the environment in advance of the child's arrival. Gather specific supplies and equipment in advance, and place them out of sight, but within easy reach, at the location where they will be used. Place supplies in a crate out of sight or behind a bench that is turned on its side to form a divider. Take out only the supplies needed at the time.

Place items in clear view if you want the child to see them. Use those items to guide the child from activity to activity. Store large pieces of therapy equipment (such as platform and tire swings) behind a partition, or stack them neatly in a corner until needed.

Put away all equipment when finished with each task. Be aware that you can lose control of the child at the same time you lose control over the environment. Assist the child to put toys in the appropriate containers. If it is inappropriate to spend time on clean-up, move the used supplies out of the child's visual field and progress to the next activity. Once the child is engrossed in the new activity, put away the previous supplies or stack them neatly out of sight.

Sensory Environment

Noise levels, visual distractions, odors, and the number and proximity of other children contribute to the sensory environment. Make sure the environment meets each child's sensory needs. A child who is hypersensitive to auditory stimuli may have a very difficult time functioning in an open classroom, a large clinic, or a room in which many children are making a lot of noise; but a child who is hyporesponsive to sensory stimuli may thrive in that environment. The stimulation may raise that child's level of arousal sufficient to help him (See Chapter 3, Sensory-Based Obtaining and Avoidance Behaviors.)

Emotional Environment

Nurturing, positive, and supportive environments bring out the best in all children. It is important to understand the individual child, encourage his participation, and respond based on his needs. People in the child's environment must be able to see his positive aspects along with his weaknesses. Children innately sense when people believe in them and their abilities, and they respond positively when the environment reflects trust and mutual respect. A positive emotional environment is projected through verbal and nonverbal behaviors.

Maximize Strategies and Systems

What happens within the environment has an impact on the child's ability to function as much as the environment itself. Children with autism have difficulties interpreting social innuendo and abstract concepts, and they function best when they know what to expect and what will occur next. Anxiety is reduced and compliance increased by controlling these children's activities. Some children function best when they can have some say in what will happen next. Whenever possible, allow choices. This will motivate the child, increase his investment in the task, and decrease challenging behaviors. See Table 4.3 for some simple systems and aids that can help the child to feel comfortable within the environment.

Schedules and Planned Activities

Schedules come in different forms and have different purposes. Therapists are accustomed to working from a treatment plan in a prescribed manner; and how the treatment plan is implemented often is at the therapist's discretion.

You may organize the treatment session in many different sequences. Follow a logical sequence in activity choice and progression. Progress from:

- Highly structured activities to less structured activities (for example, fine motor tasks while sitting at a table, progressing to sensory-based total-body activities)

- An enjoyable gross motor activity to a hard, exercise-based activity

- Sensory-based to nonsensory-based activities

Progress through specific phases of treatment. When organizing a session by phases, the treatment phase is defined by the pattern of activities selected. The session may begin with preparation activities such as total-body, sensory-motor activities that prepare the child to function. The second phase may be the activation phase—the heavy workout section of treatment that involves specific exercises and activities geared at remediating underlying problems. The third phase may be the function phase in which the child practices specific functional skills.

TABLE 4.3   Strategies and systems to increase performance

Schedules and planned activities	Provide organization and format to the activities selected for each session. • Start with highly structured activities, progressing to less structured activities. Provide a logical structure: • Preparation (for example, sensory-based activities) • Facilitation (for example, hard work and strengthening exercises) • Functional tasks (for example, writing) Alternate hard-work activities with sensory-based fun activities. Let children anticipate the planned sequence of events, or at least the next activity.
Down time	Minimize waiting time and time between activities. Be prepared, with all needed supplies at hand. Keep activities moving at a constant or rapid rate. Keep the child busy or mentally involved.
Transitions	Begin each session with the same activity. Prepare the child for the change. Give advance notice verbally. Use visual reminders. Use a preferred item as a distraction.
Choices and control	Choose activities that enable choices.
Defined rules	Teach rules that will help children succeed. Specify rules clearly and concisely. Be sure the child understands the rules and the consequences, if any. Help children link the action with the consequence. Enforce rules consistently. Post the rules. Review them with the children before each session.
Concise instructions	Limit extraneous verbalization. Monitor your instructions. Be brief and concise. Do not ask whether a child wants to do something unless you are prepared to let him decline. Keep verbalizations specific to the task. Use gestures with verbal instructions. If necessary, limit instructions to one or two words.
Interesting activities	Tasks that are interesting, motivating, and challenging keep children engrossed.
Quantified tasks	Let the child know the end point of the task. Specify how many items are to be completed. Break tasks into component parts that appear manageable.

While activities vary within each phase, the types of activities within each phase remain the same. Predictable schedules and activities and logical activity progressions help the child relax within the environment. Stress-free environments promote optimal functioning.

Children function optimally when they know there is a basic schedule for each session and within each environment. Some children function best knowing the entire schedule start to finish, while others need to know only the next activity. You may choose not to verbalize the schedule ("After we do ___, we will do ___."), but instead visually indicate the next activity by placing it within the child's visual field.

Schedules and planned activities are abstract concepts that do not exist in the *here and now*. They are projections of the future and require an understanding of time and space. The child must have *feedforward*, an understanding and anticipation of the future. Visual schedules can help the child anticipate the next activity as well as the sequence of activities. They provide a definite end to the tasks.

A visual schedule can be as simple as writing the sequence of activities on the chalkboard. Teachers often post the class schedule with the time frame for engaging in each activity. Depending on the child and the therapist's goals, plan the schedule with the child's cooperation at the beginning of each session. Write out the sequence of therapy activities, giving the child choices where possible.

Picture System Schedule

You may want to use pictures to provide concrete visual schedules. Select pictures to depict each activity. Then arrange them on a board to show the sequence of activities that will be performed. When each activity is completed, let the child take the picture off the board or turn it over.

Down Time

Minimize down time. Challenging behaviors can surface during unscheduled time between activities. Although teaching a child to wait patiently may be a therapy goal, usually it is not a primary goal. Treatment sessions that minimize down time can maximize the child's quality time with the therapist and increase the child's ability to function.

Preparation is the key to minimizing down time. Have all needed supplies at hand. Keep activities moving at a constant or rapid rate to prevent the child from *spacing out* into self-stimulation or inattentive behaviors and keep his interest throughout the session.

There may be times when down time cannot be prevented. During those times, keep the child busy and mentally involved. Most children will not sit quietly while the therapist leaves the area to get needed supplies. Engage the child physically or mentally with an activity before you leave to get the supplies. If you have no activity, ask the child to count to 10 forward or backward, or have him close his eyes and count to 10. Closing his eyes will help him avoid visual distractions. If you cannot engage the child physically or mentally during down time, incorporate the time into your treatment and have the child go with you.

Transitions

Change makes many children anxious. Transitions between activities represent change that can trigger anxiety, stress, and behaviors that are difficult to manage. Several techniques are effective in helping a child through transitions.

Begin each session with the same *first* activity. This practice will decrease the anxiety associated with the transition and prepares the child for success by assuring compliance. You may begin the session by saying, "We will go to point A and remove our socks and shoes before we play." Be sure the child understands the rules.

Schedules prepare children for the sequence of activities, but often they need preparation for the end of the task. Give advance notice of the end. Whenever possible, use visual reminders or verbal concrete ends before moving to the next activity. For example, say, "We will do five more"; and then count backward from five as the child completes the task ("We have only four more . . . Three more," and so on).

If the child is anxious about the task you are about to introduce, use a preferred item as a distraction. For example, if the child is anxious about paper-and-pencil tasks but loves a certain character action toy, distract his attention from the difficult aspect of the task to the pleasant aspect—the character—to help the anxiety pass. For example, place the character toy on the child's desk for writing tasks. Let the child play with the toy for a few minutes before you begin the session; or ask the child to write about the character. This distraction enables ample opportunities for positive feedback and reward before the child refocuses on the task at hand.

Choices and Control

Rather than fight with children over task selection, it may be helpful to give him control over the tasks or activities. Every activity can enable choices without sacrificing the therapeutic value of the task at hand. For example, ask the child, "Do you want to use crayons or colored pencils?"; "Do you want to do the scooterboard or the net swing?"; "You choose the next activity. Then it is my turn" or "You choose the activity, and I will choose how you will do it" (indicating on one foot, half-kneeling, and so on).

Defined Rules

Almost all environments have rules. However, we cannot assume that children with autism will pick up the nonverbal cues that govern the rules. They need to be taught the rules that will help them be successful. State the rules specifically, clearly, and concisely (for example, "No running allowed"). We also need to be sure that they understand the consequences, if there are any. Have them repeat the rules and the consequences of breaking them. It is important that they be able to link what they did with the consequences. ("What were you doing? Were you running? You were running. What happens when you run?") When there are rules, they must be enforced consistently. You may want to post the rules as a visual reminder, especially if the rules apply to everyone within the environment. Review the rules before beginning each session.

Concise Instructions

Children often have difficulty with auditory processing and understanding verbal directions and instructions. Auditory instructions are abstract and difficult for many children to understand. Often, talking too much can confuse these children. Give short, concise instructions that sometimes consist of only one or two words. Using gestures or demonstrations with verbal instructions adds a visual component and helps increase comprehension.

Limit verbalizations to the specific task or command, especially when a child is just learning words. Extraneous verbalizations serve only to confuse the child. Off-task questions or statements (for example, "Are we having fun?" or "Did you know this game is ___?") may distract and confuse a child who is having difficulty following the original direction.

Do not ask a child, "Do you want to do ___?" unless you are prepared to let him decline.

Interesting Tasks

Activities that are interesting, motivating, and challenging are more likely to keep the child engrossed in the task.

Quantified Tasks

Let the child know the end point of tasks or how many items he will need to do. Place the items in front of the child. For example, if you want the child to put ten pegs into the pegboard, place ten pegs on the table. This becomes very important when the item is difficult.

Break tasks into component parts that appear manageable. Do not overwhelm the child. Rather than telling him that he will have to put all the pegs in the pegboard, tell him he needs to put all the red ones in. When he finishes the red ones, he can do the blue ones, and so on, until all the pegs are put in the pegboard.

Use delayed reinforcement techniques. When you observe the beginning signs of fatigue, identify the number of items the child needs to complete in order to terminate the activity. Challenging behaviors are often exhibited when a child does not see the end to a difficult task.

CHAPTER 5

Behavioral Issues

Treatment Strategies That Facilitate Positive Outcomes

Carolyn Murray-Slutsky

W e have seen that challenging behaviors first develop to meet a need. They serve as coping strategies; if they are effective, the child repeats them until they become automatic responses. These behaviors persist because of the secondary rewards. The child is comfortable with the routine and the behavior, his needs are met through the behavior, and he receives satisfaction and reward from his environment. To change the challenging behavior, we must modify our response to the behavior while giving the child more effective coping strategies.

 ## Secondary Reinforcers

Negative Attention

We must thwart any impulse to punish or reprimand negative behavior. Negative attention is often given in a loud voice with strong sensory experiences tied to it—the firm hand grasp, swift removal of an object, and one-to-one attention. A darting glance of disapproval, time out, and various forms of punishment are forms of negative attention that can serve as strong secondary reinforcers to the behavior you are trying to stop.

Unexpectedly, Michael lunges at you. You quickly grasp his hands, look him in the eyes, and say, "Don't do that!"

Without thinking, you have just given Michael deep touch input (grasping his hands firmly), eye contact, and negative attention. Michael just learned that when he wants something, lunging at you gives him comfort (deep touch) and immediate one-to-one attention.

We must give more attention to on-task and appropriate behaviors. Anticipating the child's behavior helps us intercede before the negative behavior. We may be able to prevent the behavior from occurring and teach the child better coping strategies. When the unwanted behavior (here, the lunging) occurs, lightly encircle the child's wrist with your fingers while redirecting his hands functionally. Avert the child's gaze by looking away, and stay calm. When the child demonstrates on-task behavior, give eye contact and specific reinforcement. By doing so, you have turned negative attention into positive feedback and quiet on-task behavior.

Behavioral Philosophies and Strategies

The goal of intervention is to protect the child from failure and help him build self-confidence and a sense of mastery over his environment. We must give the child new skills and behaviors that replace ineffective ones. The new behaviors must receive more attention and rewards than the old behaviors. This means that tantrums must be ignored or made ineffective, attempts to throw objects must be quietly redirected to a functional task, and fleeing behaviors must not result in task avoidance.

Once we know the primary underlying cause of the behavior, it would be nice to wait to see what happens as we work on improving the child's coordination, strength, sensory-motor skills, and overall processing. However, the child can't lose the time waiting until the underlying problem is *cured* and therapy is effective. The child has developed ineffective coping strategies and challenging behaviors that interfere with therapy, learning, and living. Even if we are able to eliminate the behaviors and *cure* the underlying sensory, motor, communication, and learning problems, the child will not have the skills needed to be successful in the environment.

We must treat the underlying problem causing the challenging behavior, while giving the child coping strategies and behaviors that work *now*. This involves a proactive approach. We must know which behavior we want to develop, and provide the child the tools, the time, and the environment to practice these new behaviors and strategies. Often we must use behavioral strategies to extinguish the interfering behaviors that block the child's skill acquisition and active participation in therapy. Facilitation techniques are needed to teach coping strategies and skills. Being proactive, intervening before the problem has occurred, and using some basic behavioral strategies can help improve the quality of therapy sessions, resulting in quicker functional improvements.

Intervene Before the Challenging Behavior Occurs

Once the behavior is displayed, we are in a position where we need to deal with it. Usually this is exhausting and emotionally draining. While techniques for effectively dealing with challenging behaviors are discussed in Chapter 6, we want to avoid the need for using them. If we are proactive, we can intervene before the behavior occurs and teach the child positive coping skills.

Proactive strategies focus on the child's positive, constructive, on-task behaviors while ignoring or redirecting off-task behaviors. Behavioral strategies become important in accomplishing this. See Table 5.1.

TABLE 5.1 Effective treatment strategies

Identify the target behavior.	Identify the behavior you want to occur, not the challenging behavior you want to stop.
Attend to on-task behavior.	Give more attention to on-task behaviors than to negative behaviors. Provide reinforcement every time the new behavior is displayed.
Avoid punishment and verbal reprimands.	Negative attention, reprimands, and punishment reward the exact behavior you are trying to stop.
Reinforcers	Describe the targeted behavior and appropriate reinforcer. All rewards and forms of reinforcement must be motivating to the child. Reinforce only the targeted behavior. Reinforce the targeted behavior immediately. Reinforce the targeted behavior consistently. Grade reinforcers from primary to secondary, and from consistent to intermittent. To function independently, a child needs to be internally motivated and respond to secondary motivators provided intermittently.
Delayed gratification and reinforcement	Teach the child to tolerate delayed gratification or reinforcement while they continue to work. Wait until just before the child reaches maximum level; present a concrete end to the task slightly beyond the child's tolerance; then provide reinforcement.
Prompting and facilitating	Never use prompts until you know the child's baseline functioning without prompts or assistance. • Physical prompt or facilitation—Therapist provides physical assistance and guides the child through the activity • Visual prompt—Therapist provides visual cues, drawings, symbols, or written rules or instructions that assist the child to sequence the task • Demonstration—Therapist demonstrates the desired response while the child imitates it. This requires that the child have a good sensory-motor concept of his body. • Modeling—A child models the desired response for another child. • Auditory or verbal prompts—Therapist assists the child with verbal directions. Prompts can be given by varying voice volume and inflections. Combine prompts to gradually decrease the assistance provided.
Shaping the response	Used to teach a behavior or skill that is not in the child's repertoire • Forward chaining—Task is broken into component parts. Child is taught to independently perform the steps, from the first to the last. • Backward chaining—Task is broken into component parts. Child is taught to independently perform the steps, from the last to the first.
Time out	Taking time out—Child with sensory overload, anxiety, or regulatory disorders is taught to take time out to reorganize. Keep atmosphere positive and compassionate. Giving time out—A reactive approach usually used as a form of punishment. Avoid it. Therapist's time out—Technique used to interrupt attention-seeking challenging behaviors in order to reward appropriate behavior. Therapist stops and shuts down all work, averting gaze for 15 to 20 seconds; then rewards next appropriate behavior.

Reinforcers

The first step in using reinforcers is to identify a specific desired behavior. It is not enough to know which behavior we do not want; we also must mold the correct behavior. The second step is to identify a reward that is reinforcing to the child. The third step is to give the reward consistently, immediately, and *only* for the specific desired behavior.

Because behaviors that are followed by positive events are more likely to be repeated, we need to know what the child views as positive and motivating. This can be the single most important factor in designing a successful therapy session. During the initial session, pay particular attention to what motivates the child. If the child responds better to negative attention, analyze the components to discover the motivating characteristic. Is the child seeking the high volume, the intensity, the firm touch? Apply these traits to praise, thus transferring the negative attention-seeking behavior to positive-seeking behavior. Vary the reinforcers and motivators throughout the therapy sessions depending on the level of difficulty and sensory components of the task and the child's interests and functional level. Reinforcers follow a natural hierarchy and may be graded from primary reinforcer to secondary reinforcer and from being applied consistently to intermittently.

Primary Reinforcers

Primary reinforcers are activities and tasks that are naturally reinforcing. The reinforcer is inherent in the task or object. Foods, drinks, and snacks are examples of common primary reinforcers. When using food as a primary reinforcer, use very small portions or single objects so that it is not filling, lessening its effectiveness. Many sensory-based activities can be primary reinforcers, depending on the individual child's preferences. For a child who craves proprioceptive input (into the joints) or vestibular input (movement), jumping on a trampoline, being thrown in the air, and swinging are primary reinforcers. A child with decreased sensory feedback in the hands may like to use resistive clothespins. Children, who find sounds reinforcing, enjoy having sounds paired with movements (for example, vocalizations paired with pencil strokes). Singing and rhythmic activities are primary reinforcers for many children.

Secondary Reinforcers

Secondary reinforcers have qualities that the child likes. These include praise, attention, a privilege, stickers, tokens or money, smiley faces, and nonsensory-based toys or activities. When using a small toy as a secondary reinforcer, many people give the child the toy for a few seconds, then take it back and progress to the next task. It is important that children move from using primary to secondary reinforcement. To accomplish this, we need to link primary with secondary reinforcers. For example, praise the child (secondary reinforcement) for successful task completion while rewarding with a primary reinforcement (jumping on a trampoline or a food reward). Then gradually decrease the frequency of giving the primary reinforcer while increasing the frequency of the praise.

Grading Reinforcers

It is essential to grade reinforcers from primary to secondary and from consistently administered to intermittently. Consistently administered reinforcers are effective in *developing* a new behavior; however, they must be given every time the desired behavior occurs (no matter what environment it occurs within), or the behavior will not become established. New behaviors must be reinforced consistently and more frequently than the behaviors you are trying to extinguish. This is very labor intensive.

Intermittent reinforcement, the strongest form of reinforcement, is less demanding and more effective in *maintaining* a behavior. It is less labor intensive and is used to maintain a child's internal motivation and drive. It also is responsible for maintaining desirable as well as undesirable behaviors. In the case study mentioned before, when Michael lunges at you, redirect his behaviors into a functional task; then reward his on-task behavior. Because this is a new behavior for Michael, it must be reinforced consistently, at first often linking both primary and secondary reinforcers. As the new behavior becomes established and the negative attention-seeking behavior diminishes, he may be moved to intermittent reinforcement of on-task behavior. However, if he is successful *even once* in obtaining the negative attention he desires, he has received intermittent reinforcement, and the undesired behavior will persist.

Because rewards can be a method of helping the child through difficult tasks, the reinforcers may need to be changed based on the difficulty of the task. You may need to use food as a primary reinforcer for a new task, while using secondary reinforcers for others. Primary reinforcers also may be needed to reward the child for performing tasks that are necessary for functioning, but are not intrinsically motivating. For example, a child not driven to speak will not be intrinsically motivated to repeat words or make verbal utterances. Primary reinforcers of desirable sensory experiences or foods may be linked to repeating sounds or words. Once the child produces the desired response, it can be linked to both the primary and the secondary reinforcer of praise.

The goal is to tap into the child's internal motivation and drive. If the child learns to function only with external rewards, we are failing to teach coping skills. To function independently, the child must be internally motivated, responding to secondary motivators (praise) only intermittently.

Delayed Gratification and Reinforcement

Teaching a child to tolerate delayed gratification or a delay in reinforcement is another technique that is easily integrated into therapy sessions and is effective in staving off attention-seeking and avoidance behaviors. Learn to recognize the child's tolerance and frustration level-the point at which he begins to lose interest in an activity. Wait until just before the child's maximum level, where the challenging behavior is about to be exhibited, and intervene at that point. Specify the number of repetitions or time needed to complete the work, end the task, or gain the desired activity or reward. When the child reaches the specified point, release him from the task and give positive reinforcement. Gradually increase the amount of time the child must wait before ending the task.

> Aaron has difficulty with fine motor tasks. Working with his therapist, he is placing pegs in a board. Normally, Aaron can put only four pegs into the board before he becomes frustrated and starts throwing things. After the third peg, Aaron begins to shift

around in his chair and his tension increases. The therapist encourages and praises him for his good work and gives the command to delay gratification, saying, "Aaron, only two more and you can jump on the trampoline." The therapist then takes away all pegs except two. Aaron's tension decreases as soon as he knows there is an end to the task. He does not need to use his challenging behaviors to escape. The therapist gets Aaron to complete five pegs, rather than four. As Aaron's skills increase, the target number is increased. The therapist reads Aaron's nonverbal cues of frustration, gradually pushing his tolerance for the task and delaying reinforcement further.

Teaching tolerance for delayed gratification also is an effective method of teaching self-awareness and communication strategies and rewarding on-task behavior. Be specific when facilitating the communication request and rewarding the on-task behavior.

Alex is swinging in the net and playing basketball. His affect is animated, and he is engrossed in the game. The therapist is using vestibular input to strengthen his extensor muscles throughout his neck, back, and shoulder girdle. Alex starts showing signs of fatigue. His face becomes serious, and he begins to shift in the net. He tries to cross his legs over to give himself more stability. If left to continue, he will become silly, distractible, and try to get out of the net and run away. The therapist stops him. Ending the task here would be logical, but Alex needs to recognize how he feels and learn socially acceptable ways to communicate his feelings before he displays challenging behaviors. The therapist asks, "How do you feel? Is your neck tired? Are you tired?" Alex answers, "I'm tired." The therapist says, "You're tired. Put your head down for a few minutes, and rest. Then we'll do two more and quit." After a break, Alex continues the exercise. On subsequent sessions, he is able to request a break, saying, "I'm tired."

Time Out

Time out can be a positive or negative technique depending on when and how it is used; that is, whether you are taking time out, giving time out, or taking a therapeutic time out.

Taking Time Out

Taking time out is an effective technique to teach self-regulation to a child who is experiencing anxiety or sensory overload from the environment. When a child is escalating, becoming overwhelmed, or is overwhelmed and out of control, time out can give the edge he needs to regroup and reorganize. Teach the child to recognize signs of escalating behaviors and techniques that will help him reorganize. Visual aids such as using cards with the colors of a stoplight are often helpful in teaching self-awareness. Green means "You're fine," yellow means, "You're escalating," and red means, "Take time out." Give a color card to the child and guide him to take a time out; or just turn over the card and nod, and the child will take a time out until he is calm and ready to return to the group or activity. Taking time out must be used compassionately as a method of getting the child out of the situation so he can pull himself together; it cannot be used as a form of punishment. It must not have a negative connotation, and your voice quality and volume must be calm. Whenever possible, allow the child to be involved in choosing where the time out will be taken. Be sure that the child does not take time out to avoid a task.

Giving Time Out

Giving time out usually is used as a form of punishment and has a negative connotation. A person giving time out is usually reacting to the behavior rather than being proactive in preventing it. Avoid giving time out. It is important to analyze the cause of the child's behavior. If it is caused by fear or avoidance of the task or event, the time out rewards the behavior and provides the escape the child is seeking. Giving time out is beneficial only when a child is engaged in an attention-seeking *nonproductive* behavior that the child views as pleasurable. The time out then removes the child from the pleasurable activity for a brief period of time in order to elicit and reward on-task behavior.

During the time out, it is important that the child does not receive reinforcement. No one should talk to the child, make eye contact, or attend to any ploys to get attention. If the child's behaviors cannot be ignored, he may need to be physically removed from the area. Using a timer is an effective way of monitoring the time out.

Alex is working on a coloring project at his desk. His classmates are nearby and working hard. Intermittently, the teacher appropriately acknowledges both Alex's on-task behavior and that of his classmates. Alex suddenly begins to engage in self-stimulatory, attention-seeking, disruptive behavior. He begins with loud vocal play and giggling, progressing to rolling his crayons between his fingers, throwing them, and grabbing other children's crayons. The vocal play and tactile input from the crayons provides pleasurable sensory feedback, which increases in frequency as the teacher and the classmates ignore him.

The teacher quietly walks to Alex's desk, visually and verbally attending to the *other* children's on-task behavior. Without making eye contact, the teacher places Alex's hands in his lap and turns his chair away from the desk and the other children. She tells one child, "Robby, I like how quietly you are working," and another child, "MaCris, you are keeping your crayons neatly on your desk. Good work!" As soon as Alex quiets down, she turns his chair around and places a crayon in his hand. When he begins to work appropriately, she acknowledges his work and tells him, "Alex, I like how quietly you are working."

Therapist's Time Out

This time out is used to interrupt attention-seeking challenging behaviors. Stop, shut down all work, and avert your gaze for 15 to 20 seconds. This technique is effective when working one-to-one with a child who uses loud vocalization or attention-getting behaviors that are difficult to ignore. By shutting down and averting your gaze, you wait for an interruption in the child's behavior to reinforce quiet behavior. Time outs that last longer than 20 seconds can have a reinforcing effect on the challenging behavior, and therefore they must be closely monitored.

Prompting

Prompting or facilitating a child's response is a technique that is used frequently. Therapists who are skilled in neuro-developmental treatment (NDT) techniques have perfected physical handling and facilitation techniques to obtain desired motor movements. Prompting or facilitating a child's response becomes important when you want to help a child learn a movement, behavior, or skill.

Prompts can be provided in many ways. Physical prompts or facilitation, verbal instructions, physical assistance, demonstration, visuals, modeling, gestures, voice inflection and volume, glances, and facial expression are methods of prompting a child through a task or response. Prompts should never be given unless the child needs the assistance. At the beginning of each session, assess the child's current level of functioning before prompting. Grade prompts within each session, and diminish or fade the amount of assistance given.

Physical Prompts

These prompts involve physically guiding or assisting the child to complete a desired activity. They can be completely dependent, in which the therapist controls the child's full movements (such as in hand-over-hand assistance); or the child can do the majority of the activity and the therapist is available to prompt the child when he might stop. Physical prompts also may be used to teach compliance to a verbal request (for example, saying, "Sit down" while giving a gentle push for the child to sit). Children who are easily overwhelmed by verbal instructions respond favorably to physical prompts. They help the child stay organized and in control in difficult environments. For example, following complex directions in an open, unstructured environment could lead to negative interactions and frequent negative reprimands for a child who has difficulty staying focused in that environment. With physical prompts, the child can be successfully guided through the instructions and environment. Positive feedback and interactions can be facilitated, and both the therapist and the child can feel good about the interaction.

Physical prompts also are effective in modifying undesirable self-stimulation behaviors that interfere with task performance without paying direct attention to and negatively reinforcing the behavior. Self-stimulation behaviors that are repetitive and serve no sensory purpose can be easily redirected into a functional task. For example, when a child starts flapping her hands during fine motor tasks, the therapist can subtly guide her hands back to the functional task or into a quiet position. Extinguish self-stimulation behaviors (such as hand flapping, rapid eye movement, spinning or fingering objects, and obsessions with small objects and strings) by not reacting, removing the object, providing some other type of activity, and redirecting the hands into productive positions and responses. Reward appropriate behavior immediately.

Visual Prompts

Physical assistance provides the greatest amount of assistance; visual prompts provide less. Visual prompts may include:

- Visually cueing the child to the correct response (such as pointing to the correct response)

- Cueing the child to visually scan the answers by moving your finger from left to right across the page

- Visually placing the correct answer closer to the child to increase the likelihood that he may choose it

- Physically gesturing the meaning of a word (such as *stand up* or *sit down*)

- Visually glancing in the direction of the child to keep him on task

Drawings or symbols also are visual prompts that remind the child of what he needs to do. Rules posted on a wall, schedules written on a chalkboard, and pictures that depict the next activity are other examples of visual prompts. The pictures may depict skills the child needs to practice. Visual prompts are an effective way of transforming abstract concepts into more concrete images. They can be effective in serving as a method of teaching self-monitoring and self-awareness.

> Steven's occupational therapist is frustrated over his lack of compliance. Sessions have become battlegrounds in which Steven refuses to comply with any request, even if it is clearly within his capability. In the past, Steven used task refusal as a method of coping with decreased processing skills. When he did not understand what was being asked of him, he would say, "No, I don't want to do this, I want to do that." By controlling both the request and the activity, he could assure that he both understood the request and could complete the activity. He learned to link negative responses with whining behaviors, reverting to the latter when "No" did not work.
>
> Steven's behavior now is a learned response that occurs automatically and spontaneously to any request or demand. It is interfering with his learning to improve both his processing skills and his functional skills. The negative tension also is counterproductive and interferes with his internal motivation and drive. The therapist is working on decreasing his negative and whining behaviors while improving his self-awareness and self-monitoring. A scoreboard-type sign is posted above Steven's workstation. He is asked to begin a task. He impulsively responds, "No." Without attending to his negative behavior, the therapist places a mark in the No column on the scoreboard. The task is reintroduced. Steven retorts, "No, I don't want to," and another mark is placed in the No column. This is done without emotion or a sense of punishment. By the fourth request, Steven responds with whining. The therapist asks, "Did I hear whining?" and describes whining behavior. The therapist moves a hand toward the Whining column

as if to mark it, and Steven yells, "No! Don't mark it. It's not whining. I said, 'I want to do it.'" The therapist repeats, "You want to do it. That's wonderful!" and moves away from the sign, rewarding the appropriate behavior. By the end of the session, the therapist has only to move in the direction of marking the sign to serve as a visual reminder of the desired behavior. Steven monitors what he is saying, stopping mid-sentence to self-correct.

Responding with "No" or whining was an automatic learned response that helped Steven cope when he could not process instructions. Now he has the skills to process instructions, but still he responds automatically to avert the task. By extinguishing the learned response, Steven was forced to process the verbal instructions. He realized he understood the request and that he had the skills needed to do the activity. What appeared to be lack of task compliance was actually a display of learned behavior.

Using cards with the colors of traffic lights (see page 51) can be used to monitor undesirable behaviors, escalating silliness, or off-task behaviors, while allowing children time to self-correct and get their behavior back in control. Stop signs also may be used at hallways where children need to stop and line up. In the classroom, teachers often list or post pictures of desirable behaviors. The children have matching lists or pictures on their desks, and the teacher gives smiley faces every 5 minutes or when the children display the desired behaviors. Rewarded behaviors may include sitting quietly in place, raising their hands, keeping hands to themselves, and not talking.

Demonstration and Modeling

Demonstration of the desired response by the therapist is considered an abstract form of visual prompting. Rather than providing physical assistance, you may assess whether the child has grasped the whole concept and is able to follow your demonstration. This is similar to imitation and requires that the child have a good sensorimotor concept of how his body moves in space. The child must first understand his body and how it relates to the environment before he can comprehend and imitate the bodily movements of others. This will be discussed further in Chapter 13, which addresses foundation skills to learning.

Modeling of a desired response by a peer is another abstract form of visual prompting. Modeling can be provided unobtrusively by pairing children. A child with stronger verbal skills may serve as a model for a child who is just learning to use functional language, or a child with more advanced fine motor skills may work next to a child who needs to acquire those skills. Rewarding the desired behavior in both children is critical. When the child is not attending to the appropriate behavior that is being modeled, draw attention to it by positively reinforcing the child who is modeling the desired response or behavior. ("Matthew, I love how you are holding the pencil. Your thumb is exactly where it should be"; or, "Matthew, you are writing beautifully. Your letters are coming just to the line"; or, "Look! Matthew is standing on one foot without holding on.") You may need to provide physical prompts to the second child in order to elicit the desired motor response. As soon as the second child begins to display the appropriate behavior, give praise immediately.

Controlled competition

Modeling may require more intense intervention, structure, and guidance. Adding a touch of controlled competition is often effective. Teaming two or three children and taking turns often works to model higher-level skills. In the following example, a game involving large cube blocks is chosen to teach verbal directions involving pronouns and colors.

> Steven is having difficulty following multiple-step directions and taking the work seriously. Matthew is available to model the desired response. Steven is given the instructions, " Put the blue cube on the red cube." He strolls to the cubes, picks up the blue cube, and places it between the yellow and red cubes. Steven is told, "No. Matthew, it's your turn." The therapist assures that Steven is attending, using physical prompts if needed. The same instructions are given. Matthew follows them exactly and is praised. "Steven, it's your turn. Put the blue cube on the red cube." Steven runs to the cubes, completes the instructions exactly, and is praised.
>
> At this point, the game can be increased in difficulty. Steven can be offered the opportunity to model the desired response for Matthew by asking, "Who wants to go first?" Steven can be chosen to model desired responses that are within his capability or slightly beyond. Matthew is available to guarantee Steven's success by modeling difficult responses.

Maintain control of all children used as models. They will have a tendency to want to play teacher and instruct the child with the lower skill level. Keep the atmosphere positive and empowering to the child with the lowest skill level.

Verbal Prompts

Receptive language skills are normally a weak area for children with autism. Verbal instructions can be confusing and often overwhelming. Our goal is to help children comprehend and follow verbal directions and instructions. Using verbal prompts or linking verbal instructions with visual cues, such as gestures or physical prompts, can be helpful. Grade prompts from the most concrete (physical prompts) to the more abstract (auditory prompts). Through linking prompts (that is, physical with verbal, then fading the concrete physical prompt), we can help children comprehend verbal instructions.

Voice inflection and volume

The simplest forms of verbal prompts are voice inflection and changes in voice volume. Use these to help children comprehend the aspect of the command they need to focus on. "Place the blue cube *on* the red cube," "Give me your *hand*," or "Give me *your* hand" are examples of how changes in inflection can be used as cues or prompts.

Changes in voice volume also can help children with sensory registration difficulties who tune out or do not attend to auditory information. (See Chapter 10.) Variations in volume and inflection may produce the change needed to help them register auditory information. Linking exaggerated verbal gestures can further enhance registration (for example, say, "What is it?" while shrugging your shoulders and opening your arms and hands as if to say, "I don't know").

Shaping Behaviors

Shaping is a technique that is used to teach a behavior that is not in the child's repertoire. It is another method of teaching the steps involved in a task and linking them. It is often associated with forward or backward chaining techniques. When using any chaining technique, break the task into its component parts.

Forward chaining focuses on having the child independently master the first step in the chain while you prompt or assist the later steps. The child is progressively asked to accomplish more steps in a forward direction as you decrease your amount of assistance. The advantage of this technique is that the child learns to master the technique from start to finish. The disadvantage is that the child may become frustrated when he associates task completion with independently completing the last step. Moving through all steps also can be time-consuming.

Shoe tying is an example of forward chaining; that is, following a progression through a task:

- Step 1. The therapist teaches the child to cross the strings; then:
- Step 2. Looping the top string under
- Step 3. Pulling tight
- Step 4. Making a right loop
- Step 5. Wrapping the left string around the loop
- Step 6. Pushing the left string through the hole from back to front
- Step 7. Pulling the loop through the hole
- Step 8. Holding one loop in the right hand and one in the left hand
- Step 9. Pulling tight.

Using forward chaining, the therapist works through all nine steps every time. The child is asked to complete Step 1 independently, is reinforced for successful step completion, and is guided through the remaining eight steps. Assistance is progressively decreased and the child is asked to complete steps 1 and 2; then 1, 2, and 3; and so on until the task is mastered and all nine steps are linked into task completion.

Backward chaining focuses on the child mastering the last step in the sequence first. The child then works backward until the first step in the chain is mastered. Again using shoe tying as an example, the therapist starts at Step 1, providing physically assistance through all subsequent eight steps. The child then completes Step 9, independently pulling the loops tight. The child then works backward to complete steps 8 and 9; then steps 7, 8, and 9; and so on. The advantage of backward chaining is that the child is rewarded for the last-step task completion.

This technique is effective when a child is afraid of failure or believes he cannot accomplish the task. The child will see immediate results. Many children will have renewed excitement over the feared activity, declaring, "I can tie my shoes!"

It is critical that everyone working with the child is familiar with the technique and promotes the same positive attitude. Asking the child to perform a partially mastered skill in another environment (such as at home) without the physical assistance for unlearned steps will result in failure and frustration. Techniques can be taught easily to parents and professionals working with the child, resulting in the child's success in completing the task and increasing his self-esteem.

Approximating Desired Behaviors

Shaping behaviors may involve rewarding behaviors that closely approximate the desired response. When you reward any movement in the desired direction, the child will begin to associate the desired response with the reward. Gradually give the reward only for the desired response or behavior. As frequency of the desired response increases, grade the rewards from primary to secondary, and from frequent to intermittent reinforcement.

CHAPTER 6

Behavioral Issues
Intervention Strategies

Carolyn Murray-Slutsky

We have analyzed the child's behavior, tracked the events that preceded the behavior, and identified secondary reinforcers. We know the environmental factors that make the behavior more or less likely to occur, and we can design an environment for optimal functioning, eliminating the secondary rewards to the challenging behavior. We have looked at the primary causes of the behaviors and have developed a theory of what causes the behavior to occur. We have examined whether the child displays obtaining or avoidance behaviors, and we have pinpointed exactly what the child is attempting to obtain or avoid. We understand that the child's behaviors are displayed to meet these needs. Now we need to identify intervention strategies that address the underlying problems. We will look at the behaviors and intervention strategies based on the basic needs they serve.

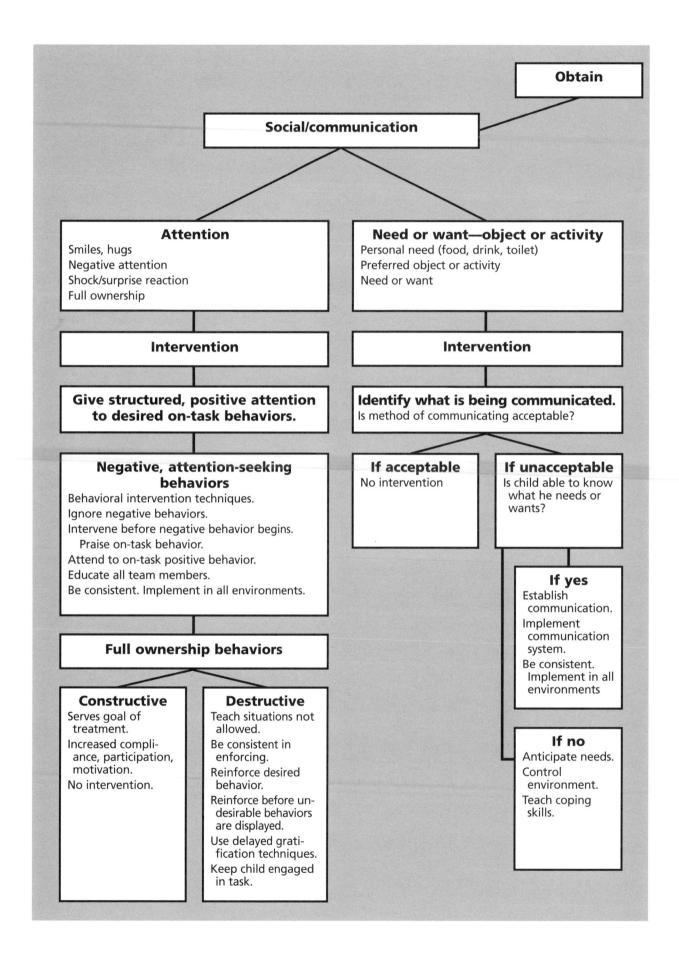

Obtain

Social/communication

Attention
Smiles, hugs
Negative attention
Shock/surprise reaction
Full ownership

Need or want—object or activity
Personal need (food, drink, toilet)
Preferred object or activity
Need or want

Intervention

Intervention

Give structured, positive attention to desired on-task behaviors.

Identify what is being communicated.
Is method of communicating acceptable?

Negative, attention-seeking behaviors
Behavioral intervention techniques.
Ignore negative behaviors.
Intervene before negative behavior begins.
   Praise on-task behavior.
Attend to on-task positive behavior.
Educate all team members.
Be consistent. Implement in all environments.

If acceptable
No intervention

If unacceptable
Is child able to know what he needs or wants?

If yes
Establish communication.
Implement communication system.
Be consistent. Implement in all environments

Full ownership behaviors

Constructive
Serves goal of treatment.
Increased compliance, participation, motivation.
No intervention.

Destructive
Teach situations not allowed.
Be consistent in enforcing.
Reinforce desired behavior.
Reinforce before undesirable behaviors are displayed.
Use delayed gratification techniques.
Keep child engaged in task.

If no
Anticipate needs.
Control environment.
Teach coping skills.

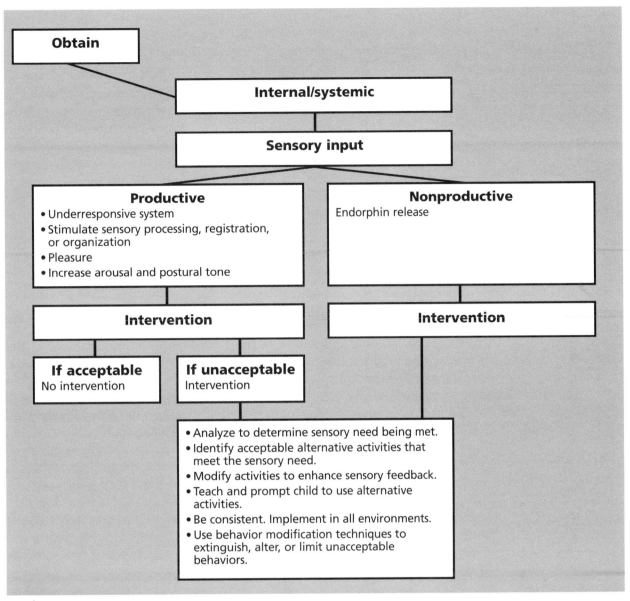

 FIGURE 6.1
Intervention for obtaining behaviors

 ## Intervention Strategies for Obtaining Behaviors

Social-Communicative Behaviors

Attention

Attention-seeking challenging behaviors require behavioral intervention strategies, and negative experiences need to be transformed into positive, productive encounters. The goal is to create good behaviors, reward the positive, and ignore the negative. Adults must be made aware of the child's need for attention; and a consistent program must be implemented to reward positive, on-task behavior, while ignoring attention-seeking behaviors. Positive attention must be specific, rather than general, leaving no room for interpretation by the child. By using the child's name in conjunction with praise, the child will learn to associate the name with positive experiences. ("Anna, nice looking at me"; "Anna is sitting quietly. Very good!"; "Anna, I like how you asked Luis to help you.")

Negative, attention-seeking behaviors are reinforced by consequences and secondary reinforcers. We must control the factors in the child's environment that reinforce and reward the unwanted behaviors, while simultaneously prompting and modeling the desired behaviors. All team members must be educated not to react or visually attend to the child's negative behavior, and to reward all desired behaviors. Consistency is critical; the child will learn quickly who will and will not respond. Anticipating when the child will display the negative behavior, interceding just before that point, and rewarding on-task behavior is an effective method of blocking the negative behavior.

Full ownership

Full ownership is an attention-seeking behavior in which the child demands the full, uninterrupted attention of one adult in the environment. Any deviation of attention from that person results in the child's challenging behaviors. Full ownership can be a desirable behavior in some environments. For example, a therapist working one-on-one with such a child will find that the child is fully vested, displaying increased compliance with task demands, motivation, and participation in therapeutic activities. In other environments, however, this behavior can be stifling for the adult and frustrating for both adult and child. Modifying the behavior may be environment- or situation-specific. The child must be taught the exact situations in which the behavior is allowed. Consistency in enforcing the rules is critical. The child may be confused as to why he can have his mother's full attention in one environment and not in another. Delayed gratification and reinforcement techniques are effective. Interceding before disruptive behaviors occur, specifying how long the child must wait for attention, and consistently following through will help the child delay gratification. Gradually increase the time the child must wait before receiving attention. Engaging the child in a distracting task is another effective technique for maintaining on-task behavior.

Object, Need, or Want

The first step in designing an intervention program is to determine what the child is trying to communicate through the challenging behavior. Analyzing the events that preceded the behavior as well as the events that occur after the behavior will provide insight into what the child is trying to communicate. Then we need to look at how the child is communicating and how can we enhance his communication abilities.

Assess your expectations of the child. Are they realistic? In many situations, it is not realistic to expect the child to comprehend or communicate what distresses him or to analyze what he is trying to obtain from an experience. The child may not possess the self-awareness (that is, internal awareness) to discriminate the details of the event or activity. He may not realize what he is seeking; he only knows that he is disappointed, unhappy, or frustrated. When this is the case, we must anticipate the child's needs, interpret his responses, structure the environment effectively, and teach basic communication and coping skills.

Children need to have avenues to constructively request their needs and communicate them. Assess the child's current abilities and expand his communication skills in order to constructively redirect his behaviors. We will discuss various communication systems in Chapters 15 and 16.

The child may desire an activity that is not appropriate for the time or setting. Anger and frustration, increased stress, and escalating behaviors may occur as the child attempts to obtain a desired activity or complete it in a specific manner. When the activity is not in the child's best interest, several strategies are effective. The easiest is to set up the environment; simply do not make the activity available to the child. This is important in the case of obsession toward an object or toy.

An obsession is an internally driven fixation in which the child has a compulsion or preoccupation with a specific toy, activity, or sequence for completing an activity. Examples include lining up objects in a row or stacking them methodically, seeking out numbers or letters from any environment and arranging them in order, tapping puzzle pieces three times before placing them, and spinning small toys. An uncontrollable need to have a specific toy or activity is another form of obsession.

Do not attempt to rationalize the obsession toward the object. This will only tend to escalate the child's anxiety. Remove the object from the child's sight. Do not attend to the obsessive behavior, and continue with the desired task. Prompt the child through the transition.

Some children will respond to firm limit setting. If the child appears to comprehend what you are saying, let him know that you understand what he wants. Explain what you want him to do. Be consistent and persistent in having him complete the desired activity. Establish a routine so the child can anticipate the activities you expect him to follow. Make changes gradually.

If you can give the child the desired activity, it may work well as a reward. Establish specific criteria that the child must accomplish in order to obtain the desired activity. Another option is to use the activity within your therapy session.

For example, playing with a toy bird, Jonathan's desired activity, is used as a reward. Jonathan is told that he may have the toy after he picks up five pennies and places them in a bank without screaming or dropping them. The toy is used within the session when the child is asked (by the bird) to place them in the bank or in the bird's mouth. Every time a penny gets in, the bird jumps up and down with excitement.

Sensory-Seeking Internal/Systemic Behaviors

Children engage in sensory-seeking activities in both productive and nonproductive methods; some are socially acceptable, and some are unacceptable. The key to therapeutic intervention is to analyze the activity the child is engaging in to determine its basic sensory component. Then analyze the response it has on the child, and determine whether it is productive, organizing, and socially acceptable. If the activity is not acceptable, teach the child constructive alternative activities.

Activities that are viewed as constructive and acceptable in one environment may not be appropriate in another. Jumping on a trampoline may be organizing and an appropriate activity for home, but it is inappropriate and not acceptable at school. However, the sensory component received from jumping on the trampoline may be extracted from the activity and a socially acceptable method integrated into the classroom to help the child become organized. Proprioceptive and vestibular alternatives might include using an inflatable cushion on the classroom chair that enables the child to bounce lightly, giving periodic breaks to jump on a mini-trampoline, or integrating an exercise program into the child's scheduled activities.

Some children engage in sensory-seeking behaviors that are nonproductive and have no organizing benefit. These self-stimulating behaviors are disorganizing and interfere with the child's functional abilities. However, they are not always nonproductive. Hand flapping, finger flicking, hand patterning, and deep-head pressure are examples of behaviors that may meet a sensory need while appearing unacceptable socially. A therapist who is knowledgeable in sensory integration must assess the child's sensory behaviors, needs, and response to the input before classifying the behavior as being sensory nonproductive. Children learn and use many unusual and sensory-based behaviors to help them organize their behaviors. If the behavior is necessary for the child, we must find productive alternatives while systematically extinguishing the undesirable behavior.

Integrating specific sensory-based activities into the child's environments at home, school, and play will help the child overcome the need for specific sensory activities and self-stimulation patterns. While meeting the sensory need is important in extinguishing the inappropriate behavior, behavioral intervention techniques also are necessary. The behaviors have served a purpose and are a learned response. Most children will not give up these self-serving behaviors without assistance, encouragement, and reinforcement for the alternative behaviors. We must determine whether we need to stop the behaviors, limit them, or simply alter them. Then teach alternative behaviors, establish reinforcers, and redirect old behaviors into new ones.

Intervention Strategies for Avoidance or Escape Behaviors

Avoidance of Attention, People, and Events

Children with autism avoid new activities, the attention of familiar as well as new people, new social situations, and new events. These children find safety and comfort in routine and consistency. They may view new situations as a violation of their routine and a threat to their ability to function competently. They can neither control the event that occurs if it is new, nor assure that they will be able to function effectively. They have difficulty grasping the *whole picture*; they tend to focus in on what appears to be irrelevant aspects of the environment, and have difficulty reading the implied meaning and gestures associated with social situations. Our goal is to help children learn to cope with new social situations by teaching basic social skills and integrating them into daily activities. This may lessen the stress and anxiety that these children associate with new places, events, or people, and help them feel more confident.

Many children with autism have difficulty registering changes and initiating actions, and they may not register a new person in their environment. If they register the person, they may not know the appropriate response or greeting or be able to initiate it. We must teach social innuendoes and implied meaning associated with social situations. Prompts, modeling, and verbal mediation are useful in teaching appropriate social skills.

Basic social skills include looking at people when they talk, saying hello, saying or waving good-bye when they leave, and responding when another person says hello or good-bye. These basic skills must be practiced in every environment until they become automatic. Establish a standard greeting routine every time you and the child meet before the therapy session. This may include stooping down to the child's level, making eye contact, getting the child's attention, saying hello, and prompting the appropriate response.

Rhythmic activities and songs are excellent classroom or group activities to teach basic social interaction. Develop interactive songs that prompt the child to initiate the appropriate response. For example, sing, "Hello Adam. How are you today?" and have Adam sing his response. Fade the prompts to facilitate the child's full independence in social situations.

Prepare the child for new social situations. Help him anticipate all of the aspects of a new situation and learn how to respond to many of the demands that will be placed on him. Teach the skills he will need to succeed in the new situation. Whenever possible, use pictures, model the desired responses, and read or develop social stories that center on the person or new event. Reward the child for all appropriate behaviors as soon as they occur. A child who understands delayed gratification may work for an end reward for behaving in a pre-specified manner.

Sophi, 5-years-old, has a difficult time with new situations. In those circumstances, she often exhibits challenging behaviors. She throws herself on the floor, screams or makes loud squawking noises, bangs her head, and lunges at people nearby.

Sophi was scheduled to participate in therapeutic horseback riding. Her teachers, parents, behavioralist, and therapists worked together to help her make an easy transition to the new experiences associated with horseback riding. Many activities in the classroom, home, and therapy revolved around horses. Pictures of horses were cut out and posted on the chalkboard and walls at home and school. There was discussion about what horses eat, where they live, the texture of their hair, and how big they are. Hay was brought into the therapy room so Sophi could connect the sight, smell, and feel of the hay with the horse. Riding the horse was discussed, and Sophi practiced wearing a helmet and sitting in a saddle attached to a peanut ball. She associated bouncing (which she enjoys) with the saddle and the word *horse*. She practiced saying the word *horse*, making the clucking sound that signals the horse to move, and learned a song about horses.

On the day she first rode a horse, all discussions centered on horses and riding, with emphasis on *today*. Sophi carried a picture of a horse with her while she was being driven to the stables. She made the transition easily, with excitement and enthusiasm. She was guided and prompted up the mounting

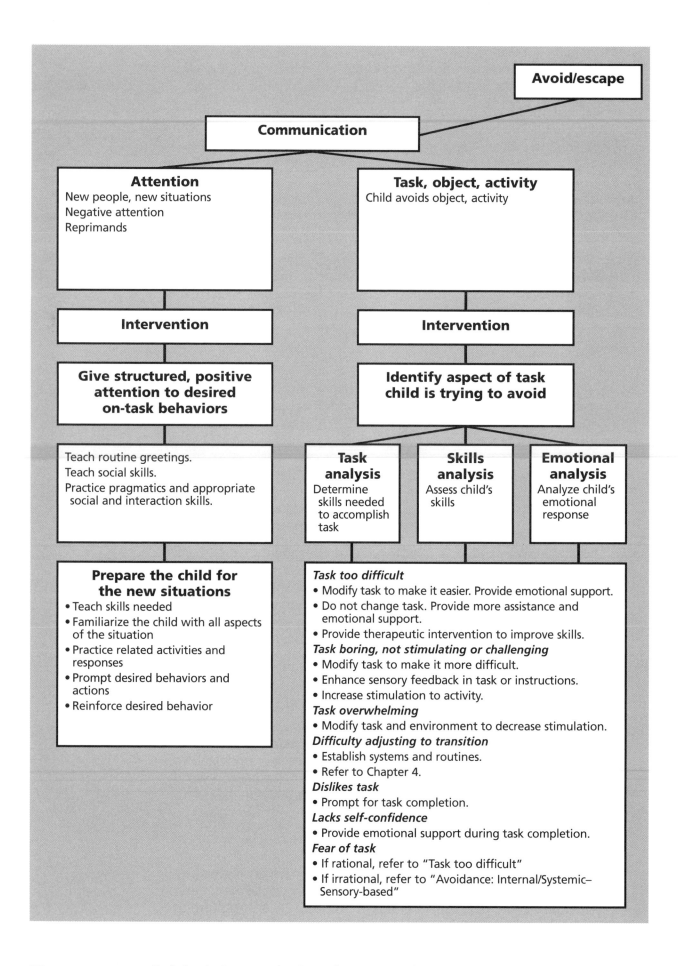

Avoid/escape

Communication

Attention
New people, new situations
Negative attention
Reprimands

Task, object, activity
Child avoids object, activity

Intervention

Intervention

Give structured, positive attention to desired on-task behaviors

Identify aspect of task child is trying to avoid

Teach routine greetings.
Teach social skills.
Practice pragmatics and appropriate social and interaction skills.

Task analysis
Determine skills needed to accomplish task

Skills analysis
Assess child's skills

Emotional analysis
Analyze child's emotional response

Prepare the child for the new situations
• Teach skills needed
• Familiarize the child with all aspects of the situation
• Practice related activities and responses
• Prompt desired behaviors and actions
• Reinforce desired behavior

Task too difficult
• Modify task to make it easier. Provide emotional support.
• Do not change task. Provide more assistance and emotional support.
• Provide therapeutic intervention to improve skills.
Task boring, not stimulating or challenging
• Modify task to make it more difficult.
• Enhance sensory feedback in task or instructions.
• Increase stimulation to activity.
Task overwhelming
• Modify task and environment to decrease stimulation.
Difficulty adjusting to transition
• Establish systems and routines.
• Refer to Chapter 4.
Dislikes task
• Prompt for task completion.
Lacks self-confidence
• Provide emotional support during task completion.
Fear of task
• If rational, refer to "Task too difficult"
• If irrational, refer to "Avoidance: Internal/Systemic–Sensory-based"

Avoid/escape

Internal/systemic

Sensory
Overarousal
Overstimulated
Modulation disorders
• Auditory   • Tactile   • Olfactory
• Visual   • Postural
Attempts to calm and organize

Systemic/visceral
Pain or discomfort
Hunger
Auto-immune response and histamine reactions
Illness or impending illness

Intervention

Intervention

Identify sensory systems and environmental aspects contributing to overload
• Decrease environmental stimulation.

Assist parents to differentiate between sensory-based versus medically-based concerns

Identify appropriate and effective sensory-based activities
• Teach alternative activity for calming.
• Teach child to identify signs of sensory overload.
• Guide child to use alternative activity.
• Integrate calming sensory-based activities into child's schedule.

Refer to appropriate medical professionals

Remediate underlying modulation difficulty

Systematically increase tolerance for and scope of new activities

FIGURE 6.2
Intervention for avoidance or escape behaviors

block and onto the horse, and she helped to put on her riding helmet. The horse started to move, and she quickly associated the movement with the horse. Sophi knew what to expect and how to respond. There was no anxiety, stress, or fear of the unknown, but only pleasure and excitement.

Avoidance of a Task or Object

It is critical to determine whether the child possesses the skills needed to complete the task, the child's perception of his skills, and his perception of the task.

The first steps in intervention are task analysis and skills analysis. During task analysis, ascertain the aspect of the task that the child wants to avoid. Is the task threatening, difficult, or overwhelming? Is it unstimulating and boring, or new and out of the child's routine?

Next, analyze the child's functional skills to determine whether he actually possesses the skills needed to complete the task at the level of independence in which it is being presented. Consider the child's sensorimotor awareness, the appropriateness of the task, the child's actual skill level, and his confidence in his ability to accomplish the task.

Then analyze the child's emotional responses to the activity. Determine whether the child's emotional response is based on lack of confidence or self-esteem, or if it appears rooted in fear. Fear may be rational or irrational, but it is a real feeling. The child may believe that a particular task is beyond his capability, or he may fear failure. The fear is characterized by lack of confidence and self-esteem.

The fear may cause an autonomic nervous system reaction of "fight or flight" with increased heart rate, dilated pupils, and flushing of the skin. When children demonstrate an autonomic nervous system reaction to fear, they are reacting with very strong, life-preserving emotions. If you ignore this emotionally charged state and persist in pushing the child to perform, you can expect aggressive behavior. The aggression may be turned inwardly in the form of self-abuse, biting, or head banging; or turned outwardly, and you may be bitten, slapped, or pinched.

> Jason is asked to walk across a balance beam that is placed six inches off the ground. He exhibits fear, crying, screaming, and clinging to the therapist. Task analysis determines that the child must be able to narrow his base of support to stand on one foot, possess adequate awareness of how his body moves through space, and have adequate balance and equilibrium reaction to correct his balance when he starts to lose it. Skill analysis determines that Jason does not have sufficient balance reactions to self-correct when he loses his balance. He can stand on one foot, but he does not have sufficient sensory awareness to move his body safely along a balance beam. He is posturally insecure. The therapist determines that his fear is rationale.

With irrational fear, task analysis and skill analysis show that the child possesses the skills needed for the task and has the confidence to complete the activity. The fear response is a true, emotional reaction that is disproportionate to the threat.

Irrational fear must not be discounted. It is a primary symptom of a modulation or regulatory disorder. When rational or irrational fear is exhibited, the task must be modified to the child's level of functioning, and support and encouragement must be provided. (For more information on fear responses, see Chapters 10 and 11.)

Task Is Too Difficult

When a task is beyond the child's capabilities, we have two choices: modify the task down to the child's level of functioning, or keep the task at the current level and provide assistance to assure successful task completion. Grading the task down to the child's level of functioning, or modifying the task, promotes independent functioning and prevents challenging behaviors from surfacing. Positive reinforcement and praise can be linked with the task, thus promoting opportunities for emotional support and encouragement. Gradually increase the difficulty of the task as the child's skills increase.

When choosing to keep the task at the current level, provide specific assistance and guidance to help the child master the part of the task that is too difficult. Both physical and emotional assistance will be needed.

Any time a task is beyond the child's capability, it is important to determine the underlying problem that is preventing it from being mastered. Therapy must focus on increasing the child's skill level and improving the underlying problem. In Jason's case (page 68), he must be given the sensorimotor skills needed to know how his body is moving through space, the balance and equilibrium reactions needed to self-correct postural difficulties, and the pelvic stability to narrow his base of support. Skills need to be addressed through therapy sessions, home programs, and other types of direct intervention.

When the child possesses the skills needed for the task, but does not believe he possesses them, it is usually due to lack of self-confidence, self-esteem, or lack of awareness or exposure to successfully completing the task. Intervention must positively reinforce the child's skills as he gradually increases independence in task completion. Keep the task at the current level of difficulty while providing support and encouragement. Delayed reinforcement and prompting the child through the task are excellent techniques to gradually increase a child's confidence and task compliance without triggering frustration.

In all situations, the child needs to be taught communication techniques.

Task Is Boring, Not Challenging or Stimulating

When a child is not stimulated or motivated by a task, three problems become evident when analyzing the task and the child's skill level:

1. The task is below the child's functional skill level.

2. The task is not stimulating or it lacks meaning for the child.

3. The task may be presented in a manner that is overwhelming to the child.

Task is below skill level

When the task is below the child's functional skill level, he may become bored. Activities that are not stimulating often result in the child's inattention, acting out, or presenting other challenging avoidance behaviors. A major problem occurs when the therapist, professional, or parent underestimates the child's potential. A child often will rise to the occasion when another person expects more and believes in him. It is helpful to gather information from all team members regarding the child's capabilities. Videotaping the child's performance in various settings also is helpful in obtaining a complete picture of his potential. When one person in the child's environment is able to get him to perform at a higher level, it is important that we not discount this, but find out what it is about that person or environment that enables the child to thrive. We need to draw from these experiences to challenge the child effectively.

Task is not simulating or it lacks meaning for the child

For children with sensory-processing deficits, activities that provide no inherent sensory feedback often lack meaning. As a result, the child is not motivated or stimulated to perform the task. A child who lacks sensory feedback may not attend to instructions presented in a dry, flat, monotonous fashion. An underaroused child may need enhanced verbal instructions, instructions presented with enthusiasm, fluctuating voice volume, and inflections.

> Michael has decreased awareness of his hands and arms and finds little interest in writing or coloring. He tunes out verbal instructions and seldom listens. It is difficult for him to attend to and process instructions. He has difficulty feeling the pencil in his hand and moving it. The therapist needs to modify verbal instructions for enhanced sensory feedback by adding enthusiasm, varying inflections, and verbal and visual prompts. Sensory feedback must be added to the activity to increase the challenge and stimulation. This includes using a vibrating pen, placing sandpaper under the drawing surface, and using an incline board.

Activities are often perceived as boring when they lack sensory feedback or challenge or are presented in a dry format. Children with autism often lack the initiative to change the activity, the ability to communicate their boredom, and the skills to make the task more interesting. They rely on others to appeal to their interest levels and keep the activity stimulating. Environmental modifications and systems to increase our efficiency are often helpful in maintaining the attention and motivation of these children. Some of these include:

- Being prepared

- Being organized

- Decreasing down time between activities

- Being animated, as necessary

- Appealing to the child's developmental level (for example, using fantasy and creativity in symbolic play)

- Increasing the child's investment in the activity

- Building reward systems into the activity

Task presentation is overwhelming

The activity may be within the child's capabilities, but presented in a disorganized or overstimulating manner, thus causing the child to *shut down*.

The presentation of a task and the environment in which it is performed can account for the child's varying functional levels and the differing reports from professionals. When analyzing and grading tasks for structure and stimulation levels, consider:

- The room size (Large, open room versus small, quiet room)

- People in the environment (1:1 ratio versus many children)

- Noise within the environment

- Clutter within the environment (Are all unnecessary supplies out of the child's visual field?)

- Amount of structure provided

- Quantity of work

- Instructions and verbal directions given

Providing structure, small enclosed rooms, and minimal verbal instructions with more visual instructions and demonstrations initially allows the child to function optimally. Break the task into its component parts, and gradually increase the difficulty level to challenge the child. Avoid irrelevant or distracting instructions (that is, too many words). Present one item at a time. Structure the task, and keep the environment and work area free of clutter. Use visual aids whenever possible.

If the child is continually overstimulated and overaroused, he may have a modulation disorder. Refer to "Avoidance of Sensory" information, pages 72–73.

Change in Routine and Activity

Change in routine, interruption of a desired activity, and introduction of a less desirable task can result in avoidance and escape behaviors. Change and transitions are difficult. The ability to anticipate change often helps the child prepare for a less desirable task and accept a transition with less anxiety, stress, and challenging behaviors. Systems to enhance performance become critical in helping him prepare for change. Review Chapter 4 for systems and strategies to improve the child's performance. Visual aids, schedules, clocks, timers, picture systems, and simple verbal reminders with visual gestures are helpful. The Time-Timer™ transforms the abstract concept of time into a visual depiction. The amount of time the child must work is displayed in red, and as the minutes pass, the red area decreases.

Some children are able to make smooth transitions to the next activity with advance notice, while others *get stuck* during the transition. Prolonging the transition, discussing the transition as it occurs, being disorganized, or having increased waiting time between activities only increases these children's anxiety. Help the children quickly through the transition without attending to any challenging behaviors, and reward them once they are through the transition and back on task.

Anger, Frustration, and Escalating Stress

Anger, frustration, and increased stress and escalating behaviors may occur as the child attempts to avoid or escape the activity, transition, or change. Attend to the warning signs of frustration and stress, and intervene before they escalate. Intervention requires that we give children the tools they need to effectively communicate what they want or do not want. To do this, we must establish and maintain communication with them. They must understand that we know or are trying to understand what they want or do not want. If they know that we care, often their frustration will escalate at a slower rate.

Internal/Systemic, Sensory-Based Avoidance Reactions

When children avoid or try to escape from sensory stimulation, often they are trying to block out information entering their nervous systems. This occurs when the child is overaroused, overstimulated, or has a modulation or regulatory disorder. (See Chapters 10 and 11.) The goal of intervention is to help these children achieve and maintain the optimum level of arousal needed to function.

Nonverbal children may bang their heads, bite, grind their teeth, hide under objects, and rock when overstimulated. All of these behaviors provide deep proprioceptive input that neurologically calms the child's nervous system. Rhythmic movements, such as rocking, also calm the system and provide a sense of organization through slow vestibular input. Self-abusive behaviors trigger the release of endorphins—pain inhibitors—and children may use them in an attempt to calm and sedate themselves.

Challenging behavior reinforces itself. When children engage in these behaviors to avoid and block out sensory stimulation, the response within their nervous systems reinforces the behavior. Attempts to extinguish the behavior without meeting the underlying sensory need will result in other undesirable behaviors.

Intervention requires that you identify the system or systems—visual, auditory, proprioceptive, vestibular, olfactory, tactile—that are contributing to the child's overarousal, as well as the systems that the child is using to calm and organize himself. Once the system or systems are identified, decrease the amount of that stimulation in the child's environment. Guide the child through the desired activity or task while decreasing the sensory input associated with it. This may involve modifying the method and volume of your instructions. It may be necessary to decrease verbal instructions and, instead, use gestures and physical guidance; and demonstrate or model the desired behavior or response.

Therapeutic intervention also must address applying calming and organizing techniques. (See Chapters 10 and 11.) Identify alternate activities that meet the sensory need. When the child engages in the challenging behavior, move him immediately into the alternative activity.

> When overwhelmed, Lauren bites her arm or squeezes the skin on other people's arms, causing injury to herself and others. She continues this behavior until she feels calm and quiet. Lauren is seeking deep-touch and proprioceptive input. Introduce an alternative activity. For example, make fists of Lauren's hands and push them together, or push them hard and steadily into her lap

or onto the floor. This isometric exercise provides similar input to the nervous system. Teach Lauren the alternative activity and the exercise's calming input. Then consistently redirect the undesirable behavior by having her substituting the alternative activity.

Sensory-based activities that can be strategically interjected into the child's schedule include carrying a heavy book bag, moving heavy objects, morning or evening exercise routines, bicycle rides, trampoline exercises, swimming, weight-bearing exercises, and massaging the child's hands or feet. It is important to teach the child to identify the warning signs of sensory overload. Then teach him therapeutic techniques that work to calm the nervous system, effective methods of obtaining satisfaction of his needs, and ways to communicate those needs to others.

Children, who no longer experience sensory overload or modulation difficulties, may continue to exhibit avoidance behaviors. Their sensory-based behaviors may persist as learned behaviors that previously served a function, and they may not realize that they no longer need to use these behaviors. This is commonly seen in children with tactile or oral defensiveness and sensory modulation disorders. Once the underlying modulation difficulty is remediated, these children may continue to avoid the activities that created discomfort. They need to be emotionally supported while learning that the textures and activities are no longer painful or unpleasant. Avoidance behaviors need to be extinguished, while slowly and methodically increasing their tolerance for and scope of new activities.

Internal/Systemic, Visceral-Based Avoidance Reactions

Children may be experiencing changes inside their bodies and be uncertain of what they are. These internal sensations may be as simple as hunger, or more intense as pain or discomfort from an injury. Other possibilities include illness or impending illness, allergic reaction to food or to something they touched, or a histamine reaction to an insect sting. Children experiencing sensory overload may learn techniques to block out the input or calm their systems; but with internal systemic reactions, those techniques may be ineffective in alleviating the discomfort. Challenging behaviors may erupt out of frustration or the disorganization experienced within their systems.

The therapist must be an advocate. Rule out basic causes for the discomfort, such as hunger, thirst, or soiled diapers or clothing. Look for signs of pain or discomfort and impending illness, such as fever. Observe for signs of allergies, such as irritability, circles under the eyes, irritations on the skin, swelling or histamine reactions, runny nose, and watery eyes. Talk to parents and teachers to determine whether there were any unusual environmental factors or foods the child may have eaten that may be contributing to the behaviors. The child may be reacting erratically to environmental factors such as airborne fumes, carpet cleaners, perfumes, or smoke.

Help parents understand the signs and symptoms of sensory-based problems and how sensitivity to environmental factors can cause internal distress, disorganization, and internal visceral reactions. Be cautious; a child who is perceived as having a sensory regulatory disorder actually may have an internal systemic cause for the symptoms. Parents need to rule out medical causes for behaviors. Therapists must help them discern and systematically rule out causes for the behaviors that are out of their control. We must guide them to the appropriate medical professional, who may be a pediatric neurologist, optometrist or developmental optometrist, allergist, immunologist, nutritionist, or other specialist.

 ## Temper Tantrums and Challenging Behaviors

Inevitably, you will be challenged. A child will test you to see how far he can push you or find out whether you really mean what you say. He may throw himself on the floor screaming, bang his head uncontrollably, kick, scratch, lunge at you, bite himself or you, throw things, spin toys or himself, or lash out at you verbally. You will need to make decisions and take actions immediately. Knowing the most productive thing to do is challenging for even the most experienced professionals. Some strategies are listed in Figure 6.3.

> A child lunges at you and starts to kick and hit. Your automatic instinct is self-protection and anger. Your heart rate escalates and your body prepares for a fight. These are strong emotions and feelings that will interfere with handling the behavior objectively.
>
> A child bursts into tears and throws herself on the floor, crying uncontrollably. Your instinct is to protect and cuddle the child. These nurturing emotions also interfere with handling the behaviors objectively.
>
> A child starts screaming and tries to run away. You try to guide her back, and she screams louder. Nothing you do quiets her; she continues to escalate, screaming and now fighting. There's no logic to it. You try to comfort her and hold her. She takes a solid bite out of your shoulder, inflicting pain. You scream.

Do not react! It is difficult, but critical. What we need to do is not natural. (No wonder it's so hard to handle challenging behaviors!) We must fight our natural urges to comfort someone who is crying, to fight back when we are attacked, to run away when we are frightened, to blame someone when something goes wrong. Too often, we charge these behaviors with emotions and personalize the experience. We blame the child. Our feelings may surface into statements like, "He hurt me! That child is just mean!" or, "She's spoiled! Someone needs to teach her a lesson." These feelings and thoughts reflect a lack of knowledge about the child, the child's behavior, and what the child is trying to accomplish. You must control these thoughts in order to handle the challenging behavior constructively. The child's behavior is not a personal attack; he is not maliciously attacking you or attempting to annoy you. He is trying to tell you something in the only way he knows. He is using learned behavior that has worked in the past.

By remaining calm, you can control every aspect of your response. You must respond exactly as if the behavior were not occurring. Your voice must not change inflections or rise in volume. Avoid even the smallest change in body language and facial expression. Do not escalate with the child. If necessary, breathe deeply and slowly. Do not say "No!" Do not address the behavior or even look at the child. Children are sensitive to the smallest changes and will pick up on the subtlest cue that you have responded. By attending to the child and the behavior, you will only reinforce the behavior.

Anticipate challenging behavior.
Teach alternative skills.
Avoid temper tantrum or challenging behavior.

Temper tantrum or challenging behavior occurs

Remove yourself from potential harm

Ignore challenging behaviors
- Continue to work as if behavior is not occurring.
- Maintain your nonverbal behaviors. Monitor your:
  - Voice volume
  - Breathing
  - Movements
  - Eye gaze and attention
  - Stress level
  - Facial expression

Do not react! Remain calm!

Protect the child and others from potential harm

Be objective. Analyze purpose of the behavior.
To obtain? To avoid or escape?

Obtaining
Communication (attention or task)
  Determine appropriate method to request and obtain.
Internal sensory
  Determine sensory need and appropriate method to request and obtain.

Avoidance or escape
Communication (attention or task)
  Determine appropriate level of task compliance or communication expected.
Internal systemic
  Determine cause for overarousal or response.
Modify environment for optimal function.

Determine appropriate response
What do you want to occur?
What is the appropriate coping skill?

Facilitate, prompt, or shape the desired response
For task avoidance, child must work through the task.

Off-Task behaviors
Ignore and withdraw reinforcement.

On-Task behaviors
Reward and attend to all movement toward desired response.
Praise and reward appropriate behaviors.

FIGURE 6.3
Temper tantrums and challenging behaviors

Protect yourself, other children in the area, and the child from harm. Maintain a calm, controlled affect. Assess the environment to assure that no one will be hurt. Unobtrusively move dangerous objects from the area without attending to the child's behavior. Be prepared to quietly step out of the way of flying arms or feet, and to monitor the child for changing muscle tone that may indicate sudden advances. Whenever possible, maintain your hands gently on the child. You can feel quick changes in muscle tone before you can see them.

The next step is to analyze the situation. Review the sequence of events and analyze the probable causes for the behavior. What just happened? What is the child trying to tell you? Does he want something (obtaining behavior), or is he trying to escape (avoidance behavior)? By taking time to analyze the behavior objectively, you can *buy time* to control your emotions.

Determine a constructive course of action. What do you need to have happen, or what do you want the child to learn from this episode? The answer will be based on your analysis of what triggered the behavior and what the child is trying to obtain or avoid.

There are some basic rules to follow when determining an intervention program and avoiding secondary reinforcement to the challenging behaviors.

- Reward all constructive and positive behaviors. Reward them immediately, and reward them frequently.

- The instant that challenging behaviors occur, avert your eyes to be sure not to reinforce negative behaviors. Discontinue any positive praise.

- Prompt desired positive responses, and shape appropriate responses. Reward all attempts in the correct direction.

- If the child is using the behavior to avoid a task, do not permit him to succeed. Ignore the behavior and work through the task. Be sure that the task is appropriate for the child. If necessary, modify the task for fewer repetitions. Be sure the child knows how many repetitions are expected.

- A child may need to be removed from the situation or calmed if he is unable to regain control of his behavior. The child may become so disorganized, frantic, and anxious that he is not in a state to comprehend the alternatives or constructively implement alternative behaviors. Sensory-based activities may be used to calm him. Distracting him from the anxiety-provoking activity also may be effective. Engage him in a distracting task, and reward him for appropriate responses and on-task behavior. Once the child is calmed and organized, place him back in the original situation that he was trying to avoid. If the child succeeds in avoiding the original task, the negative behavior will be reinforced and will continue. The goal is *not* to complete the task, but to reengage the child in the task and make it a positive experience.

If the child is using the behavior to obtain an object, activity, or event, determine whether it is possible to give him what he wants. If so, how can you get him to constructively work for it or ask for it? Let the child know that you know and have what he wants (but do not attend to the negative behavior).

> Karen is working at her desk on a coloring task that is difficult for her. Suddenly, she bolts across the room toward a box of toys.

Her effort to reach the box is blocked, and she is physically placed back at her desk. She screams, kicks, and starts to scratch at the therapist. Without emotion or eye contact, the therapist redirects Karen into the activity, beginning with hand-over-hand assistance, decreasing it as Karen calms down and resumes her work. Karen is praised for her on-task behavior. The therapist quietly goes to the box, opens it, and removes the toy that was inside. Karen watches attentively, gesturing that she wants the toy. She is prompted to request the toy. The therapist praises Karen for asking, and tells her, "When you finish coloring the page, you may have the toy." When the page was completed, Karen looked at the therapist and asked for the toy.

Define in your mind the behavior or response that you want. In Karen's case, the therapist wanted Karen to complete her work and to ask for the desired toy. Her attempt to get the toy served to avoid a difficult task; therefore, she had to complete the work. However, the toy was used to motivate her and teach her to communicate.

Prompt the positive response, and reward any positive behavior or gesture. Karen was physically prompted through the task and verbally prompted to request the toy. She was praised for on-task behavior, and she was rewarded with the toy when her work was completed and after she had asked for it constructively.

A child lunges at you and starts to kick and hit. You calmly step aside, and the child's lunge misses you. The child is in an open area and can't get hurt. You attend to another child in the area, reward that child for good behavior, and ignore the first child's tantrum, remaining out of his reach.

A child bursts into tears and throws herself on the floor, crying uncontrollably. You analyze the situation and realize that she is trying to avoid the task you brought out for her to do. You analyze the appropriateness of the task, and know it is at her level. You bring her to her chair and begin to work with her, hand over hand, to have her complete the task. She tries to throw herself into extension, but you calmly continue. When she quiets for one second, you praise her good work and continue to work with her.

A child starts screaming and tries to run away. You try to guide her back, and she screams louder. Nothing you do quiets her; she continues to escalate, screaming and now fighting. There's no logic to it. You assess the situation and regain your composure. You are unsure of what is triggering the behavior. Is it sensory modulation? Task avoidance? An expression of a want or need? You lower your voice, breathe slowly, watch for a moment. You take the child's hand and guide her from the classroom. You reassure her that you want to understand and help her. You engage her in a familiar activity, physically prompting her to complete the activity, obsessively counting each repetition aloud. She starts to count with you. She calms down, and you return to the classroom. You work on resistive activities that help her organize herself further, and then present the original task. She quietly completes the activity.

Consistency is critical when responding to challenging behaviors. Each professional who works with the child must address the challenging behavior in the same manner in order to extinguish it. Once the behavior is exhibited, it must be addressed calmly and systematically. Secondary reinforcers, such as attending to the behavior, will cause the behavior to persist.

Anticipating the Challenging Behavior

A word of caution: Choose your battles wisely. Children respond for very specific reasons. Those reasons can be predicted and anticipated. Read the warning signs, anticipate the behaviors, and divert the crisis when possible.

Anticipating the child's behaviors is the most effective method of teaching coping skills. Keep alert for the signals that the behavior is about to occur, intercede as you start to see the signs, and teach the child alternative methods of responding. Do not allow yourself to be distracted by others in your environment. When you let your guard down, you will miss the warning signs and most likely will experience a challenging behavior that could have been redirected. Learn from each experience. Whether teaching coping skills or handling a challenging behavior, always try to end on a positive note.

 ## Working Together as a Team

Parents often invest extensive time and energy in attempting to understand and explain their children's behaviors and intentions. This is exhausting and time consuming. It requires sensitivity to the multiple causes in the children's environments and within their bodies as well as keen sensitivity to the children themselves. Parents are invested in their children and, in some regards, overly sensitive to the children's needs, behaviors, and wants. The children rely on the parents to meet their basic needs. While driven by love and a need to do the best for their children, it is often hard for them to be objective regarding their children's behaviors and the causes. As the children grow older, secondary rewards become more complicated and the causes are not limited to a single factor. Parents often need and seek out the help of professionals who will respect their opinions as full, vested members of the team and will share their love and compassion for their children.

Professionals have a responsibility to assist the parents. They must respect the opinions of the parents as team members who have valuable insights into their children and how they function across multiple environments. The parents also often possess an innate sense of their children. It is the professional's responsibility to help the parents examine such information objectively and provide in-depth insights into their children.

Each specialist must assist in the development of effective remediation strategies and coping skills. This requires a comprehensive team approach between the behaviorist, occupational therapist, speech-language pathologist, physical therapist, special education instructor, augmentative communication specialist, parents, and physician. Working together, they develop and implement a comprehensive intervention program. Such a program is aimed at eliminating challenging behaviors that interfere with the mastery of new skills, remediating the original underlying problem that causes the behavior, and providing emotional support and encouragement.

Collecting data, identifying and analyzing problems, and developing an intervention program must be objective in nature. However, the success of an intervention program often depends upon the relationship between the professional and the child. In implementing the intervention program, the professional working with the child must *like* the child. Each child possesses strengths along with weaknesses, and anyone who expects to be effective in working directly with the child must be able to see the child's positive aspects and strengths.

Just as parents have an innate sense about their children, the children have an innate sense about the people around them. A child can sense when a professional is afraid of him, appalled at his behavior, or just doesn't like him. Love and compassion toward another human being is projected through verbal and nonverbal behaviors. Mutual trust and respect are inherent in this relationship. To effectively change challenging behaviors, we must not only provide emotional support and encouragement, we must *like* the children we work with.

CHAPTER 7

Sensory Integration Theory and Treatment

Betty Paris and Carolyn Murray-Slutsky

Sensory Integration (SI) is a theory and technique developed by A. Jean Ayres, a psychologist and occupational therapist. Her career was devoted to the organization and development of theories and then the testing of those theories that related to sensorimotor integration. She began her work in SI during her postdoctoral work at the National Institute of Mental Health Training Program, Brain Research Institute, and Division of Child Development at the Center for the Health Sciences at the University of California in Los Angeles in the 1960s. Her work spanned the next three decades.

Initially, Ayres' interest and research focused on the impact of visual perception and motor control on learning. She quickly expanded her research to include the other sensory systems including the vestibular, proprioceptive, and tactile systems (Ayres 1964, 1969, 1975a, 1977). Dr. Ayres postulated that sensory processing could have a direct impact on a child's ability to learn and perform. She developed standardized tests to measure the visual, vestibular, tactile, and proprioceptive systems. The test measures were combined with clinical observations of muscle tone, postural control, and balance as further measures of neuromotor maturation. Factor-analytic studies were then completed to analyze patterns of dysfunction among learning-disabled children. Through these factor-analytic studies, Ayres identified dysfunctions in the sensory processing of tactile, vestibular, proprioceptive, and visual systems that interfere with motor planning, language, behavior, cognition, and emotional well-being. The theory of Sensory Integration evolved as a direct result of Ayres' interpretation of this data.

Ayres made several assumptions underlying SI theory. The first is that of *neural plasticity*, the ability to change or modify the central nervous system. Dr. Ayres believed that the brain—especially the young brain—is naturally malleable and capable of change, given the correct input. The concept of treatment was and is based upon the belief in the ability of the young brain to change how it functions. SI theory was based upon observations of clusters of behaviors in Ayres' cluster-analytic studies (Ayres 1974). The improvements in those behaviors, attributed to sensory integrative treatments, has led proponents to hypothesize that changes can and do occur within the brain as a result of the treatments. The brain changes are not readily observable to the practitioner, but the improved performances certainly are. By giving enhanced sensory experiences within the context of meaningful activities that involve the planning and execution of an adaptive response, we can increase sensory integration and improve learning.

The second assumption was the belief in the *nervous system hierarchy*. Ayres recognized that the brain functions as a whole, but that *higher-level functions* such as abstraction, perception, reasoning, language, and learning, evolve from and are dependent upon the integrity of the *lower level* (subcortical structures) of the brain. Lower-level structures were believed to develop and mature before the higher-level structures. Ayres postulated that sensorimotor experiences—sensory intake, sensory integration, and the interconnecting associations—occurred mainly within the lower centers, and therefore, the development of higher-level cortical functions was dependent upon the integrity and integration of the information from the sensory systems (Ayres 1968, 1972c, 1973, 1975, 1980, 1989). Later, Ayres recognized that the suppression of input was as vital to the process of neural integration as was the activation of input, and that sensory integration is an intricate and complex process performed at all levels of the central nervous system (Reeves 1998).

The brain is no longer thought of as a hierarchal processor; rather, it is believed to process information from many different areas within the brain in a parallel or distributed fashion. The information is processed simultaneously and, if processed accurately and efficiently, the result is successful adaptive responses to environmental conditions, regulated emotional tone, and higher-level cortical functions.

The third assumption is that of *developmental sequence*, or the belief that SI in the normal child occurs in a developmental sequence. It assumes that the brain is immature at birth and develops in a progression. Ayres believed that higher-level functions are the result of sensory integrative processes that occur at lower levels of the brain and develop early in life. SI postulates continue to believe that deficits in sensory input result in deficits in conceptual and motor learning. SI theory hypothesizes that through systematically providing therapeutic sensory motor experiences geared at facilitating normal neuromotor development, we can assist the brain to function more normally and develop according to normal developmental sequences. Treatment is aimed at providing therapeutic sensory and motor experiences that will address brain levels (that is, subcortical functions) that will facilitate the processing of information needed to develop the higher-level skills.

Through using specific sensorimotor experiences developmentally designed to address both the sensory integrative needs and those within the nervous system (that is, facilitating the integration of the lower-level or subcortical structures of the brain), we can enable the brain to work more efficiently as an integrated whole. Throughout the remaining chapters, we will examine SI theory, key components to assessing a child's needs, prioritizing intervention, effective treatment intervention strategies, and integrating various intervention strategies into SI.

Sensory Integration

We are constantly bombarded by external and internal sensory input. The process of sensory integration involves receiving the sensory information from one or more of our sensory systems, registering the stimuli, and constantly analyzing which stimuli are important or unimportant. On a conscious or unconscious level, we make decisions about which stimuli to attend or react to and how much of our attention to direct to it. This is how we are able to make appropriate responses to the stimuli.

Problems arise when a person has difficulty organizing the information bombarding the system. A child, who is unable to interpret or understand auditory input, may be unable to discriminate verbal instructions or conversation from the buzz of the fluorescent lights, the hum of an air-conditioning or heating system, and the sounds from just outside the window. That child will be unable to follow even the simplest directions and may be accused of being stubborn or ill-mannered. A child, who is unable to understand and interpret tactile input, may be bothered by the textures in the food he is eating and the clothes he is wearing. He may be so threatened by the unexpected touch of someone brushing up against him that he becomes confused and unable to perform tasks such as controlling a pencil. A child, who is unable to interpret the messages sent from his proprioceptive system, cannot know accurately where his arms and legs are in space. Efforts to move, reach, grasp, walk, or play become unpredictable and confusing. Inadequate, threatening vestibular information can lead the child to be unaware of when he is upright or to be threatened by changes in position or support surfaces. Impaired ability to organize and process the sensory input and to respond appropriately can lead to irritability, impaired ability to concentrate, discomfort, clumsiness, frustration, and a host of other emotions and behaviors.

Children with a sensory integrative disorder are not always easy to understand or to deal with. They may appear explosive, picky, or rude. They may become either very clingy or very controlling in order to organize the quantity and type of sensory input that bombards them. They may withdraw or push people away because they are threatened by uninvited touch. They may not accept being cuddled by their family members. They may demand certain articles of clothing or food, while refusing others. Often they cannot verbalize the causes of their problems. They themselves don't know what is wrong.

Ayres described SI as the "organization of sensation for use" (Ayres 1979). In Sensory Integration theory, SI is referred to as a neurological process that occurs naturally within the brain with little conscious effort or attention. The process is multifaceted and very complex. It is the processing and integration of external and internal information within the brain, and the ability to use this information functionally through appropriate adaptive responses. Ayres and her followers believe that the process of sensory integration has an impact on our development, learning, motor control, emotions, and behavior.

The Senses

Sensory information is received into our nervous systems from our environment or from within our bodies. This sensory information includes not only the senses most people think of, but also a host of other sensations that arise from within our bodies. These sensations include the following:

- Auditory (hearing)
- Visual (seeing)
- Olfactory (smell)
- Gustatory (taste)
- Tactile (touch)
- Vestibular input
- Kinesthetic/Proprioceptive input
- Pain
- Pressure receptors from the internal organs
- Chemical input

Processing and Decoding the Information

The sensory information is comprised of differing forms of energy, which are converted by the receptors into electrical or chemical energy that the body can decode, transport, and use. For example, in the eye, specialized receptors have specific decoding functions. One type of receptor transmits light, another color, and so on. The images we see travel down the nerves via tiny electrical impulses to an area in the brain that converts those electrical impulses into chemically transported bits of information within the visual cortex. The result is transformed into a picture of what we see. Receptors within the body decode information to indicate such diversities as the rise or drop in blood pressure, the temperature of blood within the body, the pH of the fluid within the brain and spinal columns, or indication of the need to void. Chemoreceptors are those that are stimulated by a change in the chemical composition of the environment in which they are located. These include the receptors of taste as well as those perceiving changes in oxygen levels, blood sugar states within the body, and others.

The receptors are divided into various classifications. Distance receivers are the receptors concerned with events at a distance, or removed from the immediate vicinity of the body. They make us aware of the external, remote environment. Exteroceptors are those concerned with the external, near environment. These make us aware of people and things in our immediate environment. Interoceptors are those concerned with the internal environment responsible for pain, temperature, and other feelings. Interoceptors also are concerned with the proprioceptors, which provide information about the position of the body in space at any moment in time. In an adequately functioning system, these receptors enable us to discern whether the stimulus is in the external environment, whether near or far from the body, or coming from the internal environment. In a child whose system is not functioning well, we see evidence that he is unable to discern himself well from his environment.

While information is received from each sense separately, once it enters the nervous system the information begins to be combined, compared, and contrasted. These basic senses are closely connected to each other and form interconnections with other systems within the brain. The interplay among the various senses is complex and requires a thorough knowledge of both the sensory system and its neurological pathways.

Simplistically, the impulses travel from the receptors up through the spinal cord, brain stem, and midbrain. Some go to the cerebral cortex and some to the cerebellum. The information is decoded, synthesized, and dealt with at a variety of way stations.

The following outline represents a very complex system of dealing with all of the input from our internal and external environments. Specifically listed are areas that have been cited as being involved in autism.

Spinal Cord Level

Spinal cord reflexes are generated at this level. The muscle stretch reflex is a typical example of the simplest form of reflex. The stimulus that initiates this reflex is a stretch to the muscle. The reaction is a contraction of the muscle. This reflex is protective in nature, in that it acts to prevent the muscle from injury when the muscle is stretched to the point of tearing. Other examples are the knee-jerk reflex, in that tapping on the patellar tendon under the kneecap produces the knee jerk, or reflexive kick of the lower extremity.

Brain Stem and Midbrain

Reticular (activating) formation

Activity in this system produces the conscious-alert state that makes perception possible. It courses through the pons, hypothalamus, and thalamus. The reticular formation is a network of interconnections between ascending sensory tracts, but also forms interconnections from the trigeminal, auditory, and visual systems and the olfactory system. This system has the capability of heightening or dampening the information passing through it. Further, the number of neuronal connections and the fact that so much sensory input converges upon this area can literally negate the specificity of any sensory modality. Therefore, it is believed that most neurons within the reticular formation are activated equally by a variety of sensory stimuli. (See Ganong 1975.) The system is therefore *nonspecific* and can be activated by many types of sensory input, as compared to the classical sensory pathways that are activated by specific types of sensory stimulation. Disorders in regulation, arousal, and emotion are believed, in part, due to problems within the functioning of the reticular activating system, or RAS. Since the RAS is nonspecific and can be activated by many types of sensory stimuli, this area is believed to contribute to difficulties with modulation of sensory input and regulation of behavior, a problem often seen in autism.

Pons

This is the area of the brain that houses all of the regulatory or vegetative functions of the brain—respiration, blood pressure, heart rate, and others. Changes within this area of the brain result in alteration in respiration rate, blood pressure, and so on, and are recognized as measurable and observable indicators of neuronal regulation.

Hypothalamus

The functions of this area of the brain include some fairly discrete visceral reflexes and other complex behavioral and emotional responses. Certain autonomic responses are triggered here, including hormonal reactions involved in rage and other strong emotions. Stimulation of areas within the hypothalamus causes increased levels of epinephrine and norepinephrine to be produced within our bodies and are thought to be the chemical transmitters that contribute to arousal levels, sensory regulation, and levels of stress and anxiety.

Thalamus

This is the communication center for all sensory information as it is processed into the central nervous system or out of it to the rest of the body. It serves as a way station for all types of sensory relays to the cerebral cortex and other structures. Much of the information processed is both site and sensory system-specific or modality-specific, but some is not. The thalamus is thought to aid in focusing attention to relevant stimuli by the processes of correlation and integration that occur within. A small portion of this structure has a very large reciprocal relationship with the frontal lobe and is involved with emotion and behavior. It is also a way station for outward-traveling information from the cortex to other areas within the brain. Its messages may be facilitating or inhibiting to the system.

Cerebellum

The cerebellum is responsible for coordinating muscle groups in synergy throughout the body. It is responsible for the timing and sequencing of muscles for synergies of actions so that movements are performed smoothly and accurately, while combining information with the proprioceptive system to ensure the movements are graded appropriately to the task. In order to do this, the cerebellum is constantly informed of commands being issued by the cerebral cortex and pyramidal systems via the thalamus. All sensory modalities, including tactile, auditory, and visual stimuli, feed their impulses to the cerebellum. After evaluation of these signals, the cerebellum is able to make automatic and appropriate corrections for mistakes or inaccuracies in muscle activities.

The cerebellum also is believed to be involved in the control of emotions, behavior, and learning of some motor skills, and has been cited as a key area of the central nervous system involved in autism.

Cerebral Cortex

Limbic system

This is an area of cortical tissue surrounding the hilum of the hemisphere. It is comprised of the hippocampus, its central structure, and the amygdala. The limbic system is responsible for integrating cortical and hypothalamic functions. Limbic system circuits have been noted to have a prolonged after-discharge following stimulation. This has been offered as an explanation in part, that emotional responses are generally prolonged and will outlast the stimuli that initiate them. Another characteristic of this system is that there are relatively few connections between it and the cortex, and therefore relatively little opportunity for cortical influences. The limbic system also is involved in the process of learning. There is evidence that avoidance and defensive behaviors are orchestrated by mechanisms within this area of the brain (Gray 1991; Pribram 1991; Ledoux 1996).

- **Hippocampus**. This structure communicates input from the cerebral cortex to the hypothalamus and thalamus and sends information back to the cerebral cortex. Therefore, it is involved with learning, memory, cognition, motivation, and emotion.

- **Amygdala**. The amygdala has been cited as an area involved with the ability of the system to psychologically prepare for action, and has been identified as an area of involvement in those with autism. The amygdala works with the hypothalamus to control biologic rhythms and sexual behavior, and it contributes to motivation.

Neuronal regulation or transmission occurs via chemicals called neurotransmitters, released at the cellular level within each area of the central nervous system. These neurotransmitters determine whether excitation or inhibition will occur. Each neuron within each area of the central nervous system is constantly bombarded by adjacent neurons sending both excitatory and inhibitory input at the same time. The competition of input is integrated by the neuron through neuronal integration, which determines whether a cell will fire (Kandel et al. 1991).

The interconnection of all of these systems provides for inhibitory and excitatory mechanisms that regulate attention and arousal, generate adaptive responses to our environment, aid in regulation of emotional tone, and control our ability to function. If neuronal excitability becomes too intense, the disintegration in interaction between multiple systems can occur. It can cause confusion, irritability, fluctuations in emotional tone, and disorganization within the system. Simple tactile stimulation may be perceived as aversive or threatening, vestibular information may be disorienting, auditory stimulation may become maddening, and visual stimulation overwhelming.

However, if the information is received and coordinated accurately with other sensory information, a person is able to interpret a situation accurately, control emotions and behaviors, and make an appropriate organized response.

The integration of sensory information has an impact neurologically on multiple areas of functioning. See Table 7.1.

TABLE 7.1 Functions of the brain

Executive functions	Thinking	Learning	Perception	Language	
Motor control	Gross motor	Fine motor	Oral motor	Speech	
Emotions and behavior	Emotions	Behavior	Arousal	Attention	
Vital functions	Heart rate	Respiration	Blood pressure	Autonomic nervous system	Parasympathetic nervous system

In normally developing children, sensory integration is an ongoing process that occurs on a subconscious level allowing for the development of body scheme or body image, and of skills across many areas including cognitive, motor, social, and emotional realms. Sensory integration is what allows us to take all of the continuous streams of information from within our bodies and the environment around us and use the information to learn, plan, and organize our behaviors.

The Sensory Systems

Sensations that arise from within our body include pain, temperature, heart rate, blood pressure, and signals associated with other visceral or bodily functions. The kinesthetic and proprioceptive input from our muscles and joints enable us to know how our bodies are moving and how much pressure to exert for a given task, while the vestibular system enables us to interpret body orientation in space and with relation to things around us.

Tactile System

The tactile system is the most pervasive system. It is comprised of all the touch receptors of the body. The skin is the primary receptor, but the sensory receptors within the oral cavity or mouth also are tactile receptors. Separate from taste, they perceive texture through tactile input.

The types of sensations carried within these systems are dealt with, for our purposes, by two primary pathways within the central nervous system (brain and spinal cord): the anterolateral system and the dorsal column medial lemniscus system. The anterolateral system is sometimes referred to as our protective system, while the dorsal column medial lemniscus system is referred to as our discriminative system.

Anterolateral System

The anterolateral system consists of a diffuse bundle of nerve fibers that convey pain, temperature, and crude and light touch. This system extends through the spinal cord and brain stem, supplying input to many areas. It is slow moving and poorly organized and provides less discriminate spatial or temporal information. As the information passes through the reticular formation portion of the brain stem, it is integrated into our levels of arousal and our emotional tone. The information is relayed first to the hypothalamic structures and then to the limbic system and is highly integrated with emotional behaviors that provide for emotionally charged responses to the sensations. Integration at this level enables the "fight or flight" type of response to pain, high temperature, or other potentially dangerous, threatening situations. The anterolateral system also projects to the thalamus, which is the communication center for all sensory information as it is processed into the central nervous system or out of it to the rest of the body. All of these areas are involved in processing the information from the anterolateral system and in coordinating responses generated from the cortex.

Dorsal Column Medial Lemniscus (DCML) System

The dorsal column medial lemniscus system processes tactile, vibratory, touch-pressure, and proprioceptive input. It is a highly discriminatory system that conveys deeper pressure and spatial and temporal localization and allows for tactile discrimination. In contrast to the anterolateral system, this system is fast moving and efficient. It, too, projects through the reticular activating system to the thalamus so that information may be coordinated with other incoming and outgoing sensory processing before going onto the primary and secondary somatosensory areas of the cortex.

Tactile information must be accurate for visual perception and basic concept development. In normal development, infants first perceive things in two dimensions. Later, through tactile exploration with their hands and mouths and through gross motor explorations, they begin to perceive the world in a three-dimensional reference. However, if tactile processing is impaired and unreliable, spatial and temporal concepts are not solidified.

Adequate tactile information enables the child to perceive where his tongue is within his mouth and how to position the tongue to make sounds and produce speech. The tactile system enables him to tolerate varying food textures, manage food within the mouth, move his mouth to chew, and time the movement of the food for successful swallowing.

Tactile processing can impede interpersonal relationships. Children who interpret touch as aversive may lack the ability to bond adequately with their caregivers. This can alter developing social and cognitive skills. The child may be *on alert* constantly against all of the tactile input in his environment and not be able to focus on or tolerate people and things in his world. He may spend most of his time trying to avoid people and things in the environment. He may develop the use of aggressive behaviors or body language that puts people off. He may develop language skills that drive people away. He may simply flee or withdraw and become *asocial.* Conversely, the child who does not perceive tactile information at normal intensities may develop clingy behaviors and may touch or mouth everyone and everything in the environment.

Because the tactile system is so extensive, the input at any moment is both abundant and continual, and it can act to excite and arouse the system or to calm and sedate it. The effects of the tactile system can be dramatic and are integral to adequate functioning.

Proprioception

Matthews (1988) described the function of proprioception to be the provision of the motor system with a clear and unambiguous map of the external environment and of the body. Proprioception, combined with vestibular information, provides

Exploring the Spectrum of Autism and Pervasive Developmental Disorders

the central nervous system with a stable frame of reference against which other sensory input is interpreted. The proprioceptive system is comprised of a variety of receptors within our muscles, joints, ligaments, and tendons. The receptors located in the muscles are the muscle spindles and Golgi tendon organs which sense elongation of muscle fibers and tension, or the force being exerted by the muscle. These receptors give us our stretch reflex as a protection against injury and the ability to cortically override the stretch reflex. Impulses from the muscles reach the cerebellum without affecting consciousness and provide us with the automatic background activity; that is, postural tone and balance.

Conscious awareness of various parts of the body depends upon impulses arising from the receptors around and in the joints themselves. Velocity receptors discharge during changes in joint angles, and position receptors give us information about joint angles that is not dependent upon movement at the joint (at rest).

The information from these sources is conveyed through the dorsal root of the spinal cord via the DCML, lateral spinothalamic, and spinocerebellar tracts yielding vital information essential for awareness of the position of our limbs and about their movements. Most proprioceptive impulses that reach the central nervous system do so on an unconscious level. The information passes through the thalamus, where it is analyzed against all other incoming or outgoing sensations before being relayed to the cerebellum. The cerebellum uses the full gamut of the information to predict, judge, and correct the motor act to achieve the correct force, direction, and rate of muscular contraction and relaxation. This allows us automatic, unconscious motor control. The pons (which houses the reticular formation) exerts either a facilitating or inhibiting influence on the information; and the hypothalamus allows the emotional response to stimuli and is responsible for eliciting increased muscle power when needed. The parietal lobe is responsible for the motor response to the stimulus.

The somatosensory system is responsible for the sensations arising from both the tactile and proprioceptive input. It is referred to as a system because, although each system has specific information to deal with, our bodies functionally rely on the co-mingling of the input from each system. The comparison of data perceived within the tactile system is compared with and contrasted to the information from muscles and joints. The combination of these systems operating as a team enables us to develop spatial and temporal concepts and to perform movements automatically without depending upon other systems.

An infant, who perceives his world in a two-dimensional reference, begins to move within his environment to reach a toy. As he exerts himself and moves through space, his proprioceptive system combined with the tactile information begins to map out his world and his body. As he manipulates toys and objects, the combination of proprioceptive and tactile information tells him about shapes, dimensions, weight, and texture. His world gradually becomes three-dimensional.

When we reach into our pockets, it is the combination of tactile and proprioceptive input that allows us to identify and discriminate objects such as a dime from a quarter, or a nickel from a key, without having to use our visual systems to do so. Once the selection is made, we may choose to validate our actions through the use of the visual system, thereby reinforcing or giving feedback to our systems.

Vestibular System

This system tells us if we are moving, in what direction, and whether or not we are upright. It also signals to us when our balance is threatened. When it cannot be relied upon to deliver this information accurately, the world becomes a very confusing and frightening place. Nothing makes sense. Vestibular information is the reference point against which other sensory input is measured (tactile, proprioceptive, auditory, and visual). This comparison is what allows localization of a stimulus, concepts of spatial and temporal relationships, and body orientation to the environment.

The cornerstone of the vestibular system is comprised of a set of receptors within the inner ear. They consist of the semicircular canals that respond to acceleration and deceleration of the head as well as angular displacements of the head. The utricles are concerned with movement in relationship to gravity (linear accelerations and the position of the head in space). The saccule is believed to be a receptor for vibratory stimulation to the face and head and may influence eye movements. Receptors within this system are triggered by gravity and give us a sense of orientation—our *internal compass*. The sensations or input gathered here have a direct bearing on our sense of balance, head control, eye gaze, and on our postural and antigravity extensor muscle tone.

Impulses descending within this system reinforce the tone of the extensor muscles of the trunk and extremities, enabling us to be upright against the pull of gravity. Conjugate eye movements occur in response to head movements and to the position of the head in space, and are directly influenced by this system. Without a stable head, conjugate eye use is less than optimal. Vestibular reflexes combined with optic reflexes enable the eyes to remain fixed on a stationary object while the head and body are moving.

Inadequate vestibular processing can be the cause of many different problems. An infant with a poorly functioning vestibular system will have difficulty calming himself. Developmental milestones such as rolling, sitting up, creeping, or walking may be delayed or clumsy. Problems in academic performance can surface as a result of inadequate vestibular processing. The inability to sustain an upright sitting posture in a chair and to use the eyes well for learning may be interpreted as attentional deficits, can result in underaroused states, and will have an impact on learning. Inadequate vestibular processing can impede the muscular efforts needed for school-related tasks such as coloring, tracing, and writing. It will impede bilateral, gross motor coordination needed to walk, ride a bicycle, or play. It can cause a fear of movement, nausea, and dizziness. It can make visual information confusing and unreliable, adding disorganization to the picture.

Sensory Integration and Normal Development

Development is a spiraling process. Skills are acquired in many different domains at the same time. For example, babies learning to eat with a spoon are receiving and integrating sensory information from:

- *Touch receptors* from the spoon and the textures in the mouth and on the face

- *Proprioceptive receptors* from the jaw as they chew, from the weight of the spoon, and as they guide their arm movements

- *Visual receptors* as they guide their arms from the plate to their mouths

- *Olfactory receptors* from the smell of the food

- *Gustatory receptors* from the taste of the food (salty, sweet, sour)

As babies effectively integrate the information, the following functions are mastered:

- *Gross motor* skills of posture (staying upright, stabilizing the head, opening and closing the jaw), balance, and hand-to-mouth pattern

- *Fine motor* skills of hand control, tool usage (spoon), and eye-hand coordination

- *Oral motor* control of the tongue, lips, and jaw

- *Executive functions* of planning and sequencing

As children get the spoon to their mouths, they get the feedback from the successful completion of the task, and they will be able to use this new skill as a building block for more complex activities.

For another example, as babies begin to move through space, crawling and eventually walking, and later as toddlers learn more complex motor skills such as somersaults and climbing a jungle gym, they are gaining valuable information from their senses. They are receiving and integrating information from the:

- *Proprioceptive system* as their muscles and joints work to push, pull, kick, and climb

- *Tactile system* as their bodies struggle against the carpet or tile in learning to crawl, as the head touches the ground for somersaults, or their hands and feet struggle to hold onto the bars of the jungle gym

- *Vestibular system* as the head changes position in learning to roll and sit up, and as they begin to move through space

- *Visual system* as they use their eyes to monitor orientation in space, guide movements, and judge the distances so as not to bump into items or fall

As children integrate the information from these senses, they master the following functions:

- *Motor control:* Balance, postural control, trunk control, coordination, gross motor skills, grading arm movements, strength

- Executive functions:

  — *Concept formation and cognition.* Not only are they working on motor control, but they are producing an impact on their cognitive or executive functions by learning spatial concepts and concept formation such as *under, over,* and *through.* They also acquire problem-solving abilities.

  — *Motor planning and sequencing.* They are working on timing and sequencing of motor movements, body scheme, bilateral integration (using their arms and legs together in a coordinated fashion), and motor planning.

— *Language*. As they connect words to their movements, they are integrating language with motor movements to develop a method of explaining their actions and desires.

Sensory integration in normal children develops automatically, spontaneously, and continuously. Without conscious awareness, children will take the information from multiple sensory experiences, analyze it, combine it, and use it to develop more complex skills. Each bit of information or sensory input received into the nervous system is a contribution toward giving the child a rich, whole learning experience and will be used to make a complete picture from which the child can build and learn progressively complex tasks.

For developing children, sensory integration is fun and provides the internal motivation or drive to meet the challenges of mastering and producing an impact on their environments. Through child's play, valuable sensorimotor experiences are realized. Driven to play and interact with their environments, children experience successes and failures through their attempts. Sensory integrative processing is what enables them to benefit from the success or failure, alter their ensuing attempts, or repeat them in order to accomplish the desired tasks successfully. Each challenge requires that children adapt to the environment and organize their responses. The drive to master the environment, coupled with the actual physical interaction that produces sensory stimulation and the adaptive responses it requires, helps organize the brain.

Under normal circumstances, each interaction yields a sensorimotor experience which in turn, focuses, hones, and sharpens the sensory integrative process; and each sensorimotor experience can be used to build foundation skills and scaffolding for effective social, cognitive, emotional, academic, and functional performance. These foundation skills provide the base from which children can acquire attention and arousal needed for learning gross and fine motor skills, reading and writing, self-care activities, and motor planning skills.

Children often test their limits during play as they attempt to accomplish tasks just beyond their reach. Motivation and inner drive are vital components to healthy play experiences. Games provide motivation, structure, and challenges; and they stimulate creativity, initiative, and rewards, both real and imagined. During play, children take risks and follow their inner drive to produce physical activity in which they master their environments and bodies. They are energized by curiosity, competitive spirit, and the need to succeed.

Young children will create very elaborate imaginary game scenarios, and then use toys and items in the environment as imagined tools, weapons, modes of transportation, geographical barriers, and rewards. A paper towel roll becomes a sword, a packing box becomes a cave, a bed becomes a cliff, and rocks become treasure. They will roll, run, climb, swing, jump, fight, and compete to gain the coveted reward.

School-age children will participate in team sports to provide the structure, competitive motivation, and forum in which to hone their skills. They will accept the challenges and meet them with verve and voracious tenacity. They will perceive that they are able to jump higher, run faster, and throw farther than their peers. They learn spatial concepts, role delineation, cause and effect, social interactions, and how to deal with anger and frustration; and they learn how to make their movements more skilled and effective.

These are the times to try out new behaviors, new tasks, and get feedback from oneself and others. It is a time of creativity, imagination, a time to stretch reality and experiment without fear of repercussion. Play provides the child with multi-sensory experiences and socialization opportunities.

 ## Sensory Integrative Dysfunction

Sensory integrative dysfunction occurs when the brain is not able to organize sensory information for use. Information coming in from the senses may not be accurate. The input may not be efficiently interconnected within the brain, and the child may have difficulty putting together the information from the various senses. It is as if the brain were not connecting what is being heard, with what is being seen, with how the child is moving. Experiences may lack meaning or be distorted. Without good sensorimotor experiences that are meaningful, the child may not develop the foundation skills necessary for building more advanced skills.

There are no diagnostic tests for sensory integrative dysfunction. Parents may take their child to a physician who will run medical tests and find nothing significant. Consequently, the physician may tell the parents that nothing is wrong with the child medically, and that what they are seeing is a behavioral problem or a problem that the child will outgrow.

Ayres defined sensory integration dysfunction as a malfunction, believing that the areas of the brain involved with sensory integration were operational, but not efficiently functioning. She believed that, lacking evidence of actual damage to the brain structure, the problem could be at least partially corrected through therapeutic intervention (Ayres 1979).

Based upon Ayres' reasoning, the presumption of SI theory is that the sensory systems are all present within the brain and at least deemed capable of functioning in and of themselves. The child is capable of the executive functions of thinking, learning, and language. Motor skills are intact. The child is capable of the motor control for gross, fine, oral motor, and language skills. The child also is capable of normal emotional and behavioral development. The parts of the brain governing these functions are intact and presumed capable of normal operation.

The problem may arise in:

● The ability to perceive and/or process the incoming information

● Inefficiencies in organizing the information, therefore affecting the output in one or more areas

— If the communication between systems is poor, the output often becomes disorganized, ineffective, and unpredictable.

● The ability to effectively use the sensory information for function

When a child has a sensory integrative dysfunction characterized by inefficiencies in organizing the sensory information within the nervous system, we often see inconsistencies in performance. On a given day, a child may come into the clinic or school and process efficiently, with all areas of the brain communicating well. The child functions beautifully and is happy and well-behaved. The teacher and parents see the child's tremendous potential and capabilities. Each area of the brain is capable of full functioning, and the parents and teachers are thrilled to see the child's capabilities. On another day, the child's system may not function or communicate well, and he becomes disorganized, inefficient, and unable to function and perform adequately. The poor communication results in multiple areas being affected. The parents or teachers become frustrated by the unexplained inconsistencies in performance. The child is admonished for being lazy or exhibiting behavioral problems. In reality, the child is suffering from sensory integrative dysfunction. Because of inefficiencies in the processing of information within the brain, he is not effectively able to function.

A child who has a problem perceiving and processing sensory information will pass along this problem through multiple systems. When information going into the nervous system is inaccurate, the child's motor output will be inaccurate. Because of the interconnections within the nervous system, a problem in processing one type of sensory input will have an adverse impact on multiple areas of the child's functioning.

For example, a child with decreased tactile processing may have problems because the tactile information from his tongue and mouth is not perceived or processed adequately. The child won't know how to position his tongue for speech or move food around his mouth for eating. However, a tactile processing problem also will affect how the rest of the body is perceived and functions. Fine and gross motor skills also will be affected. The disorganization caused by impaired tactile processing will have a direct impact on the child's emotional state and the behavioral reactions to his performance. Disorganization of the continuous stream of sensory information, combined with the child's ineffectual and laborious efforts, leads to confusion and frustration. Controlling or avoidance behaviors, tantrums, and aggression are a direct result of the impaired tactile processing. See Table 7.2.

An intervention program must focus on addressing the underlying problem of tactile discrimination while promoting integration within the nervous system on multiple levels. A program that focuses only on improving the outcome or skill acquisition, such as the fine motor skill or behavioral problems, rather than addressing the underlying inefficiency within the central nervous system, will result in several problems.

Improvements often will be in the development of splinter skills. Through repeated repetitions of an activity, a child may make improvements in a particular

TABLE 7.2   Example of a child with tactile-processing problems

Decreased Tactile Processing		
Oral Motor Issues	Fine and Gross Motor Issues	Emotional, Behavioral, and Sensory Issues
Impaired awareness of tongue and mouth	Impaired coordination of finger movements	Disorganized emotional state
Difficulty moving food around in the mouth	Decreased fine motor abilities	Inconsistent emotions
Pocketing of food, chocking, gagging, aspiration	Motor incoordination awkardness	Fear of new foods
Impaired awareness of how to position tongue for sound production (articulation)		Withdrawal or avoidance
		Self-stimulation, aggression, head banging, hand biting

skill or motor movement. However, he may fail to generalize this skill; and development of the motor control and sensory motor awareness needed for other tasks may be limited.

1. When you are working on skill development, rather than improving the ability of the brain to receive and process sensory information, often a child will appear to plateau. Parents, teachers, and therapists become frustrated at the child's inability to generalize skills and the slow degree of improvement.

2. The targeted behavior or self-stimulation pattern may stop, but another one may replace it to meet the child's sensory or communicative need.

When the program effectively addresses the underlying problem as well as the central processing problem within the nervous system, improvements can be seen across many of the areas that are impacted by the sensory system, even when intervention does not directly address that problem skill. For example, a program designed to address the underlying decreased tactile processing, if effectively and aggressively designed, can have an impact on oral motor control, food preferences, speech, and fine motor skill development, even though the actual treatment only addressed the sensory systems and gross motor skills.

The hallmarks of sensory integrative dysfunction are inconsistencies in performance, difficulties in attention, arousal, organization of behaviors, motor planning and coordination, and fluctuations in emotions and behavior. *We are describing a central processing disorder*. If therapy or behavioral intervention does not address the central processing component and merely works on strengthening or practicing specific fine, gross, or oral motor components, we will see some improvements in those skills. However, in the child with sensory integrative dysfunction, a plateau will develop in his performance. Therapy must address the central processing component in order for progress to be realized, because it is the central processing that has been ineffective. The goal of treatment is to get the child to organize the input and to make successful and effective use of that input.

Impact on Development

Sensory integrative dysfunction can have a very pervasive impact on a child's life and a direct and adverse impact on his development. If poor sensory processing or communication exists from the time of birth, it will have a direct affect on what that child learns, his perception of the environment and his body, and on his development.

The child misses important stages or components of his development. His motor control, problem-solving skills, and perceptions are impacted. Thus, you may see delays in cognition, language development, and motor coordination. You may see awkward postures, immature grasp patterns, a sluggish or hyperactive child, or one who is reluctant to join in with other children.

Children are always growing and developing. Normal development requires that they develop certain skills before moving on. Even though children learn on multiple levels and never truly master one skill before moving to higher ones, they still need to master skills along a certain continuum. Often these children need more than just sensory integrative treatment. Often they have developed splinter skills after years of attempting to function without a sound sensorimotor foundation. The *holes* in their development are so large that their nervous systems can't automatically adapt. They have learned so many coping strategies and developed so many fears that they won't allow themselves to attempt a task even though their nervous systems now are ready to integrate the information. They are unwilling to take the risk to develop. Predictability and consistency are safer than taking the chance at failure.

Through our years of experience in working with children with sensory integrative dysfunction, we have come to believe that many of these children need more than just sensory integrative intervention. Treatment programs aggressively designed according to sound SI principles, which also address the functional, neuro-developmental, behavioral, and communication problems, have resulted in dramatic improvements in these children.

Key Components of SI Intervention

The evaluation is the foundation for effective intervention strategies. Through a sound evaluation of the sensory systems and by using a method of tracking and trending the evaluation findings, we are able to analyze the areas of difficulties in order to determine a clustering of problems within various sensory systems. By identifying the underlying problems within specific sensory systems, we are able to design a treatment program that promotes the integration of sensory information, rather than simply teach and develop splinter skills within a single domain.

Sensory integration has three main postulates (Stancliff 1998):

1. Normal persons take in sensory information from the environment and from their own movements, process and then integrate the sensory input within the central nervous system, and use this information to plan and organize behavior.

2. Deficits in sensory input result in deficits in conceptual and motor learning.

3. By being given enhanced sensory experiences within the context of meaningful activities and the planning and production of an adaptive behavior, a person can enhance sensory integration and improve learning.

The goal of sensory integration is to help the child organize sensory information for use (Ayres 1972a). This entails improving the child's ability to process and integrate information within the brain. In order to accomplish this, we must adhere to four specific components of treatment:

1. The adaptive response

2. The child's inner drive

3. Treatment technique and equipment

4. Individualization and variety

The Adaptive Response

The first component is that the child must be an active participant in the treatment and must produce an adaptive response. In order to make the interconnections within the brain, the child must be doing the work. We cannot do *for* or *to* a child and expect integration to occur. For example, providing the child with sensory experiences in which he is a passive recipient is not sensory integration. No integration of sensory input within the brain is required, because there is no output (response) expected. In this case, the child is receiving sensory stimulation rather than sensory integration. Therefore, sensory integrative treatment requires that the child perform a purposeful, goal-directed activity that provides feedback. Swinging on a swing for the mere pleasure of the sensation does not demand an adaptive response once balance reactions are instilled in the individual and are automatic. However, a task that requires a child to maintain balance on the swing while throwing beanbags at a target demands sensory integration. As the child throws the beanbags, he will get visual, auditory, and kinesthetic feedback. He will adjust his performance based upon the feedback of successful and unsuccessful attempts. Through this feedback, the brain can develop models of movement that can be used as the foundation for more complex motor planning.

The Child's Inner Drive

The second component is a similar concept. In order to facilitate the processing, analysis, and integration within the brain, the child must be actively involved and motivated to succeed or do something. Effective treatment and sensory integration rely on tapping into the child's inner drive and intrinsic motivation to interact with the environment and, in many cases, *conquer* the world. For many children, this is difficult, but it can be accomplished. It often requires finding what is referred to as the just-right challenge (Koomar and Bundy 1991). This represents a task that the child views as being challenging and which has the sensorimotor experience the child needs. Providing the just-right challenge requires skill in reading the child's cues and responses and adjusting the activity ever so slightly to guarantee success while providing challenge. The therapist must take into account many factors:

1. Listen to the child's needs and interests, and help him create the needed challenge or task.

2. Provide the needed sensorimotor experience within the task or throughout the task. Often, the sensorimotor input provided by the activity can contribute to the motivation driving the child to accomplish the task.

3. Design a task that is at or beyond the child's level of functioning. A task that is too easy and is viewed as boring or not stimulating may result in shutdown.

4. Consider the child's perception of the task. It may be perceived as difficult, but it must be perceived as being able to be accomplished. A task that is too hard will frustrate the child.

5. Consider the difficulty level of the task. The activity must be graded appropriately in its level of difficulty, the amount of integration of input required, and the output or response required. The amount of assistance provided also must be graded and reduced as the child increases his skill and confidence.

6. Be prepared to provide the energy needed to drive and often coax the child into and through the activity, facilitate the play experience while providing encouragement, and offer verbal praise and feedback.

Treatment Technique and Equipment

The third component that is important in SI intervention is the actual treatment technique and equipment. SI is often a blend between being child-driven and therapist-guided treatment. It is typically characterized by equipment that is large, provides multisensory input, and is capable of being used in many ways. SI is considered a hands-off approach in that the therapist often assumes a passive role or a role as a facilitator rather than a *doer* or *handler*. It is the child's responsibility to do the work and the therapist's responsibility to design the environment for the appropriate challenge and sensorimotor experiences. The child must be actively involved in connecting auditory, tactile, and visual input with what his body is doing in order to make sense of his world and accomplish ever more challenging tasks.

The environment usually is spacious, allowing room to run, jump, and motor-plan novel tasks. Suspended equipment, often textured, is used for new multisensory experiences. Treatments often lose their effectiveness when the child learns or masters the skills needed for the task. Once the task is learned, the challenge is over and the effectiveness of the treatment diminishes if it remains unchanged. The demands that variations in environment, equipment, activities, and challenges place upon the child force the brain to organize sensory information from many origins, analyze the information, organize a response, monitor its success or failure, benefit from feedback, and refine further adaptive responses.

Individualization and Variety

The fourth component is that treatment must be individualized to meet the needs of each child. The child's needs may vary daily, hourly, or within a session. The therapist must be sensitive to the child's needs and constantly adapt the program to meet them. The environment and activities must be set up to meet the individual needs of each child, and treatment must be based on a thorough and comprehensive evaluation and ongoing analysis.

Summary

This, then, is Sensory Integration-large rooms, suspended equipment, and individualized, multisensory experiences that enable an endless array of novel, unique challenges from which to build increasingly more complex tasks.

CHAPTER 8

Neuro-Developmental Theory and Its Integration Into Treatment

Carolyn Murray-Slutsky and Betty Paris

Neuro-developmental treatment (NDT) is a treatment technique that was developed by Berta Bobath, a physical therapist, and her husband Karel Bobath, a medical doctor. Mrs. Bobath's work started in the 1940s and spanned the next several decades. As Mrs. Bobath worked with children with cerebral palsy in her clinic, she devised theoretical approaches to handling techniques. Karel Bobath became interested in his wife's work and began to research possible neurophysiological explanations for her findings. This pairing of information progressed into a treatment technique widely used throughout the world for the treatment of a variety of diagnoses that involve movement dysfunction. Many of the beliefs put forth by the Bobaths also can be applied to children with autistic spectrum disorders.

 ## Key Components of NDT

Current theory as set forth by the NDT Association consists of four basic tenets:

1. Human behavior and function are based upon the continuous interaction between the individual, the environment, and the task. NDT holds forth that the individual is composed of many subsystems that interact with and

are interdependent. Those systems are dynamic in that they change and adapt to both internal and external stimuli.

2. For proficient motor function, the individual must use a combination of infinite numbers of movements and coordinate those into desired functional activities under a wide range of circumstances. Learning and adaptation of motor skills involve a process associated with practice and experience.

3. Impairments in motor control can limit the person's ability to function. A maladaptive performance or the inability to function can result in far greater degree of impairment, new impairments, and possibly other pathophysiologies.

4. The intervention process begins with the assessment of the individual's functional performance and an analytic approach to problem solving. Treatment uses therapeutic handling and focuses on increasing function by building on the individual's strengths while concurrently addressing any existing problems.

These tenets can be applied to children with autism. The sensory issues within autism lead to alterations and deficits in how the subsystems relate, communicate, and affect the system's ability to function adequately. The individual with autism must be able to use a combination of infinite numbers of movements and coordinate those into desired functional activities under a wide range of circumstances. Autism alters the innate ability of the individual to develop the varieties of movement strategies and to generalize and adapt those skills to a wide range of circumstances. Maladaptive performance or the inability to function can result in far greater degree of impairment, new impairments, and other deficits found in autism, such as cognition, language, behavior, motor planning, and emotional well-being. Learning and adaptation of motor skills involve a process associated with useful feedback, practice, and experience, all of which may be provided in treatment. Treatment of the child or individual with autism should include therapeutic handling and focus on increasing function by building on the individual's strengths while concurrently addressing any existing problems.

A Living Concept

NDT is a living concept that continues to evolve and to emerge new theoretical models and new information in the movement sciences. The theory allows that the individual is comprised of many interactive and interdependent subsystems; and that those subsystems are plastic and adaptive to changes, both from the internal and the external environments.

Sensory Integration theory also continues to evolve. Based upon the work of Ayres, we have ever-increasing data of how the sensory systems impact on our ability to interpret and respond to the environment. The treatment techniques are being developed and honed so that function may be improved.

Importance of the Sensorimotor Experience

Mrs. Bobath's work addressed the importance of sensorimotor development in learning. She believed that the baby's ability to learn and to develop is based upon the sensorimotor experience. He learns about himself through the movement of his body and hands, through touching his face, trunk, and legs. The normal child gets to know his body by putting fingers in his mouth and by playing with his hands. He learns about his mouth and tongue through this exploration. Appreciation of textures and shapes develops as he touches and mouths objects. As he learns to reach, crawl, and climb, he learns about his own size in relation to people and things in his environment. Spatial perception is developed as he masters rolling, creeping, crawling, and walking. His perceptual, visual-motor development and overall intellectual ability is influenced by his physical development (Bobath 1972).

Mrs. Bobath also professed that a paucity or lack of movement leads to a lack of development of sensory information about the movement, and that the sensory information gained through abnormal movement is abnormal. She also believed that equilibrium reactions and postural control are the foundations for normal patterns of control.

The sensory issues in children with autism are well documented. Ayres' description of the hyper- or hyporeactive systems helps explain why. The infant or child may be hyper- or hyporeactive to tactile, proprioceptive, and vestibular stimuli. This could explain the root problems in the child's inability to sustain antigravity postures or muscular efforts, his inability to make sense of tactile experiences, and his inability to map an accurate body scheme. Thus the child misses important hand explorations and weight-bearing experiences early in his development due to intolerant or underreactive systems.

Ayres' belief that impaired sensory processing leads to impairments in motor function also is borne out in children with autism, who often exhibit impaired sensory reactions and abnormal movement strategies. The result is impaired body percepts that impede motor output. The hyperreactive systems described by Ayres cause the child to perceive tactile experiences as being painful and vestibular experiences as being threatening; thus the child avoids those experiences. The avoidance of touch and movement leads to diminution of somatosensory awareness, balance, and postural mechanisms and function. Ayres' description of hyporeactive systems helps to explain how these systems cause the tactile, proprioceptive, and vestibular components to be missed or avoided during play experiences. Subsequent compensatory movements or motor control strategies reinforce poor body scheme. The result is the absence of body awareness or the development of impaired body awareness. The child lacks an adequate body scheme and the awareness of how to make his body work effectively for him. Consequently, he has ineffectual or limited movement repertoires.

Atypical Development in Autism

The theory continues to reiterate Mrs. Bobath's belief that development follows a typical sequence and that a maladaptive performance or the inability to perform within that framework can result in greater impairment. This set of postulates can be applied directly to children with autism or any of the autistic spectrum disorders. These children often have delayed, missed, or lost developmental milestones during the course of their development, resulting in abnormal or missed movement patterns and alterations in the muscular system affecting motor control. The maladaptive motor performance seen in autism may well lead to impairments in concept formation, perception of spatial relationships, and impairments in body scheme and motor planning skills. The causes of the maladaptive performances seen in autism are due only in part to problems in sensory processing.

Often, children with autism have a low postural tone base with poor ability to sustain postures against gravity. They resort to use of compensations that alter their posture and choices of position and movement. We see anteriorially tipped or rounded shoulders, poor pelvic stability, and fluctuation between anterior or posterior pelvic tilts (between a pot-bellied or flat back posture) and locking of middle joints (elbows and knees).

These children miss the normal processes that elongate and activate multi-joint muscles to develop:

- The muscles required for internal stability of the joints

- Isolated muscle control

- Control over the two sides of the body

- Control of their arms, legs, hands, and feet

They may refuse to sustain or tolerate being on their stomachs, and therefore miss opportunities to develop their back and upper-arm muscles by pushing up against gravity. They suffer in the development of graded or accurately calibrated upper-extremity control and proximal stability and manipulative skills, thereby compromising hand function. They may be unable to develop the flexor muscles to complete a sit-up maneuver (supine flexion) or avoid positions of ring- or tailor-sitting. They will often choose to use a W-sitting posture for stability, rather than develop the internal postural control and balance to function in other floor-sitting or chair-sitting postures. They do not develop the smooth, controlled weight shifts and the ability to transition between postures, because the W-sit posture effectively blocks the development of these skills. They steadfastly refuse to use or sustain tall-kneel or half-kneel in play because of a basic lack of postural control, and will never gain the control over their hips and pelvis required for single-limb postures, normal gait, and running and jumping. They also fail to develop the body awareness affecting foot placements, and they lack extremity control for raising and lowering body weight. The separation of the medial and lateral borders of the feet required for normal balance reactions is sacrificed because of decreased weight-bearing and movement experiences. Feet that don't develop tactile discrimination can't discriminate the surfaces that they walk across or stand on, further impeding balance. Impaired balance and coordination are the by-products of impaired sensory processing in the tactile, proprioceptive, and vestibular systems. These individuals may be described as hyperactive because they are unable to sustain attention. However, through our knowledge of NDT, we recognize that an inability to sustain postures can be one component of attentional deficit.

Integrating Treatment Techniques

Each of the two techniques offers treatment approaches that are valuable in the treatment of the individual with autism. NDT techniques offer a hands-on approach to addressing the issues of motor learning and control. Out of NDT has come the use of facilitation strategies to use in activating specific muscles or groups of muscles, a working knowledge of how the baby progresses through the developmental framework and thereby acquires equilibrium reactions, postural,

and motor control that serve function. Sensory integration has factored out not only clusters of symptoms linked to specific sensory systems, but also has identified specific groups of symptoms that comprise sensory integrative dysfunctions. SI theory enables us to deduce the problems and sensory issues that must be addressed to improve function. Although the two theories present different approaches to treatment, the integration of both theories affords a holistic view of the problems and explains the methodologies to use in addressing them.

NDT acknowledges the importance of the sensory experience in the development of motor control. As Mrs. Bobath professed, the normal child learns through his senses. As the mother of a normal infant handles her child in dressing, feeding, and play, the baby learns to distinguish himself from his mother (Bobath 1972). NDT attempts to provide the sensorimotor experiences through handling just as the child experiences it throughout development.

By using the tactile, proprioceptive, and vestibular components offered through NDT techniques, we can provide children with autism the opportunities to experience areas of their bodies that they may not be perceiving well. Through hands-on techniques, we can teach these individuals how their bodies move and help them organize and sequence their efforts. NDT facilitation techniques use vibration, tapping, and traction or compression in order to manually cue muscles or groups of muscles to work, while providing tactile and proprioceptive input to increase the child's sensory experiences. The vestibular components addressed through the use of NDT include those gained from the child's movement through different postures or positions. As we handle the child, we attempt to aid him in accurately interpreting those experiences, assist in the development of engrams of normal movement patterns, and facilitate the expansion and development of more complex motor sequences so that learning may occur.

However, it is through SI theory and the information yielded by Ayres' factor-analytic studies that tell us which systems contribute to various clusters of functions and which systems and modalities (tactile, vestibular, proprioceptive) must be addressed in treatment to improve the central processing underlying the impediments to function. Through Ayres' work, we know when to use vestibular input and which types of input to use. We also learn how and when to apply tactile and proprioceptive input to develop the somatosensory awareness needed for functional responses.

NDT techniques emphasize the importance of *grading* the handling. The therapist places hands or *key points of control* on the child, either proximally (close to the trunk) or distally (away from the trunk), so as to enable the child to do as much for himself as he can and yet provide a more normal sensorimotor experience. In this way, the child will gain information about movement that he can use in perfecting his own efforts as the therapist's hand placements are altered and the child takes on more individual control of the movement. The drawback is that NDT, although recognizing the importance of sensory input in handling, does not address the issues with the same level of sophistication as does SI theory. NDT does not address the issues of the hyper- or hyporeactive systems and how to alter or grade handling in order to be effective. It also does not address the issues of sensory modulation and how to manage the volatile nature of that disorder. Through the use of SI, handling and treatment can be graded appropriately for a hypo- or hyperresponsive system. SI theory teaches us to provide the "just-right challenge" to the child in order to foster and nurture motivation needed for integration and learning to occur and for our treatments to be more effective.

Function is the Goal

Originally the NDT technique was criticized for not improving the child's ability to function. However, early in its development, children undergoing therapy were not allowed to practice skills until they could perform with normal motor control. Is it any wonder that they didn't improve? This attitude led to a decrease in function and fewer opportunities to initiate and experience the sensation of movement and, therefore, motor control. NDT now acknowledges that the child must be allowed to problem-solve the motor act in order to learn it. An initial lack of quality is inherent in the problem-solving process, and many repetitions are required before skilled, normal movement develops. In normal development, infants who lift their hands initially to reach in prone do not do so with a smooth, controlled effort. Rather, they make an effort, usually miss what they were reaching for, and come crashing down. It is not until they have practiced a thousand times that the movement becomes controlled and skilled. Similarly, after practice and through the benefit of experience, motor engrams are formulated and hard-wired into the central nervous system, allowing automatic, functional, and successful environmental interactions.

The goal of SI is to increase the child's ability to adapt within the environment. The adaptive response so ingrained in the theory is function. However, a basic tenet of SI theory is that in addressing or teaching someone how to adapt to a changing environment, you must alter the adaptive response needed through engineering the environment.

A child with an autistic spectrum disorder may have missed important aspects of development because of abnormal movement patterns or missed developmental sequences. Now, he may need to back up to develop and practice those aspects. Therapy may be needed to help him in developing the ability to register, analyze, interpret, and synthesize the sensory information. It also may be required to help him develop the motor control needed to improve his functional interactions.

A thorough knowledge of how NDT theory looks at the components of normal development enables the skilled practitioner to assess what is missing and what is needed. NDT allows for the hands-on guidance or training of a motor act or its components in order to assist the child in problem solving and learning the motor engram necessary to function. The techniques use the developmental framework as its reference; that is, skills are facilitated or developed basically following the normal (developmental) sequence. The child will need to practice the motor act thousands of times in order to perfect and make use of it.

NDT attempts to address the quality of movement by providing normal sensorimotor input to improve postural tone, by facilitating active adaptive responses with the child as an active participant in the treatment, and integrating postural reactions into the treatment. The specific (NDT) handling techniques enable the child to learn the sensation of moving in more normal patterns. As he does so, he develops a higher degree of motor control and motor organization (Bobath 1972).

Children with autistic spectrum disorder often have poor quality of movement. We must develop and perfect their adaptive responses in order to address issues in their postural tone, eliminate stiffening of their limbs, and enhance the sensations of moving in more normal patterns.

SI attempts to address the quality of movement by providing sensorimotor input while demanding that the input be put to use to produce an adaptive response. That response may be better sustained postural or muscular reactions in an anti-gravity posture, a balance or equilibrium reaction, a fine motor skill, or a projected action sequence. Through carefully applied sensory input, appropriate sensorimotor outputs are facilitated. The child learns to accurately interpret, analyze, synthesize, and use the sensory information available to him in order to function optimally and to generalize skills across varying environments.

Grading the Treatment Session

The Bobaths' ultimate emphasis was on normalizing movement. They believed that movement and function were intertwined. The foremost component in treatment is the evaluation process. (For specific components for the evaluation, see Chapters 3, 9, 11, 13, and 14.) Not only is there an initial evaluation performed, but evaluation or assessment must be ongoing in order to monitor the child's needs at any point in treatment.

During one of our NDT certification courses, we were introduced to the treatment progression concept. This concept dictates a good evaluation or assessment of the child and involves setting a goal for each session and then dividing treatment into three general phases: preparation, facilitation and strengthening, and function.

Preparation

The NDT concept professes that alignment dictates function. This first phase of treatment looks at issues of alignment and abnormal muscle pulls. This is where we identify what is missing, what is blocking function. (What do I need to give this child or take away in order for this child to function?) We identify what ranges need to be increased or decreased, what muscles need to be elongated, what mobilizations need to be done, and what other steps need to be taken in order to prepare the client for movement. In treating a person with autism, we also must include preparing the sensory systems and bringing them into the calm-alert state needed for learning and optimal function.

Facilitation and Strengthening

During this segment, we work on the facilitation or activation of the muscles required for postural control and the development of fast, reliable equilibrium reactions in a variety of positions. We may concentrate on specific muscles or groups of muscles needed in order to perform a task, whether fine motor, gross motor, or oral motor. From the SI perspective, we provide the sensory input required to serve the facilitation and activation of those muscles, equilibrium reactions, and postural control mechanisms. We also provide the sensory base to facilitate fine motor, gross motor, oral motor, and visual-perceptual or visual-motor functions as they relate to the functional outcomes desired. Included within this phase of treatment are the therapeutic interventions needed to maintain a calm-alert state for function through sensory modulation or regulation.

Function

During this phase, the child is allowed to practice the movement patterns and skills in a functional capacity. We must weight whether to follow an NDT theory

base and allow the repetitions needed to convert movement patterns to motor engrams for smooth and automatic function, or to use a SI approach to allow for generalizing the skills across variable tasks and conditions.

It is our strong belief that function must be incorporated into each treatment in order to assure carryover of what is gained in therapy. The function phase of treatment may consist of practicing a certain skill, such as gait training with the physical therapist, fine motor skills with the occupational therapist, communication with the speech therapist, or the development of foundation (sensorimotor) skills needed for learning.

Integrating the Two Theories

Sensory integrative postulates continue to believe that deficits in sensory input result in deficits in conceptual and motor learning. SI theory hypothesizes that through systematically providing therapeutic sensorimotor experiences geared at facilitating normal neuromotor development, we can assist the brain to function more normally and develop according to normal developmental sequences. Through using specific sensorimotor experiences developmentally designed to address both the sensory integrative needs and those within the nervous system in order to produce adaptive responses to the environment, we can enable the brain to work more efficiently as an integrated whole. Treatment is aimed at providing therapeutic sensory and motor experiences that will address brain levels (that is, subcortical functions) that facilitate the processing of information needed to develop the higher-level skills.

Treatment is individualized, includes work with the child's family, and is aimed at acquisition of normal muscle tone and facilitation of normal movement patterns, be they of the head, arms, trunk, legs, or tongue (Bobath 1970). The environment is engineered by the therapist to provide opportunities for varied sensory and sensorimotor experiences, and the child is allowed to problem-solve the motor act with sufficient assistance to assure success.

Children with autism require that assistance to register, plan, organize, execute, and benefit from a more normal sensorimotor experience. We must identify the elements that may have been missed in their development and create a treatment plan by which they may obtain those needed catalysts for development. By giving enhanced sensory experiences within the context of meaningful activities that involve the planning and execution of an adaptive response, we can increase sensory integration and improve learning. By using the components of obtaining biomechanical alignments, facilitating normal muscle actions, and enhancing the tactile, proprioceptive, vestibular, auditory, and visual components during handling, we can help children with autism map out body scheme, organize their movement strategies, and achieve better control over their bodies. The outcome will be to promote increased function across many environments and skill levels.

By combining the two theoretical bases and the treatment techniques, we can enhance the sensorimotor experiences to improve sensory processing, postural control, enhance motor planning, and concept formation through increasingly more complex adaptive responses. We can make the tasks intrinsically motivating, and we can enhance learning.

CHAPTER 9

Sensory Modulation

Carolyn Murray-Slutsky

*T*o *modulate* means to adjust or adapt to a certain proportion: to regulate; to temper (Melzack and Wall 1965).

We are constantly adjusting and regulating things in our environment to help make us more comfortable and to aid in organizing the information around us. When the sound on the radio gets too loud, we modulate it by turning down the volume (inhibiting it). When it is too soft, we turn up the volume (facilitating the sound). When the sounds in our environment overpower the volume of the radio, we choose to either turn up the volume or turn it off, depending on what our nervous system needs or our mind wants.

Within the nervous system, there are neurons that facilitate or excite as well as ones that inhibit or quiet. One of the jobs of the nervous system is to prioritize and balance these impulses. As facilitating input comes in from one part of the brain, inhibiting input comes in from another to balance it. Facilitating input alone would spread uncontrolled throughout the nervous system and quickly overwhelm us. Inhibiting impulses block out irrelevant information and help the nervous system operate in a calm, well-regulated or modulated fashion, blocking out irrelevant information, while increasing the intensity of important, relevant information. *Modulation within the brain* refers to the brain's ability to organize and regulate its own activity. This includes suppressing irrelevant information while facilitating and attending to important messages.

Normal Sensory Modulation

Sensory modulation refers to the ability of the nervous system to regulate, organize, and prioritize incoming sensory information, inhibiting or suppressing irrelevant information and prioritizing and helping the child focus on relevant information. A well-modulated nervous system adapts to changes in its environment, has a level of arousal and attention appropriate for the task, blocks out irrelevant information, attends to relevant stimulation, and responds appropriately in direct proportion to the input.

Sensory modulation occurs in three phases:

- Registration

- Orientation

- Arousal (preparation for action or effort)

Habituation occurs when we recognize familiar input and no longer need to register or orient to it. Habituation enables us to tune out background information, such as the hum of the air conditioner or the sound of the computer running, in order to focus on relevant information.

> David, a student in third grade, has good sensory modulation. He sits quietly in the classroom, attending to the teacher. He is surrounded by 35 classmates. David is able to block out and inhibit the auditory input from the movement of the other students around him, the constant hum of the air conditioner, and the sounds of people walking through the hallway outside. He also is able to suppress the tactile input he receives from his shirt touching his skin and the hard surface of the chair beneath him. He is able to intensify the sound of the teacher's voice and the visual images being written on the board. As he begins to drift off for a second, he subconsciously starts to kick his foot in and out quietly but quickly under his desk. He shifts in his chair and bounces up and down several times. He increases his arousal level enough that he no longer drifts off.

> David's nervous system is organized and shows good sensory modulation. He is able to handle multisensory information effectively. He inhibits irrelevant background sensory information from his tactile, visual, and auditory senses. He is able to integrate and use multisensory information by attending to and registering relevant visual and auditory information. He also is able to modulate his level of arousal and alertness to maintain his attention and focus. He maintains a calm-alert state, optimal for learning.

Sensory modulation requires that we:

- Register, orient, and attend to relevant stimuli in the environment
- Respond appropriately to the sensory stimuli (in direct proportion to the degree of input provided)
- Have the ability to shift focus and attention to varying demands
- Suppress or habituate to irrelevant sensory information and filter out extraneous information
- Process multisensory experiences occurring simultaneously
- Obtain and maintain an arousal level appropriate for the activity

Sensory Registration

Sensory registration is the acknowledgment of sensory information. It occurs in relationship to movement, touch, olfactory, visual, or auditory sensory information. *Diminished sensory registration* is a delay or failure to respond to the information.

Vinogradova (1970) defined registration as the ability to perceive the stimulus. Registration asks the question, "What is it?" When registration occurs, there is a phasic physiological response, or arousal, to the input that occurs. This same physiological response occurs when any change to any parameter to the stimulus is present (Pribram and McGuinness 1975).

A child arouses briefly to the stimulus, then begins to answer the question, "What is it?" To do this, the child will check his memory to see whether it has stored any similar sounds or situations to compare with the new stimuli in order to give it meaning. These patterns of memory are called *neuronal models*. When the stimulus becomes identified and its meaning is established, the arousal response decreases. However, when there is any change to the stimulus or if there is a mismatch to the neuronal model or memory of the sound or situation, the child will reorient to the stimulus and his arousal response will increase again.

> David sits quietly in the classroom, attending to his teacher. Suddenly he hears a loud sound in the back of the room. The sound registers and produces an arousal response. David turns and asks himself, "What is it?" He sees a child leaving the classroom next door, and he recognizes the sound as the door slamming shut. He used his memory—previous neuronal models—to recognize the sound. The next time David hears the sound, he will know what it is and will not need to turn and register the information.

Orientation

Orienting to the stimulus occurs next. After sensory information registers, the child will orient to it, evaluating its significance. An involuntary tonic physiological readiness to respond occurs. It causes us to ask, "What is to be done?" This orientation phase contributes to the construction of neuronal models in that it assesses the feedback available from the outcomes of behaviors (Pribram and McGuinness 1975). The child must look through his memory of similar events and determine what action needs to be taken. If a child has no neuronal models from which to draw, he will orient to the stimulus and prepare for action or arousal.

> David is attending to the teacher when he hears the door open in the back of the classroom. He turns and sees the principal walk in. She walks to the front of the room and talks quietly to the teacher. Then the teacher announces the names of three children who will be dismissed early to practice for the school play.

David registered the sound of the door opening, oriented to the principal, and was in a state of physiological readiness. The principal had never come into the classroom before. David had no neuronal models to pull from. After the announcement, he asked himself, "What is to be done?" His name was not called, and he answered his question with, "Nothing." However, he built a new neuronal model. In the future, when the principal walks into the room at about the same time, David may not need to orient to her or get into a state of physiological readiness.

Arousal

The final phase is preparation for action, the exertion of effort or attention. This is now a voluntary mechanism in which effort and energy must be expended. The child's memory of prior events can be an important factor in the degree of energy, effort, and attention generated. For example, had David's name been one of the three called, his arousal level would have increased higher and he would have prepared for action. However, if he had a bad experience with the principal, or if had he done something he should not and was afraid of being caught, his arousal level would have increased dramatically. His past experiences would have influenced the amount of arousal he experienced.

Sensory Modulation Disorders

Sensory modulation disorders are registration, orientation, or arousal (ROA) difficulties that are predictable or fluctuating and may involve defensive behaviors.

- Predictable sensory ROA disorders are discrete problems of over- or under-responsiveness involving sensory registration, orientation, or arousal.

- Fluctuating or defensive responses are ROA disorders characterized by inappropriate, hypersensitive, or fluctuating responses to sensory information. (See Figure 9.1.)

Sensory modulation disorders are ROA disorders that are either predictable and discrete, or fluctuating. Defensive behaviors, while often fluctuating, may be predictable and discrete.

Because fluctuating or defensive responses are ROA disorders, the overlaps make it difficult to identify whether a child has a fluctuating sensory modulation difficulty or just a problem orienting or attending to the stimuli. Understanding these differences and identifying the actual cause for the functional problems are important in order to identify and implement the most appropriate and effective intervention program.

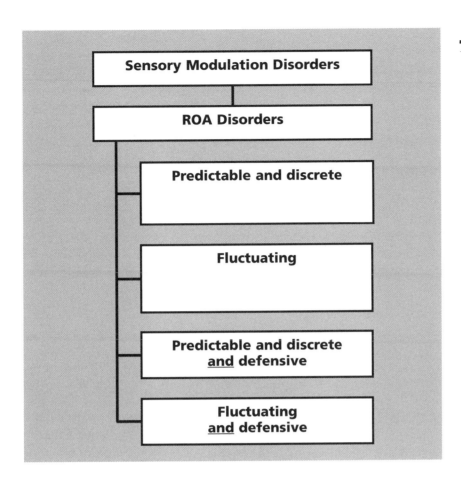

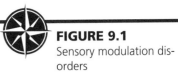

FIGURE 9.1
Sensory modulation disorders

Predictable Sensory ROA Difficulties

Sensory registration, orientation, and arousal difficulties may be a discrete problem within one or more sensory systems such as the tactile, olfactory, visual, auditory, or vestibular-proprioceptive systems. One system may be particularly vulnerable to either over- or underresponsiveness to the sensory input. With such discrete problems, the child is more predictable. He consistently either under- or overresponds to sensory information, or we can identify specific situations or times of the day in which the child experiences consistent difficulties. These may include:

- The end of the day when the child is fatigued or has experienced sensory overload

- Transitions from one activity to the next where predictability, structure, and inherent organization does not exist

- Open-field activities (activities performed in large spaces) such as gym class, an open classroom, library, circle time, or a therapy clinic

In these specific situations, the child has difficulty registering, orienting to, or processing sensory stimulation. He may either shut down or appear disorganized, emotionally labile, distractible, or hyperactive, unable to process or integrate the sensory information.

> Amelia is 11-months old. Physical development is advanced for her age, and she is not only walking, but also running. Amelia does not register or orient to most auditory or visual input. Her

mother can stand in front of her and call her name, bang pots and pans, and try to play with her with absolutely no response to either the auditory or visual input. Yet, Amelia will register the sound of her favorite videotape from three rooms away and run to get to it. She also will register the visual sight of her favorite spinning top. Amelia's sensory registration and orientation problems are predictable and nonfluctuating.

Fluctuating and Defensive Modulation Disorders

In contrast, a child with a fluctuating or defensive modulation disorder will demonstrate an ROA disorder; however, he may swing erratically and unpredictably from one end of the spectrum to the other, or he may be constantly in a state of hyperarousal or overstimulation to specific sensory stimuli. This child has difficulty controlling or tempering the internal thermostat for excitation and inhibition. Keys to identifying a fluctuating modulation disorder are:

● the unpredictability, and

● fluctuations.

The child may overregister and obsess on information or register everything in the environment, filtering out nothing. He may fail to be able to handle multiple stimuli in the environment, to organize multiple sensory experiences, or to modulate his arousal levels appropriately for the task. He may show defensive behaviors toward sensory input, demonstrating increased awareness of sensation coupled with a simultaneous craving for the exact sensory input to which he is hypersensitive. He may appear neurologically sensory-deprived and needy, yet disorganized and ineffective in being able to get his needs met.

A child with a fluctuating or defensive modulation problem may demonstrate any combination of these problems. The underlying neurological problem involves the brain's inability to organize, regulate, and assimilate incoming sensory information. The child's nervous system may be described as volatile and unpredictable. He may easily become overstimulated due to lack of appropriate inhibition of sensory information, or he may appear numb to all sensory information, oblivious to everyone and everything.

The one thing that is consistent among children with fluctuating, and often defensive, sensory modulation disorders is their inconsistency and unpredictability. The picture can change in a matter of minutes, hours, or days. Parents, therapists, and teachers all report frustration over their inability to predict what the child will be like from one moment to the next. The child's nervous system is fragile. It is not able to effectively regulate on its own. What appears to be a minor sensory experience may be unopposed within the child's nervous system, throwing him quickly and unpredictably into overstimulation. He may become frantic, disorganized, overexcited, or he may just *shut down*. His behaviors may appear illogical and difficult to explain.

Just as a child may demonstrate a problem with ROA, he also may demonstrate a fluctuating or defensive response within a specific sensory system, such as the tactile, olfactory, visual, auditory, or vestibular-proprioceptive system. Tactile defensiveness, gravitational insecurity, aversive response to movement, and poor sensory registration are common types of sensory modulation or defensive disorders defined by Fisher, Murray, and Bundy (1991).

Functional Implications

Children with problems modulating sensory input (ROA problems that are predictable, fluctuating or defensive) will exhibit problems with learning, language, and purposeful interaction with objects and people. Learning depends on registering sensory information, filtering extraneous input, and having optimal state of arousal to attend to a task. Disorders in language, social relations, behavioral organization, attention, and purposeful interactions often are related to inadequate sensory processing (Ayres and Tickle 1980). See Table 9.1.

TABLE 9.1 Sensory modulation disorders

Sensory Registration, Orientation, and Arousal Difficulties

1. The child may fail to register or respond to sensory input, people, or things in the environment or may attach little meaning to it. Sensory input may include tactile, auditory, visual, olfactory, or vestibular-proprioceptive input.

2. The child may register inappropriate changes or things in the environment while ignoring important changes or things.

3. The child may overregister or obsess on information in the environment, or register everything in the environment, not filtering out what is or is not important.

4. The child may register the sensory information or item, but may have no idea of what needs to be done. The child may not be able to identify the play potential of the object. This may lead to motor planning problems (see Chapter 13).

5. The child may not habituate to irrelevant background information.

6. The child may fail to assimilate familiar things he has seen or learned. Every time he sees it, it is as if for the first time, causing the child to constantly orient and arouse to stimuli.

7. The child may fail to handle multiple stimuli in the environment (Lovaas et al. 1971), or be able to organize multisensory experiences, resulting in disorganized responses (Ayres 1979).

8. The amount of arousal generated may be inappropriate to the task, stimulation, or situation.

9. The child may have difficulty in large, unstructured, or open-field environments such as transition times, open classrooms, large clinics, and circle time.

   a. The child may be unable to register information, running from thing to thing.
   b. The child may register specific items within the environment, but it may be inappropriate or the child may have no idea of what to do with the items.
   c. The child may register, orient to, or arouse to everything within the environment, failing to sustain attention.

Fluctuating or Defensive Responses

Inappropriate response to sensory information; overresponsiveness or fluctuating response to sensory information

---

1. The child may respond erratically or inconsistently to things in the environment. The child may fail to respond to sensory information from the tactile, vestibular, proprioceptive, auditory, olfactory, or visual modalities at one moment; and then overrespond, appearing defensive at other times.

2. The child may have an exaggerated response to sensory information from the tactile, vestibular, proprioceptive, auditory, olfactory, or visual modalities.

✳ ROA Disorders: Predictable and Discrete? Fluctuating or Defensive?

Children with autistic spectrum disorder may not respond to sensory input from their environment, displaying a form of sensory dormancy, or they may overreact to the input, displaying a form of sensory defensiveness. Fluctuations and difficulty modulating their responses also are common. The sensory input most vulnerable to ROA and fluctuating or defensive modulation disorders includes the vestibular or movement system, the tactile (touch) or oral system, the olfactory system, as well as the auditory and visual systems.

ROA Disorders: Predictable and Discrete

Predictable Problems With Sensory Registration

We have seen that sensory registration involves acknowledging that the stimulus exists in order to ask the question, "What is it?" We often see children who do not cognitively register stimuli in the environment or fail to attach meaning to this input. The parents' first concern may be that their child appears deaf. They can go behind the child and make loud, crashing noises, and the child fails to respond. The child fails to register the auditory sensory input.

Visual and tactile systems are equally as vulnerable. A therapist may wave a toy in front of a child, place a toy in his hand, and attempt to get him to register that an item exists, all to no avail. The child fails to register the visual input. Another child may be numb to pain, bumps, and bruises. He may not react when he is bleeding or has fallen. This child is displaying tactile dormancy, a failure to register information from his touch or pain receptors.

A child is seldom devoid of all registration. He may register inappropriate or insignificant changes in the environment, or he may miss important sensory input while attending to irrelevant details. When sensory registration occurs, the child searches his memory for neuronal models that attribute meaning to the experience. He may ignore experiences that have no meaning.

While the parents' first concern may be that their child appears deaf, they also report that the child does respond. The child responds, however unexpectedly, to other stimuli (such as Amelia, who hears her favorite videotape from three rooms away). The therapist also knows that the child registers visual information, even though the child does not respond to a toy in front of his face, because he registers his *favorite* toy. Children will register sensory experiences that have meaning to them.

Each child who registers inappropriate or insignificant changes in the environment will do so in his own unique way.

- One child walks into the clinic and visually scans every corner of the room. Then he obsessively collects all small rubber balls that were spread throughout the room. This child registered only the small rubber balls in his environment and failed to prioritize other sensory information present.

- Another child fails to respond when his name is called in the classroom, but turns every time a paper crumples or a page turns.

- Another child stands in front of the school bus and fails to register the sound of the bus horn.

- A child walks into the clinic and fails to register the therapist standing in front of him, but comments on the lights and a piece of equipment that has been moved since his last visit.

- Another child seemingly fails to be attentive in class, but registers and attends to the sound of the computer being turned on in the classroom next door.

Just as a child may register irrelevant information, he may overregister it, being unable to habituate to irrelevant background information. A child who constantly registers information that should not be attended to, such as fans, motors, and paper crumpling, will appear distractible, inattentive, and disorganized.

Sensory registration may vary depending on the environment. Many children have sensory registration difficulties in open, unstructured environments.

> McKenzie is 20-months old. When the door to the clinic opens or she is able to slip through it when no one is looking, she will run frantically through the clinic screeching in a high-pitched voice. She will run nonstop throughout every area of the clinic, aimlessly knocking items off shelves. As she runs and screeches, her frenzy increases, as does her arousal. Her hyperactivity is nonproductive, and she does not engage in any productive play or activity. McKenzie does not register sensory information in this open clinic environment.

Predictable Problems With Orientation

Orienting to sensory input involves evaluating its significance and preparing to be ready to act. A child will orient to an object only after he has determined that the object or sensory input is of significance. When he orients to it, he looks through the neuronal models in his memory and determines its significance. If a child is not registering relevant sensory information, neuronal models will not be built, the child will not see the significance in the input, and orientation will not occur. If the child is registering the information, but not building neuronal models because he does not see the importance of the input, then his attention will be random and less purposeful. He will appear distractible and disorganized.

Motor planning difficulties will result when a child either does not have adequate sensory registration or does not build the neuronal models necessary for orientation. Formulating the *idea* or play potential for a situation or object—a critical step in motor planning—requires both sensory registration and orientation. Motor planning deficits and interventions are discussed in Chapter 13.

Predictable Problems With Arousal

Arousal (that is, preparing for effort and attention) requires energy expended from the body and nervous system. If the child is not registering the information, he will not orient to it and there will be no effort, attention, or arousal. Conversely, the child may register, orient, and arouse to everything, unable to evaluate the significance of the sensory input or constantly arousing to what should be considered background or irrelevant input. A child who registers, orients, and is aroused by all sensory stimuli indiscriminately will appear distractible, hyperactive, inattentive, or just may shut down from overstimulation

Imagine that you are visiting Disney World or the Smithsonian Institute. On your first visit, you would have no neuronal models or similar memories from which to compare the sensory input. You register, orient, and arouse to everything around you. It is all new and exciting. You want to take it all in, running in one direction to see something, then in another direction when you see something else interesting. You expend tremendous energy, and by the end of the day you are exhausted. The next time you go, the visit is less exhausting. You now have built neuronal models and memories of what interests you and what does not. You are able to focus your attention on the activities that give you pleasure, ignoring those that do not. But if you had not built neuronal models or memories, your second visit would be as overwhelming, overstimulating, and exhausting as your first day. This is how some children experience life.

Unstructured, open-field situations are often difficult for children with ROA disorders. In these environments, three problems commonly occur:

1. The child may be unable to register the information in an open, unstructured environment.

   McKenzie is a child who did not register the sensory information in an open-field environment. She entered the large clinic running around frantically, knocking items from shelves, oblivious to specific items. She did not register any information within her environment.

2. The child may register information, but it may be inappropriate, or he may not have the *idea* of what to do with objects or stimuli in this open environment.

   Carmen entered the clinic and walked around aimlessly. She picked up every object and inspected it, turning it over, then dropping it and moving on to the next object. She is a child who registers information, but does not orient to the information because she does not have the *idea* or motor planning skills, to develop neuronal models.

3. The child may register, orient, and arouse to everything in the environment, but may not be able to process the significance of the input in order to sustain attention or effort to be productive.

   Andrew registered, oriented, and aroused to everything indiscriminately, and quickly became overaroused. He raced into the clinic and proceeded to run from item to item. He jumped onto the platform swing, throwing it uncontrollably in the air. A second later, he was off and diving into the ball pool. He jumped out and saw some balls in a bucket. After he dumped the balls and threw them in every direction, he was off again. Within two minutes, Andrew had registered, oriented, and aroused to ten activities and destroyed order in the clinic. He was unable to organize the multisensory experiences in order to sustain his attention on one task.

When a child is unable to process multisensory experiences or filter out relevant from irrelevant information within the environment, he may cope by overfocusing on familiar experiences or events that have meaning for him and for which he has built neuronal models and memories. By overfocusing, he registers, orients, and arouses only to things that have meaning to him. He limits his energy expenditure and is able to make sense of this world. A child may do this in his own unique way. He may seek out numbers, letters, items that can be stacked or lined up, or things that can be spun. To the child, these may have relevance, importance, and may provide a sense of organization.

Fluctuating or Defensive Sensory Modulation Disorder

Fluctuating or defensive modulation disorder is a very specific type of ROA problem. Any child with a fluctuating or defensive response to sensory input will have a problem with registration, orientation, or arousal. However, a child with a registration, orientation, or arousal problem does not automatically have a fluctuating or defensive problem.

This disorder is characterized by overresponsiveness, hyperarousal, and overstimulation; or a fluctuating response to sensory input in which the child swings erratically and unpredictably from one end of the spectrum to the other (from underarousal to overarousal).

The fluctuations are often due to an intricate interplay between sensory deprivation and overstimulation. A sensory defensive child is deprived of sensory stimulation and will demonstrate sensory-seeking behaviors, on his own terms. He will crave sensory input while simultaneously rejecting it. Overstimulation, shutdown, disorganization, and increased defensiveness are common responses to sensory input.

To accurately classify defensive modulation disorder requires skilled observations. It is based on several factors:

- Atypical affective response to sensory input (either over- or underresponsiveness) out of proportion to the stimulus

- The quantity and frequency of defensive behaviors present. The more (quantity of) defensive behaviors present, the more likely that the child has a defensive or fluctuating modulation disorder.

- The tendency toward high arousal levels and overstimulation. It is often associated with fluctuating responses.

Inconsistency is characteristic of neurological instability or a fluctuating or defensive modulation disorder. The child may fluctuate from lack of sensory registration of sensory input (underresponsiveness) to overresponsiveness. This may occur unpredictably and for no apparent reason. What appears to be small amounts of sensory input can quickly cause a child to become overloaded and overaroused. To identify the correct intervention, it is critical to accurately differentiate whether a child has a problem with discrete ROA or fluctuating or defensiveness.

The sensory input most vulnerable to defensiveness includes the tactile, oral, auditory, and visual systems and the vestibular (movement) system. Defensiveness may travel between systems.

Fluctuating or defensive modulation disorders are not behavioral disorders. The fluctuations and unpredictable behaviors and responses are due to neurological instability and are out of the child's behavioral control.

Registration and Orientation Problems: Defensive or Fluctuating

Defensive behaviors are characterized by overregistration and overorienting to sensory information.

- Tactile or oral defensiveness involves the constant overregistration of normal tactile input, the inability to habituate to background tactile input, and a high emotional tone associated with touch defensiveness. The child may react negatively to tags in clothing, the feel of clothes on the body, his hair being combed, textures of food, or water in a tub or pool. The negative reaction is out of proportion to the stimuli and often is highly emotionally charged, bordering on hysteria.

- Auditory defensiveness involves the constant registration of auditory input that normally would be ignored or habituated to by others, or an overresponsiveness to normal sounds.

- Vestibular defensiveness and aversion to movement involves registering and overreacting to small changes in body movements or positions that normally would be habituated to and viewed as nonthreatening.

Defensive behaviors are, in part, an overregistration to sensory input. However, the problem is much more pervasive and involves not only overregistration of the sensory input, but overarousal with aversive, almost painful response to normal sensory input.

Arousal Problems: Defensive or Fluctuating

Defensive behaviors often heighten the child's attention to the sensory input, increasing both the attention and arousal levels and making them inappropriate for the stimuli or task.

The child displays high arousal levels that often are connected with high emotional tones and autonomic nervous system responses of fight or flight. The child tends to be in a state of constant arousal and attention. He is alert for impending threats and often registers, orients, and alerts to specific sensory input. A child who is defensive to touch may go through his day in a state of high arousal, registering and orienting to any form of touch input. The higher his arousal, the more he registers and orients to touch and the less he can habituate to less invasive touch. His behavior escalates and he is unable to calm himself. He may continue to escalate or shut down due to his high arousal level. A vicious cycle pursues.

A word of caution. Defensive behaviors may originate from a discrete problem with sensory registration, rather than a true fluctuating defensive modulation disorder. For example, a child who has difficulty registering tactile or tactile-proprioceptive input (underresponsiveness to sensory input) will control all food that enters his mouth. Due to decreased tactile-proprioceptive awareness, he will not know how to move his tongue, lips, and jaw to control the food. His refusal to eat a variety of foods may be misdiagnosed as tactile defensiveness, when in fact it is the result of a tactile discrimination difficulty or a lack of registration to tactile input. Differential diagnosis is critical, because the intervention strategies are very different.

Defensive behaviors that are predictable and nonfluctuating may be a learned response. A child with a fluctuating defensive modulation disorder will learn to avoid activities and objects that are painful and uncomfortable. He will associate these activities with fear and discomfort, and will avoid them at all cost. When the defensiveness and modulation disorder is resolved, the child will continue to react to the activity with fear and avoidance.

Frequently this learned defensive behavior is accompanied by a lack of skill development because the child avoids activities. For example, a child with tactile defensiveness often avoids weight bearing on his arms and manipulating objects within his palms, which will contribute to shoulder weakness and decreased intrinsic muscle coordination within the hand (discussed further in Chapter 14). Eliminating learned defensive behaviors requires the development of the skills needed to effectively complete the task, provision of emotional support, and a gradual increase in participation in activities that caused defensiveness.

Seizures

We have seen that it is important for a therapist to ascertain whether a child has a discrete, predictable problem with sensory ROA; or a fluctuating, defensive modulation disorder. It is equally critical for the therapist to differentiate between the potential for abnormal seizure activity and problems with ROA or fluctuating or defensive reactions. The children we are describing are at a higher risk for seizures because they have medical-neurological problems. The potential for seizures is not an excuse not to treat the child; to the contrary, it is more of a reason to treat the child. We must develop sensitivity to the child, his behaviors, and the events that trigger changes in his sensory registration, orientation, and arousal. Look for specific clues that may indicate abnormal seizure activity. In these cases, you will need to guide the parents to pursue medical intervention in addition to therapeutic intervention.

Seizures may be masked as momentary inattentiveness. The child may be engaged in a task and momentarily lose focus or attention. His motor movements may stop, or he may continue with the task but lose his previous focus or investment in the task. Other subtle signs may be fluttering of the eyes, drooling, a slight decrease in sustained effort, or a change in muscle tone. After the abnormal EEG activity, the child may sit dazed; or he may resume the activity, but with strong or loud vocalizations such as high-pitched yipping sounds; or he may run frantically and automatically for no reason.

Another sign of abnormal EEG activity is that the child actually loses motor learning. A child makes progress within your session, and you feel confident that he has developed the neuronal models and effectively retained the information; but by the next session, he has lost the information. In this case, begin to question whether seizure activity may be occurring. Seizures can result in not only fluctuating performance, but the obliteration of previously developed neuronal models, adversely impacting the child's ability to learn. If seizures are the underlying problem, they must be addressed simultaneously with therapy in order to increase the child's functional skills.

Theories of Sensory Modulation

Sensory modulation disorders were identified within the tactile system as early as 1964 by Dr. Ayres. The understanding of tactile defensiveness evolved into the theories that relate to our understanding of sensory modulation. These theories become critical in understanding the disorder and designing intervention programs.

Tactile stimuli enter the nervous system through touch receptors in our skin. It is carried through the spinal cord to the brain via either the dorsal column medial lemniscal (DCML) system or the anterolateral system. Each system is very different. The DCML system transmits the sensations of touch pressure, vibration, and proprioceptive information. It is fast, efficient, and responsible for discrimination of tactile information. The anterolateral system functions to mediate pain, crude touch, and temperature. It is slow, indirect, and responsible for the emotional responses and autonomic nervous system responses associated with touch.

The DCML system transmits touch pressure, vibration, and proprioceptive input quickly through heavily myelinated pathways directly to the thalamus, the integrating center, and the reticular formation, both in the brain stem; then directly to the primary and secondary somatosensory area of cortex, as well as areas 5 and 7 of the posterior parietal lobes. Deep-touch pressure and proprioceptive input carried through the DCML system results in a calming effect (Ayres 1973). Decreased arousal is believed to occur due to its projections through the reticular formation. Its projections to the somatosensory areas of the cortex and areas 5 and 7 of the parietal lobe are responsible for localization and identification of specific tactile information used for tactile discrimination.

The anterolateral system transmits pain, crude touch, and temperature sensations; and is compromised of three pathways that are slow and indirect. Projections are sent to the thalamus, the integrating center; the limbic system, responsible for emotional tone; the hypothalamus, responsible for autonomic regulation and hormonal reactions associated with rage and other strong emotions; and the tectum, associated with the visual and auditory systems. Most fibers synapse in the reticular formation. The reticular formation, also known as the reticular activating system (RAS) due to its impact on arousal, with its interconnections to every sensory system, yields a pervasive influence over virtually every part of the brain. This connection enables the reticular formation to play a very important part in processing and integrating sensorimotor information. It serves as an arousal center that impacts the entire nervous system, either exciting the entire system or calming it down (Ayres 1979).

The anterolateral system is a protective system that activates during time of need to protect the individual from harm. Its connections to the reticular formation, the limbic system, and the thalamus charge the person with adrenaline, or neurotransmitters that result in the high arousal, which is needed to protect him from harm. It is often associated with the fight or flight response triggered by the autonomic nervous system.

TABLE 9.2   The dorsal column medial lemniscal (DCML) system and the anterolateral system

Dorsal Column Medial Lemniscal (DCML) System	Anterolateral System
Transmits tactile, vibratory, touch pressure, and proprioceptive information	Mediates pain, crude touch, light touch, and temperature
Characteristics	Characteristics:
• Heavily myelinated • Moves quickly through the system • Has a very direct course	• Slow, indirect course • Has three pathways
Course: Sends projections to the: • Thalamus within the Reticular Formation (integrating center, coordinates all information and relays it to the cortex) • Primary and Secondary somatosensory areas of the cortex; areas 5 (somatosensory and motor integrating area of the posterior parietal lobe) and 7 (Emotional/motivational tactile association area)	Course: Most fibers terminate in the reticular formation (mediates arousal, emotional tone). Projections are sent to the: • Thalamus (integrating center, coordinates all information and relays it to the cortex) • Limbic system via the hypothalamus (Emotional/motivational aspect of behavior; the limbic/reticular activating system (RAS) impacts the visceral/emotional aspect of attention) • Tectum (associated with the visual and auditory systems via the superior/inferior colliculus)
Associated with tactile discrimination or perception Provides precise information critical for tool usage	Associated with many aspects of touch (tactile defensive characteristics), arousal, emotional tone, and autonomic regulation
Impairment of the DCML results in impaired stereognosis; decreased light touch; and loss of position, vibratory, and two-point discrimination	

Ayres (1973) hypothesized that the DCML system was responsible for exerting an inhibitory influence over the anterolateral system; and that in normal development, the deep-touch and proprioceptive input transmitted through this system, as the child develops, serves as a natural inhibition to the protective system, the anterolateral system. Under stress or danger, the anterolateral system would activate and serve to protect the individual.

Ayres further hypothesized that tactile defensiveness is the result of an imbalance between the two systems. Defensiveness occurs when the DCML system does not exert its normal inhibitory influence over the anterolateral system, thus evoking strong emotional responses and defensive behaviors to normal tactile input.

She recognized the "gate control theory" proposed by Melzack and Wall (1965), and she believed that the DCML system served as gatekeeper over the anterolateral system. Ayres hypothesized that the provision of deep-touch pressure, proprioceptive, and other input mediated by the dorsal column would activate the DCML system to close the gating mechanism. This would block the protective response to touch and diminish the emotional response as well as the hyperactivity and distractibility associated with the defensiveness. She also believed that in contrast, any light-touch activities would open the gate, triggering the defensive and emotional response associated with the defensiveness. Escalating stress, anxiety, fear, or the anticipation of noxious stimuli also would open the gate, triggering the defensive response.

In the 1980s, Knickerbocker elaborated on the term *sensory defensiveness* to refer to a more generalized problem within multiple systems. She hypothesized that the problem was the result of an imbalance between inhibition and excitation within the nervous system that could result in responses of sensory dormancy or defensiveness. Symptoms observed clustered within clinically related sensory systems; the olfactory, tactile, and auditory systems (OTA triad) and the visual and vestibular systems (visual-vestibular dyad) (Knickerbocker 1980, 31–34).

Royeen (1989) hypothesized that a sensory modulation disorder included extremes from sensory dormancy (hyporesponsivity), to defensiveness (hyperresponsivity) and from failure to orient, to overorientation. Royeen believed that a modulation disorder was present when an individual either spent excessive time at one end of the spectrum or the other, or fluctuated between the two ends. A person with a modulation disorder is unable to stay in the middle of the spectrum.

These theories explain the inconsistencies we observe and the variations between sensory systems. It explains how a child can be tactile defensive one day and auditorily defensive the next, overly sensitive to environmental factors one day and oblivious and unresponsive the next.

Theories of sensory modulation emphasize the role of the limbic system as a modulating center for sensory input. Sensory information is processed at different levels of the limbic system depending on the complexity of the stimuli presented. It plays an important role in attention and orientation through determining what stimulus is important and what is not (Becker 1980). The hippocampus is believed to contribute to persistence in new tasks. Lesions of this area result in being able to begin a goal-oriented task, but not being able to stay with it to completion. The hypothalamus is the control center for the autonomic nervous system and serves a reciprocal relationship with the limbic system.

Stress and anxiety have been associated with limbic structures and components of the reticular system, hypothalamus, and cortex, as well as the action of neurotransmitters norepinephrine, epinephrine, and serotonin (Ashton 1987). Anxiety resulting from stress, apprehension, or fear can increase arousal, restlessness, and defensiveness; and can interfere with concentration.

Neurotransmitters carry either inhibiting or facilitating messages to the neurons to which they bind and play a role in the modulation of ROA. The effect of the various neurotransmitters and their role in sensory modulation is currently being investigated and discussed in neurological and psychiatric studies and journals. The impact of sensory integrative procedures on these neurotransmitters also is being discussed.

Working Theories for Intervention

A child with a modulation disorder has an imbalance between the inhibition and facilitation within the nervous system that results in either over- or underregistering, orienting, or arousing to sensory input. The limbic system and reticular formation are believed to be instrumental in obtaining modulation within the nervous system and in selecting and prioritizing sensory registration, orientation, and attention. Fluctuating or defensive disorders, such as tactile defensiveness, are believed to involve one system—the anterolateral system—operating without effective modulation of another system—the DCML system. Fluctuations also may result from an imbalance within the nervous system.

Intervention often employs strategies that impact modulation at all levels. Sensory modulation (that is, obtaining a balance between facilitation and inhibition) can be impacted through:

- Altering sensory input, integration, and organization
- Impacting the neurotransmitters
- Cortical and cognitive intervention

Maintaining optimum levels of arousal within the nervous system is critical to enhance appropriate sensory ROA. When the child is in that optimal window of arousal, he is more likely to register, orient, and attend to relevant, purposeful sensory information. The more time the child spends in this normal window of arousal, the more comfortable and normal it will feel to him.

Sensory-based activities can alter the level of facilitation or inhibition within the nervous system. Inhibitory activities often are used for an overaroused system and include deep-touch pressure; resistive and proprioceptive input; slow, linear vestibular input; or slow, rhythmic activities or songs. Facilitation activities are used for an underaroused system and include fast, vestibular input; fast rates of tactile or proprioceptive input (such as toweling or jumping); or songs that change rate or inflections. The calming or alerting influence of many sensory-based activities is believed to occur through its projections through the reticular activating formation, through activating neurotransmitters (such as with heavy work and resistive activities), or through inhibiting or facilitating cortical areas.

When sensory-based activities are used with activities that are graded to just beyond the child's ability, that are motivating and challenging to him, and require him to purposely interact with and adapt to his environment, increased processing organization and modulation can occur. Sensory information coming into the system needs to be monitored and gradually increased in order to improve the child's tolerance for and ability to process sensory and multisensory information.

Integrate sensory-based activities into the child's schedule to help him maintain normal arousal levels, and therefore optimal functional levels for learning and processing. As soon as possible, teach the child self-regulation; that is, teach him what his body needs to stay calm or alert, and appropriate activities that will help him accomplish this.

Minimize stress. Anxiety, stress, fear, and anticipation of noxious stimuli can lead to an increase in the excitation within the nervous system, and have an impact on modulation at all levels. Stress can be inhibited cognitively through relaxation techniques or rationalization, through inhibition techniques that will calm the nervous system (activating the DCML system), or through environmental modifications that redesign the environment to minimize stressful encounters.

Intervention strategies for fluctuating or defensive modulation disorders differ from static ROA due to the instability of the nervous system. Intervention strategies often employ more inhibitory input, the integration of more powerful inhibitory activities into the child's daily schedule, extensive environmental modifications, and intensive sensory integrative techniques.

Sensory-based intervention strategies must be employed slowly and carefully monitored, because the child may flip quickly from under- to overarousal. When selecting sensory-based activities, begin with inhibitory and calming input (deep-touch pressure, proprioceptive, and resistive activities). Use facilitation techniques sparingly, and monitor for adverse long-term reactions, which can occur four to six hours later.

Environmental modifications become essential for children with defensiveness; and they must continue until the child is able to integrate and modulate sensory information within more normal levels. Whenever possible, eliminate stressful activities that trigger defensiveness. Modify activities that cannot be eliminated by including inhibition techniques (those that activate the DCML system or that promote the release of inhibitory neurotransmitters). Many tasks that promote anxiety also will require systematic analysis and intervention. Modify the components that contribute to the sensory defensiveness by incorporating inhibition techniques into the task. Support and coach the child through the task, one step at a time in isolation. The goal is to eliminate the fear associated with each step.

Sensory integrative treatment procedures are geared at providing a modulating effect on the child's nervous system. By selecting specific sensory-based activities, facilitating multisensory integration in a graded fashion, and promoting adaptive responses through challenging activities (actual integration within the nervous system), we assist the nervous system to modulate, integrate, and regulate itself.

CHAPTER 10

Intervention Strategies for Sensory Modulation Disorders

Carolyn Murray-Slutsky

Intervention is a sequence of evaluation and treatment. We evaluate each child, design and implement a treatment program geared at remediating the underlying problems, and then we evaluate its effectiveness. Treatment programs must be constantly reassessed and modified, based on the child's response.

Before we can develop an intervention strategy, we must consider several factors. (See checklist, Figure 10.1.) First, we must determine the child's current state of arousal or state of the nervous system. In general, is the child in the calm-alert state, or is he underaroused, overaroused, or having fluctuating arousal levels? The second factor we need to determine is the phase at which we see the functional breakdown. Is the child experiencing difficulty with sensory registration, orientation, arousal/attention, or effort? When looking at this, we also must look at the sensory systems. Is the difficulty specific to a sensory system, or is one system adversely impacting the child's response? Then we need to determine whether the difficulty occurs in specific situations, environments, or at specific times of day. Finally, we must determine whether the child is using any coping strategies, either effective or ineffective. A child may revert to self-stimulation patterns or various repetitive behaviors as a way to increase organization and processing.

Before we can develop an intervention strategy, we must consider several factors.

1. What is the child's current state of arousal or state of the nervous system?

   _____ The calm alert state

   _____ Underaroused: Increase arousal to the calm-alert state

   _____ Overaroused: Decrease arousal and stress

   _____ Fluctuating arousal levels

2. At what phase do we see the functional breakdown?

   _____ Is the child experiencing difficulty with sensory registration, orientation, or arousal/attention or effort?

3. What are the specific problems we are observing?

   _____ The child is overregistering data; registering insignificant information in the environment; is unable to prioritize data

   _____ The sensory information has no meaning; the child has no idea.

   _____ The child registers and orients to the same information, never forming neuronal models or memories. Each time, it is new.

   _____ The child is unable to handle and process multiple stimuli.

   _____ The child is unable to habituate to background information.

   _____ The child is unable to regulate the arousal level appropriate for the task, environment, or situation. Disorganization increases.

4. Is the difficulty specific to a sensory system, or is one system adversely impacting the child's response?

   _____

   _____

5. What is the child's stronger sensory system? What system does the child seek out to help organization?

   _____

   _____

6. Does the difficulty occur in specific situations, environments, or at specific times of day?

   _____

   _____

7. Does the child use any coping strategies, either effective or ineffective? A child may revert to self-stimulation patterns or various repetitive behaviors as a way to increase organization and processing.

   _____

   _____

FIGURE 10.1
Steps in determining intervention strategies for ROA difficulties

Obtain the Calm-Alert State

Optimal sensory registration, orientation, and arousal occurs when the child is in the calm-alert state. *A calm-alert state is a window in which our ability to function is maximized.* It is the state in which the level of arousal within the nervous system is optimal for peak attention and task performance. This optimal state of arousal varies depending on the task, and it requires the child to change arousal levels as the activities change. The optimal level of arousal for listening to a teacher in the classroom is different from participating in sports or playground activities.

When we are operating within this calm-alert state, we are setting up the environment for optimum sensory registration, orientation, and arousal. In this state, we have sufficient levels of stimulation to be alert and open to learning, processing, or functioning, yet not to the point at which stimulation begins to interfere. Our first step to intervention must be directed toward getting the child functioning within this window of optimal arousal. The calm-alert state, while the first step, may change the child's sensory registration, orientation, and arousal. If the child is responding appropriately once in this state, turn to the section titled, "Facilitate Sensory Integration" (page 156).

Underaroused

Children who are underaroused, who fail to register sensory information within their environment or have difficulty processing sensory information secondary to underarousal, may appear sluggish, hyporesponsive, tired, bored, uninterested, or not mentally with you. They may resist participating in activities, preferring to read or watch TV rather than play actively or physically. Emotionally, they may react or overreact as if they are tired or not feeling well. Children who are underaroused benefit from sensory-based activities that increase the overall arousal of the nervous system. (See Table 10.1.)

Sensory-based activities that increase the child's arousal and bring him to the calm-alert state often require a period of testing and careful observation. Closely monitor the child's reaction and facial expressions as you introduce new and more aggressive sensory input. Look for an increased responsiveness and processing of sensory information. It is important to remember that each child is different and that individual preferences-likes and dislikes—enter into designing the correct intervention that will bring the underaroused child into the calm-alert state.

In general, linear vestibular combined with deep-touch or proprioceptive input has an arousing yet overall organizing effect on the nervous system. Activities that are repetitive, regular, and fast in nature also have an arousing effect. In contrast, activities that are irregular in their speed, rhythm, or movement may have an arousing effect, but often are disorganizing and should be avoided. Examples of fast, repetitive, regular activities that combine linear vestibular with deep-touch or proprioceptive input include:

- Jumping on a trampoline

- Bicycle riding

- Jumping on a pogo stick

- Bouncing while sitting on a ball
- Jogging
- Scooterboard activities
- Linear swinging in the net
- Playing tug-of-war
- Swinging in the net with the child propelling himself using a Bungee® cord

When attempting to increase a child's arousal, the entire therapeutic environment must be taken into consideration. The therapist is part of that environment, as are the lights, the atmosphere, and the room. Things to keep arousal levels increased include:

- A colorful, brightly lit room
- Loud, high-energy instruction and interactions
- Enthusiastic treatment sessions
- Verbalizations with inflection and changing pitch, gestures, and animation

TABLE 10.1 Environmental and therapeutic modification to alter arousal levels

If underaroused	If overaroused
• Use the stronger modalities to increase arousal	• Use inhibition techniques
• Use fast, regular, repetitive movement such as bouncing, jumping	• Lower anxiety. Use environmental and organizational modifications
• Use linear vestibular and deep-touch, proprioceptive, if it's a stronger modality	• Use slow, rhythmic, repetitive activities; slow rocking
• Modify the therapeutic environment:	• If calming, use deep-touch, deep proprioceptive, and/or resistive input
— Brightly lit rooms	• Use neutral warmth or swaddling for young children
— Bright colors	• Modify the therapeutic environment:
— Faster rhythms and songs	— Clutter-free, organized environment
• Modify therapeutic use of self. Use	— Low natural lighting
— Louder voice with changing inflections	— Quiet enclosed rooms
— High energy, enthusiasm	— Slow rhythmic songs
— Animation and gestures	• Modify therapeutic use of self. Use
• Oral motor activities may be arousing, such as chewing, crunching; or use flavors such as sour, bitter, spicy-hot	— Lower, softer, monotonous voice
	— Slow, calm speech
	— Avoid animation and exaggerated movements
	• Oral motor activities may be calming, such as sucking; or use sweet flavors

Exploring the Spectrum of Autism and Pervasive Developmental Disorders

Overaroused

In contrast, a child's nervous system may be overaroused or overstimulated, and therefore the child is not able to process well. He may be hyperresponsive, over-register to multiple stimuli, have difficulty filtering out the pertinent from the nonpertinent information, or not process information or assimilate it well. Organizational problems, high anxiety levels, and low thresholds of frustration tolerances are inherent in an overaroused child. The child may have difficulty sitting still to complete a task; be unable to control his impulses; have difficulty monitoring and controlling his emotions, appearing as if he is about to blow up or lose control; or be in constant yet nonproductive motion.

Children who are overaroused, have difficulty handling multiple sensory stimuli within the environment, quickly become excited, or exhibit defensiveness will benefit from inhibition techniques that are geared at lowering their arousal level and anxiety. These include modifying the environment and implementing systems that reduce anxiety. The goal is to move the child from overarousal to the calm-alert state.

Sensory-based activities to lower arousal levels need to include deep-touch and proprioceptive input. (See Table 10.1.) These activities are the most direct forms of inhibition, and therefore are calming techniques. They include resistive activities, such as:

- Push-ups performed against the floor, wall, or between two desks (arm push-ups in which the child lifts his own body weight); or chair push-ups in which the child lifts his body weight while sitting in his chair

- Isometric exercises such as clasping hands together and pushing

- Weight bearing on the arms (in which the child places his hands on the floor while supporting his knees on a chair). In this position, he may read or complete an activity.

- Animal walks, such as the crab, bear, or duck walk

- Wheelbarrow walks

Environmental factors play a major role in decreasing a child's arousal level. Clutter-free environments, quiet enclosed rooms, predictable schedules, slow rhythms and songs, and low, monotonous voices tend to be calming. Some children need to decrease environmental stimuli while receiving deep-touch input. These children benefit from having a hideout or quiet place to go to when they need to calm down and get organized. This can be a cardboard box with a top, a table placed in a corner with a blanket over it, or any small enclosure. Some children like to have pillows, foam blocks, or blankets placed in the box for deep-touch input.

Fluctuating or Defensive Disorders and the Calm-Alert State

A child with a fluctuating or defensive disorder may not be easily identified. The child may present as either underaroused or overaroused. Attempts to get the child to the calm-alert state may quickly backfire. As you use techniques to increase the child's arousal level, he may quickly and unpredictably become overaroused. The best way to anticipate a fluctuating or defensive disorder is to obtain a thorough clinical and sensorimotor history. This history should address questions such as, What upsets the child? What does the child do, once upset? How is the child calmed?

The presence of defensive or avoidance behaviors does not always indicate a fluctuating or defensive disorder. Many children with autistic spectrum disorders also have other sensory integrative dysfunction that contributes to defensive and avoidance behaviors.

- Children with a stable tactile discrimination problem (underresponsiveness to touch) may demonstrate defensiveness to baths or haircuts or certain fine motor tasks because of the inability to know where their bodies are in space or how they are moving.

- Children who are posturally insecure and do not have adequate balance reactions or trunk control may be threatened by walking on uneven surfaces, sand, or grass; be fearful of heights; or fear they will fall out of their beds.

- Children may fluctuate in their responses to sensory input due to improved sensory processing and awareness. For example, as a child with a tactile discrimination problem improves in the ability to process multisensory stimuli in the environment, he may display auditory defensiveness (covering his ears to noises). He may never have displayed auditory defensiveness in the past; but due to his improved awareness to the environment and environmental sounds, he now displays what appears to be auditory defensiveness. It actually may be an increased sensitivity and awareness to auditory input coupled with the inability to know what to do with it or how to integrate the new information for successful interaction.

While it is important to differentiate the cause of the defensive behavior in order to identify the correct intervention strategy, it becomes equally important to identify methods to help the child function and stay in the calm-alert state. The techniques described below may be helpful for children who demonstrate defensiveness as part of a modulation disorder and other sensory integrative dysfunction.

Moving the child with a fluctuating or defensive disorder into the calm-alert state often requires both inhibition techniques to decrease arousal as well as environmental modifications specific to the activity and the sensory system. Often the child with the defensiveness has learned to fear certain activities because of their sensory components. Responses are either impulsive, emotionally laden, or life-preserving reactions. Whenever possible, eliminate or modify activities that are threatening and produce anxiety, because anxiety interferes with the child's ability to learn and process information. However, it is not always possible to avoid these situations. Table 10.2 (Tactile Defensiveness), Table 10.3 (Gravitational Insecurity), and Table 10.4 (Auditory Defensiveness) address defensive responses that can occur during some necessary functional tasks. Treatments or environmental modifications are suggested that may reduce anxiety, helping the child to maintain the calm-alert state during these tasks.

TABLE 10.2   Tactile defensiveness: Common responses and intervention strategies

Tactile defensiveness: Aversive or negative behavioral response to certain tactile stimuli that others find to be non-noxious. It includes avoidance of touch, aversive response to non-noxious touch, and atypical emotional responses to touch.

Child hates having hair combed, washed, or cut	• Seat child firmly in your lap. Squeeze child between your knees (deep pressure).
	• Place your hands on top of the child's head and exert gentle but constant pressure down. (Joint compression of the neck inhibits defensiveness.) During joint compression, you must have correct alignment of the head on the spine.
	• Use a firm stroke or pressure as you comb or wash the child's hair.
	• Count or have the child count as you comb, wash, rinse, or cut the hair.
	• Give definite time limits to the task. ("Let's count to 10. Then we will stop cutting your hair.") Provide inhibition techniques immediately after.
	• Break the task into each step and item needed for each step:
	— Eliminate any unnecessary steps or items.
	— Use inhibition techniques (described above) while emotionally coaching the child through each step and familiarizing him with each item.
	— Practice each step in isolation in a stress-free environment.
	— Gradually combine steps and perform the task in the natural environment.
Child hates baths or showers	• Before bath time, do resistive exercises or activities that provide deep proprioceptive input.
	• Have the bath water drawn before having the child undress. Make the transition from undressing and getting into the tub as quick and smooth as possible.
	• If the child dislikes having his face or body washed, encourage him to wash himself. Self-imposed touch produces a less defensive reaction.
	• Use a large sponge or loofah sponge. Rub firmly to decrease defensiveness.
	• Use fragrance-free soap made for sensitive skin.
	• If the child is showering, use a hand-held shower nozzle. Let the child control the direction and force of the water.
	• Use a large towel, and quickly and firmly wrap the child in it. Avoid exposure of the wet skin to the air; the light touch may trigger a defensive reaction.
	• Provide deep-touch toweling to the extremities, hands, and feet to decrease defensiveness. If the child will tolerate it, provide a firm massage, using lotion to avoid skin irritation.
Child acts out when standing in line or starts to push and shove children.	• Position the child at the end of the line. Children bumping against him may be threatening or painful.
	• Assign a special task. Have the child go ahead to make sure the area is ready, or have him stay behind to make sure the lights are turned off.
Child withdraws or punches others who touch him lightly.	• Teach others to touch the child firmly. Discuss that the child feels light touch as alerting and as if he were being hit.
	• Approach child from within his visual field.

(continued)

TABLE 10.2   (continued)

Child reacts negatively when touched from behind or when touched by others.	• Tell the child when you are going to touch him. Always touch firmly. Assure the child that you will touch firmly and that you will not move your hands.
Child reacts negatively and emotionally when touched or touched lightly (exhibits anxiety, hostility, or aggression).	
Infant may reject cuddling as a source of pleasure and calming.	• Teach friends and relatives to show affection affirmly and directly.
Infant may prefer the father's firm touch over the mother's light touch.	• Tell the child what you will do and how you will do it. ("I'm going to hug you real hard." Respect the child's need for control.
Child may pull away when approached for a friendly pat or caress from a relative or friend.	• Make kisses on the cheek a form of deep-touch input. Hold the child firmly and give a deep, firm kiss.
Child may crave the deep-touch pressure of a hug, but try to rub off the light touch of a kiss.	• Give firm hugs rather than kisses. Take turns hugging. Have the child hug first, then return the hug. Determine who gives the best hugs.
Child may reject touch altogether from anyone but his mother or primary caregiver.	• Teach people always to approach the child from the front and always to make sure the child is able to anticipate the hug or or expression of affection.
Child may control when and by whom he is touched.	• Swaddle infants firmly. Be sensitive to their need for minimal sensory stimulation. Avoid vigorous rocking and shaking when they are upset. Rock slowly in a linear direction (up and down, side to side, or front to back). Swaddle and hold them firmly; talk to them quietly and softly.
Child is picky or dislikes certain clothing:	
Seams on socks are irritating.	• Turn socks inside out so seam is on outside. Use seamless socks.
New clothing is irritating.	• Wash new clothing to take out the stiffness. Have child help to select clothing.
Tags on clothing are irritating.	• Remove tags until child's system can tolerate them.
Child will wear only certain clothes.	• Avoid buying clothing that the child perceives as irritating. The head, neck, and abdominal area are very sensitive to touch.
Child takes off clothes inappropriately.	• Use inhibition techniques; joint compression, deep-touch, proprioceptive input.
	• When child removes clothes because they are overstimulatng or arousing.
	— Use inhibitory techniques. Have the child wear snug or tight-fitting clothes.
	• When child removes clothes because he likes the feeling of air on the skin:
	— Have him wear loose-fitting clothes for added light touch.
Child is a picky eater:	• Place the child on an oral motor program. (See pages 151–156.)
Prefers certain textures	• Before mealtime, provide deep-touch, resistive oral motor, and total-body exercises to decrease touch defensiveness.
Refuses to eat foods with lumps	
Dislikes sticky foods	• Do not introduce new foods or challenges at meal time. Set aside a separate time for graded feeding programs to remediate the underlying problem. Try to make meal time a relaxed, pleasurable experience.

TABLE 10.2 (continued)

Child uses only his fingertips. Child plays with toys, crayons, pencils, and so on, with only the fingertips.	● Before activities, provide phasic deep pressure into the palms of the hands, such firm clapping or a modified donkey game in which you hold the child on your lap, face down and parallel to the floor. Quickly lower the child to the floor, thus activating protective reactions (the child catches himself on hands). ● Progress to sustained deep pressure into the palms through resistive or weight-bearing activities. ● Grade activities from using fingertips to the whole hand. If the child will tolerate it, provide deep-touch input over the hand and writing tool.
Child avoids getting his hands dirty or using messy materials: Hurries to wash off even a speck of dirt May verbally rationalize why he can't get his hands dirty ("My mother won't let me").	● Encourage less messy activities. ● Use tools to manipulate the supplies whenever possible (for example, a paintbrush rather than finger paint). ● Before messy tasks: — Use phasic deep pressure into the palms (described above) — Use inhibitory techniques (deep-touch and proprioceptive input) to the hands and total body — Use messy materials that provide resistance, such as putties or dough mixtures. — Provide external resistance to the child's arm movements.
Child may toe walk to avoid contact with the ground.	● Check for heel cord shortening. Range must be increased in order to decrease walking on tiptoes. ● Provide deep pressure into the bottom of the feet. Seat the child firmly on your lap facing a wall. Place the child's feet flat against the all and put pressure directly through the knees into the feet. Have the child help push. ● Progress to positions such as half-kneeling. Encourage weight shift over the flat foot. Maintain pressure downward into the foot. ● Progress to static standing activities, then dynamic standing activities.
Child avoids walking barefoot in grass or sand, wading in water, or playing in sand or water at the beach or a park Becomes very nervous, anxious, emotionally upset, or aggressive.	● Whenever possible, avoid these situations until the child's nervous system is better equipped to handle it. ● When this is not possible or the child is ready to expand activities: — Before the activity, develop a densensitization routine. Start with sustained deep pressure into the feet. The position described above under "Child may toe walk to avoid contact with the ground" is effective. Progress to firm friction massages or compression into the feet, such as jumping on a trampoline. — Progress to desenitization of the hands and fingers described above under "Child uses only the fingertips." — If the child is on the Wilbarger Deep Pressure and Proprioceptive Technique (DPPT) program, initiate the treatment before performing the activity. (See pages 146–162 for discussion of Wilbarger's protocol.) — Introduce aversive activities in a fast but graded progression. ● Teach the child that these procedures will help him to overcome his discomfort. Help him to relax. Provide emotional support.

TABLE 10.2   (continued)

| Child has trouble falling asleep. | • Develop a calming routine before bedtime. Include quiet activities or inhibition techniques, such a resistive or deep proprioceptive actiities, isometric exercises, modified push-ups, yoga, and other calming activities. |
| | • Use a heavy comforter, flannel sheets, or even a sleeping bag to provide deep-touch input and deep calming. |

TABLE 10.3   Gravitational insecurity: Common responses and intervention strategies

Gravitational insecurity: Overresponsiveness to the vestibular system. Anxiety and distress stimulated by movement of the feet off a stable surface or changes in head position that normally would be viewed as nonthreatening.

The child has the motor control and balance reactions needed to perform the task, but has an aversive or atypical emotional response.

Child fears walking on uneven surfaces (curbs, gravel, mud, grass).	• Provide deep touch input before the activity.
	• Weighting the child's waist often provides deep proprioceptive input and helps the child to feel more secure.
	• Provide emotional and physical support.
Child will not sleep in a bed, but sleeps on the floor.	• Give the child a sleeping bag and a safe corner on the floor to sleep.
	• Use a weighted blanket.
Child is fearful of heights.	• Avoid these positions. The child is not getting accurate information from his vestibular-proprioceptive system and is relying on vision. If unavoidable, give deep proprioceptive input (provide steady, gentle pressure downward on shoulders) before the activity.
Child screams when lifted or placed on changing table.	• Child is fearful of movements into space or backward space. Hold the child firmly. Move with the child while holding him close to your body and supporting the head while providing deep-touch input to the body.
Child gets car sick.	• Seat the child near a window.
	• Open a window or turn on the air conditioner. Turn vents toward the child.
	• Give gentle, steady, compression downward through the head (maintaining alignment); or teach the child to give himself head compressions.
	• Give the child chewy foods or gum. Try ginger.
	• Acupressure wrist bands use acupressure points to decrease motion sickness.

TABLE 10.4 Auditory defensiveness: Common responses and intervention strategies

Auditory defensiveness: The overresponsiveness to normal sound or the registration of auditory input that normally would be ignored or habituated to.

Child covers his ears to noises, demonstrates increased anxiety or increased distractibility.	• Limit extraneous auditory stimuli in the environment. • Use rugs or carpet in the area to minimize extraneous auditory stimuli.
Child becomes upset with fire bells and alarms.	• Forewarn the child of any loud noises. • Position the child toward the front of the class to facilitate his ability to attend to auditory instructions and block out irrelevant information. • Use therapeutic listening techniques (listening to specifically modulated music through a headset) to decrease hypersensitivity and help to modulate the system.
Child becomes upset with the noise of a vacuum cleaner.	• Vacuum when the child is not around. • Use a broom, hand sweeper, or electric broom. • Prepare the child for the sudden noise. • Do not approach the child with the vacuum cleaner running.
Child becomes upset or agitated in noisy open field or public environments.	• Avoid special events, whenever possible, until the child's sensory system can accommodate them. • Have the child engage in resistive or deep proprioceptive activities before the event to lower his resting threshold and increase tolerance. • Have the child wear snug clothing or a neoprene vest (see page 161). • Have the child wear ear plugs. • Using an audiotape player with headphones. Listening to a favorite radio station often will drown out environmental noises and help the child to stay focused on an activity. • Use therapeutic listening techniques.

A word of caution: If you believe the child has a fluctuating or defensive disorder, you must be very careful in selecting your intervention strategies. The child with a fluctuating or defensive disorder has an unstable nervous system and will be very susceptible to any sensory input. He may flip from being underresponsive to being overstimulated in a matter of seconds. The goal for a child with a fluctuating or defensive disorder is to get the system in a state of homeostasis or balance, and this will require the selection of very specific inhibitory and deep-touch proprioceptive input. Facilitation techniques described in this section may be contraindicated and often cause the system to become overexcited.

Anxiety and Its Impact on the Calm-Alert State

Anxiety resulting from stress can increase arousal, amplify defensiveness, block sensory registration, and interfere with learning, concentration, and acquisition of new skills. The situation causing the stress and anxiety does not have to be rational. If the child perceives the situation as stressful or difficult, he will become anxious. Gray (1982) states that anxiety occurs when the actual experience does not match the expected response. If a child can predict what will be expected of him, and his expectations match what is actually expected, he can function with less anxiety. Therefore, according to Gray, behavioral inhibition occurs when the experience matches our expectations.

Routine, structure, and predictability help the child know what to expect. By setting up the environment for less stress, we may focus on the more important phases of therapy; that is, helping the child improve his processing and functional skills. Gradually, as we help the child lower the overall arousal level of his nervous system, we may decrease the environmental predictability and increase the child's ability to accommodate and adjust to more varied environmental demands. Making environmental accommodations and implementing organizational systems into your sessions becomes critical when dealing with a child who has a tendency to become overaroused or has a fluctuating or defensive modulation disorder. Lowering the child's arousal threshold into the calm-alert state is vital to the success of any therapy session.

To decrease the child's stress and anxiety, integrate the following suggestions into your sessions. Also use them as a guide when you provide consultative services to the child's school, home, or tutorial programs.

Initial Therapy Sessions

Initial therapy sessions are a source of anxiety for children who tend toward overarousal or fluctuating or defensive disorders. Before placing a child in this initial situation, some preliminary questions will enable you to foresee a crisis, make necessary accommodations, and set the groundwork for a healthy, anxiety-free therapeutic relationship. Questions include:

- Will the child go with someone he or she does not know?

- How does the child deal with a new situation?

- What can I expect of the child? For example, will he sit in a chair?

- What does the child do when upset? What calms the child?

- What activities does the child like?

- Is there anyone who can join the child who will decrease his initial anxiety? Is there an object or activity that the child can bring that would not interfere, but would make him feel comfortable? How do I get the activity away from him if it interferes?

Change and Transitions

Change and transitions provoke anxiety for most children with autism. Decreasing anxiety during change and transitions becomes very important in order to maximize productive time with the child and to help the child maintain optimal functioning. There are many ways to accomplish this.

- Establish a general routine or flow to your treatment session. It may be as simple as always starting with a gross motor activity or a sensory-based activity, progressing to heavier muscle work and strengthening activities, then moving into a small room for writing tasks.

- While you may choose to vary your tasks, the general activities are similar so the child can anticipate what will come next.

- Help the child anticipate when you will be transitioning to the next phase of treatment. Tell the child the sequence of activities, or use a picture activity board that visually depicts the sequence of tasks. When the task is completed, have the child turn over the activity or place it in a *finished* box. The child then can see the next activity and plan for future activities.

Some children may not see the inherent structure to your sessions; and even though you have a routine and flow, they still will become anxious. These children may need greater structure with less variability. Once their nervous systems become more flexible, you can make greater variations from session to session. You may need to complete each activity in a consistent order, making changes within the same activity rather than adding totally new activities. You also may need to use a picture activity board to depict an entire schedule.

Prepare Children for Stressful Situations

Identify the situations throughout the child's day that cause stress and anxiety. Prepare him for what to expect and what he is to do in each situation. In situations that can be distressing and unpredictable, such as fire bells and alarms, the child must learn the exact meaning of the alarm and the appropriate response. Whenever possible, learn when fire drills are scheduled, and forewarn the child repeatedly.

Provide Boundaries

Open-field situations, unstructured environments, and rooms without inherent structure, boundaries, or walls are the most difficult environments for children. Either work within defined boundaries or walls or teach a sequence of behaviors that will help them organize themselves within the unstructured environment. Establish rules, post them where the children can see them, and review them frequently. Have the children identify whether their behaviors meet the predetermined rules or expectations.

Decrease anxiety by providing structure and predictability to tasks. Within sessions and activities, give children definitive ends to tasks. For example, tell them, "You have five more to do. Then you can _____." Use a timer or visual time-prompter (such as the Time-Timer™) to provide a concrete end to the task. Be consistent in your responses. Children will relax when they know what to expect and are confident that you always keep your word. Give frequent choices ("Do you want to do A or B?"). Guide the session, and let the child feel in control.

Use Rhythmic Activities

Repetitive, regular-paced rhythmic activities and songs are organizing. Use this to your advantage. When completing tasks, have the child count out the repetitions, sing the alphabet song or other favorite nursery rhyme or song, or make up a song that includes the steps to the task. Most nursery rhymes are in lower tones and are specifically designed to be slow, rhythmic, relaxing, and organizing. Songs and activities that have erratic beats, dramatic changes in volume, a mismatch between the rhythm and the activity, or generally are fast in nature, have a more disorganizing effect.

Children respond based on the state of their nervous systems. What is calming and organizing at one moment may be disorganizing the next minute. Be sensitive to how the child is responding. Discontinue the song if the child reacts in an opposite manner to what you are trying to elicit. Read the child's nonverbal cues. If a child covers his ears, he may be indicating a hypersensitivity to the music or your voice, or he may be communicating to you that he doesn't want to sing now. Often, subtle changes in volume, voice quality, or inflection can modify the song or activity sufficiently to elicit the desired response.

Establish and Maintain Communication

Decrease anxiety by establishing an effective method of communication, interaction, and mutual trust. Children are sensitive to your nonverbal cues. If you think it, they will feel it. Project a positive attitude, trust, respect, and understanding toward each child. Let each one feel your warmth, sincerity, and concern through your touch, approach, and eye contact. Understand what each child wants and who each child is. Read each child's nonverbal cues sent through gestures and moves toward or away from certain equipment. If you can't understand the child, ask someone who can. If there is no one who can help you, let the child know you are sincerely trying. Then work with other therapists to set up a method of communication that helps the child communicate more effectively.

Foresee Emotional Crisis

Learn to sense when the child is about to lose control and remove him from the situation or circumvent the crisis. Look for the warning signs. What triggers the crisis or overload? Analyze the environment and situations that preceded the breakdown, and change the environment for optimum learning and sensory processing.

Monitor the environment for sensory overload. If the environment is overstimulating (too many people, too much noise, too many demands), change it before the child loses control. Warm emotional tones reduce stress. Voices that are quiet and calm, low lights, low noise levels, rooms without clutter or distractions, slow rhythmic songs, and slow linear vestibular input or rocking motions are all relaxing and inhibitory.

Create a Positive Atmosphere

Predictability, safety, and trust set the environment for optimal levels of arousal and learning. Each person working with the child is part of the child's environment and contributes to the entire atmosphere. Project a consistent, controlled, positive, and trusting attitude. Keep your frustrations under control, and do not permit your emotional responses to be triggered. Do not reprimand or condemn. Stand back and analyze the stressful situation to determine the best course of action. Reacting impulsively in anger or fear can destroy the environment and trust that are necessary for anxiety-free learning and processing. The constant goal is to keep the child in the calm-alert state.

 # Facilitate Sensory Registration

Sensory registration requires that the child respond and attend to sensory input or things in the environment. The child must know that there is something there to interact with. Without sensory registration, no other learning can take place. Helping the child to obtain sensory registration must be your first goal; however, several important considerations must be made in order to determine how to do this. See Table 10.5.

Without sensory registration, the child will not orient to an object, thus determining the significance of the item. A child who does not identify the significance of the item will not form a neuronal model or memory of the object or event. Unless a neuronal model or memory is formed, learning will not occur. Therefore, once sensory registration occurs, it must be linked with something meaningful to the child. What is meaningful to one child may have no meaning to another.

The difficulty with sensory registration is often related to one or two weaker sensory systems. It becomes important to determine the sensory systems that appear weaker and the ones that appear stronger. For example, it is common for children to have weaker auditory skills and stronger visual skills. Functionally, we may see this when we verbally ask a child to stand up, but the child does not respond. However, when we gesture with our hands to stand up, the child immediately stands up. Many children also seek out and enjoy deep proprioceptive and vestibular input. In these cases, the child's stronger sensory systems are the visual, proprioceptive, and vestibular systems, while the weaker sensory system is the auditory system.

Within the weaker sensory systems, a child will always register something. We must identify what the child registers within the weaker system, determine what has meaning to the child, and use it to broaden the child's scope of sensory registration.

> In Chapter 9, we met Amelia, 11-months old. Amelia does not register or orient to most auditory or visual input. However, she does register to activities that have meaning to her, such as the sound of her favorite videotape and the sight of her favorite spinning top. Her auditory and visual systems are her weaker systems. Amelia's stronger sensory systems are the vestibular and proprioceptive systems. She seeks out both vestibular and proprioceptive input through jumping and running, both advanced physical skills for her age. She also loves roughhousing, crashing into things, and being thrown into the air-activities that also have meaning to her. Amelia is not in the calm-alert state. She is underaroused and does not register or process most auditory and visual information. When engaged in activities that have meaning to her and increase her arousal levels, her affect brightens and her sensory registration increases.

TABLE 10.5   Intervention strategies to facilitate sensory registration and orientation

Assessing the sensory systems

What are the stronger sensory systems?

1. What does the child register (activities)?

2. What has meaning to the child?

3. When that type of sensory input is provided, how do the child's arousal level and processing change?

What are the weaker sensory systems?

1. What does the child register within the weaker system?

2. What has meaning to the child?

What do we need to do to move the child into the calm-alert state?

Treatment plan to increase sensory registration

The child needs to be moved into the calm-alert state.

The activity must register. We need to get into the child's registration.

The activity must have meaning to the child. The child must view it as being positive and enjoyable.

The child must actively interact or do something. This will enhance the development of neuronal models and memories.

Treatment strategies

Use a stronger sensory modality to move the child into the calm-alert state.

1. If underaroused: Use the stronger modalities to increase arousal.

   a. Use fast, regular, repetitive movements.

   b. Use linear vestibular and deep-touch, proprioceptive (if it is a stronger modality).

   c. Modify therapeutic environment and therapeutic use of self (voice inflections, high energy, enthusiasm, animation, and so on).

2. If overaroused: Use inhibition techniques.

   a. Lower anxiety. Use environmental and organizational modifications.

   b. Use slow, rhythmic, repetitive activities.

   c. If calming, use deep-touch and proprioceptive input.

   d. Modify therapeutic environment and therapeutic use of self (lower voice, slow and calm speech; avoid animation and exaggerated movements).

(continued)

TABLE 10.5 (continued)

Activities to facilitate sensory registration and orientation:

1. Couple a stronger sensory modality with the weaker modality to give the activity meaning and facilitate registration and orientation. The child must view the activity as being pleasurable.

2. Couple a pleasurable sensory experience with an undesirable task.

3. Use a preferred meaningful activity, if necessary, to couple with the weaker sensory modality or undesirable activity to get registration. Immediately make the intended activity meaningful to the child. At this point, the child must actively participate in order to produce a meaningful response.

4. Fade out or modify the child's preferred activity (especially if the child tends to overfocus on the activity), once the child appreciates the original activity (is able to register and orient to the activity). This will occur only when the original activity has meaning to the child.

5. Maintain sensory registration. A mismatch from the original stimulus must occur. Therefore, the input must systematically be changed in order to assure that the child continues registering and orienting to the session.

Develop neuronal models and memories; link the activity to a functional output. The child must link the activity with the idea. If necessary, complete the activity hand-over-hand to help the child receive the satisfaction from the output. The activity must have meaning to the child.

Intervention requires that we move the child into the calm-alert state. We must get the child to register information that is necessary for the development of functional skills. Once the child registers the information, he must actively interact or do something with the activity. This will enhance the development of neuronal models and memories and facilitate learning.

Sensory registration and orientation often can be accomplished by linking a stronger sensory modality with a weaker modality. However, when this is done, the activity must be one that the child views as being pleasurable. Amelia's weaker auditory skills can be linked with her stronger vestibular-proprioceptive skills to enhance auditory processing. For example, she loves to jump. The vestibular and deep proprioceptive input from jumping also increases her arousal to the calm-alert state. To increase her processing, we may link the *words*, "Amelia, let's jump" with the action *jump* to increase her sensory registration of auditory cues. She can link the positive experience of jumping with the words. Eventually we can increase the time between the auditory cues (the words) and the action, making Amelia process the auditory words before having the sensory experience of jumping.

There are many exciting ways to enhance sensory registration, orientation, and processing, once you know the child's stronger and weaker sensory systems and have identified what the child will respond to.

- When asking a child to look at a particular point, link auditory input with visual input by placing an object within the child's visual field, obtaining visual contact with the object, then moving the object to the place where you want the child to look. Reinforce the words (for example, "Look up") with the appropriate response.

- When asking the child to process words that require physical movement (for example, "Stand up"), link the word with the physical act and reward the child's good performance with vestibular-proprioceptive input. The added sensory input will further reinforce the word (auditory input) with the physical movement. For example, use a platform swing on a linear suspension. To reward the child for standing up, use up-and-down or bouncing or jumping movements on the swing.

- When asking the child to discriminate between words, such as ball and boat, use objects with strong tactile or olfactory components. Use balls that are scented or textured, or boats that have small moving parts. Link tactile or olfactory input with auditory input.

- When using a picture to reinforce a word, bring the picture toward your lips so the child will look at your face and the word formation. Link auditory with visual input.

When the child registers the sensory information and has developed neuronal models or memories for the activity, you may choose to fade out the other stronger sensory modality to see whether the child will register and process the weaker modality or the undesirable activity.

If Amelia were older, we might be interested in having her register and orient to a fine motor task of coloring or scribbling. Visual skills also are a very weak sensory modality for Amelia. We could use her stronger modality of deep-touch and proprioceptive input as a method of increasing her sensory registration as well as give sensory-based pleasure from a non-sensory activity such as coloring. We might position the activity on an incline surface with rough sandpaper placed behind the paper and select a picture of the character in her favorite videotape. We can use hand-over-hand assistance to provide deep proprioceptive input, or use heavy circular or linear strokes in a fast movement pattern to increase sensory registration. The activity then would link a pleasurable sensory experience with Amelia's weaker sensory modality (visual input).

Another effective technique involves coupling a preferred activity with a weaker sensory modality or an activity that has no meaning. Amelia's love for spinning tops, while a form of overregistration, can be used advantageously. Because Amelia will register this activity:

1. It can be used as a reward for registering a weaker modality or participating in a less desirable activity.

2. It can be linked to a weaker modality and used as a method of drawing the child in to an activity that has no meaning to him. Once engaged in the activity, if it is pleasurable, registration will occur.

Amelia could benefit from working on a platform swing that has been modified with vertical suspension to allow for up-and-down movement. However, Amelia is resistive to any change in activity and failed to actively attend to or register the swing. Attempts to place her in the swing were met with hysterical screaming. Her preferred toy, the spinning top, was strategically placed on the platform swing. Amelia struggled to play with it, and eventually she climbed onto the platform swing. She registered the swing, but did not orient to it; it had no meaning to her. Once she was on the swing, we provided the vestibular input she likes through the up-and-down movement. As Amelia connected the swing to the pleasurable sensory experience, the preferred activity—the top—could disappear. New activities could be introduced that can be linked to the swing. The next time Amelia came to the clinic, she registered and oriented to the platform swing as well as to the visual tasks she completed while on the swing.

Changing the original stimulus or providing a *mismatch* increases the sensory registration, orientation, or arousal response. This technique is effective within a session when the child was registering the information but has stopped. While change increases the orientation response, it also may increase the child's anxiety level. Make change in the original stimulus systematically and slowly, in small increments, until sensory registration occurs to the desired sensory activity. It becomes important not to be totally predictable so that the child will not habituate to you and your requests.

 hen a child is able to make the connection between the activity and its meaning, he will develop neuronal models and memories from which to build future experiences and learning. The child must be able to look at an activity, register the use and meaning for the activity, and have the appropriate level of arousal. To have this occur, we must be sure the activity has meaning to the child and that the child is able to derive the end results from the activity. This requires that the child must actively participate in the task, be motivated and enjoy it, and complete the task sufficiently to understand the end product. This process must be graded rapidly within treatment sessions.

Our goal is to have the child develop the neuronal models, or memories of the appropriate sensorimotor experience. If we can link the activity the child is registering to something the child views as meaningful, we may facilitate the development of those neuronal models or memories that may aid in the processing of more complex information.

Facilitate Normal Levels of Attention, Arousal, and Effort

Intervention strategies are effective when the child becomes comfortable functioning within the calm-alert state and when he is able to alter his arousal levels to promote optimal functioning in each activity. Children need to learn what it feels like to function in the calm-alert state. They need a norm from which they can judge future behaviors. If a child has never known normal levels of arousal, he will never have that norm from which to judge future behaviors. The goal is to have the child functioning in optimal arousal. This involves obtaining better modulation within the child's system, teaching the child to know what his body needs for optimal arousal levels, seeking out activities that meet his needs, and increasing his comfort and the amount of time spent within this state.

Strategies effective in altering arousal levels use several overlapping neurological principles. These include:

- Using cortical or cognitive intervention strategies. These strategies often teach the child to cognitively function and modify the environment. It has an impact on the nervous system from the cortex downward through the nervous system. They employ techniques such as:

  — Applying environmental modifications and controls: Altering and controlling the child's environment for optimal functioning

  — Teaching strategies for communication, social interactions, stress management, and behavioral control

  — Teaching self-regulation

- Altering emotions and arousal on a cellular and synaptic level (neurotransmitters) through specific sensory-based activities

- Altering sensory input and improving sensory integration and organization within the nervous system. These strategies work from the peripheral receptors through the brain stem and midbrain structures to higher centers, helping the child to integrate, process, and organize sensory information to improve performance. This technique employs:

  — Sensory integrative activities

  — Sensory diets

  — Self-regulatory activities

  — Oral motor activities

Coping Strategies

We must identify both the child's coping strategy and the intervention strategy that is effective in helping the child organize his nervous system. Most children will use coping strategies; some are effective, while others are ineffective. For example, a child who is overstimulated by the noise in a room may run out of the room or around it, screaming. His coping strategy is to flee and use auditory input (screaming) to block out the stimulation in the room. Some other children revert to various repetitive or obsessive behaviors in order to help them organize themselves and the environment. Self-stimulation patterns characterized by deep-touch and proprioceptive input are used by other children to calm and organize themselves. These behaviors include end-range fixing of joints, such as excessive wrist flexion or extension, hyperextension of the elbows, toe walking, hand fisting, or hand biting. To help the child develop effective coping strategies, we must understand the sensory base of stereotypic behaviors. See Table 10.6.

Children who have low arousal levels and secondary problems with attention may use self-stimulation patterns as an attempt to increase their arousal levels and attention.

> At school, Matthew, 5-years-old, works hard to stay focused. Although his teacher reported that he is somewhat disorganized, Matthew shows no self-stimulation behaviors. When he arrives

TABLE 10.6   Sensory input provided by stereotypic and disruptive behaviors

Initially, stereotypic, disruptive, and destructive behaviors may be provoked by a specific event or need. Then the behaviors are reinforced and maintained by:

The sensory stimulation the child receives
The success encountered within the child's environment:
- Effectiveness in meeting the child's needs (calming, arousal, organizing)
- The attention received (obtaining)
- Termination or acquisition of the activity or event (avoidance or obtaining)

Behavior	Sensory Input Provided
Rocking	Linear vestibular; rhythmic motion
Spinning self	Rotary vestibular; visual (if eyes are open)
Pacing	Linear vestibular; rhythmic motion; proprioceptive input
Running	Fast vestibular (linear, rotary, or angular depending on direction); proprioceptive
Jumping	Linear vestibular and deep proprioceptive
Throwing self to floor; crashing, playing too hard	Vestibular, deep-touch and proprioceptive
Lunging	Vestibular (angular), proprioceptive (especially when stopped by someone)
Head banging	Linear vestibular, vibration, proprioceptive, deep-touch, rhythmic motion
Masturbating	Deep-touch pressure, proprioceptive
Hanging upside down or lying with head inverted	Intense vestibular input
Shaking extremities or hands	Vibration, proprioceptive
Rubbing hands or fisting them together	Deep-touch, proprioceptive; visual (if in visual sight or near face)
End-range fixing or patterning (for example, bending wrist, fingers, or elbows into extreme flexion or extension; also seen as knee hyperextension and toe walking)	Proprioceptive and deep-touch input
Hitting self or others	Deep-touch and deep proprioceptive input
Scratching or rubbing	Deep-touch and proprioceptive input
Pinching, pushing, or attempting to be pulled	Deep-touch and proprioceptive input
Finger flicking	Visual; some proprioceptive input
End-range fixing or angling of eyes, crossing eyes, overconvergence of eyes	Proprioceptive from end-range fixing; visual
Spinning objects	Rotary vestibular and visual (visual-vestibular integration)
Mouthing clothing and objects	Proprioceptive and tactile; gustatory (if the objects have flavor)
Chewing on clothes or items	Deep proprioceptive and deep-touch input
Teeth grinding	Deep proprioceptive; vestibular from the vibration; auditory
Biting self or others	Deep proprioceptive, deep-touch input
Pressing hand to mouth or teeth firmly	Deep proprioceptive and deep-touch input
Ear flicking	Vestibular (vibration and sound); proprioceptive; tactile
Covering ears	Auditory
Humming, singing, self-talk and other quiet, steady vocalization	Rhythmic auditory and vibration; proprioceptive from generating the vocalizations
Screaming nonstop	Auditory and vestibular input
Smelling and sniffing objects and things	Olfactory and gustatory; strong systemic input

home, he is exhausted, but excited to be home with his five brothers and sisters. As soon as he walks through the door, he starts running around the house, flapping his hands and squawking uncontrollably for hours. His excitement continually mounts throughout the evening, and his ability to attend and focus deteriorates. He has used all of his energy to stay focused throughout the school day. At home, he attempts to arouse himself with vestibular input. His attempts at arousing himself work, but they are disorganizing, ineffective, and frustrating to his parents.

By analyzing the activities or self-stimulation patterns that a child chooses, we gain insight into the type of sensory input he needs to either increase or decrease his arousal. Then we can teach effective and appropriate sensory-based activities that can bring the child into the calm-alert state. Attention and processing are optimized when the child is operating within this window.

✦ Empowering the Child to Maintain the Calm-Alert State

Although we can modify the environment, the real solution occurs when the child learns to modulate his own nervous system, selecting sensory-based activities that will arouse him when he needs arousing and calm him when he needs to be quiet. As the child adopts socially acceptable activities to meet his sensory needs, he no longer needs the less desirable or challenging behaviors and they may be extinguished. This is a gradual, ongoing process in which control is handed back to the child.

Sensory Diets

The term *sensory diet* was coined by Wilbarger (1984, 1995) to describe the principles related to sensory processing theory. A nutritional diet was used as a metaphor to explain the key ideas about sensory diets. While daily nutritional diets involve three well-balanced meals and a snack, most people acknowledge that the study of nutritional diet planning involves special knowledge about many complex factors. Sensory diet needs are similar to nutritional needs, requiring the right combinations of sensory input to keep an optimal level of arousal.

Similar to snacks, some sensory-based activities might change our mood or state of alertness for short periods of time. Others, similar to nutritious meals, have longer-lasting effects on behavior and performance. We can achieve and maintain optimal levels of arousal for performance by timing and carefully selecting our sensory-based activities. This is important for any person, but it is especially important for those with a disruption in sensory experiences or a decreased ability to engage in activities (Wilbarger 1995).

Some activities, like nutritious meals, have a modulating effect on the nervous system. Activities that include deep pressure, tactile, vestibular, or proprioceptive input are believed to have the most pervasive effect on behavior. Examples include aerobics, weight lifting, jumping on a trampoline, play wrestling, and playing hard on playground equipment. Some of the most important changes in the nervous system come from knowing how to choose activities for long-lasting effects. The effects of specific vestibular activities or movements can last four to eight hours or longer. The effects of proprioceptive activities that involve the whole body, joint traction, co-contraction, or heavy muscle action generally have a two-hour duration. The Wilbarger protocol for summated deep-touch pressure and proprioceptive technique (DPPT) is effective for one to two hours (Wilbarger 1995).

Other activities, like snacks, are mood changers. Their transient effect can elicit emotional responses, meet changing needs, and help the child let off steam or deal with everyday situations. These activities include tactile, visual, auditory, olfactory, oral, and respiratory input (Oetter et al. 1995), and include (among others) sucking on candies, chewing gum, fidgeting with toys, and listening to music.

To develop an individualized sensory diet, carefully analyze the child's sensory needs, daily routines, and arousal states throughout the day. Then implement an individualized sensory diet into the child's schedule to help him maintain an appropriate amount of arousal for performing functional tasks throughout the day.

Teach Self-Regulation

Teaching self-regulation and coping strategies to a child requires a thorough understanding of the child's sensory needs. Through history forms or interviews with parents and teachers, and through direct observation of the child, determine:

1. The child's responses to experiences involving touch, tactile or food choices, and vestibular, proprioceptive, vision, auditory, olfactory, and gustatory input.

2. Activities that the child uses that are effective in calming, arousing, or organizing himself. It may be helpful to look at what sensory-based activities the child seeks or avoids, as well as the sensory components of any challenging or unusual behaviors displayed. Challenging behaviors develop initially to meet a sensory need, and then are maintained by the sensation they provide and the responses they receive in the environment. (See Table 10.6.)

The next step is to analyze the child's arousal and activity levels throughout the day. Wilbarger (1995) recommends analyzing the sensory qualities encountered in two typical days: a structured school or work day, and an unstructured day during the weekend. Record where the child sleeps, the textures he prefers in sheets and pajamas, his state when he gets up in the morning, and so on. Address general questions, for example, during what part of the day is the child the most organized? During which part of the day is the child disorganized or his behavior or performance diminished? Under what conditions does the child display low arousal levels versus high arousal levels? Are these predictable cycles?

Develop an Action Plan

Develop an action plan based on careful analysis of the child's likes, dislikes, and needs.

1. Identify the child's likes and needs, factors that contribute to the child's ability to function. This includes:

   — Activities or sensory-based activities that are calming, pleasurable, and organizing for the child. Identify the activity, if it is socially acceptable. For activities that are not acceptable or desirable, identify the sensory component.

   — Time and situations in which the child functions optimally and operates in the calm-alert state. Define specific factors that appear to contribute to this.

2. Identify negative factors, activities disliked or avoided, and activities that contribute to sensory overload or shutdown:

   — Times and situations throughout the day in which the child does not function optimally. Define specific factors that contribute to this.

   — Environmental factors that have an adverse impact on the child's functional performance and contribute to sensory overload. Consider organizational aspects, sensory components, arousal levels, activity demands, frustration levels created by the activity, and so on.

   — Coping strategies that are either not effective or are not socially acceptable for the environment.

3. Establish an action plan.

   — Identify several powerful sensory-based activities that are socially acceptable and effective in either raising or lowering this child's level of arousal into the calm-alert state. Determine the length of effectiveness of each activity.

   — Establish therapeutic routines to increase the child's attention, organization, and arousal levels to optimize performance. Develop routines that incorporate sensory-based activities that meet the child's arousal and organizational needs into all daily activities: waking up, dressing, throughout school hours, during transitions, meal times, leisure activities, bathing, bedtime, and so on.

   — Modify the child's environment for optimal states of arousal and, therefore, function.

   — If necessary, teach the child how to perform and use the sensory-based activity in order to derive the sensory experience.

   — Teach the child self-regulation. Teach him to identify signs of escalating behaviors or low arousal levels, and to seek out appropriate sensory-based activities to obtain the arousal level appropriate for the activity.

The majority of children we treat react in similar ways throughout the day. They have stable and predictable sensory registration, orientation, arousal, or attentional problems that are characterized by either under- or overarousal to sensory information. Select and use activities that address the individual child's arousal needs.

Activities geared at increasing the child's arousal level must be used cautiously for a child with a fluctuating or defensive disorder, which results from an unstable and volatile nervous system. Activities that increase the child's arousal level may contribute to the instability of the child's condition. Use activities that incorporate deep-touch and deep proprioceptive input, and therefore have an impact on the limbic system and reticular formation of the brain.

Initially, the child cannot independently and easily perform therapeutically based sensory activities. The child may need to be taught activities such as bike riding or the use of sensory boxes or hideouts. Teach him how to physically complete the activity as well as to learn the organizing effects provided by the activity. Help the child's family or teachers to gradually and strategically integrate the activities into the child's routine. Emphasize that sensory-based activities must never be used as a punishment, but only as a pleasant organizing experience.

Children often are unable to objectify or perceive their own behaviors, responses, or needs without assistance and guidance from an adult. We must help them understand and objectify what they are feeling or want. Once the child can identify the need, he can be directed toward the activities that will meet the need. Eventually the child will be able to identify his own warning signs of escalating behaviors or sensory needs and will independently choose activities that help him maintain the calm-alert state at home, school, during play, and eventually during work.

Erin is a 3-year-old with a sensory modulation disorder characterized by fluctuating levels of arousal. In most environments, she quickly becomes overstimulated, running frantically in circles, screeching at the top of her lungs, and flapping her hands. Her attempts to organize herself are nonproductive and serve only to further increase her arousal level. The only way she can effectively calm herself even slightly is through biting on anything or anyone.

Erin needs deep-touch and deep proprioceptive input. She loves to sit on a platform swing with a tire on it. We pack the tire with soft Gertie—balls or beanbags. The tighter we pack her, the happier she is. She is able to attend well after receiving the deep input. Erin has learned to tell us when she has had enough and is ready to face the world.

At home, Erin receives 20 hours per week of one-on-one discrete trials. When she becomes frustrated, she quickly escalates out of control. When she is out of control, she is not able to register or process sensory information. Behavioral techniques are ineffective because her nervous system is not allowing her to respond rationally. She is in a hyperaroused state and cannot process until she gets back into the calm-alert state. Erin cannot self-regulate her behavior and arousal levels. The only thing that works is deep-touch and deep proprioceptive input combined with calming techniques.

Our goal was to integrate activities into the home that were organizing and that could be used before Erin became out of control. That way we could teach Erin to self-regulate her behaviors within her home environment. Eventually, as she gains the motor control she needs, we would like to have her learn various sports and extracurricular activities that have the same organizing effect.

To begin our efforts to teach self-regulation, her mother created a hideout for Erin—a large cardboard box filled with her favorite soft pillows and stuffed animals. The top was left on, but flipped back so it was out of the way. Erin enjoyed sitting in the box, and on several occasions she was allowed to sit inside it while she watched her favorite videotape. This helped Erin view the box as a reward rather than a punishment. The box was kept in the room where she performed her discrete trials. Initially, Erin was guided to the box as a form of positive reinforcement after successfully completing several sessions. In the box, she was encouraged to sing her favorite songs, which helped her relax. It became critical to use the box before Erin became frustrated and lost control, so that the box was never used as an escape or reward for a tantrum or losing control. Gradually, Erin learned that sitting in the box was a way to become relaxed and calm, and she began to request the box as her reward for difficult discrete-trial sessions. Eventually, she was able to tolerate higher and higher stress levels and could effectively use the box to reorganize herself before she lost control.

Zachary, 8-years-old, is in a varying exceptionality class. He is mainstreamed for math and art and shows advanced skills in these areas. While the majority of the time he is able to stay organized and focused, there are times throughout the day that are difficult for him and his teacher. When Zach arrives at school, he is anxious and disorganized and proceeds to run around the classroom screeching. Once he is able to settle into his classwork, he calms down. He also has a difficult time transitioning to reading. During this time, the children in the class move from their desks into an unstructured area of the room. Again, Zach runs around the room, pulling items off the shelves and distracting others in the room. His teacher is unable to calm him down sufficiently to participate in the class activity. Once they move back to their desks, Zach will calm down after 20 minutes or so.

During therapy sessions, Zach calms and organizes himself with deep proprioceptive and resistive activities. Therapy sessions are always begun with Zach performing weight-bearing activities on his arms while working on resistive hand tasks. As he works, the therapist discusses and negotiates the sequence of activities for the therapy session. After this initial activity, Zach seldom has problems with organization, attention, or arousal.

To help Zach maintain organization, attention, and arousal at school, his schedule was modified to meet his sensorimotor needs. Two major problem areas were addressed: the beginning of the school day, and transitions to, and participation in the less-structured activity of reading. To start the day, Zach needed deep proprioceptive and resistive activities. His father, who normally goes out jogging every morning before work, decided to see whether Zach could ride his bicycle next to him while he jogged. Bike riding is an excellent form of linear vestibular and resistive proprioceptive input. Zach worked easily into the routine. He looked forward to getting up in the morning, riding the bike with his father, then getting ready for school. His behavior showed dramatic changes and he was able to start the school day in a calm and organized state.

On days when weather conditions kept him from riding his bike, a routine was established in which he would arrive 15 minutes early for class. He and another child played board games while weight-bearing on their arms. Zach knew that his days would start with resistive activities and in a predictable fashion. He could get up in the morning, check the weather, and know whether he would ride his bike or go to school early to start with weight bearing.

Transitions to reading occurred midday and required a different approach. The reading session lasted for 20 minutes. Zach was given a five-minute warning before the session. During that time, he reviewed what he needed to do. (Initially, he was prompted through the review.) Then, two minutes before the class transitioned, Zach was released from his seat so he could put on his weighted vest and proceed to the reading area. Once there, he stood between two desks and did 20 arm push-ups, then sat in his seat. By the time his classmates arrived, Zach was organized. The resistive arm exercises and the deep proprioceptive input helped him maintain his organization throughout the reading session.

Oral Motor Programs

Many children display oral motor and feeding difficulties. The causes may stem from a wide variety of sensory-based and behavioral issues. Children with defensive modulation disorders and overarousal can respond to food or oral motor activities with limbic system reactions of fear and hysteria. Children with underarousal, low muscle tone, and decreased active muscle control within the mouth may have similar hysterical responses when food is introduced. The response may be rooted in a basic survival response, fear of aspiration due to decreased sensory awareness, motor control, and poor suck-swallow coordination. While oral motor programs are needed for both groups, the child with overarousal and modulation difficulties will need a program focused specifically around providing deep-touch and proprioceptive input into the oral areas. The child who is underaroused, has a tactile discrimination disorder, or has poor oral motor or respiratory control may need a more comprehensive program that is discussed in Chapter 12.

Oral motor programs that encompass deep-touch and proprioceptive input may be necessary for both groups. The mouth has extensive sensory nerve endings and is one of the primary areas for tactile discrimination. It is often the first place to start therapy intervention. This can have an organizing effect on the child's entire behavior. Children often mouth objects or bite on towels, shirts, and other objects to help them organize and calm themselves. Heavy pressure both outside and inside the mouth is an effective treatment strategy.

Minimize Anxiety

Take care to minimize anxiety. Oral motor and feeding programs are stressful for children who avoid new foods and textures. Gradually desensitize the child by addressing the sensory, motor control, and behavioral issues simultaneously.

- The child will feel less threatened when his active participation is encouraged and sensory input is not imposed upon him.

- When anxiety starts to mount, it is often helpful to provide deep proprioceptive input while counting to 10 with the child.
  - Provide gentle, steady, deep proprioceptive input downward through the shoulders or head. When using joint compression, take care to assure biomechanical alignment of the head with the spine. Deep compressions also may be provided by gently but firmly squeezing the child at the hips or shoulders.
  - Deep proprioceptive input will assist in calming and organizing the child.
  - Counting to 10 serves many purposes:
    - It take the child's mind off the task at hand, engages the child cognitively, and helps the child relax.
    - It is a familiar structured task. Children often relax to tasks they are familiar with.
    - Counting to 10 is not threatening, and provides an end to the task.

You may choose to use the strategy of counting to 10 when introducing a new item or technique. Tell the child that when you finish counting to 10, the technique will be stopped and the child may relax. Children often are able to tolerate the technique for ten seconds without undue anxiety. Although the child may not like the technique, he will realize it is not as bad as he originally thought and will allow you to repeat it for another ten seconds or longer.

Deep-Touch Pressure

Face

Many children crave deep-touch input to the outside of the mouth and face, such as firm pressure massages. Lotion may be used if the child is not defensive. Children who lack facial expression or who have low facial tone, weak or garbled speech, or decreased movement of the tongue or oral musculature may be appropriate candidates. Apply a small amount of lotion to your hands to help them glide smoothly across the child's skin. With the child sitting on your lap facing away from you, firmly stroke the child's face. Whenever possible, direct the firm pressure in the direction of hair growth. Start at the child's midline and work out to the sides. Firmly and consistently move your hands across the bridge of the nose; then under the nose, moving down and out across the face; and under the chin; and then from the forehead out to the sides. While the child is in this position, you can easily provide gentle but firm, steady compressions through the child's shoulders, head, or trunk.

Some children may be more sensitive outside of their mouth than inside. If the child will not tolerate sensory input to the outside of the face, progress into the mouth.

Mouth

Heavy pressure across the roof of the mouth usually is calming. Often, the easiest way into a child's mouth is through a preferred food or dessert. If the child does not bite, an Infa-Dent® placed on your finger (over a glove) is a nice texture to begin with. The short bristles provide a comfortable deep-touch input. Dip the Infa-Dent into the child's preferred food and provide deep-touch pressure into the roof of the child's mouth, downward into the center of the tongue, and, eventually, into the gums, using a back-and-forth movement. You may perform the same activities using a toothbrush with soft bristles, a Nuk® brush, or a washcloth.

Jaw and Teeth

Deep pressure down into the jaw also is recommended to facilitate biting and jaw action. Biting, using the back molars, can provide resistance and deep proprioceptive input needed to decrease oral defensiveness, promote stability of the jaw and base of the tongue, and decrease teeth grinding. A child may be encouraged to play bite and tug with tubing, a washcloth, pieces of licorice, or beef jerky. Food textures that encourage biting and crunching also are effective (Oetter et al. 1995).

Some children work well with chewy necklaces. Make a chewy necklace using a round, flexible, stretchy string and a piece of thick, round, hollow rubber tubing. Cut off a necklace-length of rubber tubing, and place a pencil grip over the tubing. Cut a slightly longer length of stretchy string, thread it through the tubing, and tie a firm knot. The child now has a stretchy necklace that can be pulled, or the child can chew the tubing or pencil grip when deep proprioceptive input is needed. To assure safety, monitor closely when the child is using the necklace. Precautions are listed on page 228, Chapter 12.

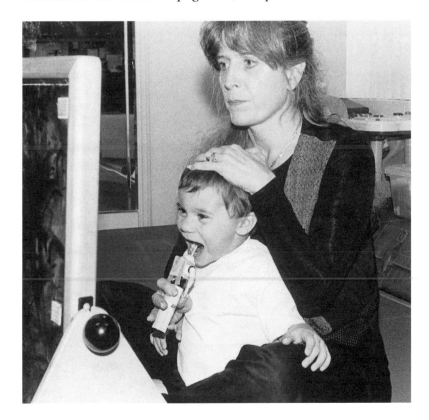

ILLUSTRATION 10.1
Gentle head and neck compression offers the proprioceptive input required for calming while the child uses a battery-operated lollipop to provide deep-touch input to the tongue and roof of the mouth.

Cheeks and Lips

Some children with low tone and lack of active facial expression or muscle activation need facilitation to the muscles of the cheeks. They may tolerate deep-touch input into the cheeks. Gently place your index finger into the child's mouth (over a glove or with an Infa-Dent). Firmly grasp the cheek between your thumb and index finger. Apply gentle, even pressure and gently oscillate as you move your finger out of the child's mouth. Then have the child actively use the muscles for activities such as blow toys.

When a good seal is obtained, blowing provides both deep-touch and proprioceptive input to the lips, cheeks, and lungs. Use whistles, balloons with whistle stems, and other blow toys to increase lip closure, forced exhalation, and breath control while providing good sensory input into the oral mechanisms. Try out the toys yourself, and look for ways to increase the natural resistance.

Respiratory Control

Respiratory control is vital for sensory modulation, self-centering, speech and language, and oral motor control. It involves inhalation, exhalation, strength, duration, timing, and coordination of these, and coordination of breathing with sucking, swallowing, eating, and speech.

Resistive activities that focus around sucking air in or blowing air out, as well as increasing the coordination, timing, duration, and strength of these will improve respiratory control. Examples include drinking-straw games in which the child uses a straw to blow cotton balls in a race or to make bubbles from a soap solution. Other activities that work on resistive inhalation include drinking thick liquids through a straw or picking up checkers and placing them in a cup by creating a suction with a straw.

ILLUSTRATION 10.2
The child works to coordinate lip closure with breath control to keep the ball afloat.

To increase strength and duration, use a longer straw or tubing, or use a medium that provides greater resistance.

Emphasize timing, coordination, and sequencing by increasing the amount of precision, stops and starts, or sequences required when humming, vocalizing sounds and patterns, whistling, and blowing musical instruments such as kazoos, harmonicas, or whistles.

Food as a Tactile and Sensory Experience

Tactile experiences with food in the mouth are the easiest, most natural ways to give tactile stimulation and deep-touch input into the mouth and jaw. Look for snacks and foods that offer resistance and require the jaw and tongue to work hard. Teething biscuits are an excellent medium for young children to obtain both deep-touch and deep proprioceptive input through biting. Chewy and crunchy foods have a different impact on the sensory system. Chewing is resistive and organizing, while crunchy foods are alerting. Chewy foods include bagels, gummy candies, cheese, gum, and granola bars. Crunchy foods that are alerting include popcorn, pretzels, bread sticks, crackers, fruit, nuts, and raw vegetables such as carrot or celery sticks.

Wrap gauze around strong-flavored candies so you can control the placement of the candy from outside the child's mouth. Move the candy around the child's teeth or molars to distribute the deep input, promote the tongue to work in different ranges, and teach the child to chew things rather than swallow them.

TABLE 10.7   Sensory characteristics of foods and snacks

Chewing is resistive and organizing. Chewy foods include:
- Bagels
- Gummy candies
- Cheese
- Gum
- Granola bars

Crunching is alerting. Crunchy foods include:
- Popcorn
- Pretzels
- Bread sticks
- Crackers
- Dry cereal
- Fruit
- Nuts
- Raw vegetables such as carrot or celery sticks

Sour foods are alerting, arousing, and organizing. These include:
- Lemon balls
- Sour balls
- Mega WARHEADS®

Hot, spicy, or bitter flavors are more alerting. These include:
- Cinnamon candies (for example, Ferrara Pan® Red Hots)
- Atomic FireBall® candies

Cold food temperatures can be used to:
- Decrease sensitivity
- Increase low tone and arousal

Flavors and temperatures of candies and foods can be used to your advantage. Sour foods, such as lemon sour balls, are alerting, arousing, and organizing. Hot, spicy, or cinnamon candies and bitter flavors are even more alerting. A sour candy or a tablespoon of frozen lemon concentrate may help a child who is having difficulty attending or waking up. A child who is oversensitive in the mouth may react better after using ice pops, ice cubes, or frozen juice cubes. Cold food temperatures are useful to decrease hypersensitivity and to increase sensitivity in most cases of low tone and underarousal. When using ice to increase oral tone and oral movements, do not let the child suck the ice for more than one minute at a time. Take a short break (one minute), and then let the child resume sucking.

Oral Motor Program Schedules

Oral motor programs must never be done haphazardly. Schedule oral motor programs for specified times throughout the day. The best time to do a program is just before the child needs oral motor control. The oral motor program will enhance the child's sensorimotor awareness and motor control for the functional task. Schedule the exercises for five to ten minutes before meals, as well as before or at the beginning of a speech therapy session.

Give sensory-based snacks throughout the day. Although the arousal and integrating effects of candies and snacks are short-lived, they can give the child the start he needs to stay on task or attend to difficult lessons. Oral motor activities, characterized by deep proprioceptive input, will help the child stay calm and organized for longer periods of time.

Biting is often an indication of a sensorimotor need. Discourage children from biting themselves or others to organize and calm themselves. In these cases, an oral motor program characterized by deep proprioceptive input may need to be implemented more frequently, along with total-body deep-touch activities that have a longer period of effectiveness. Intersperse these activities frequently throughout the child's day in order to meet the child's needs. Use behavioral intervention techniques to extinguish the biting while assuring that the sensory need is met. Having specific times for oral motor intervention that incorporates deep-touch input, and offering approved chewy substances that the child is allowed to bite, will help decrease the need for biting. Consistency in enforcing the schedule and providing approved biting chewy substances is critical in extinguishing the biting. Inconsistencies will only confuse the child and reinforce the biting behaviors.

 ## Facilitate Sensory Integration

Signs of improved sensory integration for a child with registration orientation, arousal, or modulation difficulties often include many of the following:

- Improved organization of behaviors

- Better arousal states

- Increased vocalizations and language

- Improved coping strategies with less frustration

- Greater flexibility and ability to tolerate changes

- Improved functional behaviors and physical performance

- Better sensory modulation with less overarousal or defensiveness

- Decrease in stereotypic behaviors

- Improved registration and orientation of sensory information with better ideational skills

- Better processing of information from multiple sensory systems

- Improved learning

Enhanced Sensory Activities

Sensory integrative techniques assist in changing the resting state of the nervous system, and work to alter arousal levels and improve processing primarily through the limbic system and reticular formation. These techniques encompass activities that create enhanced opportunities for deep-touch pressure, linear vestibular, and proprioceptive input.

Deep-touch pressure comes from deep-touch input to the skin, while proprioceptive input comes from heavy muscle work, compression to the joints, or traction to the joints or extremities.

Linear vestibular input is elicited from horizontal or vertical movements of the head or body, usually from moving up and down or forward and backward. These sensory-based activities work to calm and organize the nervous system.

Enhanced sensory activities are not inherently integrating, but serve as a vital component to treatment.

Trampoline Activities

Trampoline activities provide excellent opportunities for both deep proprioceptive and linear vestibular input, but must be closely supervised because they may be dangerous. Use small trampolines, three feet wide, for structured activities such as jumping up and down. The more direct the sensory input, the more organizing the effect.

Children may not know how to obtain direct input through their extremities or trunk, but will jump in a disorganized, haphazard fashion. Integrating neurodevelopmental handling techniques into the activity for a few minutes can enhance the sensory input. The key point of control may be the child's hips. Firmly plant your hands on the child's hips. As the child jumps, be careful not to move your hands from their original location. Moving the hands or putting them on and off will increase the child's discomfort and may trigger a defensive response. Guide the child firmly down into the trampoline while giving joint approximation through the hips. As the child propels upward, release the pressure without moving your hands. Provide approximation and compression as the child jumps down. Progress from consistent joint compression, to intermittent compression, to hands off. To increase the difficulty, chalk a circle in the center of the trampoline. Have the child jump with feet together into the

ILLUSTRATION 10.3
Joint approximation, provided downward through the pelvis as the child lands, provides proprioceptive input and reinforces correct alignment, coordination, and body scheme.

center of the circle, and then with feet apart outside the circle. Let the child choose a sequence or pattern to jump (for example, two jumps in the center and two out).

- Large trampolines are effective for games and similar activities.

- Play games that reinforce social songs, such as having two or more children playing "Ring around the Rosey" or "Duck, Duck, Goose."

- Play games that reinforce body parts or create general body awareness.

- Have a child jump up, drop onto his knees, then get back on his feet.

- Following directions can add a level of difficulty. Either give directions, or let one child give commands while another child follows them.

Net Hammock Swing

Prone activities in a suspended net are excellent. A child who is working at the end ranges of extension and supporting body weight against gravity is receiving deep proprioceptive input. This may be enhanced by having the child actively propel himself in the net or reach interactively for resistive activities. Deep-touch input is provided by the net itself when the child's trunk is swaddled by the net. Linear vestibular input is provided depending on the activity selected. Take care to encourage linear vestibular input rather than rotary or erratic movements that can have a disorganizing effect. Linear vestibular input will facilitate prone extension, which in turn will provide greater proprioceptive input. When in the net, the child is physically contained and provided with natural boundaries. Choose this activity when a child needs boundaries, deep-touch input, a restricted environment, and linear vestibular input.

- Have the child lie prone in the net and use his arms to climb up a rope or ladder to reach an object.

- Encourage the child to climb or swing to reach rings, slap bracelets, or Mardi Gras beads and then put them in a designated place.

- Have the child play basketball games while lying prone in the net. This will facilitate end-range prone extension with full spinal arching and arms forward. Place the target forward and high so that the child will fully extend and arch. Monitor for smooth spinal extension with no cervical hyperextension. Have the child propel himself using a Bungee cord that is attached below and perpendicular to the net; or propel the child while he focuses on the activity.

Total-Body Activities

Adapt total-body activities for deep-touch and proprioceptive input. Use various environments to create a playful yet enriched sensory environment.

- Have the child climb and crawl over and under pillows or mats, climb on play structures, hang from play structures or trapeze bars, and climb over or through difficult obstacle courses that require physical exertion.

- Jumping and crashing activities provide deep-touch input into the skin and offer proprioceptive input into the joints. Let the child jump and crash from various height surfaces, such as from a bed or couch, onto cushions or pillows on the floor and into bean bag chairs. Wrestling activities also may be beneficial.

- Linear vestibular and proprioceptive input are obtained from jumping on the trampoline, bouncing on therapy balls, or performing activities while suspended in a net or hammock.

Weight-Bearing and Resistive Upper-Extremity Activities

These activities have an organizing effect and can be integrated throughout the day as forms of deep proprioceptive input. Examples of isometric exercises or pushups include:

- Hand clasps. The child clasps his hands together in front of his chest and pushes the hands together to a count of 5 or 10.

- Wall push-ups. The child stands two to three feet from a wall, places his hands on the wall, and slowly lowers his body to the wall, then back.

- Floor push-ups. The child is positioned with his hands on the floor, hips and feet on a chair, so that he is facing the floor and his body is parallel to the floor. He gradually lowers his head to the floor, then returns to the original position.

- Table arm push-ups. The child stands between two tables with hands firmly placed on each table. He lifts his legs and full body weight to a count of 5 or 10.

- Chair push-ups. The child sits in a chair with or without armrests. Placing his hands on either the seat of the chair or the armrests, he lifts his feet and body out of the chair for a count of 5 or 10. To increase the level of difficulty, have the child gradually raise or lower his body.

Weight bearing onto the arms can be an effective method of deep proprioceptive input, and has the secondary benefit of strengthening the arms, elbows, and hands. The child lies prone with legs supported on a chair or peanut ball, hands on the floor, bearing weight on his arms. Carefully select the height of the chair, starting with a low chair in which the body is parallel to the floor. Gradually increase the height as the child becomes stronger. The higher the chair, the greater the degree of inversion (vestibular input) and the greater the strain on the arms. In this position, the child (or several children positioned the same way) can play board games and other interactive, turn-taking games.

Neuro-developmental principles need to be kept in mind when monitoring children in this weight-bearing position. Watch for hyperextension of the elbows; turning in or out of the hands causing shoulder internal or external rotation; hands flipping up into the tripod position or metacarpal-phalangeal (MP) hyperextension, thereby overstretching the ligaments of the fingers; sagging trunk; hyperextension of the cervical spine or lumbar spine; or difficulty shifting weight over the shoulder due to instability or weakness. When these factors are observed, modify the activity to enhance its therapeutic value. (Principles of motor control are discussed in detail in Chapter 14.)

ILLUSTRATION 10.4
Weight-bearing and resistive upper-extremity activities provide proprioceptive input and can have a calming, organizing effect.

Push-Pull Games

Modify these games and activities for enhanced vestibular and deep-touch and proprioceptive input. Develop push-pull games in which the children push heavy equipment or balls from one place to another, or develop games that incorporate these components while fostering social interaction.

- Body pulls. Play relay games in which the children pull their bodies across the floor using only their arms.

- Scooterboard activities. Sit on the scooterboard and have the child lie prone on your lap. Then have the child place his hands on the floor and propel the scooterboard. For a variation, have another child and adult play this activity as a relay race.

- Therapeutic wrestling. Resist and guide the child's movements under the guise of playful wrestling.

Resistive Equipment

Use weighted equipment to enhance deep proprioceptive input.

- Have several children stand in a line. Give the first child a large, heavy ball, and have him pass it to the next child in line, and so on. For variation, have the children pass the ball overhead, making sure that each child stays in alignment. This exercise provides deep-touch input through the arms, trunk, and legs.

- Use Thera-Band® activities to build in resistive work to moveable equipment such as scooterboards, tire swings, and net swings.

- Strap Thera-Band to the legs of the desk while the child sits there. Encourage the child to resist the Thera-Band while he is sitting at the desk, thus obtaining proprioceptive input.

- Have the child wear a weighted vest during total-body activities to increase the sensory feedback into the extremities and provide deep touch into the trunk.

Neoprene and Weighted Vests

Use neoprene vests, weighted vests, weighted blankets, weights, and other forms of consistent resistive or deep-touch input throughout the day to help the child stay organized and focused. These forms of deep-touch input have an immediate calming effect on a child with stable, predictable arousal difficulties. The effectiveness lasts for approximately 20 minutes, when the child acclimates to the touch or resistance and the therapeutic value is lost.

Children with fluctuating or defensive modulation disorders often respond to the deep-touch input with increased arousal and hyperactivity. The calming effect is often noticed after approximately 10 minutes.

Neoprene vests, which provide a snug wrap to the trunk, have been worn successfully for longer than 20 minutes. The conformability and constant touch pressure to the trunk provides stability to the trunk, shoulder girdle, and pelvis, and provides the child a sense of midline. This centering point provides internal stability and organization to the body.

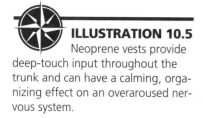

Carefully monitor the effectiveness of the equipment. Use weighted or neoprene vests at intervals when the child needs help staying focused. These include open-field situations such as circle time, gym class, library time, and other less structured or transition times.

Deep Pressure and Proprioceptive Technique (DPPT)

Wilbarger and Wilbarger (1991) described an intensive, systematic technique for providing deep-touch pressure to clients ages 2- to 12-years of age with varying degrees of sensory defensiveness. They recommended using a nonscratching surgical scrub brush to apply firm and rapid touch pressure to the client's arms, hands, back, legs, and feet. This is followed by gentle joint compression to all major joints. The deep-touch pressure, compression or traction to the joints, and heavy muscle action together acts as a special combination to reduce or eliminate sensory defensiveness. This procedure is effective in decreasing or eliminating sensory defensiveness when it is used every 90 minutes to two hours, during the day, for a period of approximately two weeks.

The Wilbarger protocol includes:

- Making a list of defensive characteristics

- Establishing scheduled routines that include:

  — Sensory diets of powerful sensory-based activities

  — Implementation of the DPPT

  — Environmental modifications

- Therapeutic intervention

A word of caution: This aggressive intervention strategy should be implemented and monitored by a therapist who is knowledgeable in the technique. It can be very effective when used on the right child and implemented in the correct format. Carefully select the child and the appropriate environment. While taking only two or three minutes to complete, the technique requires in-depth knowledge, dedication, and commitment. Certain environments are more effective than others. The individuals who will be implementing the program must be educated thoroughly in this hands-on technique. This includes viewing educational videotapes and observing the technique, as well as demonstration and counter-demonstration on an adult before implementing it on the child. The activities and time schedule must be clearly established in advance.

Sports and Extracurricular Activities

One of the long-term goals of sensory integrative activities is eventually to get the child actively involved in sports and extracurricular activities that help him modulate his own nervous system. Often this is a very gradual process in which we constantly work toward increasing the child's skills and functional abilities. In addition to direct intervention, we must move the child toward increased independence in activities that provide linear vestibular and deep-touch or proprioceptive input.

Sports and extracurricular activities must be carefully selected for each child, based on the child's interests, physical abilities, and individual sensory needs. It may be best to increase a child's independence in the specific activity (for example, skating) before enrolling the child in a class. Classes need to be monitored closely because they can have a disorganizing and overwhelming effect on the child.

Activities that a child might complete independently and that provide the needed sensory input include swimming on top of the water or with a kickboard, bicycle riding, jumping games on a trampoline, roller-skating or roller-blading, jumping rope, and jogging. Extracurricular activities that often provide the desired sensory input include gymnastics classes, horseback riding, swimming lessons, and karate.

Principles of Sensory Integrative Treatment Sessions

The basic premise of sensory integration prohibits a cookbook approach. While activities can be described that provide enhanced deep-touch proprioceptive or linear vestibular input, it is not the activity that creates the integration. It is the motivation of the child, the grading of the activity to the child's functional level or just beyond, and the facilitation of the adaptive response from the child. SI also requires that as the child masters an activity on one level, it must be modified for increased challenges at other levels. The process of grading activities for increased levels of difficulty must be an ongoing process that the therapist facilitates throughout the session.

Structuring the therapeutic environment demands considerable professional skill. Planning and executing movements provide the major means through which the brain organizes stimuli (Ayres 1973).

The child's internal drive and urge toward sensorimotor development and expression appear to be directly related with the integrative process. Designing the therapeutic environment to foster the child's internal motivation and move him toward self-actualization—the state in which the child is experiencing a fulfilling, organizing, and integrating experience—requires professional skill and sensitivity.

All children possess the capability to be motivated and driven toward sensorimotor development and self-actualization experiences. Most children experience this drive intensely throughout their first years of life. Their inner urge for action and growth drives them to experience more. Their behaviors are emotionally charged with enthusiasm and a zest for the experience. While this inner drive exists in children with autism, often it is buried deep beneath fears, rituals, and behaviors.

Unlocking the child's inner potential and drive requires skillful manipulation. We must bring out in the child what the child cannot bring out in himself. Sensitivity, skill, and creativity contribute to activating the child's inner drive. We must enable the child to gain contact with that drive in order to maximize the response to treatment. We must watch carefully as the child performs, monitor his moods, emotions, and motor movements, and gradually move him into greater involvement in the task. As the child gains pleasure from the task, we must analyze the component that gives the child pleasure and gradually coax the child further.

We must make critical choices between establishing structure and enabling freedom. Free play does not inevitably, and in itself, further sensory integration. Structure may be needed to push the child forward and help him work through the fears that block his potential. Structured permissiveness creates an atmosphere of exploration while providing intervention to help the child control his behavior. Once the child starts to respond, having a controlling structure may defeat the purpose of nurturing his potential and ability to self-direct his interactions with the environment. We need to help create the environment in which the child is driven to excel and create the situations necessary for the child to respond in a manner that will foster maturation of his nervous system.

When the child's internal drive is activated, it will be obvious by his response. He will clearly indicate that at some level of consciousness, he recognizes the significance of the event. Often the child will take over the direction of the treatment in a generally constructive way. His response will be characterized by intense emotional involvement and excitement. He will persevere with the task, refuse to try anything else, and resist the need to terminate the session. The extent to which a child's potential is realized through his sensory experience is usually reflected by his enthusiasm for treatment (Ayres 1973). He will engage in the therapy session merely for the feeling of success and power derived from his accomplishments. While external rewards may be needed initially to motivate a child, when you have activated his internal drive, motivation, and desire and ability for self-actualization, the reward is in the child's success. There is no reward more powerful.

Negative responses are a warning to stop and analyze what is happening. As a rule of thumb, do not to force a child into an activity that he doesn't want to do. Forcing the child may increase his anxiety, adversely affect the therapist-child relationship, and have an adverse impact on the therapy session. Carefully analyze what component of the activity the child is reacting too. There may be another way to approach the problem. If the child fears a new activity, move back to a familiar activity and gradually change it until it evolves into the desired activity. If the child is reacting to a position, such as prone against gravity, distract him through activities that he enjoys and gradually modify those activities until the child is in the prone position. If the child still responds negatively, look critically at the activity's sensory requirements. The activity simply may not be appropriate for the child.

The goal of sensory integrative intervention is to strengthen neural integration, especially the neural integration that underlies learning and behavior. Motor learning and motor skill development are not the objectives of sensory integrative treatment (Ayres 1973). However, motor acquisition can be enhanced by skillfully providing the child with the sensorimotor foundation and processing skills he needs. Treatment programs that are skillfully graded to enhance the sensory integrative skills, build the motor control needed, and integrate these into the performance of more difficult functional skills, will result in improved skill development simultaneously with improved sensory processing.

> Roberto is an 8-year-old boy with autistic spectrum disorders. He receives outpatient occupational therapy twice a week for one-hour sessions. Clinically, Roberto presents with a fluctuating defensive modulation disorder. His nervous system fluctuates from underresponsiveness to overresponsiveness, and his nervous system and his emotions are often described as volatile. He has a tendency toward overarousal and hyperresponsiveness to auditory, tactile (touch), and vestibular (movement) sensory input. Although he is capable of being pleasant and charming, he can quickly become emotionally unstable and cranky. His resting threshold for stress and sensory stimuli is very low, and he becomes overstimulated and explodes with the slightest stimulation or threat. When overloaded, he becomes snappy, cranky, emotionally labile, inattentive, and disorganized.

> In order to function, Roberto has developed his own coping strategy. He uses his strong verbal skills to augment a very controlling, inflexible personality. He controls exactly what will occur throughout the day, who touches him, how he is touched, where he goes, and what is demanded of him.

> Roberto has poor somatosensory processing (tactile and proprioceptive), which contributes to poor body scheme and motor planning. His general movements are awkward, and he has difficulty planning and learning new motor tasks. He has poor vestibular-proprioceptive processing. His arm movements are characterized by overshooting and subtle tremors with skilled movements. His balance is poor, and he has difficulty with most gross motor tasks. He cannot stand on one foot or balance when his base of support is narrowed. He is posturally insecure and fearful of any position that threatens his balance. His fear is rational, because he does not have the equilibrium or balance reactions to help himself if he should fall.

The outpatient, medically based treatment plan for Roberto includes activities to

- Improve his tactile, proprioceptive, and vestibular processing in order to improve his
  - Total-body motor planning
  - Ability to monitor body movements without visually monitoring
  - Trunk control, balance, equilibrium reactions
  - Grading of arm and leg movements; decrease in tremors
  - Functional hand skills
- Improve his sensory processing
  - Multisensory processing
  - Sensory modulation, arousal, and attention

Roberto arrives at the clinic for therapy after six hours at school. He is anxious, disorganized, and has a very low threshold for stress. His breathing is rapid and his voice is high-pitched. He demands to control the first activity; but once he tries it, he fails because he cannot organize himself sufficiently to be successful. The therapist takes gentle control over the session and guides him through a treatment progression geared at lowering his threshold and providing him with improved sensory processing and motor control.

Preparation. Roberto must be brought into the calm-alert state. The net swing was selected to provide linear vestibular with proprioceptive input. It also provides deep-touch input to his trunk and enables his extremities to be free. Roberto was eager to participate in the net activity. He demanded to play a basketball game while swinging in the net. The therapist set up the basketball hoop at a height that would require Roberto to extend full range against gravity and make him reach into extension to get the ball. At first, the therapist convinced him that he would get more points if she helped propel him, pushing him firmly for greater linear vestibular input. Roberto kept his head, neck, and trunk extended against gravity and his eyes fixed on the target. He received immediate feedback as he hit the target. As his points and enthusiasm mounted, Roberto screamed, "Let me do it! I can push myself and get the points!" The therapist turned over the control to him. As he continued to be successful, the therapist asked, "Shall I make it harder?" With Roberto's permission, the therapist began to raise the height of the target, gradually making him propel himself harder and reach higher to make the target. He was working hard, his breathing was regular, his voice volume was strong and well modulated, he was more organized, and he enjoying the challenge and his success.

When he started to show signs of fatigue, dropping his head and grabbing the back of his neck, the therapist said, "You really are too good at this game. We need something more challenging. How many more of these should we do?" Roberto yelled back, "We'll do three more. Then we need a dangerous game. What can we do that is dangerous?"

Facilitation. Roberto couldn't think of what to do next that would be challenging, and he asked the therapist for help. After hearing several games, he screamed, "The alligator game! I want to play the alligator game! It will be dangerous!" The therapist and Roberto set up the trapeze bar with a bench in front and behind it. Roberto meticulously adjusted the distance between the two benches, stood on a bench, held onto the trapeze bar, and swung out to land on the other bench. He made believe that he was flying over water that held dangerous alligators, and tried to land safely on the *islands* (the benches) on either side. At first, he could barely land on the islands, and he demanded that the benches be brought closer together. When he felt safe, he screamed, "Where are the alligators?" Small green bolsters (alligators) were placed in the area between the two benches. Roberto's excitement mounted; he loved the danger and the challenge. He flew over the alligators, almost falling into the water. After several successful flights over the dangerous waters, he screamed for more alligators. The benches had to be moved apart to make them fit. He knew he could do it, even though it was much harder.

In this activity, Roberto's arms received proprioceptive input through the traction and resistance they received as he pulled his body weight from bench to bench. He had heightened awareness of where his trunk and legs were while he worked to make them safely set down on land. He received linear vestibular input as he flew through the air. Most of all, he worked on motor planning. Because the activity offered less support than the net, it required him to plan and execute total-body movements; that is, he had to plan in advance where his body needed to land, and make it happen.

Roberto loved the excitement and the challenge. As his excitement started to decline and he mastered the challenge of the alligators, the therapist suggested that perhaps he would consider saving some children in another room. They needed someone strong and brave to save them. Roberto enthusiastically jumped down, shouting, "I'll save them!"

The next room had a tire swing suspended from the ceiling. On the walls, there were six small pictures of children. The therapist asked, "Here are the children. Why do they need you to save them?" Roberto replied, "They are being held captive on an island. I need to swing over and free them." Lying prone through the tire swing, he tried to propel his body to swing toward the pictures. He couldn't see his legs, and they moved awkwardly and dug into the mat below him. The more he struggled to move the tire, the more resistance his legs received and the more proprioceptive feedback he received. He struggled to move the tire swing in the direction of the children. He swung a few feet, and the tire rebounded in the opposite direction. Originally, Roberto thought he would pull the pictures off the wall to save the children, but it was obvious that this would be too difficult. His enthusiasm started to decline as he began to lose faith in his ability to save the children. The therapist said, "You can save them by touching them. Just touch the children and they are free. You can do it, Roberto!" His motivation rose, and he propelled forward again. Finally, he was able to touch a picture. He screamed, "I saved her! I'll save the rest!" He struggled, moving his feet and legs without seeing them, balancing on the tire on his stomach, balancing his upper body with his lower body as his balance shifted from the movement of the tire, reaching, and timing his reach. When he finished saving all six children, he dropped to the mat, exhausted but proud of his accomplishments.

This activity was much harder than swinging on the trapeze. While it provided linear vestibular and proprioceptive input, it required total-body motor planning, sequencing, and timing. Roberto had to oppose gravity and coordinate his head, trunk, arms, and legs as they resisted gravity. If he had been upright, he wouldn't have had to fight gravity.

Roberto asked if he could do a scooterboard crashing game next. He set up a wall of cushions and crash mats at the end of the room. The therapist sat in front of the crash wall, and Roberto sat on the scooterboard facing the crash wall. A long piece of Thera-Band was looped around his waist, with the therapist holding each end. He held onto the band and used his feet reciprocally to push himself back, away from the therapist and the crash wall. The therapist held tight and resisted his movements. When he reached a distance of five feet, the therapist directed him to stop, gave him a warning, then had him extend his legs. The therapist moved out of the way, and Roberto flew forward, crashing into the wall. After the crash, he rolled off the board laughing uncontrollably, then picked up the scooterboard and prepared to do it again.

Roberto could now tolerate this activity. He had the balance to sit on the scooterboard without falling off, and could reciprocally move his legs against resistance. Each time he lifted a leg against resistance, his balance was thrown off and he had to use his muscles to regain control. The activity was loaded with deep proprioceptive input from the resistance to his legs as he pushed away, the resistance to his abdominal muscles as he picked up his legs to propel forward, and the deep-touch input to his legs and body as he crashed into the wall. Linear vestibular input came from the speed of the scooterboard. Roberto loved the speed and danger associated with this challenging crashing game.

Function. To finish the session, Roberto needed to incorporate the newly acquired skills into a functional activity that would be integrated into a home activity, such as bike riding. He had been threatened by the sensory and motor components involved in this task. During the session, he had worked on both the sensory and motor components needed for bike riding, and he appeared to be prepared for the task. His two-wheeled bike with training wheels was used. The therapist manually resisted the bike as Roberto attempted to ride it forward, enhancing the proprioceptive feedback as he pedaled. As he mastered the reciprocal lower-extremity movements, the therapist lightened the resistance, gradually grading the task for success.

When the session was over, Roberto begrudgingly ran to the waiting room to tell his mother about his successes. He had flown over alligators, saved children that were held captive, and crashed into walls. He was most proud of the fact that he did dangerous things and that he was strong and brave. Later, his mother reported that when he arrived home, he did his homework easily without complaining and was calm, motivated, well behaved, and pleasant throughout the evening.

The Comprehensive Treatment Program

Many children with autism need a multifaceted, comprehensive treatment program that includes clinic-based outpatient therapy, school-based therapy, and therapeutic sensory activities integrated into their lives. Coordination of services is important to assure that children receive intervention that directly impacts their functional performance in every environment.

Roberto received such a comprehensive treatment program. In addition to clinic-based outpatient services, he received a sensory diet that was aimed at helping him stay organized through difficult times in his day. He was in the second grade in a class for children with varying exceptionalities (VE). Roberto had a difficult time starting the day. He arrived at school disorganized and upset. In class, he couldn't stay in his seat, couldn't organize his work, himself, or his desk, and frequently fell out of his seat. He stayed disorganized through most of the day. His worst times were in reading class, where he could not stay focused, and after lunch, when the class did writing activities. He frequently fell apart after lunch, crying hysterically or having outbursts of anger. In the cafeteria, Roberto experienced sensory overload from the noise levels (auditory) and being shoved and pushed (tactile). His anxiety was high because of sensory overload and his fear of the unknown, his inability to control the people in his environment, and his fear of being bumped (touched) or losing his balance (postural insecurity).

His parents, teachers, and therapists worked together to develop a sensory program that would help him. He needed to arrive at school more organized. The therapists knew that he became calm when provided with deep proprioceptive input and resistive exercises. They arranged for him to arrive at school early wearing an extra-heavy backpack. He was escorted to the indoor basketball court, where he walked laps around the court until classes began. He was instructed to count each lap and record it in a log book. The backpack provided deep proprioceptive input (resistance) through his trunk and legs, as well as deep-touch input through his back.

The teacher noted that if Roberto could walk for 20 minutes before class, he could stay focused until about 11:00 a.m. (2½ hours). At 10:45, when Roberto was beginning to lose his concentration and self-organization, the teacher asked him to deliver a crate of heavy books to a room down the hall. Previously, the teacher had made arrangements with another teacher to expect the books to be delivered and picked up at different times throughout the day. The teacher always thanked Roberto for being so helpful, so he felt a sense of responsibility. The crate was packed with heavy books, thus providing deep proprioceptive input. Roberto carried or pushed the books to the other classroom; and just before the afternoon reading session, he was sent to pick up the books.

Just before lunch, the teacher had him do table push-ups, standing between two tables and lifting his legs for the count of 10. This helped Roberto lower his threshold in the cafeteria.

After lunch, Roberto and the entire class needed extra help to stay on task and reorganize themselves before they could participate in the writing class. With the help of the therapists, the teacher designed and initiated a 10-minute isometric exercise session. The class did table push-ups, wall push-ups, chair push-ups, jumping in place (if they needed increased arousal), and isometric arm exercises or chest pushes (hands clasped together in front of their chests). They shook their hands to loosen them, and they did simple coordination exercises for their fingers. After the exercises, Roberto was able to organize himself and sit down to complete his work.

The teacher worked with the occupational therapist to make several other classroom modifications.

- Roberto did best when sitting in the front of the class where there were less visual and auditory distractions.

- He also needed to be seated away from the PA system and the air-conditioning vents, both of which tended to increase his agitation and distractibility. Also, he needed a two-minute warning before the bell rang or a fire drill was called.

- He was given a Movin'Sit™ wedge cushion to use on his chair. This enabled him to shift his weight and receive vestibular input that he needed to maintain postural tone. As an added benefit, by shifting his weight forward he received proprioceptive input through his legs and feet. This helped reinforce his legs and the correct position for sitting.

- A weighted vest was made available during the reading session. Roberto learned to recognize when he was having difficulty staying focused and needed to use the vest.

- He used a tall, clear acrylic incline board during all written and reading work. The incline board helped him maintain his posture while sitting at his desk, and therefore helped him to attend to his work. It also positioned his hand for writing tasks and improved his handwriting and legibility.

Roberto often became disorganized and angry over after-school activities. He would forget his schedule and become upset with what appeared to him to be a change. To remedy this, he was given a seven-day schedule that listed the days of the week, his school schedule, and all special activities or field trips and the times they occurred. The schedule was pasted to the front flap of his homework notebook. On his way to school, he verbally reviewed the day's schedule and plan. On the way home, when he would ask his mother where they were going, she would direct him to look it up on his schedule. Roberto learned to look at his schedule and take responsibility for knowing and preparing himself for the day's activities.

Roberto benefited from:

- A program to improve his sensory modulation through a sensory diet, self-regulation, and environmental modifications

- Direct intervention from his school occupational therapist to improve his fine motor control and functional performance at school

- Activities provided by his school physical therapist to help improve his gross motor control and ability to perform in his physical education class.

- Clinic-based intervention to improve his sensory integration, motor control, and motor planning

CHAPTER 11

The Somatosensory System and Tactile Discrimination Disorders

Carolyn Murray-Slutsky

The somatosensory system is comprised of both the proprioceptive and tactile systems. Somatosensory perception refers to the combination of tactile and body position sense.

The tactile system encompasses sensory nerve endings or receptors that are located in the skin and mouth. It carries sensory information from the skin and mouth into the central nervous system (CNS). This is the largest sensory system, and its influences are very pervasive. Tactile nerve endings—large fibers with fast conduction rates—that mediate tactile sensation from the skin are responsible for discriminating between surfaces, shapes, and textures. The system provides precise, discrete information necessary for skilled hand and tool use.

Pain and temperature sensation also are received from the skin receptors; however, they are transmitted through the CNS via slow, thin fibers that travel a different course. These receptors serve the purpose of protecting the individual.

The proprioceptive system encompasses sensory nerve endings that are located within the joints and muscles. It carries sensory information from the muscles and joints into the CNS to provide information about body position, muscle contractions or tension, the rate timing and sequencing of our movements, and the amount of force being exerted. It detects and registers changes in position of the arms and legs, skin stretch, and the strength and degree of muscle contractions or muscle tension. The latter is important in grading the pressure and force of a movement.

The tactile and proprioceptive systems are intimately intermingled from both a developmental and neurological perspective. The close relationship between touch, joint, and body movements often cannot be separated. For example, when a child reaches for and obtains an object, the child receives proprioceptive information from his arm moving through space, and tactile information as he touches and manipulates the object, learning about its texture, surface, and shape. He also receives proprioceptive information as his fingers close around the object and measure its weight in order to judge the amount of resistance needed to pick it up. While functionally and developmentally it is difficult to separate tactile-proprioceptive sensory information, it is equally difficult to separate it neurologically. Discriminatory tactile and proprioceptive sensory information, once in the central nervous system, travels through the same fast fibers, terminating at the primary somatosensory cortex.

 ## The Tactile and Proprioceptive Systems

Normal Development

The tactile system is the first system to develop *in utero*. At birth, it is the most mature system, surpassing both the visual and auditory systems. The child first learns about the environment by means of the tactile system. Gottfried (1984) identified that early tactile information may be important in the development of:

- Tactile perception

- Development of parent infant attachment

- Stress coping mechanism

- Sociability

- Cognitive development

Oral Motor

The mouth is described as one of the most precise tactile discriminators in infants. It is the first source of tactile information available to infants after birth. Babies automatically mouth objects and toys to learn about their qualities and features. Mouthing objects of interest, detecting the qualities and characteristics of objects, may continue until the objects of interest are too large and complex for adequate oral exploration (Getman 1985), until tactile discrimination in the hands is adequate to glean the same information and body scheme is formulated. Mouthing of objects is important for decreasing oral hypersensitivity and facilitating oral-motor development. It also may be important for environmental learning, and may contribute to the early development of bilateral hand use (Henderson and Pehoski 1995).

Oral and tactile exploration of the body parts develops gradually and helps form the foundation for body scheme, the internal model of the body. Mouthing of the hands may occur as early as birth. Sucking of the hands and fingers (fisted) often occurs naturally during the first month. Physiological flexion—total-body flexion that is present at birth—biomechanically positions children's hands near their mouths. Accidentally at first, the hands find their way into their mouths, and they learn that sucking helps them maintain a calm and organized state. The flexion enables them to use their hands to explore their faces and heads, further defining their body schemes. Physiological flexion gradually dissipates after the first month, and infants must develop active muscle control over their arms to further explore their faces, heads, arms, fingers, and legs.

Kravitz, Goldenberg, and Neyhaus (1978) indicated that infants use their fingers to explore their:

- Head and face within hours of birth

- Fingers at approximately 12 weeks

- Legs at 16 weeks

- Feet at 19 weeks

At an early age, children begin to explore their bodies through touch, and they begin to use this tactile feedback to develop their body percept. This is reinforced and confirmed as they move through space.

Body Scheme

A child's body scheme is largely unconscious and is built on somatosensory information. It is the child's internal model of the body in action. A well-organized body percept enables the child to *feel* what the body is doing without looking at it. This internal map enables the child to navigate and plan body movements with ease, coordination, precision, and well-regulated, smooth, and accurate movements. It contributes to the ability to grade the pressure, force, and speed of arm and leg movements, and has a direct influence on the ability to perform gross motor activities in a coordinated, accurate fashion.

The development of body scheme is dependent upon the syntheses of sensory stimuli from touch, proprioception, vestibular input, and vision; it provides the child with valuable information about where his body is in space and how it is moving. Early development is characterized by intense tactile and deep proprioceptive input into all aspects of the child's body. As he moves against gravity, resisting the pull of gravity, he receives proprioceptive input into his joints. He moves from prone to prone on his elbows, to extended arms and quadruped, and eventually to sitting and standing. As he progresses, the child spends valuable time working his muscles against the resistance of gravity and his body weight. This proprioceptive and tactile input contributes to the child's internal concept of his body and its interrelationship with movement.

Every time the child moves through space and touches an object, he receives tactile information. When he looks at the object, this tactile information is intermingled with visual information, confirming not only the shape and size of the object, but the relationship of the object to the child's body. As he moves through space, his muscles contract, sending proprioceptive input to the brain. The vestibular receptors also fire, sending information about the movement against gravity. These impulses intermingle with the visual and tactile information within the brain. This sensory information provides information regarding the makeup of the body and its relationship to the environment and other objects.

Much of our knowledge of the world begins with our bodies. Visual space perception begins with understanding the spatial relations on our own bodies. Concepts such as *above* and *below* are internalized as we learn that our eyes are above the nose, that our hair is above the mouth, that our legs are below the trunk, and that our feet are below our knees. These concepts can be generalized to objects long before the child can use words to describe them. Number concepts also have a reference to the body. Children learn that they have one nose, but many fingers. Later, they learn that they have two ears, eyes, hands, and feet; five fingers on each hand; and five toes on each foot. Without adequate knowledge of the body, a child is handicapped in learning processes involving visual spatial perception and skilled motor tasks (Ayres 1961).

Imitation, a skill needed for learning, relies on the child having good tactile discrimination and body scheme. Most children learn through imitation. To imitate requires that the child first have a good perception of his own body, how it is connected and how it moves. Imitating the movements of others requires that the child knows where his extremities are moving and how they are connected, and he must have the praxis or motor planning skills necessary to duplicate the movement.

The child's body scheme—the somatosensory percept of the body—forms the basis for motor planning. A child with a good body scheme receives accurate information from his tactile, vestibular, and proprioceptive receptors, has a good internal map of his body, can perform unfamiliar movements automatically, and plan and coordinate them quickly and smoothly.

Fine Motor Development and Haptic Exploration

Babies receive deep proprioceptive and deep-touch input through the arms and upper extremities almost immediately. At 1 to 2 months of age, babies when placed prone receive deep input through the face, shoulders, and forearms. The natural fisting of the hands provides both deep-touch and proprioceptive input, which is further enhanced at three months when children push prone on their elbows, and again at 4 or 5 months as they push higher against gravity to prone position on extended arms. The hands stay fisted during prone weight-bearing on the arms for almost 5 months. This prepares the hand with the mobility needed for further skill development. Children receive 5 months of resistive proprioceptive and deep-touch input into the forearms and hands before they bear weight on the hand with the fingers extended. Weight bearing with fingers extended enables further muscle length and mobility required for more precise hand skills.

In early development, children work prone against gravity, a natural form of resistance, to develop the muscle control and muscle length needed for skilled hand usage. The struggle to raise their bodies up on their arms against gravity is characterized by intense deep-touch, proprioceptive, and vestibular input. This input not only helps children lengthen the muscles needed to function, but also reinforces their internal body schemes, connecting the hands to the forearms to the shoulder, and so on. In prone, the higher the child moves against gravity, the more the muscles throughout the hands are lengthened. As the child actively moves, shifts weight, and reaches in positions such as quadruped, the arches are developed and established.

This weight shifting over the fingers (which now are extended) helps children begin to isolate the fingers and develop the muscles that support the arches (balance reactions) of the hands that are necessary for skilled hand use and object manipulation. This process continues to provide deep-touch and proprioceptive input throughout the hand and upper extremities. By 12 months, children have developed a mature reaching pattern while sitting, and they continue to develop the skill and coordination needed for more advanced fine motor and object manipulation.

Somatosensory (tactile and proprioceptive) sensation is important in:

- Guiding hand exploration
- Orientation in space
- Body scheme
- Regulating the manipulation of objects
- In-hand manipulation
- The coordination necessary for object manipulation

A synthesis of information derived from somatosensory receptors provides the hand with a picture of the body and its orientation in space (body scheme) (Gardner 1988). Research suggests that body scheme—the internal picture of the body—serves as a template for interpreting the spatial properties of objects (Gibson 1962). Somatosensory sensation also contributes to the ability to manipulate objects within the hand and to regulate the physical manipulation of objects. To use the somatosensory information received from the hands, the individual must be able to make rapid and frequent changes of speed and sequencing of hand movements and regulate force during object manipulation (Hollins and Goble 1988; Johnson and Hsiao 1992). These elements of fine motor coordination are thought to be dependent on the processing of tactile, proprioceptive, and kinesthetic sensations for their execution (Brooks 1986: Johansson and Westling 1990).

Haptic exploration is the ability to obtain and interpret tactile properties through physical manipulation of the object. It is the ability to identify by touch or manipulation what you feel or touch. Haptic exploration is characterized by moving the fingers over the object and manipulating it to derive information about its size, texture, and shape. It requires a blending of feedback from tactile, proprioceptive, and kinesthetic sensations (Gibson 1962).

Infants use both the mouth and their hands to derive haptic information about objects. By either manipulating objects with their hands or exploring them by placing or manipulating them in their mouths, babies learn about the characteristics and qualities of the object. Haptic exploration using the mouth emerges as early as one month, while exploration using the hands develops closer to 2 months of age. As children improve in their ability to manipulate, rotate, bang, and finger objects, thus deriving greater haptic perception from the hands, mouthing of objects diminishes.

Piaget and Inhelder (1948) concluded that the ability of children to identify objects through touch progressively improved with age.

- At 2½ to 3½ years of age, children are able to correctly recognize common objects, but are unable to recognize shapes.

- At 3½ to 5 years of age, they are able to match topologic forms.

- At 4 to 4½ years of age, children are able to recognize geometric figures. They are able to differentiate curvilinear shapes (circle and ellipse) from rectilinear shapes (square and rectangle).

- At 4½ to 7 years of age, children are able to recognize greater numbers and levels of complexity of geometric figures.

Haptic perception is closely associated with visual perception. As children manipulate objects and learn about their qualities and characteristics, they match the information to what they visually observe. They learn to recognize what objects look like by physically manipulating them. By 6 months of age, infants can integrate visual and haptic perception because they were able to visually recognize a shape after only tactile contact with it (Rose, Gottfried, and Bridger 1978).

Summary

In early development, the infant receives intense tactile and proprioceptive (somatosensory) input. Normal somatosensory processing contributes to the infant's development of oral motor control, body scheme, fine motor skills, visual perceptual and environmental learning, as well as emotional, social, and cognitive development.

The development of oral motor control needed for both speech and normal eating relies on normal somatosensory sensation in the mouth. The child needs to have good sensorimotor awareness and control over the tongue, lips, jaw, and cheeks. Normal sensory awareness is characterized in the early years by mouthing of objects that contributes to decreasing oral hypersensitivity, increasing haptic perception of objects, and bilateral hand usage. Oral motor exploration contributes to environmental learning.

The development of the child's body scheme, or internal awareness of how the body is put together, relies on somatosensory sensation integrated with vestibular and visual information. This internal awareness is necessary to understand general concepts needed for academic learning, directionality, and spatial concepts.

Somatosensory awareness contributes to the ability to grade the pressure exerted during arm and leg movements, coordinate the timing and sequencing of movements, and master gross motor skills. To motor plan new tasks requires a good internal knowledge of the body and its relationship to the outside world. Motor planning is needed for effective interaction with new situations, toys, games, and tasks that are not already learned, and for successful adaptation to changes in their environment.

Fine motor skill development and object manipulation relies on normal somatosensory awareness. Normal development is characterized by intense tactile and proprioceptive stimulation that lengthens and activates the muscles throughout the hands and upper extremities. This muscle development and activation contributes to the ability to haptically explore objects. Haptic exploration involves the child manipulating the object in order to learn its sensory qualities. Somatosensory sensation is important in regulating the ability to manipulate objects and developing in-hand manipulation and coordination, fine motor skills, and general hand usage and object manipulation. It contributes to our awareness of objects' orientation in space and general visual perceptual skill development.

Neurological Pathways for Somatosensory Processing

Somatosensory sensations are received from the periphery. Tactile stimuli enter the nervous system through touch receptors in our skin, while proprioceptive information is received from the joints and muscles. Somatosensory information is carried through the spinal cord to the brain via the dorsal column medial lemniscal (DCML) system. The DCML transmits touch pressure, vibration, and proprioceptive information. It is fast, efficient, and responsible for discrimination of tactile information. (See Table 9.2.)

The DCML transmits touch pressure, vibration, and proprioceptive input directly to the thalamus, the integrating center. From the thalamus, the DCML travels directly to the primary and secondary somatosensory area of the cortex, as well as areas 5 and 7 of the posterior parietal lobes.

Projections from the DCML to the somatosensory areas of the cortex and areas 5 and 7 of the parietal lobe are responsible for the discriminatory skills associated with tactile discrimination. These are tested through stereognosis, light touch, finger identification, position sense, and haptic exploration of objects, and involve the specific localization and identification of tactile and proprioceptive sensory information. Sensory information transmitted via the DCML system contributes to skilled tool usage, motor planning, and bilateral integration and sequencing.

Impairment of the DCML System

Impairment to the DCML system results in impaired stereognosis, decreased light touch, and loss of position sense, vibratory, and two-point discrimination (the ability to localize two points of touch input simultaneously). These specific sensory modalities are associated with the precise interpretation of tactile and proprioceptive information needed for tactile discrimination, haptic exploration, and skilled tool usage.

In addition to discrete sensory discrimination difficulties, researchers have found the following problems associated with lesions to the DCML:

- Decreased attention, orientation, and anticipation (Wall 1970)

- Decreased initiative to actively explore the environment and to initiate voluntary movement (Wall 1970)

- Impaired manual dexterity, thumb-to-finger opposition (Wall 1970)

- Clumsiness in handling objects in space; slow and inept finger movements during specific tasks (Mountcastle et al. 1975)

- Decreased supine flexion (Ayres 1979; Wall 1970)

- Decreased anticipation of projected action sequence, or feedforward (Melzack and Southmayd 1974)

- Impaired complex movement sequences (Wall 1970)

Since the DCML is involved in the processing of tactile and proprioceptive sensory input, it appears to play a role much larger in scope than just discrimination of sensory information. It is involved with skilled manual dexterity, the manipulation of objects in space, selective attention, orientation and anticipation, as well as the programming and execution of complex movement sequences (Fisher, Murray, and Bundy 1991). Deficits in these areas often are associated with tactile discrimination disorders or motor planning disorders such as somatodyspraxia.

Tactile Discrimination Difficulties

Poor tactile discrimination is a problem within the somatosensory system that results in difficulty with haptic exploration, the identification of the temporal and spatial qualities of touch, and the perception and organization of incoming touch information for discrimination and use. Tactile information cannot be separated from proprioceptive sensory information because of the intimate relationship between the two systems, both neurologically and developmentally. Therefore, a child displaying tactile discrimination problems will demonstrate difficulties with sensory discrimination of both proprioceptive and tactile sensory information.

Poor tactile discrimination is thought to be a central processing disorder that involves the DCML. It is an underresponsiveness to somatosensory sensory input. Because of poor processing of somatosensory information, the child will demonstrate discrete problems.

Tactile discrimination can be identified through sensory testing and clinical observation. A child with a problem will score poorly on sensory tests of two-point discrimination, localization of touch, finger identification (Sinclare 1981), stereognosis (Chusid 1979), and the ability to explore an object using touch (haptic exploration).

With tactile discrimination difficulties, the underlying problem is either that the child is not perceiving incoming tactile-proprioceptive sensory information accurately, or the child is not able to organize the information within his nervous system. When this problem occurs, no matter what the cause, the child will have problems across most or all of the areas that are impacted by the system. It is a central processing problem, rather than a problem specific to an extremity or a localized area such as the mouth or hands.

It is a stable problem that does not fluctuate radically from day to day (as in a fluctuating or defensive modulation disorder). A child exhibiting problems with tactile discrimination will consistently demonstrate an underresponsiveness to tactile-proprioceptive sensory input.

The child also may show secondary difficulties in the following areas:

- Fine motor skills
- Body scheme
- Gross motor skills
- Oral motor control
- Motor planning

Imagine that for one day, you are asked to wear a thick snowsuit, boots, and mittens. The temperature in the environment is controlled, and you are not hot. However, you do have to maneuver throughout the day in this thick, awkward clothing that prevents you from feeling with your fingers and receiving accurate information from your extremities.

You sit down for breakfast, hardly able to feel the chair under you. When you try to pick up your spoon, the mittens make it difficult to feel the spoon in your hand, and you drop it under the table. Now you need to retrieve the spoon. You see it and reach for it with your hand, but you can't feel it. You realize that you need to look at it as you reach; as you reach, you lose your balance and start to fall out of your chair. You try to grab the table with your arm to keep from falling; but instead of the table, you grab your glass of milk. The milk spills everywhere. Grabbing was a reflex action; you tried to protect yourself, but you missed grabbing the table because your eyes were focused on the spoon.

You grab your book bag and fumble to get your arms through the straps. The first try is unsuccessful, and now the straps are twisted. You feel trapped, and you fear you can't get the book bag off. Your hands can't feel the straps through the mittens. You shake and wiggle until the bag is thrown off your back. The contents fly out. You scoop them up and throw them back into the bag, and you try again. This time, you get it onto your back. The weight reconfirms your success.

You run to get the bus, because now you are late. As you run in the awkward boots, your foot gets caught on some twigs and you almost fall. Your arms and legs feel heavy, and you have difficulty judging where your body ends and other objects begin. You turn a corner too sharply, and your arm hits a pole. You don't feel it. At the bus, you reach for the railing to help you up the steps, but it's hard to grasp because you can't feel it through the mittens. Finally you make it to your seat and plop down. You're not about to take off your book bag; it's too much work. You reach for the safety belt, but you can't see it or feel it. You have to ask for help.

Now imagine how the day will progress at school. Think of how you will do when you are asked to write with a pencil, cut with scissors, perform in physical education class, or just play on the playground. By the end of the day, how will you feel? What coping strategies might you use? Would you give up?

This exercise simulated what it might be like if your tactile input to your hands and body were diminished by a snowsuit, boots, and mittens. However, to realistically depict a systemic problem of the tactile system, your mouth also would have to be affected. It might be as if you had been to the dentist and had just been injected with a numbing agent. Imagine the same scenario complicated by the inability to effectively feel your tongue and mouth. When you eat cereal with the spoon, you have more cereal on your clothes than you have in your mouth, because you can't feel the spoon in your hand or the food in your mouth. When you speak, your words are slurred and you keep biting your tongue. When you run to the bus, you are working so hard to maneuver safely that you don't realize your mouth is open, and soon the front of your shirt is soaked from drool.

While this activity may simulate some of the characteristics of a tactile discrimination disorder, it is important to realize that we are imagining how decreased tactile input might feel like in a normal, well-integrated, fully developed nervous system. However, we need to look at the problem in a broader scope. Children with this problem have never known normal tactile discrimination or had normal integration of tactile input within their nervous system. They have never known what it is like to manipulate an object with the small muscles of their hands, deriving specific sensory information about its qualities. They have never integrated tactile, visual, and proprioceptive input to develop a comprehensive, functional model of the object and its orientation in space. Tactile discrimination is more than just diminished feeling; it is diminished tactile discrimination and integration.

When you imagine yourself with a tactile discrimination problem, it's easier to understand why these children may

- Appear awkward and clumsy in both gross motor and fine motor activities

- Mouth objects or drool

- Be accident prone and safety hazards

- Insist on using their vision to monitor where they are going and what they are doing

- Appear to be controlling and demanding

- Be easily frustrated and give up

We can better understand their basic personalities and coping strategies.

Personality Types and Behavioral Responses

Children who are experiencing tactile discrimination difficulties are being deprived of sensory stimulation. How they initially respond to this lack of input from their touch receptors depends on their basic personalities. Usually, children will respond in one of two ways: either they will shut down, or they will aggressively attack the world, demanding to receive sensory information.

Children who shut down show no interest in exploring their environment. Their inner drive is disrupted, and they are not motivated to explore and learn from all the sensory experiences available to them. When children cannot derive sensory satisfaction or pleasure from activities that other children find motivating and exciting, they may fail to care about the activities. As in the previous case study, everyday interactions and activities are simply too frustrating and exhausting. Thus, they revert to the coping mechanisms of shutting down or controlling their environment.

In contrast, children may learn that if they aggressively attack the world, they can obtain satisfaction and sensory feedback from their environment. In early development, children are motivated to receive primarily sensory feedback from their environment. They repeat activities over and over again to experience the sensations they elicit. Children with tactile discrimination disorders, once they understand that they can receive sensory information from their environment, are motivated by the same sensory need. However, to obtain sensory experiences, they attack the environment by rocking, head banging, crashing into things, roughhousing, mouthing things for additional sensory information, and moving about as fast as they can. Sometimes, these children have a poor sense of safety and will take chances without ever understanding the risk involved. They become safety hazards and must be watched carefully. While they demand and crave sensory input, the quality they receive is still not normal. Their central processing disorder will have an impact on their overall functioning.

Soon after beginning occupational or physical therapy, most of these children begin to realize that there is a world out there that can provide sensory feedback. They learn that certain sensory-based experiences help them know where their arms and legs are. These sensory-based experiences and their new awareness often activate an inner drive to explore. When this happens, they may aggressively attempt to obtain the sensory feedback they need, showing extensive sensory-seeking behaviors such as crashing, jumping, roughhousing, or exerting greater pressure when playing. They also may seek out activities, such as writing or coloring, that were boring or uninteresting before. The same thing may occur with children who are low toned, underresponsive, and have decreased sensory awareness of their tongue, lips, or cheeks. After beginning an oral motor and sensory-based program, these children may aggressively try to mouth everything.

Behavioral changes from passivity to sensory-seeking should be looked at positively, but monitored carefully to direct the child into more normal sensory-based activities. These children are seeing and feeling the world for the first time; while they are receiving sensory information from the environment, it still is not normal sensory feedback, nor are their sensory-seeking behaviors always appropriate. While they receive therapeutic intervention to help them integrate and process this sensory information, they also need to be taught appropriate methods of obtaining the enhanced sensory input they desire and crave.

Characteristics of Tactile Discrimination Difficulties

Tactile discrimination difficulties are characterized by an underresponsiveness to touch and proprioceptive input. See Figures 11.1, 11.2, 11.3, 11.4 and Table 11.1 for characteristics of children with tactile discrimination disorders. Behaviors described include general characteristics, total-body awareness, fine motor characteristics, oral motor behaviors, and stereotypic and disruptive behaviors.

Although many children may demonstrate the following characteristics, children have individual differences and personalities. The characteristics that they may display will reflect their unique differences as well as the degree of integration within their nervous systems.

General Characteristics and Behaviors

_____ Enjoys touch pressure, being squeezed, held tightly

_____ May not respond or register to hugging, cuddling, or tickling

_____ Does not notice when food is on face, nose is running, or hands are messy

_____ Does not notice when pants are soiled, diapers are wet, or clothing has fallen off

_____ Is a messy dresser (shirt is seldom tucked in, shoes are untied, pants are twisted)

_____ Needs to touch and feel everything; seeing is not enough. Must run hands along the walls and over furniture, handle toys, test items, and so on

_____ Needs to bump into and touch others. Has trouble keeping hands to self

_____ Shows little or no reaction to pain from scrapes, bruises, cuts—even injections

_____ Plays roughly with toys, objects, other children, adults, animals

_____ Does not realize degree of force exerted; may hurt others or break toys

_____ Does not understand the pain others can feel; may have no remorse for hurting others

_____ Likes to scratch or rub surfaces; may scratch or rub skin excessively; may bite self

_____ Dislikes the dark; needs to see surroundings

_____ May display motor planning difficulties (See Chapter 13.)

FIGURE 11.1
Tactile discrimination disorders: General characteristics and behaviors

Total-Body and Body Awareness Characteristics

_____ Is unable to identify without looking where touched on the body

_____ Is not bothered by falls

_____ Enjoys crashing into other people, objects, mats, balls; likes to fall or throw self on or off of equipment

_____ Enjoys intense sensory experiences, such as movements that provide strong sensory feedback, jumping from high places, vibration, crashing into things with great force

_____ Is a safety risk; is unaware of physical danger to self

_____ Does not know where body parts are and how they relate to one another

_____ Does not appear to know that legs are connected to the body

    _____ Does not use the legs to stabilize self in a chair; frequently falls out of the chair

    _____ Legs appear awkward and uncoordinated when running

_____ Is not able to imitate new movements or learn through imitation

_____ Is awkward in attempts to get dressed

    _____ Has trouble orienting arms to go into a shirt, figuring out how to get feet into socks and shoes, orienting pants and getting legs into them

_____ Is constantly in motion

    _____ Appears to excel in fast movements, but arms and legs lack coordination and midrange control

    _____ Uses only end ranges with poor grading of arm and leg movements

    _____ Does not have the slow, sustained postural control needed for slow movements

    _____ Runs from place to place, thing to thing; is unable to stay on task

_____ Is constantly climbing to high places; or does not have the motor control to climb or jump

_____ Has low muscle tone

    _____ Muscles seem mushy and inactive; may hyperextend midjoints and/or display a lordotic posture (rounding forward of shoulders with hyperextension of the lumbar spine and hyperextension of the knees)

    _____ Moving and playing require effort

    _____ Tires quickly with minimal exertion

    _____ Prefers sedentary activities, such as reading or watching videos or TV

FIGURE 11.2

Tactile discrimination disorders: Total-body and body awareness characteristics

Fine Motor Characteristics

____ Hands appear disconnected from the body; hands seem like unfamiliar appendages

____ Hand movements are uncoordinated

    ____ Lacks isolated finger control, in-hand manipulation skills, ability to oppose the thumb to each consecutive finger

    ____ Fingers move as a unit, as if wearing mittens

    ____ Cannot imitate finger movements; has difficulty showing thumbs up, the peace sign, or "How old are you?" on fingers

    ____ Has difficulty controlling the fingers for precise tasks

____ Must visually monitor hand movements

____ Drops things, but fails to realize when things are dropped

____ Has trouble identifying and understanding the physical properties of objects (textures, shapes, size, density, weight)

____ Is unable to identify familiar objects by touch alone

    ____ Must use vision when reaching into the desk, under a table, or in a box to get an object

    ____ Cannot identify items in own pocket or get them out

____ Uses a mouth as a third hand to stabilize objects or hold them in order to help the hands

____ Uses mouth to provide more sensory information about objects

    ____ After the age of two, uses mouth to learn about the qualities of objects

____ Has difficulty holding and using tools (crayons, pencils, scissors, spoons and forks)

____ Has learned to use the hands, but does so in strange ways; puts on socks, shoes, gloves in unusual ways

FIGURE 11.3
Tactile discrimination disorders: Fine motor characteristics

Oral Motor Behaviors

____ Barely moves lips, cheeks, or tongue

____ Cannot imitate tongue movements or facial expressions

____ Facial expression appears flat; does not move cheeks or facial muscles to express emotions or during conversation

____ Has difficulty sucking through a straw, blowing a whistle, blowing kisses

____ Bites the cup when trying to drink from it; bites the straw or whistle when blowing

____ Does not move tongue much when talking or eating

____ Drools or loses liquid when drinking from a cup

____ Is a messy eater; appears unaware when face is messy, covered with crumbs or food, or liquid is dripping from mouth

____ Stuffs the mouth with food when eating; does not appear to know there is food in the mouth unless it is packed

____ Refuses to eat anything but familiar and comfortable foods and snacks

     ____ Has definite food and drink preferences

     ____ Must visually inspect any new foods and snacks; reacts to foods based on appearance, not on taste

     ____ Cannot physically handle foods of varying textures or qualities; eats only familiar foods that are exactly the same in size, texture, and quality

____ Mouths everything (toys, objects, clothing, washcloths, towels)

____ Vocalizations lack variety

____ Has articulation difficulties

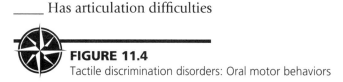

FIGURE 11.4
Tactile discrimination disorders: Oral motor behaviors

Initially, stereotypic, disruptive, and destructive behaviors may be provoked by a specific event or need. Then they are reinforced and maintained by the sensory stimulation the child received and the success encountered within the child's environment (effectiveness in meeting the child's needs, the attention received or obtained, and the degree of avoidance or obtaining received).

Children who have tactile discrimination difficulties often display behaviors that are characterized by their need for increased somatosensory (tactile or proprioceptive) input such as in Table 11.1.

TABLE 11.1 Stereotypic and disruptive behaviors associated with somatosensory or tactile discrimination disorders

Behavior	Sensory Input Provided
Jumping	Linear vestibular and deep proprioceptive input
Climbing to high surfaces; or climbing and jumping	Linear vestibular and deep proprioceptive input
Throwing self to floor, crashing, or playing too hard	Vestibular, deep-touch, and proprioceptive input
Shaking extremities or hands	Vibration, proprioceptive input
Rubbing hands or fisting them together	Deep-touch, proprioceptive, visual input (if in visual sight or near face)
Hitting or biting self or others	Deep-touch and proprioceptive input
Scratching or rubbing	Deep-touch and proprioceptive input
Pinching, pushing, or attempting to be pulled	Deep-touch and proprioceptive input
End-range fixing or patterning (for example, bending wrist, fingers, or elbows into extreme flexion or extension; also seen as knee hyperextension and toe walking)	Deep-touch and proprioceptive input
Mouthing or chewing clothing and objects	Deep proprioceptive and deep-touch input; gustatory, if the objects have flavor
Grinding teeth	Deep proprioceptive input, vestibular input from the vibration, auditory input
Firmly pressing hand to mouth or teeth (often causing skin breakdown on index finger)	Deep proprioceptive and deep-touch input
Head banging	Linear vestibular, vibration, proprioceptive, deep-touch, rhythmic motion input
Masturbating (or similar appearing behaviors)	Deep-touch pressure, proprioceptive input

Evaluation Findings

Identifying a child with a tactile discrimination problem requires a thorough analysis of findings. Identifying the underlying sensory problem for the child's functional problems requires careful and methodical tracking and analysis from the following:

- Sensory and activity history

- Clinical testing of sensory and functional skills

- Analysis of the child's academic, cognitive, and visual-motor and/or visual-perceptual skills

- Clinical observation

Sensory and Activity History

Obtain sensory and activity histories by talking with the child's parents, primary caretaker, and teachers. The purpose of completing a sensory history is to analyze the child's behaviors and likes and dislikes in order to gain insight into the effectiveness of the child's sensory system. Videotaping is an effective technique for observing the child in various settings and helping nonprofessionals describe the behaviors the child is displaying. If parents are interested in videotaping their child, ask them to do so during both easy and difficult times throughout the day. It is helpful to view the child's performance in various settings—at school, home, play, and in one-on-one training sessions.

Record the child's likes and dislikes as they relate to general behavior, total-body awareness, gross and fine motor skills, oral motor and feeding skills, performance of self-care and daily-living activities, and unusual or stereotypic behaviors. (See checklists in Figures 11.1 through 11.4 and Table 11.1.)

Sensory Testing

Sensory testing may clearly identify tactile discrimination difficulties. Several sensory tests can be used, including:

- Localization of tactile stimuli
- Two-point discrimination
- Finger identification
- Stereognosis and haptic exploration of objects
- Graphesthesia

It is important to realize that traditionally, sensory tests have low validity. Because of this, a child cannot be diagnosed as having a tactile discrimination problem exclusively by low tactile scores. The low scores must be substantiated by low performance across multiple areas of somatosensory processing.

Gross Motor Testing

Gross motor testing may indicate problems attributed to an underresponsive system. Because of the involvement of the tactile and proprioceptive systems, the child may have difficulty with:

- Low muscle tone
- Hyperextensibility of the joints
- Standing posture characterized by lordosis and hyperextension or locked knees
- Mushiness of muscles when palpated
- Body scheme
- Coordination and timing of movements
- Midrange joint control
- Grading of arm and leg movements
- Slow, sustained postures that are difficult for the child
  — Prone extension
  — Supine flexion
  — Single-limb stance
  — Romberg position—the child stands either with feet together or heel-to-toe (tandem) with eyes closed
- Holding and maintaining supine flexion—the child may be unable to hold the chin tuck or full-trunk flexion
- Motor planning activities (see Chapter 13)

Fine Motor Testing

Fine motor problems are characterized by a lack of sensory awareness that may contribute to decreased coordination and tool usage. In addition to low scores on sensory tests, functional problems will become evident when vision is occluded. The child may have difficulty with:

- Haptic exploration of objects

- Thumb-to-finger opposition (alternating finger movements)

- In-hand manipulation (especially when vision is suppressed)
    - Translation of the object from the finger to the palm, or palm to finger
    - Shifting an object between or among the fingers
    - Rotation of an object

- Decreased timing and sequencing of arm or finger movements

- Isolated finger control; ability to move the fingers in isolation rather than as a unit

- Skilled tool usage (using a pencil, scissors, spoon or fork)

- Grading of arm movements and the pressure needed to play with toys, write, or perform skilled hand movements

- Imitating finger postures (motor planning skills)

- Functional hand skills

Oral Motor Testing

Oral motor problems also are characterized by decreased sensory awareness that is exhibited through decreased coordination and control. The child may have difficulty with:

- Low facial muscle tone, characterized by paucity of facial expressions and muscle tone in the face, lips, and cheeks

- Chin tuck and sustained neck flexion contributing to decreased stability of the base of the tongue and jaw, resulting in difficulty isolating and grading tongue and jaw movements

- Activating the cheeks, lips, tongue, or oral muscles for
    - Blowing a whistle, blowing kisses
    - Sucking through a straw
    - Articulating sounds
    - Moving food around the mouth
    - Maintaining lip closure and preventing drooling

- Grading jaw movements and pressure

- Sequencing and timing of oral musculature

- Speech

- Eating

Maximum Potential

A major goal of clinical testing is to ascertain the child's average and highest functional levels. Initially, it is important to administer clinical tests according to specified protocols; however, by modifying the instructions to elicit the child's maximum functional performance, we can obtain valuable information and help validate the underlying problem. The evaluation should be viewed as a combination of both evaluation and treatment. After we know that the child has met his highest functional level on a test item, we need to identify what we can do to help him perform even better. We must modify the instructions and implement intervention strategies until we feel we have obtained the child's maximum performance. If we are effective in improving the child's performance, we will validate the underlying problem and the effective intervention strategies.

Academic, Cognitive, Visual-Motor, and Visual-Perception Skills

Academic learning, abstract thought and reasoning, visual-perception, and visual motor integration are the end products of sensory integration. When a child has a problem with academic performance, often it is a warning sign of a deeper problem—a symptom rather than the problem. Somatosensory awareness contributes to visual-perception, spatial orientation, the understanding of basic directional and abstract concepts, visual-motor integration, and motor planning of new tasks. If the child has difficulty in these areas, the academic weaknesses must be used to track the child's underlying sensorimotor problem. Similarly, the child's strengths can be used to identify the child's coping strategies and stronger sensory modalities.

Clinical Observation

Clinical observation occurs throughout the entire evaluation process, whether it is previewing an introductory videotape of the child in various environmental settings, observing the method in which the child completes clinical tests, or observing the child during free play or structured play situations.

Tactile discrimination can be observed. However, you must have an in-depth knowledge of how somatosensory deficits can impact performance in order to correctly identify it. The child's motor control, when movements or extremities are not visually monitored, must be observed.

It is possible to complete a full evaluation on a child who will not comply with clinical testing. However, the clinical tests will need to be completed as clinical observations during structured or unstructured play-based activities. You may choose to videotape the initial session. This will enable you to replay the video in order to validate the clinical observations. Structure clinical observations to elicit all of the information outlined previously.

CHAPTER 12

Tactile Discrimination Disorders and Intervention Strategies

Carolyn Murray-Slutsky

A tactile discrimination problem is a disorder of the somatosensory system in which tactile and proprioceptive sensory information is either not effectively received from the receptors in the skin, muscles, and joints, or is not effectively transmitted through the dorsal column medial lemniscal system to other areas of the brain. Integration of sensory information is inefficient and results in impaired body scheme, gross motor, fine motor, and oral motor development. Secondary academic, cognitive, and perceptual problems may be present and are a direct result of inefficiencies in somatosensory processing.

Effective intervention strategies employ five basic principles.

1. Work through the dorsal column medial lemniscal (DCML) system to increase its efficiency in receiving and integrating tactile-proprioceptive information, thus promoting tactile discrimination

   — Use facilitation techniques to activate the system

   — Increase muscle tone through linear vestibular input

   — Enhance tactile, proprioceptive, touch pressure, and vibratory input

   — Use techniques from normal development to add resistance and increase awareness

2. Facilitate integration of sensory information by developing an adaptive response and multisensory or system integration

— Create the just-right challenge

— Require an adaptive response

— Tap into the child's inner drive

3. Grade intervention from requiring general total-body responses to requiring discrete discriminating responses

— Develop body scheme

— Progress to discrete, discriminating responses of the hand, foot, or mouth

4. Grade activity progression within treatment sessions to facilitate maximum functional performance

— Preparation

— Facilitation

— Function

5. Redirect inappropriate sensory-seeking behaviors into appropriate activities that meet sensory needs

— Identify the purpose of the behavior and sensory need being met

— Meet the sensory need through a sensory-based program and alternative activities

— Eliminate inappropriate behaviors

Through providing enhanced sensory input specifically through the tactile, vibratory, touch pressure, and proprioceptive receptors (DCML system), we may increase the child's sensory registration of somatosensory information. Through intense sensory stimulation, we may activate the child's sensory registration within the dorsal column.

Sensory stimulation is not sensory integration. Sensory stimulation may wake up the DCML system, but it does not integrate the information and result in improved discrimination skills. The sensory-seeking and self-stimulation behaviors that many of children engage in do not result in better integration of their systems, but instead serve as a source of stimulation and pleasure. If sensory stimulation resulted in improved discrimination, many children who engage in sensory-seeking and sensory-stimulation behaviors would have the best discrimination skills. Sensory stimulation wakes up the system, but an adaptive response is required for a functional outcome that creates integration. The adaptive response must be challenging, motivating, and integrating. This requires that we grade intervention for increased levels of difficulty and integration.

Begin graded treatment sessions with intense sensory-based activities that are physically challenging, provide enhanced tactile and proprioceptive input, are motivating, and elicit a response that requires some interaction or purpose. This may start out as a general response. Within the session, it is critical that the response presents increased challenge and requires increased skilled discrimination.

Increased precision and skilled discrimination are the end products of activating and integrating the dorsal column. Always test and evaluate the effectiveness of each session. Sessions that do not challenge the child will not effectively facilitate integration or tactile discrimination.

Grading activities within treatment sessions requires us to read the child's responses, knowing how hard and fast to push and how to facilitate a gradual increase in integration. Break the treatment session into three phases: preparation, facilitation, and function.

Preparation. The preparation phase is the warm-up or beginning of the session. During this time, prepare the child's nervous system, activate the DCML system, and obtain the calm-alert state. This phase may include total-body activities that provide enhanced deep-touch, proprioceptive, or tactile input while requiring a challenging but less skilled response.

Facilitation. The facilitation phase requires intense work and integration, but will be guided by the therapist's specific goals. The sensory demands continue to be intense; but the output, challenge, and skill requirements steadily increase.

Function. The function phase is the final phase—the cool-down. During this time, test the effectiveness of the session by evaluating for improved discrimination and skilled functional performance.

 # Improving Body Scheme

Body scheme refers to the child's internal model of his body in action—the unconscious knowledge of the relationship of the arms and legs to the trunk and the way it moves. It is based on somatosensory information.

If the information received from the somatosensory receptors is inaccurate, the child will have a poor foundation from which to build body scheme. The child's internal model—that is, the engrams or memories of how the body moves and is put together—will be inaccurate. Accurate information is critical to the ability to motor plan total-body movements, and contributes to the ability to produce smooth, accurate, and well-regulated movements.

Children who have impaired body scheme secondary to decreased somatosensory processing look clumsy and have difficulty grading, sequencing, and timing their movements, imitating new postures, sustaining postures, and motor planning new or complex movements. Postural insecurity—that is, fear of moving against gravity—is common among these children because they do not have the postural control to balance against gravity. Decreased sensory awareness of their arms, legs, and trunks contributes to difficulties performing almost all gross motor tasks that require slow, skilled coordination.

Specific problems that require intervention include:

- Poor somatosensory processing of sensory information

- Low muscle tone and an underresponsive somatosensory system

- Decreased ability to sustain slow postures, with

  — Difficulty maintaining prone extension

  — Difficulty maintaining supine flexion

- — Pelvic and shoulder instability
- — Inability to balance when the base of support is narrowed (one-leg stance or Romberg position)
- Decreased grading of arm and leg movements with poor midrange joint control
- Decreased total-body motor awareness and control
  - — Decreased sequencing and timing of body movements
  - — Decreased gross motor skills

Treatment strategies must combine activating the system, integrating the information, and developing the postural and motor control needed to improve the ability to function.

Preparation

Before you begin the treatment session, first determine the function that you hope to obtain from the session. Then assess the child to determine his current state of arousal. What is the state of his overall organization? Is he underaroused? Overaroused?

While the majority of time, children with tactile discrimination problems will be underaroused, there may be times when they are overaroused and disorganized. In these cases, use inhibition techniques that include calming, deep proprioceptive, and deep-touch input.

Facilitation techniques will help increase the child's base muscle tone and help him become aware of his arms, hands, legs, and feet. A child who does not know he has feet will not be able to use them for balance activities. The same child will not be able to interact functionally with the environment if he doesn't know he has hands or arms. Sensory stimulation through the dorsal column medial lemniscal system can help wake up the system, preparing the child for function and success.

Facilitation techniques to increase sensory awareness of the trunk and extremities include deep pressure or lotion massages and toweling to the extremities and sensory-based activities to activate the deep-touch and proprioceptive receptors.

Lotion massages that provide deep-touch pressure, joint traction, and compression can activate the proprioceptive receptors within the muscles. The tactile receptors are activated through the deep-touch pressure, the massage, and by toweling—that is, removing the lotion from the extremity using a towel. Fast, vigorous, reciprocal movements can be effective in stimulating the tactile nerve endings.

Lotion massages and toweling are excellent techniques for home programs. Parents can give lotion massages before bedtime as a relaxation technique or toweling after bathing. All children with underresponsive sensory systems enjoy this technique when it is provided with deep-touch input, and parents enjoy bonding with their child during this pleasurable activity.

Mobilization and myofascial release techniques can be integrated into massage techniques for children who have tightness throughout the intrinsic muscles of the hands or tightness with decreased arching throughout the feet. These techniques are discussed in Chapter 14.

A child who is underresponsive to touch may not register sensory information at the normally accepted intensity. Either exercise creativity in enhancing the sensory input, or follow the child's lead. The child will show you what he likes, what he registers, and what is integrating for him.

Sensory-Based Activities

Southpaw® sensory shaker. A large, porous (breathable), cocoon-like bag filled with balls provides deep-touch input. Children enjoy playing the washing machine game in which they climb into the bag, the top is closed, and the bag is agitated until the child is clean. The child controls both the degree of agitation and duration, reporting, "I am really dirty and need to be cleaned harder" or "I'm clean now and we can stop." The sensory shaker also can function as a ball pool for therapists working with space constraints.

Foam box. Fill a cardboard box with foam pieces. The child climbs in, covering his arms. Play washing machine, shaking the box from side to side until the child says, "I'm clean now."

Sand box or rice box activities. Bury the child's arms and feet under the sand, or let him pour sand over them. Encourage the child to feel the sand or rice and resist against it.

Neoprene vests and body garments. (See Illustration 10.5.) Neoprene body wraps provide deep-touch input throughout the trunk. Children who display the need for deep-touch and proprioceptive input or children who have difficulty focusing or attending may benefit from wearing neoprene body garments.

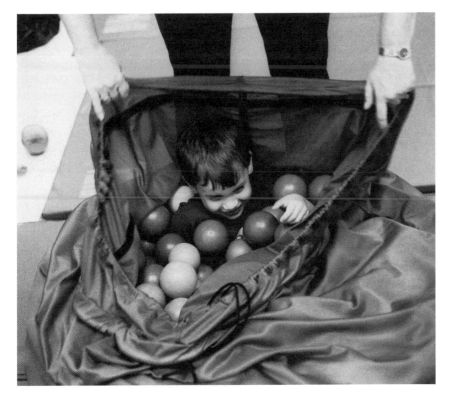

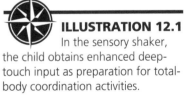

ILLUSTRATION 12.1
In the sensory shaker, the child obtains enhanced deep-touch input as preparation for total-body coordination activities.

Low muscle tone is characterized by mushy muscles, hyperextensibility of the joints, and poor midrange control. To treat this problem of vestibular-proprioceptive processing, provide linear vestibular input to stimulate the vestibular system through the utricle. The utricle receptors are within the three semicircular canals and are concerned with gravitational motion (linear acceleration) involving the position of the head in space. Linear vestibular input acts to stimulate anti-gravity extensor muscles (Fisher and Bundy 1989) that facilitate tonic postural and support reactions.

Swinging in a net hammock. Provide linear vestibular input by having the child work while prone in the net hammock. This activity is effective in stimulating the utricular hair cells within the inner ear, promoting tonic postural extensors and increasing muscle tone. Because the child is underresponsive to most sensory input, he may not respond with increased extension to mild linear vestibular input. The vestibular input may need to be fast to elicit an increase in muscle tone, arousal, and postural extensors.

A word of caution. When working in the net to facilitate postural extensors:

- Adjust the height of the net high enough to assure that the child's feet will not hit the floor when he swings back. This could result in hyperextension of the child's knees.

- Have the child take off his shoes to decrease the possibility of having his feet hit the floor, which would result in knee hyperextension.

- If the child cannot maintain trunk extension, take care to assure that he does not fall out of the net due to trunk flexion while swinging. To assure trunk extension:

    — Select activities that promote postural extension. Any activity that promotes postural or even head or eye flexion could result in the child collapsing into total-body flexion and falling out of the net. Once the child has sufficient postural control to isolate head flexion from total-body flexion, modify the activity.

    — NDT facilitation techniques, such as tapping the gluteal muscles, often are effective in increasing hip extension until the linear vestibular input can have an impact on the system, promoting tonic extension. Tap firmly to elicit firing of the gluteal muscles. The child is underresponsive to proprioceptive input and will not register the sensory input unless the intensity of this technique is enhanced beyond what is traditionally used during NDT procedures.

Trampoline or peanut ball. Provide linear vestibular input by having the child jump up and down on any form of equipment that provides a rebound. Linear up-and-down movements provide resistance to the legs as the child moves against gravity. To promote the tonic postural extensors, the rhythm must be regular and the child's movements linear (straight up and down or forward and backward). If the child is off-center or loses his balance, the result will be phasic rather than static postural control. As the child loses his balance, angular movements are produced that facilitate the semicircular canal, not the utricle, and promote phasic transient postural reactions (Fisher 1989).

Children who do not have adequate postural reactions, body awareness, or motor planning skills to jump up and down in a linear fashion will quickly improve when enhanced proprioceptive input and joint compression are added to the activity.

Firmly place your hands on the child's hips. As the child jumps up, release the pressure. As the child jumps down, provide firm joint compression downward into the jumping surface. Maintain your hand hold on the child until you feel he is able to jump in a linear up-down motion. Step back and allow the child to enjoy his center of gravity.

Facilitation

The facilitation phase of treatment is the *heavy work* section. It is the time when the child exerts the greatest degree of effort and output. There is no clear division as to when preparation ends and facilitation begins. Make it a gradual transition that is governed by your observations of the child.

During this phase of treatment, focus on helping the child develop body scheme. He needs a working knowledge of how his body moves and is connected. The goal is to give him normal engrams so he can plan new movements in a coordinated fashion.

Engrams, motor patterns that provide motor instructions for the control of actions that do not require motor planning, may be characterized by motor incoordination and poorly planned and timed movements. To improve the child's motor coordination and engrams, we must address the underlying problem. We must improve the child's sensory awareness, sensory processing, and integration within the nervous system. This is accomplished by providing enhanced sensory input and grading the responses from total-body to discrete discriminating responses and sustained postures to activities that require timing, sequencing, and planning, facilitating the adaptive response and the just-right challenge (Koomar and Bundy 1991).

Enhancing Sensory Input Through Active Physical Involvement

Provide sensory input (deep-touch, proprioceptive, vibration, tactile input) through external means (for example, with textured or resistive equipment) or through internal resistance such as that provided by active, physical muscle exertion.

Internal resistance

This sensory input will reinforce how the child's extremities are connected to his trunk. The most effective form of resistance and deep-touch proprioceptive input is the child's own muscle effort. When the child exerts effort against gravity (his

ILLUSTRATION 12.3

Textured balls provide enhanced sensory feedback to increase the child's ability to register, motor plan, and coordinate needed movements.

Exploring the Spectrum of Autism and Pervasive Developmental Disorders

own body weight); or receives joint traction or compression from his own body or body weight; or exerts effort to control or maintain his balance, he is receiving intense, deep proprioceptive and deep-touch input that reinforces his body scheme. This input is similar to how developing babies master their bodies. They receive intense proprioceptive and deep-touch input through every joint and muscle, first lengthening their muscles, then activating them against gravity. Children with autism can gain a healthy body scheme through a similar method.

External resistance to body movements

Equipment and supplies also may provide enhanced sensory input and resistance to total-body movements, therefore reinforcing the child's awareness of his arms, legs, and trunk. Equipment may include weights, weighted vests, body socks, Thera-Band, neoprene or fabric tunnels, and Bungee cords. When using resistive equipment, the goal is to provide enhanced sensory feedback to help the child learn how and where their arms and legs are moving. When using external resistance, closely monitor the activity. The sensory input should be accurate and reinforce healthy engrams or motor movements, rather than erratic, uncoordinated movements.

Body Sock™. This stretchable sack, with hook-and-loop closures, provides resistance to arm and leg movements when the child actively stretches against the fabric. It also provides deep-touch pressure downward through the head, back, face, or chest areas, depending on the movements the child is performing.

At first, many children are afraid to get inside the body sock. They may need to have their feet placed in it and learn to feel the resistance on their feet. Soon they find pleasure from the activity and will allow the therapist to place it over their shoulders and eventually over the head. Some will need to have their faces exposed, while others will be comfortable as long as they know how to get out of the sock.

ILLUSTRATION 12.4
The Body Sock provides resistance to total-body movements, thus increasing the child's sensory awareness of his body's movements without allowing him to visually monitor those movements.

Once in the body sock, many children create elaborate games. Activities such as Simon Says, backward flips over a therapy ball, calisthenics, total-body motor planning activities while wearing the body sock, or ghost-walking (with arms and legs held out to their sides) are effective ways to provide resistance to arm, leg, or total-body movements.

Improving Slow, Sustained Postural Control

Prone extension

Prone extension can be facilitated most effectively in the hammock net swing, using linear vestibular input to further facilitate extension. Facilitate an adaptive response to promote sensory integration rather than to provide pure sensory stimulation. Position activities to further facilitate trunk, head, and neck extension while promoting visual attention to the task. The following are sample activities that can be used while in the net.

Bungee cord net swing game. Anchor a Bungee cord perpendicular or at a right angle to the net swing and directly beneath it. The cord must be low enough that the child will not catch his hands or feet when he swings over it. The child holds onto the Bungee cord and uses his arms to propel himself forward and backward. Take care that the child does not look down at the cord, because this may promote trunk flexion and result in the child getting his arms or feet caught in the cord. To avoid this, have the child focus on a spot ahead of him. The cord may be used in combination with other games (for example, basketball) or in sequencing more complex motor planning tasks.

Reaching net activities. Initial activities may focus on having the child actively reach and place objects while swinging in the net. Propel the child while he visually attends and focuses on the object he is to obtain.

IILLUSTRATION 12.5

The child uses a Bungee cord to propel himself. This strengthens postural extension and the shoulders and elbows. It also works to improve sustained visual attention and timing and sequencing of movements.

Exploring the Spectrum of Autism and Pervasive Developmental Disorders

Moving and reaching for a target requires motor planning (feedforward). Some children may not be able to comprehend the task while moving or be able to time or sequence their reach to secure the object. You may need to teach the task while the child is stationary. Progress to having the child swing forward, and stop him momentarily in midair so that he may reach and obtain the object. As the child masters the timing and sequencing, decrease assistance.

For variations, have the child swing forward and push bowling pins into a barrel or grab onto a bar held in extension.

Basketball net games. The child flies forward in the net hammock swing, reaches into extension to secure the ball, then throws it at a target as he comes forward. This requires sustaining head, neck, trunk, and arm extension; keeping the eyes visually fixated on a target; and timing, sequencing, and projected action sequence (feedforward), or motor planning.

Gradually increase the height of the target to facilitate greater extension. As the height is increased, the child's speed (or excursion) also must increase to enable him to see the target.

For variations, have the child throw balls at targets, reach for objects positioned near the ceiling, or place slap bracelets on a bar positioned in extension.

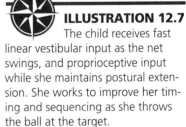
ILLUSTRATION 12.7
The child receives fast linear vestibular input as the net swings, and proprioceptive input while she maintains postural extension. She works to improve her timing and sequencing as she throws the ball at the target.

Scooterboard games. Sustained prone extension can be elicited on a scooterboard only if the arms are held off the ground into extension. Activities that require the child to propel the scooter will not facilitate tonic holding of the extensor muscles. Initially, he may need to hold onto a bar in order to obtain the proximal stability (shoulder control) required to hold his arms up against gravity. Holding onto a bar provides a distal point of stability from which he can activate the shoulder muscles. See Illustration 14.10.

The child may hold onto a bar or large plastic ring while you pull him down the scooterboard ramp or in a linear direction. While the child is being pulled, he receives traction to the shoulders, elbows, and hands, further facilitating a grasping and holding patterns.

Grade activities from providing the control to having the child actively participate. For variations, have the child hold a ring in both hands and place it on a cone at the end of the ramp; or have him hold a wand in both hands, parallel to the floor, to knock down a large foam block or wall.

As the child understands the task and obtains the proximal control needed, he may actively propel himself down the ramp, holding his arms into forward extension as he pushes over blocks, secures rings suspended in extension, and plays other games. See Illustration 14.15.

Supine flexion

While linear vestibular movement can facilitate postural extension, there is no special technique other than hard work that can promote trunk flexion. It often is easiest to begin facilitating total body flexion through phasic, transitory movements, and then progress into activities that promote tonic, sustained holding.

Head, neck, and eye flexion. For children who have very weak neck flexors that cannot hold against gravity, work to promote neck and trunk flexion with downward gaze. Gradually position the child so that he is working against gravity. By positioning the child on a moveable surface, such as a therapy ball, you can quickly increase the level of difficulty as he begins to demonstrate head and neck flexion. Activities may include working a small hand-held tape recorder and stringing beads that are positioned between his legs to facilitate increased trunk flexion with reach. While stabilizing the child at the hips, gradually move the ball backward so the child is working against gravity.

Sit-ups. Phasic supine flexion exercises for younger children include sit-up games. Have the child straddle your lap, facing you. Extend your legs and lower the child backward. Stabilize the child at the hips while he reaches for a toy or puzzle piece, secures it, then sits up and places it to either side. To assist the child, simply bend your knees or traction his pelvis in the direction of the sit-up. This is an excellent home activity. The child can sit up to whisper a secret or give the parent a hug or kiss.

Foot basketball. Elicit supine flexion by playing foot basketball. Position the child supine on either a low bench or the floor. The child takes large beach balls or lightweight balls with his feet and places them in a barrel over his head. This requires a balance of trunk flexion and extension to stabilize the trunk to prevent falling over to the side. If the child continues to fall to the side, encourage him to hold onto the bench or floor to assist in stabilizing the trunk. If additional assistance is needed, place your hand on the child's abdominal muscles to stabilize the lower trunk.

For variations, have two or three children lie on the floor with their heads positioned by the next child's feet. The first child picks up the ball with his feet and places it over his head onto the next child's feet.

Static supine flexion on a scooterboard. (See Illustration 14.10.) Securely anchor a rope across the room. The child lies supine (on his back) on the scooterboard, holds onto the rope with his hands, and crosses his ankles above the rope. Looking at the end of the rope near his feet, the child curls his chin and upper chest into flexion as he pulls himself along the rope. He must propel in the direction of his feet and must look in the same direction to promote flexion of the head, neck, and trunk. This game allows for imaginary play. The child may pretend to be crossing a mountain on a rope, being careful not to fall off the mountain; or he may try to save people (small balls or objects), carrying them to safety on another mountain.

Flexion disc or T-bar. Activities for these swings are described in Chapter 13.

Improving Slow, Sustained Pelvic and Shoulder Stability

Improved pelvic and shoulder stability can occur through most of the activities described above. In prone, when the arms are suspended in forward extension against gravity or the pelvis is extended against gravity with full hip extension, proximal strengthening occurs. Weight-bearing postures on the upper or lower extremities are excellent methods of increasing proximal stability of the pelvis and shoulders. Positioning the child in weight-bearing while on a moveable surface further increases the muscle control required, and therefore the internal stability.

Inflatable airmats. (See Illustrations 12.8 and 14.19.) The Southpaw® walrus, dolphin, and seal airmats are plastic inflatable cushions of different sizes. These are excellent for balance activities that promote graded arm control, shoulder and pelvic strengthening, and slow, sustained midrange postural control. The moveable surface enables the child to maintain developmental postures, such as quadruped, kneeling, tall kneeling, or half-kneeling. To increase the difficulty, either progress the child to higher developmental postures or make the activity more challenging. For example, while the child is in quadruped, have him raise a leg or an arm; or have him pick up and place objects in various locations, such as in a bucket or on a rope suspended from the ceiling.

A word of caution: When working with children on the whale or walrus, monitor closely to prevent falls. Thickly pad the area, or stabilize the equipment to prevent extremes of movements.

Peanut ball activities. Develop activities that require the child to assume tall kneeling or half-kneeling on the peanut ball. Provide linear vestibular input through bouncing, to facilitate increase joint co-contraction, and therefore stability. Grade the activity, having the child work first against a stable surface such as a wall, progressing to sustaining the posture in free space.

ILLUSTRATION 12.8
Balancing on the walrus, the child strengthens his pelvis and graded lower-extremity control. He strengthens his hands while using clamps to pick up objects. Proprioceptive input is provided by the dynamic surface of the walrus and through the resistive hand tools.

Glider swing. (See Illustrations 12.9, 14.20, 14.21, and 14.22.) This is a rectangular platform that provides linear movements. It is effective in maintaining various developmental postures on a moveable surface. Have the child propel the glider swing while in quadruped, tall kneel, half-kneel, or standing position. While the child is standing on the swing, use activities that require him to maintain midrange balance. For example, have the child pick up beads from the platform and string them, place clothespins on the ropes of the swing, or fish with a magnetic fishing pole with clothespins representing fish.

Scooterboard activities. Prone scooterboard activities to promote proximal strengthening must promote sustained gluteal control. In other words, the hips must be straight, with some arching of the back into extension. When the hips fall into flexion, sustained extension, and therefore pelvic stability, is lost. Activities in which the arms are sustained in forward extension also promote strengthening of the shoulders.

Improving the Ability to Narrow the Base of Support

The ability to narrow the base of support to stand on one foot, climb onto equipment, or balance while in slow motion requires postural extension and flexion as well as pelvic stability. Activities are described in Chapter 14. In general, activities that place the child in single-limb stance or tandem position are beneficial. Have the child stand with one foot supported on a step or ball; or have him stand tandem, heel to toe, while performing an activity. To increase the challenge, use a balance beam; or enhance the sensory feedback by having the child balance while standing on large foam blocks.

Grading Arm and Leg Movements

To improve the grading of arm and leg movement, work within the middle ranges. Grading arm and leg movement in free space (without a distal point of stability) requires more control than activities in which the hand or foot are stabilized against a surface (that is, a distal point of stability is provided). To improve the ability to grade arm and leg movement, begin by working against resistance throughout the middle ranges with a distal point of stability, and progress to working the extremity against resistance in space. Resistance may be provided through the child's own body weight, by pushing against resistance, or by using weights or weighted equipment.

Graded arm control

To improve graded arm movements, resistance is provided throughout the middle ranges of both shoulder and elbow movements while the hand is stabilized.

- Propel a glider swing in quadruped to knock over blocks or objects

- Push a heavy ball through a cloth or stretchable fabric tunnel (See Illustration 12.11.)

- Perform an activity while weight-bearing on the upper extremities with legs supported on a surface

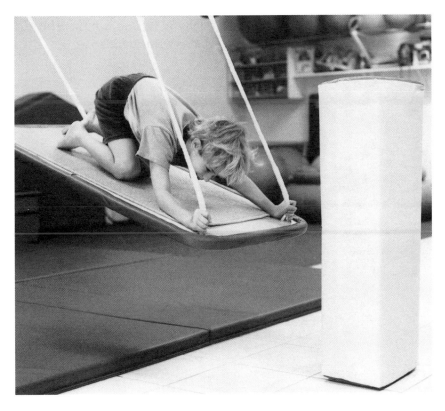

ILLUSTRATION 12.9
Graded arm control and proximal stability are strengthened as the child motor plans to have the glider swing knock over the block.

ILLUSTRATION 12.10

Weight-bearing and resistive upper-extremity activities provide proprioceptive input; strengthen the shoulders, elbows, and hands; and can have a calming effect.

Graded lower-extremity control

To improve graded lower extremity control, the knee must be worked through the middle ranges. This may occur by having the child:

- Ascend or descend stairs or high inclines such as ramps

- Balance while standing on a platform swing

- Propel a glider swing while standing with one foot in front of the other

- Push a heavy ball through a cloth or stretchable fabric tunnel. The child must be in tall-kneeling position to push the ball through.

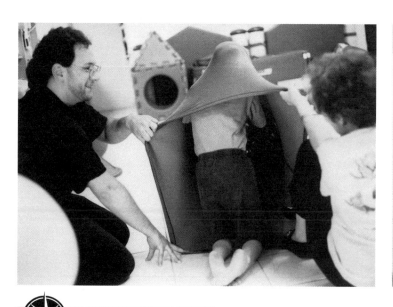

ILLUSTRATION 12.11
As the child pushes a therapy ball through the stretchable tunnel, graded arm and leg movements are facilitated and deep-touch input and total-body resistance are provided.

Improving Total-Body Awareness and Motor Control

This involves using improved static motor control for dynamic activities. It requires dynamic internal body awareness and the ability to adapt to the environment.

Function

In the function phase of treatment, work is concentrated on improving the child's total-body motor control and awareness; and the timing, sequencing, and coordination of motor movements. While this is the final phase of treatment, it also should be considered the starting point. When designing the child's individualized program, be aware of the child's functional goal. What functional activities does he need to improve in? Set up a general treatment progression designed to have an impact on these areas, set up the environment, and guide the child through them. Functional total-body activities include:

- Dressing activities: putting on and taking off shoes, socks, shirt, pants

- Age-appropriate gross motor tasks

- Standing on one foot, hopping

- Galloping or skipping

- Riding a bicycle

- Dressing independently

- Catching, throwing, or hitting a ball

- Sports-related activities such as roller-blading, baseball, basketball

 Improving Fine Motor Control

Fine motor problems are characterized by a lack of sensory awareness, low scores on sensory tests, decreased coordination and skilled tool usage, and functional hand problems when vision is occluded. Children who have fine motor difficulties secondary to poor somatosensory processing look clumsy and awkward in their hand and arm movements. They tend to use their fingers as a unit rather than in isolation, avoid fine motor tasks altogether; or be very good at fine motor tasks when allowed to use vision to guide movements, but unable to function when vision is occluded.

The underlying problem is decreased somatosensory processing with decreased sensory awareness of the fingers and how they are moving. Secondary functional and motor control problems also may be present; however, they are secondary and a direct result of poor sensory awareness.

Problems that have an impact on fine motor control and require intervention include:

- Poor somatosensory processing of sensory information with

  — Decreased fine motor control when vision is occluded

  — Decreased haptic exploration of objects

  — Decreased ability to imitate finger postures (motor planning skills)

- Low muscle tone and an underresponsive system

- Slow, sustained postural control

- Shoulder and scapular instability

- Grading of arm movements and pressure exerted to play with toys, write, or perform skilled hand movements

- Isolated finger control and haptic exploration

- Thumb abduction and prehension

- In-hand manipulation (especially when vision is eliminated)

  — Translation of the object from the finger to the palm, or palm to finger

  — Shifting the object between or among the fingers

  — Rotation of the object

- Timing and sequencing of arm or finger movements

- Skilled tool usage (using a pencil, scissors, spoon, fork)

Preparation

During the preparation phase of treatment, we must lay the sensorimotor foundation skills that the child needs to function. This is continued and intensified during the facilitation phase. If the child is underresponsive and displays low tone, the preparation phase must focus on increasing the child's level of arousal, basal resting state of muscle tone, and ability to register somatosensory information. Facilitation techniques are required to wake up the child's system and prepare him for function. Concentrate sensory input on using deep-touch pressure, proprioception, and vibratory and tactile sensory input, with the goal of activating the DCML system.

Massages

Deep pressure or lotion massages to the extremities provide deep-touch pressure, joint traction, and compression. Use toweling techniques to activate the tactile receptors.

Myofascial Release Techniques

During the preparation phase, address secondary muscle shortening and muscle tightness as a method of preparing the child for improved ability to function. This usually involves techniques to elongate the muscles within the hands and forearm, molding the arches of the hand and elongating the muscles that prohibit full thumb abduction. These techniques are very effective in promoting sensory awareness and biomechanical alignment of the muscles within the hands. Advanced training in these myofascial release techniques is necessary. For additional information, read *Improving Upper Body Control* by Regi Boehme, OTR; or contact the Neuro-Developmental Treatment Association (1550 S. Coast Highway, Suite 201, Laguna Beach, California (1–800–869–9295); (www.ndta.org).

ILLUSTRATION 12.12

Deep lotion massages, myofascial release techniques, and toweling can elongate shortened muscles while stimulating the tactile and proprioceptive nerve endings to increase sensory awareness of the hands or feet.

Sensory-Based Activities

Use enhanced sensory activities to activate the deep-touch and proprioceptive receptors. Because the child is underresponsive to touch and may not register sensory information at the normally accepted intensity, you must either exercise creativity in enhancing the sensory input or follow the child's lead. He will show you what he likes, what he registers, and what is integrating. Activities include:

- **Southpaw® Sensory Shaker, sand or rice box activities, and foam box activities**. For descriptions, see Chapter 12 (see Illustration 12.1).

- **Ball pool**. The child emerges himself in the ball pool. Hide a toy at the bottom and have the child find the toy. The child must move the arms when in the pool.

- **Beads**. Buckets of Mardi Gras beads provide an excellent form of tactile input. Have the child begin by rubbing beads across his hands and fingers. Progress to a tug-of-war game that facilitates isolated finger control.

Muscle Tone, Arousal, and Slow, Sustained Postural Control

Children who exhibit low muscle tone and low arousal levels may need linear vestibular input against gravity to warm up their muscles and begin developing slow, sustained postural control. This may be accomplished through the following activities:

- **Net hammock swing activities**. See Chapter 12, Illustrations 12.5, 12.6, and 12.7. These work the anti-gravity extensor muscles while using linear vestibular to facilitate the extension. They also facilitate head, neck, and trunk stability needed for functional hand skills and stabilization of the eyes.

- **Peanut ball activities; Trampoline activities**. For descriptions, see Chapter 12, Illustration 12.2.

Facilitation

During the facilitation phase of treatment, continue to provide enhanced sensory input while helping the child connect his hands and arms to his body. Progress from total-body treatment that requires less-discriminating responses, to more skilled discrete responses of the hands and upper extremities. The child must actively adapt to the demands, progressing from general responses with enhanced sensory input, to very specific discriminating responses. Gradually decrease the enhanced feedback as the child registers and processes the sensory information.

Facilitation may need to address basic postural control. Sustained attention and postural control will be necessary for any functional hand task. You may need to emphasize both slow, sustained extension, using linear vestibular input to facilitate postural extension, and sustained flexion of the head, neck, and trunk.

Shoulder Stability and Graded Arm Control

Improving shoulder stability and the ability to graded arm movements is important to enhance functional hand skills. Children with decreased shoulder stability have difficulty controlling their arms away from their bodies. Often they use compensatory techniques, such as hiking the shoulders in extreme shoulder elevation to provide needed stability. This position provides biomechanical stability and compensates for weak shoulder and scapular muscles. Shoulder instability and difficulty grading arm movements often are caused by underlying low muscle tone as well as poor proprioceptive monitoring of arm movements. If the child does not use compensatory techniques, he may exhibit subtle tremors of the hands or overshooting of the arm as he tries to control his arms away from his body. To enhance proprioceptive feedback and provide greater mechanical stability for the shoulder, begin activities with the hand stabilized against a table, floor, or wall. Weight-bearing activities provide distal stabilization of the hands.

Weight bearing on the arms or working the arms within the middle ranges against resistance will improve the child's ability to grade movements. During these activities, monitor for poor alignment and positioning. Avoid having the child weight-bear in the following positions:

- On the metacarpophalangeal (MP) joints of the fingers with the fingers hyperextended, thus overstretching the ligaments of the fingers

- On a fisted hand with wrist locked in extension

- On the back of the hand

- With elbow hyperextension, which indicates that the muscles controlling the elbow are inactive

- With shoulders in extreme internal or external rotation

If these occur, modify the activity and provide more assistance to increase the child's active participation during the activities. Look for active elbow control with the hands flat on the weight-bearing surface. Also look for muscle activation within the hands. This is observed when the child's fingers push into the weight-bearing surface, often causing the fingertips to turn white.

Weight-bearing activities with enhanced proprioceptive input usually are pleasurable. Resistance and enhanced proprioceptive input are provided through the child's own body weight or by pushing against resistance. Be sure the child's hands are solidly planted on a surface, providing a distal point of stability and resistance throughout the middle ranges or at the shoulder. This may occur by having the child:

- Propel a glider swing in quadruped to knock over blocks or objects (See Illustration 12.9.)

- Perform weight bearing while in quadruped position on a walrus inflatable cushion (See Illustration 14.19.)

- Push a heavy ball through a cloth or stretchable fabric tunnel. (See Illustration 12.11.) The child must be in tall kneeling in order to push the ball through the tunnel.

- Perform activities while bearing weight on the upper extremities with legs supported on a surface. (See Illustration 12.10.)

- Play resistive scooterboard activities. Sit on the scooterboard, and have the child lie prone across your lap. The child propels the scooterboard. Your hands are free to stabilize the child at the rib cage and provide more or less assistance as needed, or to change the angle of the child's body to promote different ranges of elbow flexion or extension.

- Net hammock swing activities, using a Bungee cord to propel it. This activity promotes grading of elbow movement while facilitating sustained postural extension. (See Illustration 12.5.)

- Use therapy putty on the wall or floor

ILLUSTRATION 12.13

The child is stabilized proximally to generate greater force and proprioceptive while she pushes the putty, thus strengthening her shoulders and elbows and providing deep-touch input to her hands.

Encourage the child to push the putty with both hands to flatten it out. If the putty is placed on the floor, the child's body weight and gravity will provide a natural resistance. However, if it is placed on a wall, the child's shoulder girdle may need to be stabilized to enable him to generate sufficient force and added proprioceptive input. If the child is small, sit close behind him and let him push back into your body for the needed stability. When working with older children, provide manual stabilization to the child's back as the child pushes.

Age-appropriate games and activities

Choose games and activities that provide resistance through the middle or entire elbow range of motion, and help the child develop the graded arm control he needs. Use number and alphabet games that require the child to hold a toy with one hand and operate a lever with the other. These provide a distal point of stability (the child's hand is on the lever) and resistance through the middle ranges of elbow flexion.

Graded arm activities in free space

Often, this is very difficult for children with somatosensory problems. Working in free space does not provide sensory feedback from the muscles (proprioceptive awareness) or the proximal stability needed to complete skilled arm movements. The child may need to visually monitor his arm as it moves. If the activity is difficult or challenging, the child can no longer monitor the arms, but must concentrate on the hands or the activity. When this occurs, tremoring or overshooting of the arms may occur. Using resistive activities may enhance the child's feedback, and therefore internal awareness, as he moves his arm through space. Adding resistance and making the task harder actually may make the task easier for the child. Gradually decrease resistance as the child develops greater sensory awareness and internal muscle control. Activities may be made resistive by applying:

- Manual resistance. Develop games in which the child pushes you or objects against resistance.

- Weights. Attach light weights at the child's shoulder or wrist.

- Resistance to the activity. As resistance is applied within the hand, as is required when using resistive clothespins, the child may generate increased muscle effort within the forearm, thus generating increased proprioceptive awareness.

Isolated Finger Control and Haptic Exploration

Isolated finger control and haptic exploration of objects can be facilitated simultaneously. Isolated finger control often is tested in its purest form through opposition of the thumb to each consecutive finger. Stutsman (1948) studied children's thumb-to-finger opposition and found that this task was difficult for children under 3 years of age, but could be completed effectively by children 3 years and older. Isolated finger control plays a major part in the development of more complex hand skills. The following are examples of activities that will develop isolated finger control and haptic exploration.

Textured pulling games. Isolated index-finger control and two-point pinch often develop when children pull toys through their fingers and out of their hands. Beginning isolated finger control and pinch can be facilitated through games such as tug-of-war. For example, have the child grab colorful Mardi Gras beads as you pull them through his hands. The child receives intense tactile input into the palm while index-finger separation and thumb abduction begins to occur. Provide traction to reinforce forearm supination and prehension. As the child attempts to pull the beads from you, steady proprioceptive input is provided throughout the arms.

Resistive mediums. Therapy putty provides both proprioceptive and deep-touch input. Hide plastic bugs in the putty, and have the child work his hands in the putty to find the objects. Monitor carefully to assure that resistance is applied to the thumb. The thumb must work in abduction and opposition and not reinforce thumb adduction (thumb to the side of the index finger). Observe how the child removes objects from the putty. If he digs into the putty with only the fingers and not the thumb, or pinches the thumb in adduction against the index finger, modify the activity. Use a putty that provides lighter resistance, use larger objects to hide in it, or reposition the putty on a different surface such as an easel or wall.

Sensory boxes. Fill a box with foam pieces, rice, or other tactile media. Hide three-dimensional toys or objects inside the box. Tape the box shut so that only one hand (not both hands) can get inside. Have the child reach inside the box and retrieve objects. He will receive enhanced tactile and deep-touch input while improving his discrimination skills.

The child may need a duplicate set of objects outside of the box to visually cue him about the object he is looking for inside the box.

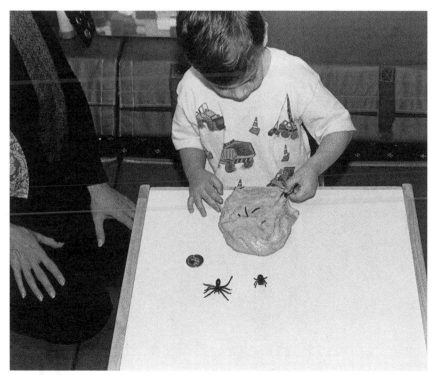

ILLUSTRATION 12.14
Objects hidden in resistive therapy putty provide enhanced proprioceptive input to strengthen the thumb and fingers and reinforce a mature prehension pattern.

The child must develop the ability to discriminate the shapes and textures of objects by touch. This becomes difficult if vision cannot be occluded and the sensory box is large, such as in a large pool of rice or beans or in a ball pool. Large rice buckets and ball pools provide good sensory stimulation, but are less effective for developing sensory discrimination, a higher-level skill.

Ball pools or the Southpaw Sensory Shaker (see Illustration 12.1) can develop the child's discriminatory skills if the activity requires the child to tactilely discriminate between the balls and other objects hidden at the bottom of the pool.

As the objects sink from view, the child is forced to rely on his tactile sense rather than vision, while simultaneously receiving valuable deep-touch input from the balls surrounding his body and arms. Requiring the child to discriminate between the hard balls and objects hidden at the bottom will help develop size, texture, and shape discrimination. Objects may include:

- Soft kick-balls

- Crumpled paper

- Two-inch balls mixed in with three-inch balls

- Small stuffed animals

- Vibrating toys or pens

- Textured balls

Fill a bucket with rice or beans, blindfold the child, and ask him to find hidden toys or objects in the bucket. To further develop the child's discrimination skills, progress from large toys to smaller, abstract shapes. Have the child describe or name the object he found in the rice while his vision is occluded.

ILLUSTRATION 12.15

The ball pool provides opportunities for deep-touch pressure, total-body resistance, and enhanced tactile discrimination. The child searches and retrieves hidden toys without using vision.

Coordination exercises increase isolated finger control, such as paper crumpling with one hand.

Tactile discrimination and haptic exploration games. Many commercially available games challenge the child's tactile discrimination skills while eliminating vision. Some examples include:

- Southpaw Tactile Activity Kit. This kit contains 50 wooden shapes, 25 shape cards, and an activity box. The child looks at a picture of an object and tries to find the object inside the box that matches the picture.

- Southpaw Textured Dominoes. This game contains 28 dominoes with seven different textures. The children play dominoes by matching the textures.

- Tactilo. The game contains 25 wooden shapes, five Bingo-type boards with the shapes reproduced on them, and a bag to hide the shapes. The children take turns reaching into the bag and identifying the objects on their game cards by feeling them.

Developing Thumb Abduction and Prehension

Developing thumb abduction becomes important in obtaining a pinch and developing more complex hand skills. Many children with underresponsiveness to somatosensory input experience weakness and instability throughout the hands, especially the thumb. Common problems observed include:

- Instability throughout the carpometacarpal (CMC) joint of the thumb with hyperextension

- Shortening throughout the web space of the thumb, preventing thumb from full abduction, and interferes with the ability to functionally oppose the index finger

- Weakness throughout the hands, with decreased in-hand manipulation skills

By approximately 12 months of age, lengthening of the muscles throughout the thumb normally occurs as the child shifts weight over the base of the thumb and vaults over the arm, hand, and thumb in a diagonal pattern. Internal stability is established as the muscles react into the surface or floor as the child moves in and out of quadruped and sitting.

Because of impaired sensory processing, many children with autism do not spend quality time in quadruped. Their hands and feet have little meaning to them, and their movements are limited in quantity and quality. Many skip quadruped altogether, moving quickly from sitting to standing to running. This often results in weakness and instability not only throughout the hands, but also in the entire upper extremity. Activities that focus on increasing the child's ability to use the hands must address both the diminished sensory processing as well as the instability that may be observed within the hands.

Treatment activities first must provide the needed length to the muscles. This can be accomplished by manually elongating the muscles and fascia, as in the myofascial release techniques, or through quality weight-bearing activities with enhanced sensory input. Then, intervention must provide both enhanced sensory feedback and strengthening in order to develop the needed internal stability.

Quadruped

The most natural way of developing thumb abduction is through the quadruped position. Activities that activate the balance reactions within the hand, while using gravity and body weight as resistance, can help develop both the length and internal stability needed throughout the base of the thumb. Working in quadruped on a moveable surface, such as the inflatable whale cushion, will challenge older children while strengthening their hands.

Tool usage

Most children are fascinated with tools. Tools often have a built-in resistance that provides enhanced sensory input while reinforcing thumb opposition. Provide resistance to all activities and games that involve tools; and combine tool use with other total-body and balance challenges. Use the following tools to strengthen the thumb and reinforce thumb abduction.

Resistive clothespins. Rolyan® Graded Pinch Exercisers are clothespins that are color coded according to the amount of resistance they provide. Most children begin with clothespins that have a one-pound resistance and quickly move up to two- and three-pound resistances. The child's thumb must be abducted on the clothespin, rather than adducted against the side of the index finger.

Escargot clamps. These tongs provide almost two pounds of resistance. The tip of the thumb must be positioned on one side of the handle with the other four fingertips positioned in abduction against it. This will strengthen the thumb in abduction, rather than reinforce adduction.

Long-handled tea bag holders. Have the child hold the handle in a manner similar to the escargot clamps.

Olive pickers. Stabilize the tool between the index finger and middle finger while the thumb depresses the plunger to open the clamp. This tool provides excellent thumb opposition with minimal to moderate resistance.

A. Tongs

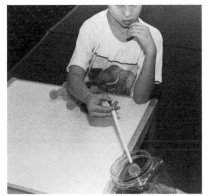
B. Olive picker

C. Escargot clamp

ILLUSTRATION 12.16

Resistive tools provide enhanced sensory input while developing strength and internal stability in the thumb for opposition. This is necessary for prehension as well as pencil and scissor control.

Pickle picker. This tool is operated in the same way as the olive picker; however, it provides more resistance. The appearance of this tool as a mechanical claw promotes creative play.

Thumb punch. This hand-held paper punch is operated by compression between the thumb and the index finger. It can be purchased at most craft stores in a variety of patterns.

Function

Developing In-Hand Manipulation Skills

Children are born with the drive to reach out and explore their physical world. By 12 months, infants have mastered a neat pincer grasp and are able to pick up small objects using the tips of the fingers. This pincer grasp must change to a manipulative pattern for true hand skills to develop. Toddlers do more than just grasp or pick up objects with a pincer grasp; they begin to manipulate objects in their fingers. When an infant picks up a cereal piece, he does so with a pincer grasp (between the thumb and index finger); but when he is given several pieces, he picks them up in a fist and puts them all in his mouth. A toddler also will pick up all of them and hold many in his hand while manipulating one out of the group to put in his mouth. *In-hand manipulation* is a term identified by Exner (1989) to describe the movement of an object within one hand.

Exner (1990) further states that in-hand manipulation develops in order to allow for more efficient placement of the object in the hand for use, placement of the object, or for voluntary release. She describes five basic types of in-hand manipulation skills.

Finger-to-palm translation. Moving an object from the finger pads to the palm of the hand. For example, pick up a coin or several coins, and one by one place them in your hand. This is an easier skill and requires the fingers to move as a unit (extrinsic muscles within the hands).

Palm-to-finger translation. Moving an object from the palm to the finger pads. For example, hold several coins in your hand and remove one coin to place it in a slot. This is a more complex skill that requires the manipulation of the object by the thumb and fingers (intrinsic muscles within the hands).

Shift. Using the finger pads to produce a slight linear adjustment of the object.

Simple rotation. Rotating an object by using the thumb in opposition to the fingers. The fingers usually act as a unit, and the object usually is rotated less than 180 degrees. This occurs when you pick up a peg in your fingertips, but need to rotate its orientation to place it in a pegboard.

Complex rotation. Rotating an object 180 degrees by using differentiation of finger movements and active thumb movements. This occurs when you pick up a pen and rotate it for placement in your hand for writing.

In-hand manipulation skills are necessary for all skilled functional hand movements. Children need them for fastening buttons and snaps, picking up cards or small pegs and placing them in a pegboard, turning pages of a magazine, or taking crayons from a container and placing them back in. They are necessary for placing and adjusting cubes when stacking, removing, and replacing small bottle lids, maneuvering puzzle pieces, putting a key in a lock, holding a pencil, and writing.

In a study completed by Exner (1990), at least 50% of the children ages 18 months to 2 years were able to perform simple in-hand manipulation skills (for example, simple rotation and moving a peg from the fingers to the palm for storage, then moving it back to the fingers). Toddlers begin to experiment with in-hand manipulation skills such as picking up and storing several small objects in one hand. By 3 years, these functions improve as they gain more control over the movements of individual fingers and refine the force of their grip. The development of complex in-hand manipulation and object rotation occurs between the ages of 3 and 6 years of age as children gain control over the intrinsic muscles of their hands. A dynamic tripod grasp begins to emerge after 3 years of age (Rosenbloom and Horton 1971), and complex object rotation after 4 years.

In-hand manipulation skills require intact tactile abilities, isolated finger control, and the development of intrinsic muscle control within the hands. A child can compensate for impaired tactile awareness through using vision as he reaches for an object. However, once the object is in the child's hands, he must rely on the tactile system to guide the object within his hand. The tactile system also helps the child determine how much pressure to use in the hand when picking up or holding an object. A tendency to use too much force when holding an object or the tendency to drop objects out of the hands may indicate tactile and/or motor control difficulties.

Prerequisite sensory and motor skills must be addressed as you work on improving in-hand manipulation skills. Sample functional activities include using one hand for:

- Finger-to-palm translation, to

    — Pick up several coins and one by one place them in your hand.

    — Pick up small discs or game pieces and nest them in your hand.

- Palm-to-finger translation, to

    — Retrieve coins that are stored in your hand, and one by one place them in a bank or slot.

    — Retrieve small discs or game pieces from your palm, and place them on the gameboard.

- Simple rotation, to

    — Pick up a peg in your fingertips and rotate its orientation to place it in a pegboard

    — Separate thin pages of a book

    — Turn a bead in your fingers to orient the hole for stringing

    — Walk your fingers down a pencil to adjust your grip

- Complex rotation, to

    — Pick up a pen and rotate it for placement in your hand for writing

    — Turn over pennies

    — Pick up a small bottle lid and rotate it to place it correctly on the bottle

    — Rotate puzzle pieces to place them correctly

- Other tasks, to
  - Fasten snaps and buttons
  - Write using translation or intrinsic movements of the fingers (dynamic tripod grasp)

Skilled Tool Usage and Adaptive Equipment

Children must acquire skills on multiple levels simultaneously. Functional home- or school-related tasks must be developed while the child masters the sensorimotor skills that make these tasks easier. Providing adaptive equipment and enhanced sensory input can help make difficult tasks easier for the child.

Incline boards

Incline boards may be beneficial during writing and many fine motor activities. They slant from a 45-degree angle to approximately 85 degrees. The paper or fine motor task is attached to the board.

By elevating the child's work onto a vertical or semi-vertical plane

- Fewer postural demands are made on the child. When using an 85-degree incline board, the child sits in an erect posture. There is little resistance from gravity, and the child may grasp the side of the board to help him maintain his posture while performing fine motor tasks. This may prevent the child from lying on the desk or falling out of the chair during fine motor tasks.

- Visual attention to the task is maximized. By minimizing postural demands and taking the physical strain off the trunk, neck, and head, the eyes are freer for visual scanning and convergence to the task. A 45-degree incline board will minimize visual and postural strain.

- The child's hands are brought into his visual field to help him monitor his movements.

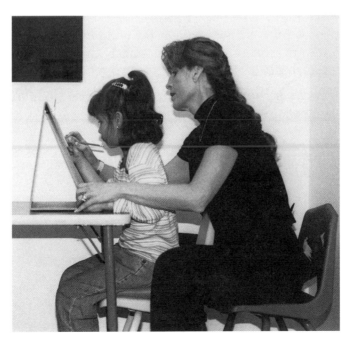

ILLUSTRATION 12.17

The child uses an incline board to improve her writing posture, stabilize the ulnar aspect of her hand, and facilitate a dynamic tripod pencil grasp.

- The child's arms and hand movements oppose gravity, thereby enhancing proprioceptive feedback through the hands, arms, and fingers. The higher the incline, the greater the feedback.

- The wrist is forced into extension, which helps activate the intrinsic muscles of the hands. Wrist extension is necessary for arching in the hand, ulnar radial separation, and radial hand control. Therefore, for skilled movements of the first three fingers (as in tracing or writing), the wrist must be extended. The 85-degree incline provides the greatest degree of stability.

- The child is biomechanically in a better position for developing the internal stability within the upper extremities that is needed for writing tasks. Use of an incline board can help the child develop internal stability in the forearm; eliminate a pronated grasp; develop a static tripod grasp and ulnar-radial separation in the hand; and, eventually, increase stability within the hand.

  — **Developing stability in the forearm**. It is very difficult for a child to scribble or color on an 85-degree incline with the forearm pronated. Biomechanically, it is difficult and uncomfortable. Reposition the tool or crayon in the child's hand so the forearm is in neutral rotation. The hand may be fisted. Encourage the child to scribble or color.

  — **Developing a static tripod grasp**. As the child colors using a fisted forearm neutral position on an 85-degree incline board, the resistance on the tip of the crayon will pull the crayon out of the child's hand into a tripod grasp.

  — **Developing ulnar radial separation of the hand**. When children consistently use a static tripod grasp for writing or tracing tasks, the next goal is to develop a dynamic tripod grasp, which requires stabilization of the ulnar aspect of the hand. Working on an 85-degree incline board, the child's arm will become fatigued. The child will rest the ulnar aspect of the hand on the incline board for added stability. This will suppress the ulnar aspect of the hand while the radial aspect (first three fingers) is actively writing.

Decrease the use of the incline board as the child develops the internal stability within the hands to function with less assistance. Gradually move the child from the 85-degree incline to a 45-degree incline, to a regular table.

Incline boards can be purchased or made. The instructions for making an adjustable incline board from a pizza box follow.

Slant-top (pizza box) writing board

Materials
Clean pizza box
Tape
Ruler
Craft knife
2 pieces of cardboard, 12″ square
1 piece of cardboard, 3″ square (or 4″ square)
2 pieces of board, 12″x 3″
Plain adhesive plastic
Optional: Decorative adhesive plastic

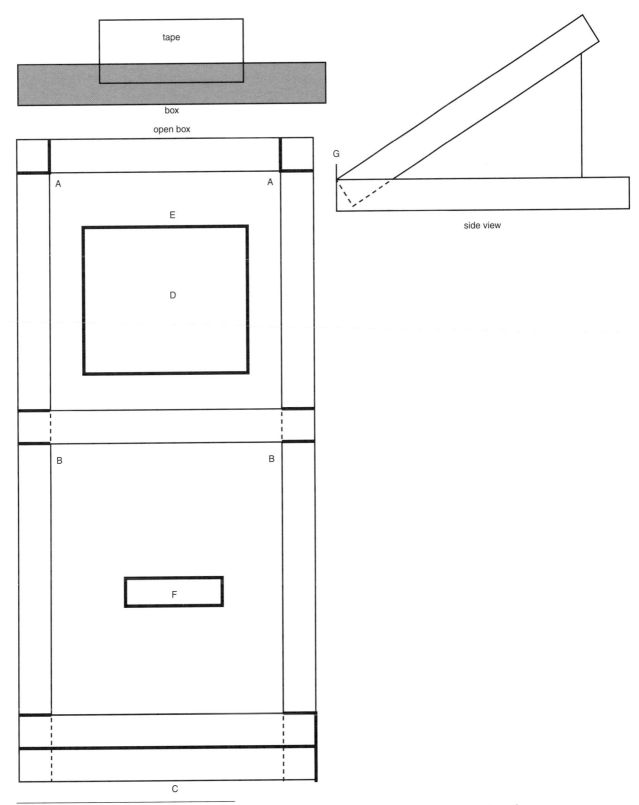

tape

box

open box

A   E   A

D

B   B

F

C

G

side view

This slant-top writing board was designed by Elizabeth A. Hagy, OTR/L, from the Occupational Therapy Class of 1995, Nova Southeastern University. The instructions and pattern are reprinted by permission.

Instructions

In almost every place where tape is used, lay it along the length of the surface-not across it. (See drawing.)

1. **Assemble the stand**. With printed side of the pizza box down, fold in on all scored lines. Along the double lines on the front bottom of the box, fold in twice over the tabs from the sides (C).

    Cut 8 pieces of tape 3 to 4 inches long. Line these up on the edge of the table so they are ready to pick up. Hold together a top front corner (A), and tape it on the outside with one piece of tape. Fold another piece of tape and fold it in half so the sticky side is out. Place the fold of the tape into the corner of the box, and smooth the two sides of the tape outward. Repeat on the other top front corner and the two back bottom corners (B) to reinforce them.

2. **Reinforce the writing surface and make the stand**. To reinforce the writing surface and make the stand. Cut two pieces of cardboard approximately 12 inches square. Lay one of these into the inside of the lid (D). Center it and tape it securely in place around all four sides. Lay the other piece (the stand) along edge E, and tape it all the way down that edge. Flip the stand back on itself and tape the other side the same way.

3. **Make the brace**. Cut a 3-inch or 4-inch square of cardboard. Fold it in half. Lay it inside the bottom of the box at F like a little tent. Tape the two long sides to the bottom of the box.

4. **Make the raised lip**. Cut a 12-inch by 3-inch piece of cardboard. Tape it to the upright edge at the lower end of the slant (G in side view).

5. **Finish the writing board**. Cover the writing surface with plain adhesive plastic to cut down on visual distraction. Optional: Cover the remaining sides with decorative adhesive plastic.

Scissors and cutting tasks

Scissors may need to be modified to facilitate ulnar-radial separation. Children may demonstrate poor stabilization of the ulnar aspect of the hand by cutting with the fingers flaring into extension as they open the scissors, and the fingers fisting into flexion as they close the scissors. Scissors need to be operated only by the first three fingers, allowing the ring and little finger to curl under to stabilize the hand.

Mary Benbow has designed scissors that are small, lightweight, and easily used to develop cutting and control within the hands. These learning scissors, referred to as Benbow Learning Scissors, are manufactured and sold by OT Ideas, Inc., 124 Morris Turnpike, Randolph, NJ 07869 (973-895-3622); (otideas@nac.net).

If the ulnar aspect of the hand continues to flare into extension as the scissors open, external stabilization may be needed. To stabilize the hand, place a makeup sponge or a small piece of therapy putty in the child's hand under the fourth and fifth fingers. Older children do well when you place a penny under their fourth and fifth fingers and ask them to cut without dropping the penny.

You may want to copy cutting activities onto thicker paper. This will provide the child with enhanced sensory feedback, and the resistance will make the task easier for the child.

Pencil grips

Because of decreased sensory awareness, some children have difficulty positioning their fingers correctly on the pencil. Pencil grips will provide needed tactile feedback and help them activate the appropriate muscles within their hands for writing tasks. As the child gains control over the pencil and his hands, gradually decrease the use of grips.

Common grips used include:

- **Thē Pencil Grip™**. This large, pear-shaped rubber grip is indented on three sides. It provides easy approximation into a tripod grasp. It is an excellent grip for helping a child transition from a fisted grasp or thumb-loop pattern to static tripod grasp.

- **Stetro™ Grip**. This small, molded plastic grip has grooves for the fingertips. It is an excellent grip for helping the child transition from a static tripod prehension to a dynamic tripod pattern. The child must be able to stabilize the thumb in abduction into the molded pad; otherwise, he will adduct over the grip.

- **Cushioned grips**. These textured cushions that fit onto the pencil are available for the child who has a static or dynamic tripod grasp, but does not have the sensory awareness to maintain the fingers correctly on the pencil. A rubber band also may be wrapped around the pencil, just above the pencil tip. This will provide the child with tactile input as to the correct placement of the fingers on the pencil.

Enhanced sensory input

Fine motor activities must have enhanced sensory input. Activities that do not provide sensory input either will be difficult for the child to perform or will require the child to visually monitor his hands. Select fine motor activities for the inherent resistance they provide. If the activity does not provide inherent resistance or

ILLUSTRATION 12.18
Resistive clothespins strengthen the opposition pattern while promoting proprioceptive input (enhanced sensory feedback) to the hands and fingers.

sensory feedback, modify it to provide some form of sensory feedback. Enhanced sensory feedback can be proprioceptive or vibratory in nature. For example:

- Use vibrating pens for writing exercises.

- Place sandpaper under the writing surface for enhanced tactile-proprioceptive input. Sandpaper may be graded from course for beginning coloring, to extra fine for cursive writing.

- Use regular clothespins or resistive clothespins with one-pound to three-pound or higher resistance.

- Use balls that are textured, weighted, or scented.

- Encourage the child to play resistive games such as alphabet or number games that require the child to hold a toy with one hand and push a lever with the other; hammer-type pop-up toys, and resistive manipulative games.

Improving Oral Motor Control

Oral motor problems are characterized by low muscle tone, lack of active muscle activation, and difficulty in speaking and eating. The underlying problem is decreased sensory awareness (proprioceptive and tactile). A child who has oral motor problems (speech and eating difficulties) because of decreased somatosensory processing will be unable to visually monitor his movements. This makes it difficult to compensate for decreased sensory awareness. The child will have no idea of how to move the muscles of his face or mouth, how to position his tongue, or how to manipulate food in his mouth.

Sensory-based oral motor problems are never seen in isolation, but are part of the child's total-body sensory-processing problems. As the child improves in somatosensory discrimination, so will his speech and eating. However, direct intervention will expedited the child's progress and confidence. The child may have difficulty with:

- Low facial muscle tone characterized by paucity of facial expressions and muscle tone in the face, lips, and cheeks

- Chin tuck and sustained neck flexion contributing to decreased stability of the base of the tongue and jaw, resulting in difficulty isolating and grading tongue and jaw movements

- Activating the cheeks, lips, tongue, or oral muscles for

  — Blowing kisses

  — Blowing toys

  — Sucking through a straw

  — Articulating sounds

  — Vocal play

  — Moving food around the mouth

  — Maintaining lip closure and preventing drooling

- Grading jaw movements and pressure

- Sequencing and timing of oral musculature

- Speech

- Eating

Intervention strategies follow the sequence of preparation, facilitation, then function. Functional goals are always related to improved speech production or eating skills. Preparation activities are directed toward increasing the child's muscle tone through vestibular-based total-body activities, progressing to tactile-based activities directly applied to the face to improve muscle tone and sensory awareness.

Facial massages that use deep-touch input and minimal lotion are an excellent form of preparation that children usually enjoy. Massages serve as a bonding experience and may form the basis of a trusting relationship. Appropriate candidates include those children who are underresponsive to tactile-proprioceptive sensory input, lack facial expression, have low facial tone and weak or garbled speech, or have decreased movement of the tongue or oral musculature.

Apply a small amount of lotion to your hands to help them glide smoothly across the child's skin. Seat the child on your lap facing away from you, with the child facing a mirror. Gently stroke the child's face. Whenever possible, direct the firm pressure in the direction of the hair growth. Start at the child's midline and work out to the sides across the cheeks. Firmly and consistently move your hands across the bridge of the nose and out to the side. Provide deep-touch pressure under the nose and gently traction in the direction of lip closure. Around the lips, direct the pressure toward lip closure.

In this position, you also can provide gentle but firm compressions through the child's shoulders, head, or trunk.

Problems Encountered

During facilitation techniques, you may encounter two problems. The first is getting inside the child's mouth, and the second is the introduction of food. To treat these problems, you must understand what causes them.

When a child has a somatosensory-based oral motor problem, he is experiencing underresponsiveness to touch. The only thing remotely similar to being underresponsive to somatosensory input in the mouth is the feeling after receiving an injection of local anesthesia in the dentist's office. Think of the difficulty with handling your own saliva, the fear of biting your tongue, the awkwardness involved with swallowing, and the inability to speak clearly. Imagine trying to eat while your entire mouth is numb. Many of us might experience a fear of choking and react with terror.

This is the fear that many of these children experience. Their response may be rooted in a basic survival response—fear of aspiration due to decreased sensory awareness and motor control. Their tongues don't work, they aren't sure what is in their mouths, and they learn how to eat only certain textures and foods. To vary the texture, size, or quality of what they eat leaves them vulnerable for aspiration. They fear eating anything new or different, yet they do not understand why.

Because the problem is in the mouth, they cannot compensate with vision. They cannot see what their tongues are doing or how they are moving. They can see only what goes into their mouths. Therefore, they visually scrutinize everything. They will eat only those foods that look the same in size, texture, or color. They develop their own rules that make sense to them.

Everyone has a basic need to feel safe and secure. Eating may threaten that basic security. The key to a successful oral motor program involves trust. The child must trust you and believe that you will not put his life in danger. You must project trustworthiness through your words and nonverbal behaviors.

Begin work with the foods the child is eating currently. Slowly expand the child's selections through using the foods he likes and finds pleasurable. Gradually vary the foods within his favorite selections. For example, if a child eats only pretzel sticks, expand the food selectivity to small, oval pretzels, to fat pretzel sticks, then eventually to small, oval crackers and regular crackers.

Conduct all oral motor programs in front of a mirror. Because of decreased sensory awareness, he will need to visually monitor what is occurring. Eventually, he will attempt facial expressions and oral motor activities in front of the mirror, experimenting with the new movements and feelings.

Facilitation

Sensory-based facilitation programs must focus on increasing the child's sensory registration and integration through the dorsal column medial lemniscal system. This means that we must enhance the registration of tactile vibratory, deep-touch pressure and proprioceptive input.

Vibration

Vibration may be used outside the mouth with toys such as the Lady Bug™ or the Humbug™. Often children will impose their own vibration to their cheeks, chin, or jaw areas.

ILLUSTRATION 12.19

Gentle head-neck compression offers proprioceptive input required for calming, while use of a vibrating toothbrush increases sensory awareness of the tongue and mouth.

Vibration inside the mouth can be done most effectively with a child's vibrating toothbrush. Some children will accept the toothbrush inside the mouth because they like the feel outside of their mouth, while others may enjoy the flavor of toothpaste or marshmallow fluff on the brush. Follow the child's lead.

Vibration input may be provided to the cheeks, tongue, teeth, roof of the mouth, and lips. Whenever possible, let the child hold the toothbrush while you guide the direction of the vibration. Follow vibration by deep-touch or proprioceptive input. Vibration is a very intense input that can be disorganizing. When the child indicates that he has had enough, respect his wishes and progress to deep-touch techniques.

A word of caution. When working with a child with a known or suspected seizure disorder, take care when using vibration.

Deep-Touch Input

Heavy pressure across the roof of the mouth is calming. Often the easiest way into the mouth is through the child's preferred food or dessert and an Infa-Dent, Nuk brush, soft-bristled toothbrush, or a washcloth. The Infa-Dent is a nice texture to begin with. The short bristles provide a comfortable deep-touch input.

If the child does not bite, place an Infa-Dent on your finger (over a glove). Dip it into the child's preferred food. Provide deep-touch pressure:

- Into the roof of the child's mouth

- Downward into the center of the tongue

- Eventually, into the gums (using a back-and-forth movement)

Follow these same procedures using the Nuk brush, toothbrush or washcloth. The child also may receive deep proprioceptive input through biting on a washcloth or Nuk brush.

A word of caution. Follow safety precautions when using the Nuk brush or Infa-Dent. The tip of the Nuk brush will come off if the child chews on the rubber tip. Monitor closely to prevent choking. The Infa-Dent® will not protect you from a child who bites. Do not use it with children who present this possibility.

Deep pressure into the jaw

Deep pressure into the jaw facilitates biting and jaw action. Biting, using the back molars, promotes stability of the jaw and base of the tongue and decreases teeth grinding.

Encourage the child to play bite-and-tug with tubing, a washcloth, or pieces of licorice or beef jerky. The easiest and most natural way to give deep-touch input into the mouth and jaw is through tactile and proprioceptive experiences of food in the mouth. Look for snacks and foods that offer resistance and require the jaw and tongue to work hard. Teething biscuits are excellent for helping a young child to obtain both deep-touch and deep proprioceptive input through biting. Chewy and crunchy foods are excellent for producing an impact on the sensory system. Food textures that encourage biting and crunching include carrot sticks, toast, bread sticks, nuts, bagels, crackers, and pieces of raw fruit (Oetter et al. 1995).

Chewies. Use of chewies is not a permanent solution to the child's need for deep proprioceptive input. Chewy substances are only a temporary assistance to the child-a form of sensory diet. Our objective is to help the child meet his sensory needs through normal daily activities such as eating, thereby eliminating the need for chewy substances.

- A chewy necklace will provide deep proprioceptive input. See page 153 for instructions on how to make this necklace.

- Tie a knot in the center of a piece of heavy tubing, and let the child chew on it.

- Loop a baby teething toy onto a length of tubing to make a necklace.

- Place a large pencil grip over tubing. (**Note:** While many therapists allow children to chew on pencil grips, these grips are not designed for oral use. Continuous chewing on the grip can cause it to break off. Monitor carefully.)

Precautions. When the child is using chewy substances, take care to assure his safety.

- When selecting the appropriate heavy tubing, read the manufacturer's recommendations. Tubings sold in therapeutic catalogs may not be suitable for oral use. Latex-free tubing is available for children with latex sensitivities.

- After determining that the child may safely use a particular product and the manufacturer's recommendations have been heeded, it still is necessary to monitor closely. If the child starts to bite through the chewy, remove it immediately.

- Monitor carefully when any object is placed around the child's neck.

Deep pressure to the cheeks

Gently place your index finger into the child's mouth (with a glove, or with an Infa-Dent on your gloved finger). Firmly grasp the cheek between your thumb and index finger. Apply gentle, even pressure and gently oscillate as you move your finger down the child's cheek. Follow by having the child actively use the muscles for activities such as using blow toys.

Rib Mobilizations

Forced exhalation with vocalization is difficult for many children. Children who are nonverbal or who have limited vocalizations often will display shallow breathing with poor breath control. Rib mobilizations will serve to lengthen the intercostal muscles, lower the rib cage on the chest wall, and place the abdominal muscles in a mechanical advantage to become more active. It also will give the child the feeling of vocalizing with inflection. The combination of vocalization with the vibration of the mobilization will force changes in pitch. A child with an underresponsive somatosensory system will enjoy the rib mobilizations with vocalizations when they are combined with using a towel for added deep-touch pressure. For more information on rib mobilization techniques, contact the Neuro-Developmental Treatment Association (NDTA), 1550 S. Coast Highway, Suite 201, Laguna Beach, CA 92651 (1-800-869-9295); (www.ndta.org).

Blowing

When a good seal is obtained, blowing provides both deep-touch and proprioceptive input to the lips, cheeks, and lungs.

Use whistles, balloons with whistle stems, and blow toys to improve lip closure, forced exhalation, and breath control while providing good sensory input into the oral mechanisms.

Prepare the child for resistive whistle games by playing games with a drinking straw. The child blows into the straw to move table tennis balls, cotton balls, and liquid in a cup.

Drinking liquid through a straw will provide resistance to sucking movements. Start with a short straw, and increase the length as the child is able to increase the ability to suck and swallow.

Establishing a Sensory-Based Oral Motor Program

An oral motor program must be practiced regularly. Develop a schedule in which the sensory-based activities are performed two or three times each day at specified times. Schedule the sessions just before meals, speech therapy, or times during which language will be facilitated. The oral motor program will prepare the child for the functional skills of eating or speech.

Do not discontinue the oral motor program because the child has improved in some of his eating patterns or because he has stopped undesirable behaviors such as mouthing toys, objects, or clothing. Regressions will occur when oral

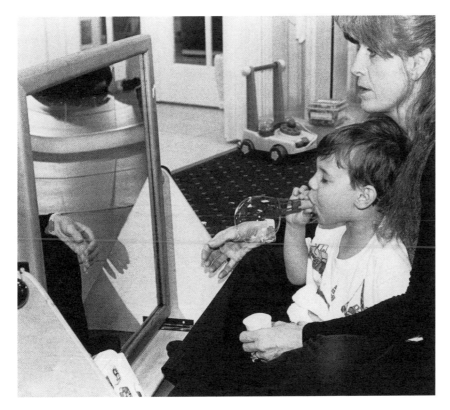

ILLUSTRATION 12.20

The child receives resistance as he uses a whistle blower to blow bubbles. This activity strengthens lip closure, activates the cheek muscles, and helps the child coordinate breath control.

motor programs are stopped before the child has improved in somatosensory awareness or developed normal eating habits. Children may maintain their progress for short periods of time—even for several weeks; but the previous behaviors or new sensory-based behaviors will resurface.

Eating as a Functional Activity

Children may need to be placed on an oral motor program for several weeks before new foods are introduced. Assess the child for increased tongue, lip, jaw, cheek, and breath control to determine whether he is ready to handle new textures and variety of foods. As he demonstrates increased oral motor skills and confidence with the oral motor program, introduce the new foods in a nonthreatening fashion.

Prerequisites to Food Introduction

There are several behavioral factors to consider before introducing food alternatives.

- Establish basic trust between yourself and the child.

- Seat the child on your lap in front of a mirror. Position yourself to be able to provide firm, steady compression through the child's shoulders, arms, and head, if needed for calming. Provide proprioceptive input downward through the shoulders or head. When using joint compression, take care to assure biomechanical alignment of the head with the spine. Deep compressions also may be provided by gently but firmly squeezing the child at the hips or shoulders.

- If the child starts to become anxious, provide proprioceptive input and joint compression to calm him.

- Engage the child in counting to 10. Use this concept when introducing a new item or technique. When you finish counting to 10, stop the technique and let the child relax. Children often will tolerate the technique for ten seconds without undue anxiety. While they may not like the technique or food, they will realize it is not as bad as they originally thought and will enable you to repeat it for another ten seconds. The child must complete the activity for the designated 10 seconds. If he wiggles out of the task, you have reinforced the avoidance of trying new techniques or foods.

- If the child becomes upset or doesn't like a food you have introduced, do not let him look in the mirror. The mirror will reinforce the child's adverse reaction. Most children enjoy watching themselves in a mirror when they are upset. Turn them away from the mirror the second they start to get upset.

- Work in small, nonthreatening steps. Vary the food choices within those foods that the child will tolerate. Teach the child to trust that you will introduce only familiar foods that he can handle.

Introducing Food

After the oral motor session, introduce the food. Begin with the exact foods that the child likes, but work with only one type or texture at a time. For example, start with either pretzels or pudding, but do not use both in one session. In addition to the favorite foods, provide a variety of foods that are similar in shape and flavor. Pretzels, if they are a favorite food, are excellent because their crunchy texture provides proprioceptive input.

Goals for food introduction

There are several goals when introducing foods:

- To have the child trust you to feed him his favorite foods

- To break the child's need to visually inspect everything that is placed in his mouth; that is, to change the child's need to react to foods according to visual characteristics.

- To have the child use his newly-acquired oral motor and sensory skills to determine the texture and taste of new foods

- To learn that the foods he fears will not hurt him

- To increase the variety of foods the child will eat

- To promote normal eating habits

- To have the child be able to eat foods served in multiple environments

Children often determine the rules of what they will eat and where they will eat it. They may learn to eat certain foods in therapy, but not at home; or at home, but not in the school cafeteria or a restaurant. Facilitating carryover into all environments is crucial to helping them develop the sensory and oral motor control needed for normal eating and speech.

Grading the program

The goal of the first session is to have the child allow you to feed him his favorite food without his visually monitoring what goes into his mouth. You may need to squirrel pretzels into your hand to keep them out of the child's sight. If basic trust is truly established, you may be able to play a feeding game with the child wearing a blindfold.

The next goal is to introduce a new item into the child's mouth. Do not give any visual clues that the item is different from the other items. If the child asks to inspect your hand, let him do so, but do not have a new item in your hand. Your goal is to get the child to use his sensory skills and oral motor control—not the visual image of the food—to determine whether he likes the new food.

Gradually, as the child accepts the new food, introduce its appearance. Gradually place the new food in its container within the child's visual field, and eventually reach into the container to give the child a taste. Let the child see the food as you place it in his mouth. Final goals are for the child to feed himself the new food, and to eat the food in different environments.

Introduce puddings and soft textures in a similar fashion. Goals are to decrease the child's need to visually monitor the food, and to transfer that to developing a taste preference.

You may want to link an undesirable flavor with a desirable one. Hide the new flavor under the favorite flavor; then gradually fade the favorite.

Sensory-Seeking Behaviors and Self-Stimulation Patterns

Stereotypic, disruptive, and self-stimulation behaviors are often seen in children with autistic spectrum disorders. When a child also has a tactile discrimination disorder, specific behaviors are often seen. See Table 11.1 for a review of these behaviors and the sensory input they provide.

Why Does the Child Do These Behaviors?

A child who is underresponsive to touch and proprioceptive input may develop and engage in these sensory-seeking behaviors for two reasons:

1. The sensory stimulation provided from the behavior

    The sensation derived from the behavior may provide the child with enhanced sensory input that he otherwise would not feel. Vigorous hand shaking, crashing, jumping, and mouthing objects provide intense proprioceptive and deep-touch input that allows a child with an underresponsive system to register sensory input. A child whose hands do not feel may finally register tactile information after vigorous hand shaking. Similarly, a child who does not have a good body scheme may finally register his legs when he jumps from a high surface.

    Behaviors must be analyzed objectively to ascertain the sensory component that the child is receiving from the behavior and the effect it has on his organization, behavior, and arousal levels. Deep proprioceptive and deep-touch input can have a calming and organizing effect, vestibular can have an organizing or arousing effect, and vibration can have an arousing effect.

2. The success encountered within the child's environment

    The behavior may be effective in meeting the child's social or communication needs. Behaviors can serve as a method of communicating needs, wants, or desires and serve as a source of receiving attention.

Attention seldom creates the behavior originally; however, it is a strong reinforcer that will keep the behavior active. A child who hits other children may receive deep-touch and proprioceptive input from hitting others. He also may receive deep-touch input when the teacher grabs his hand to stop him from hitting. But primarily, the child receives *immediate* attention that is emotionally charged. This sensory-based response will reinforce the exact behavior it is meant to stop.

Attention-seeking behaviors also serve as a method of communicating the need or want for an activity or event or the desire to avoid or terminate the activity. A child who uses stereotypic behaviors as a method of communicating, and therefore obtaining or avoiding an activity, will be reinforced every time he successfully avoids or obtains the activity. To extinguish the behavior, the child must be given a method of communicating his needs.

Eliminating Sensory-Seeking Behaviors Associated With Tactile Discrimination Disorders

One of the goals of occupational, physical, and speech therapy is to extinguish undesirable, stereotypic, and disruptive behaviors and to facilitate more normal, socially acceptable behaviors. To do this, we must meet the underlying needs (that is, sensory, communication, and environmental needs). Once the sensory need is met and the child is provided an avenue for communicating his needs, wants, and desires, the behavior must be systematically eliminated or replaced with functional, socially acceptable methods of meeting the child's needs. This is often a process that occurs simultaneously.

Three decisions must be made:

1. Does the behavior need to be eliminated? If so, does it need to be eliminated immediately?

   Many stereotypic behaviors are unusual and make the child appear different, but they do not need to be eliminated immediately. If there is no immediate need, integrate sensory-based activities into the child's activity schedule, and introduce alternative methods of communication. Once this occurs, the child may extinguish the behaviors on his own. Similarly, a behavior may be appropriate in one setting, such as jumping on a playground, and inappropriate in another, such as jumping in a classroom. In this case, limit the behavior. Consult with the child's teacher, parents, and other professionals to decide whether to stop the behavior, limit it, alter it, or see if it will extinguish on its own.

2. What sensory stimulation is provided from the behavior?

   When looking at the stimulation, also look at the intensity and duration with which the child engages in the activity. If we are to provide an alternative sensory activity, it must meet the same need as the original activity. If the child is not registering somatosensory information, the intensity of alternative activities may need to be enhanced.

3. When does the behavior occur, and what is its functional need?

   Identify whether the child is engaging in the behavior to obtain something, calm, arouse, organize, communicate, seek attention, or obtain or terminate an activity?

   Once we know these factors, we are ready to design a program geared at eliminating the need for the stereotypic or disruptive behavior as well as designing techniques to eliminate the behavior. Treatment must address:

   — Communication strategies

   — Behavior modification techniques

   — Sensory-based activities

   — Sensory integrative techniques

   — Development of functional skills to eliminate the need for the behavior

   Sensory integrative treatment strategies are needed to help the child process multisensory information and enhance the registration and processing of sensory information, thus decreasing the need for the behavior. Intervention strategies must address the areas the child is seeking or lacking. With children who have an underresponsive somatosensory system, the activities frequently are deep-touch and proprioceptive in nature.

Sensory-based activities integrated into the child's day should achieve three results:

1. To provide the sensory input before the child needs it or feels he must use the stereotypic or disruptive behavior.

2. To teach the child alternative activities that are more socially acceptable and will meet his needs.

3. To teach him to identify his need and independently and appropriately seek to have it met.

Our final goal is to develop functional skills that meet the child's sensorimotor needs. We must develop these skills through extracurricular sensory activities such as bike riding, skating, horseback riding, or playing at a playground.

> Michael is underresponsive to somatosensory information. His behaviors are characterized by sensory-seeking patterns of jumping, crashing, and bumping into walls. Recently, Michael started to bang his head when he was frustrated. The behavior provided deep proprioceptive and deep-touch input. It occurred whenever Michael could not control the activity at hand (for example, when he had to taste a new food or try a new activity). Michael was able to gesturally communicate that he did not like the activity, however he still had to complete the activity. Because he was never permitted to avoid the activity by head banging, it was not seen as an avoidance technique but as a method of communicating his frustration and trying to calm himself. The behavior had to be eliminated immediately because of its destructive nature.

> Michael receives a comprehensive clinic-based sensory integrative program to help him better process sensory information. He also has a home program that features functional activities with enhanced proprioceptive input. He spends hours on the playground, with supervision, hanging from the jungle gym, climbing across the monkey bars, and crashing into the sandpit. He is learning to ride a bike, but is not yet proficient. At home, he plays with his resistive stretch men, pulling and tugging on their elastic parts. He also completes resistive activities while weight bearing on his arms over a peanut ball.

> In the clinic, Michael finds eating and oral motor programs very threatening. His anxiety increases rapidly, and he starts to fist his hands and teeth. He quiets and calms immediately when the therapist holds him firmly on her lap and provides consistent deep-touch pressure downward through his head or shoulders. His mother was taught the technique of holding him firmly and

providing deep-touch pressure when he started to escalate. Michael consistently calmed to the deep pressure. Eventually, when he was threatened, he would go to his mother and place her hands on his head, requesting the deep-touch pressure; and he would continue to request it until he could complete the task.

Head banging had to be redirected first. As Michael started to escalate, he was caught *just before* he threw himself on the floor. Deep compressions were provided, and he calmed without head banging. If we missed our cue and he landed on the floor, he was redirected to his chair and provided with the compressions. The need for head banging was modified to a more productive but equally intense input until Michael learned the skills he needed to function effectively without the frustration.

Eventually, Michael was not threatened by new activities. His nervous system became more adaptable and his motor control more developed so that he could tolerate these activities without stress and anxiety. He learned to ride his bike, and he used the resistive activity to help him stay organized.

Communication strategies become important when stereotypic behaviors are used as a method of communication. We cannot eliminate a behavior if it is the child's only form of communication. We must provide alternative methods of communication.

Physical prompts often work to develop the desired behavior as well as eliminate the undesirable behavior. The child may be physically moved through the desired response while the undesirable behavior may be physically blocked from occurring.

During all fine motor activities, Lauren shakes her hands in front of her face and giggles uncontrollably. This behavior provides her with enhanced sensory input of her hands. However, Lauren is now using the behavior as a form of visual and sensory distraction to avoid the fine motor activity.

The occupational therapist made sure her sensory needs were met before and during fine motor tasks. Her program was graded to provide both resistive hand and sensorimotor-based activities. The therapist physically blocked any attempt at hand shaking while redirecting Lauren's hands into the fine motor activity. The physical prompts gradually molded the desired behavior and eliminated the hand shaking during the activities.

The therapist had to be sure to keep her attention focused on the fine motor task and not the hand shaking. Also, when blocking the hand shaking, the therapist had to be careful not to visually or verbally attend to it. Any attention would reinforce the behavior, making it more likely to reoccur. On-task behavior and appropriate fine motor hand movements were rewarded enthusiastically with eye contact, physical praise, and deep-touch input.

Physical prompts are effective ways to modify behaviors in the beginning; however, they should be graded and eventually faded. Prompts include verbal instructions, physical assistance, demonstration, visuals, modeling, gestures, voice inflection and volume, glances, and facial expression. These techniques are discussed in Chapter 5.

TABLE 12.1   Modifying stereotypic and disruptive behaviors associated with tactile discrimination disorders

---

Modifying or eliminating stereotypic or disruptive behaviors requires a multifaceted approach that addresses the sensorimotor, communication, and behavioral aspects of the behavior.

---

1.   Identify the stereotypic or disruptive behavior. Determine whether you need to:

- Stop the behavior
- Limit the behavior
- Alter the behavior

See whether the behavior will extinguish on its own with a sensory- and communication-based program.

---

2.   Identify the sensory stimulation that is provided from the behavior. Look at:

- Intensity of the stimulation
- Duration of the stimulation

---

3.   When does the behavior occur? What is the need met?

- Communicative, to
    — Obtain something
    — Avoid or terminate an activity
    — Communicate something
    — Seek attention
- Sensory-based, to:
    — Calm self
    — Arouse self
    — Organize self

---

4.   Design a program to eliminate the need for the behavior. The techniques that will be used will include

- Sensory-based activities
- Sensory integrative techniques
- Development of functional skills to eliminate the need for the behavior by meeting the child's sensorimotor needs

---

5.   Develop communication strategies

---

6.   Eliminate the behavior through behavior modification techniques

- Use physical prompts; then gradually fade all prompts.

CHAPTER 13

Somatodyspraxia and Intervention Strategies

Carolyn Murray-Slutsky

Dyspraxia is often referred to as a motor planning problem in which the child demonstrates motor clumsiness. However, a problem of motor planning extends far greater than just motor clumsiness. The word *praxis* refers to that ability of being able to formulate a concept or idea, organize pertinent information in order to formulate a plan, then sequence, time, and execute the movement or motor plan. It involves the ability to know what to do and how to do it (Ayres, 1972a, 1979, 1989).

One characteristic of dyspraxia is difficulty in learning new tasks. A child with dyspraxia will require more repetitions to learn the task or activity. Self-care activities and daily living skills—dressing, eating, bathing—may be difficult until the child has learned the activity and mastered it in all environments. Handwriting and writing tasks also will be difficult, because writing requires putting letters and words together in ever-changing patterns. Sports and most extracurricular activities are equally challenging. Sports enable children opportunities to perfect their timing, sequencing, speed, and coordination—all areas of difficulty for children with dyspraxia.

Gubbay (1975) believes that when using standardized psychological tests, the single most important criteria for diagnosing dyspraxia is a significantly lower performance IQ compared to a verbal IQ. *Significantly lower* is described as at least a 15-point discrepancy. This theory identifies dyspraxia as a dysfunction in which the child cognitively knows what is expected, but is motorically unable to produce the desired response. While this is one diagnostic criteria, it does present several limitations, especially for a child with autistic spectrum disorder who has limited verbal skills or who is viewed as untestable according to standardized test methods. It also does not reflect the wealth of information available that associates speech and language development with practic development. A child with dyspraxia often has associated language problems and cannot be expected to score well on language or performance items on a developmental or intelligence test (Ayres 1985). Therefore, due to low scores in both areas—verbal and performance—a child with dyspraxia might not show a discrepancy.

Gubbay (1985) noted that there is a two-to-one ratio of males diagnosed with dyspraxia as females.

 ## Types of Dyspraxia

Ayres (1989) identified four types of practic dysfunctions that are the result of factor and cluster analyses of *Sensory Integration and Praxis Test* (SIPT) scores.

Visuodyspraxia. Children have poor form and space perception, visual-motor coordination, and visual construction such as dot-to-dot designs and constructional tasks. In and of itself, it is not a true dyspraxia. Visual-motor integration is often viewed as the end product of good sensory integration. A visuodyspraxia may be the end result of a somatodyspraxia.

Praxis on verbal command. Children are unable to physically assume postures on verbal command, have difficulty with motor sequencing, and have increased scores on the postrotary nystagmus test. They do not have vestibular-proprioceptive processing deficits. It is believed to be a dysfunction of the left hemisphere and not a sensory integrative dysfunction (Ayres 1989).

Bilateral integration and sequencing. Children have difficulty using the two sides of the body together in a coordinated fashion. They often fail to develop a skilled hand dominance or preference, avoid crossing the midline of the body, and experience difficulty with anticipating movements or projected action sequences (feedforward). Difficulty with bilateral motor control may affect hopping, skipping, jumping, doing jumping jacks, and symmetrical and reciprocal stride jumping (Fisher, Murray, and Bundy 1991).

It is believed to be a disorder of praxis that is due to impaired processing of vestibular-proprioceptive information. A bilateral integration and sequencing disorder does not involve a tactile discrimination problem. If a tactile deficit is present, the diagnosis of a somatodyspraxia is more appropriate.

Somatodyspraxia. Children often appear clumsy, have poor tactile discrimination, body scheme, poor fine motor, gross motor, and oral motor problems, problems in constructive or manipulative play, difficult with feedback and feedforward (projected action sequences), and praxis-related skills.

Somatodyspraxia is a disorder of tactile processing characterized by all of the problems addressed under tactile discrimination along with a disorder of praxis and possibly vestibular-proprioceptive processing. It is the most pervasive form of dyspraxia that impacts every aspect of the child's life.

In this chapter, we will address the signs, symptoms, and intervention strategies for somatodyspraxia. Intervention strategies for the other forms of dyspraxia are effectively addressed in *Sensory Integration Theory and Practice* by Fisher, Murray, and Bundy (1991).

Characteristics of Somatodyspraxia

Children with somatodyspraxia will be underresponsive to somatosensory input (tactile-proprioceptive) and will display oral motor, fine motor, and gross motor problems because of inefficient processing of sensory information. They also will display difficulty with praxis, feedback and feedforward, and may have vestibular and proprioceptive processing difficulties.

Somatosensory Processing and Tactile Discrimination

In children with somatodyspraxia, the tactile discrimination disorder is the base problem that contributes to many of the motor planning deficits. A tactile discrimination disorder is characterized by:

- Low scores on tactile tests: The child will have difficulty with tactile test items such as finger identification, localization of tactile stimuli, two-point discrimination, and stereognosis

- Oral motor difficulties

- Fine motor difficulties with problems with haptic exploration, manipulating objects, in-hand manipulation skills, rapid alternating finger movements, and skilled fine motor and tool usage

- Poor body scheme with secondary problems in gross motor skill development

Motor Planning

Motor planning (praxis) is the process that is required in order to learn a skill. It is the conscious attention and effort required to master a new task or activity. When a child is learning to motor plan a new task, such as shoe tying, he must pay attention to his fingers and the shoe laces, and organize and sequence the task into its component steps. Once the child is able to complete the task several times, he no longer needs to concentrate on it. His fingers automatically receive the motor plan, and it becomes a skill that can be accomplished in any environment.

Children with dyspraxia have difficulty learning new tasks and require more repetition than others to learn the motor plan. Once a task is learned, it no longer requires motor planning; however, variations of the original task or completing the learned task in a new environment again will result in the need to motor plan the activity.

Parents and professionals traditionally gear demands to the child's intellectual abilities rather than to his motor planning abilities. When we see a child demonstrating a few splinter skills, we see evidence of the child's intellectual abilities and capabilities, and we tend to demand that level of proficiency in other activities. It is hard to understand that while the child is cognitively capable, he is not able to motor plan the tasks in other environments. Teaching splinter skills becomes a major concern, because children often gain skills without the ability to organize and generalize their actions.

Children with dyspraxia will achieve their motor milestones within normal limits (Gubbay 1979, 1985). Rolling over, crawling, walking, and all of the developmental milestones are centrally programmed. These actions do not require motor planning, and they do not have to be taught. For example, while parents encourage their child to walk, they do not teach the child the task of walking; the child innately knows how to do this once his nervous system reaches a level of maturity. A child with dyspraxia often will not begin to exhibit problems until he is required to interact purposefully in his environment and learn new motor skills. Most parents know when something is wrong. The child may bump into things, need more help than others his age, or show play skills that are different from those of other children. Many parents and professionals dismiss this, citing variations among individuals or hoping that the child will grow out of it. They do become concerned, however, when speech acquisition is delayed or does not develop. Speech is not centrally programmed, and often it is the first concrete sign that a motor planning problem exists.

Any task that requires learning and attention will require motor planning until it can be accomplished without conscious attention. It is required to put on clothes, eat with silverware, write with a pencil, play with tools, and participate in new games and extracurricular activities. Once the child learns the skill, his brain automatically tells his muscles what to do. This enables him to use his muscles without having to pay attention to them or exert effort and concentration. The sensations from the body (tactile-proprioceptive) enable his brain to instruct his muscles in what needs to be done. Motor planning connects the intellectual abilities of the brain with the sensorimotor aspects.

Motor planning requires a good body scheme, or internal model of how the body is put together, which in turn requires good somatosensory processing. The sensory information coming in from the child's body creates maps, or neuronal models, of how the body parts move. The more variety of movements the child has, the more accurate his body maps. The brain then refers to these maps or memories to help motor plan new, unfamiliar movements.

In children with dyspraxia, motor clumsiness and awkwardness are caused by the insufficient processing of sensory information coming in from the extremities combined with the difficulty in organizing, planning, and sequencing the motor movements. Motor control issues are always secondary problems. The body scheme is so poorly organized that the hands and feet often go the wrong way and the movements and actions become confused and disorganized. The problem is on a subcortical level and involves the brain's ability to receive, organize, and process sensory information. Automatically motor planning a task requires that the child complete the task *without thinking*. If the child does not have normal sensory processing, he will need to visually or cognitively monitor and plan all movements. This is exhausting for any child.

Vestibular input also becomes critical to motor planning total-body movements. The vestibular system is responsible for generating the muscle tone that keeps the body ready to respond. It helps us map out the space around us and determine how our bodies relate to that space. The child with dyspraxia may appear to be weak and have low muscle tone, signs of vestibular inefficiencies. Vestibular problems seldom are seen in isolation, but often are combined with problems of tactile and proprioceptive processing.

Parents and professionals often resort to two different intervention strategies: either cognitive remediation strategies, or exercises to encourage muscle strengthening. Neither strategy will be effective until the brain can process and organize the information. A cognitive approach to remediation (that is, teaching and instructing the child how to perform the action) requires the child to use higher cognitive processes. He already must think about everything he does in order to motor plan each task. Asking him to remember more directions and instructions will only confuse him further.

A strengthening approach to motor incoordination appears logical to the outside observer who observes the child's clumsiness and incoordination. Thus, parents might hire a personal trainer for the child, enroll him in strengthening classes, or place him in judo or karate classes. While this approach is effective as a home program, intervention still must focus on helping the child's brain receive, organize, and process the sensorimotor information automatically through sensory integrative procedures.

Somatodyspraxia is a problem of feedback and feedforward. Feedback involves making use of the sensory information that results from a motor act or stimulus. It enables us to judge whether our initial response was adequate and whether we need to change any of our future motor movements. When we kick a stationary ball, we obtain immediate feedback from the somatosensory system, from the sensation of hitting the ball, and from the visual system as we determine the direction and distance the ball moved. There also is internal feedback that we do not hear or see, occurring within the brain, that enables us to monitor movements before they occur or before we receive external feedback.

Feedforward motor control does not rely on sensory feedback or sensory information. It happens in advance of a motor act as preparation. It requires the child to plan and initiate movements in response to events that are moving or changing or that have not happened yet. Feedforward is often referred to as the production of projected action sequences, in which the child must project into the future the sequence of actions that will be needed. Examples of activities that require projected action sequences, or feedforward, include:

- Kicking a rolling ball

- Catching a thrown or bounced ball

- Running and jumping over a bolster that is rolling toward you

- Riding a bike through an obstacle course

- Describing verbally what you will be doing

- Jumping rope

- Playing hopscotch

- Swinging on a trapeze and dropping on a designated spot

- Walking through a crowded room without bumping into anyone

Clinical History of a Child With Somatodyspraxia

When confronted with a toy, most children know immediately what to do with it. When they see a rattle, they pick it up and shake it; they stack blocks, jump inside or roll in a barrel, sit on a swing, climb a jungle gym, and ride a tricycle. A child with dyspraxia often does not see the play potential of toys. The toys have no meaning for these children, so they may ignore them; or they may play with each toy in the same way over and over again. Instead of manipulating toys and creating opportunities for fun, these children may simply line them up in rows or look for moving parts to spin.

Children with poorly developed body schemes have difficulties with dressing and self-care activities. These children may be able to pick up a sock, but they may have no idea how to get a foot into the sock. They wiggle their feet in all directions, uncertain of how to move them to get them into the socks. Shoes, shirts, and pants all present the same problem. How does a child learn to put clothing on a body that has a poor percept? Washing and drying their hands also is difficult, because these children do not know how to move their hands and coordinate the movements. Fastening zippers and buttons and tying their shoes is difficult, as is brushing their teeth and learning to use utensils. These activities require motor planning and tactile discrimination, which are areas of deficit.

School-related tasks also are difficult. The child will have problems with any task requiring tool usage, and therefore body awareness and tactile discrimination. A poorly organized body percept interferes with writing, coloring, and drawing. Cutting with scissors, doing arts and craft activities, and manipulating puzzle pieces are difficult tasks, but they become even more so when these children have to learn to write, form letters between lines, and then attempt creative writing (taking concepts from their minds and writing them on paper). Their written work often is messy, letters are not formed within the lines, and spacing is poor. Erasing may become an obsession because of persistent mistakes, and may serve as an effective technique to avoid work.

Play skills often are limited in variety, repetitive, and lack creativity and imagination. Climbing activities may be difficult at first, but once mastered may be their movement of choice. They may climb everything, repeating the same motor movement over and over, or they may show no purposeful interaction. Nothing may have meaning to them as they walk around aimlessly, or they may register the information but have no idea of what to do or how to interact. Play is often repetitive, the same motor strategy is used for all play activities, and they are unable to use toys creatively. Learning through imitation is difficult for them because they have a poor sense of self. Imaginary play often is lacking. These children have no clear sense of their physical being; they have difficulty knowing who and what they are. This dilemma locks them into concrete play. Attempting to coax a child into imaginary play, one therapist said, "Look! You are Superman!" The child's distressed, emotionally charged response was, "No! I am Matthew!"

Riding a bike, jumping rope, skipping, playing ball, and participating in any sport will be difficult. Extracurricular activities may become frustrating as the child's clumsiness, awkwardness, poor timing and sequencing, and inability to adjust to new motor plans becomes evident. The child may have many accidents, big and small; and anxiety may rise, as more and more he fears new situations and activities.

Behavioral Characteristics

Children have an innate drive to be successful and to feel competent. The moment the child has to interact purposefully with the environment, motor planning is required. It doesn't take him long to realize that once he has mastered a task, he can successfully accomplish it only if it is done in the same environment. Therefore, to be successful and avoid stress, the child quickly learns the need to control.

He must control everything—what clothes are worn, what activities are performed, and how they are completed. He will need to control what, where, and when he eats. Because transitions and change involve motor planning new activities, which often are accompanied by anxiety and stress, the child must control where he goes. The more the child can control, the more he can assure that he will be able to function.

Often you can identify dyspraxia just by the parents' description of the child's need to be controlling from birth. This need to control is rooted in the child's need to function. The child lacks a clear sense of his physical well-being, has a poor body scheme, and lacks the sensorimotor abilities to perform a task. Avoiding new activities and events becomes a central theme. As the child improves in body scheme and motor planning skills, new activities can be introduced; and as he learns that he possesses the skills to be successful and has improved body awareness and self-esteem, his need for control will gradually disappear.

If the child has strong language skills (for example, a child with Asperger's syndrome), he actually may show a higher verbal IQ than a performance IQ. This child may prefer to talk about what needs to be done, rather than actually doing it. He may be able to describe to you the beautiful picture that he is drawing, while the actual strokes on the paper are unrecognizable. Another child may frantically beg to do every activity, but then may be unable to sustain attention or organize himself to complete any task. He may run from activity to activity, saying, "I know what I want to do. It's this . . . No, it's this . . . No, it's this."

These children are unable to organize themselves, much less their papers and desks. They always seem to have clothing disheveled, shirts untucked—a task that requires motor planning and body awareness. They forget their books, papers, and assignments. Their apparent lack of sense of time, coupled with their disorganization, results in their being constantly late. They appear distractible, inattentive, hyperactive, or disorganized as a secondary characteristic of the dyspraxia.

These children are aware of how much harder they have to work than their peers. Everything they do is a struggle that requires tremendous effort and concentration. Their emotional state is fragile and their self-confidence tentative. They realize how others react to them, and they recognize that they are awkward and clumsy. Coupled with their poor sense of self, this often results in feelings of insecurity and loss of the inner drive to successfully encounter the world. A child may demonstrate emotional lability by laughing one minute and crying uncontrollably the next. He may be unable to deal with small roadblocks, such as broken lead on a pencil, and will fall apart in hysterical crying. Another child may act baby-like and immature or be unable to separate from his parents. If the child encounters any difficulty or failure, he may never try again! If he musters up the energy to attempt a task in therapy, at school, or at home, his effort *must* be rewarded by success!

 Evaluation Findings

Identifying somatodyspraxia requires systematically tracking areas of difficulty and strengths. Meaningful clusters of scores that indicate decreased tactile discrimination, poor processing of vestibular-proprioceptive information, and a clinical history of motor planning and processing problems will point to somatodyspraxia. Evaluation findings that indicate somatodyspraxia include:

- Tactile discrimination difficulties (described in Chapters 11 and 12)
  - Low scores on tactile tests. The child will have difficulty with tactile test items such as finger identification, localization of tactile stimuli, two-point discrimination, stereognosis. Graphesthesia, finger identification and manual form perception (haptic exploration) scores on the SIPT are low (Ayres 1989).
  - Oral motor difficulties, usually with feeding and speech
  - Fine motor difficulties and problems with haptic exploration, manipulating objects, in-hand manipulation skills, rapid alternating finger movements, and skilled fine motor and tool usage
  - Poor body scheme with secondary problems in gross motor skill development

- Problems with praxis. The following tests or clinical observations correlate with difficulties with praxis
  - Postural praxis. This can be tested on standardized tests such as the SIPT or the *Miller Assessment of Preschoolers* (Miller 1982); or it may be observed clinically through the child's ability to imitate the examiner's postures and movements or demonstrate novel finger postures such as the peace sign or thumbs-up posture. The ability to imitate the movements of others is a foundation skill for praxis, learning and developing more complex skills.
  - Supine flexion: On the SIPT, low scores on supine flexion correlates with somatodyspraxia. From a neuro-developmental perspective, supine flexion actually develops during infancy as the child learns to pull up to a sitting position. The infant uses chin tuck and downward gaze of the eyes to assist the body in generating sufficient flexion control to assist with the pull to sit. Through this, the infant also develops chin tuck and downward gaze of the eyes. The tongue shares muscles with the chin and base of the neck. Chin tuck, the development of the muscles that provide stability to the base of the tongue, is critical in providing internal stability for the tongue and providing a stable base from which the tongue can move. Decreased supine flexion correlates with somatodyspraxia. It is characterized by chin jut (rather than chin tuck) and an inability to sustain trunk flexion against gravity. Since

chin tuck develops with downward eye gaze, if a child does not have chin tuck, also assess downward gaze.

- Bilateral integration and sequencing present some areas of difficulty: On the SIPT, there is some correlation with low scores on the Standing and Walking Balance Test, Bilateral Motor Coordination, Sequencing Praxis, and Oral Praxis (Ayres 1989).

- Visuopraxis test scores also may be low. This includes low scores for form and space perception, visuomotor coordination, or visual constructional difficulties.

- Clinical history that indicates difficulty with motor planning new tasks

- Clinical testing and observation of the child's performance during:

  — Fine motor activities such as rapid alternating finger movements (RAM), writing, copying, dot-to-dot-designs

  — Body scheme and gross motor activities such as kicking a stationary or rolling ball, catching a thrown or bounced ball, running and jumping over a bolster that is rolling toward the child, riding a bike through an obstacle course, jumping rope, and playing hopscotch

  — Oral motor control such as tongue movement, eating, articulation, and speech and language abilities

  — Activities of daily living tasks

Fundamental Concepts of Praxis

To have praxis, a child must be able to conceptualize a plan, organize the information, and carry out the sequence of motor acts. This is the result of sensory registration, integration, schema, and engram formation (sensory integration). Ayres (1979) identified that in order for the brain to be able to motor plan a task, first it must have the idea of the purposeful act. Then it must know how the body is designed and how it functions mechanically (body scheme). This information is provided from the tactile, kinesthetic, proprioceptive, and vestibular sensory systems.

The goal of intervention is to identify the stage that is difficult for the child, then provide the correct sensory input and challenge to facilitate the integration and execution of the task. Breaking down the child's functional status into the component parts helps us identify where he is getting stuck, and where intervention needs to start. It also guides our treatment progression and helps us objectify the child's progress. While we will present each component in isolation, each area must be addressed simultaneously, with the area of greatest difficulty receiving more emphasis. For example, a child who is not registering or orienting to sensory information will benefit from techniques to improve his registration. However, sensory registration, orientation, and ideation will never be formed unless the child carries out the sequence and accomplishes the task. Meaning must be attributed to the sensory information. Also, the ability to carry out the sequence will depend on the child's knowledge of his body (body scheme) and his ability to integrate the information and process feedback and feedforward information.

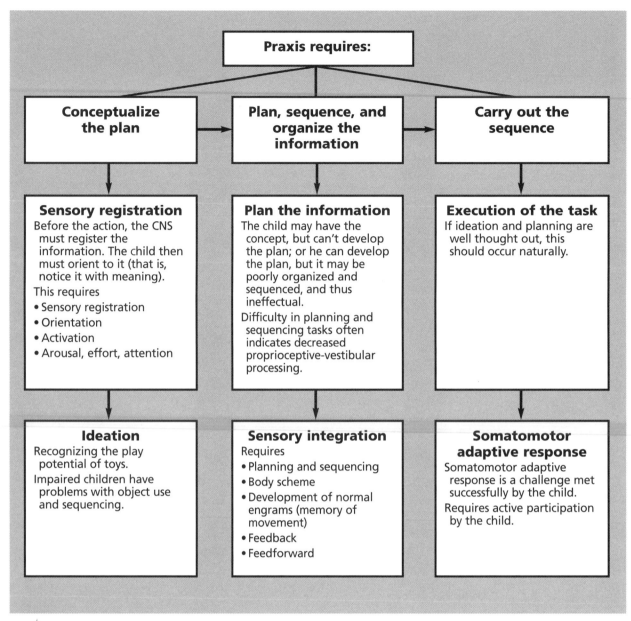

FIGURE 13.1
Fundamental concepts of praxis

 ## Conceptualize a Plan

A child is presented with a new toy or situation. To conceptualize a plan means that he recognizes the play potential of the toy or situation. He may have a problem conceptualizing the plan when he:

- Fails to respond to objects, toys, or play situations

- Avoids interacting with objects that are not familiar

- Fails to initiate play or interaction with people or objects

- Watches other children play rather than play himself

- Uses all toys in the same way

- Repeats actions over and over again

- Has problems with object use or sequencing an activity

- Runs from activity to activity with no sustained attention

- Uses equipment in simplified ways

Before a child can conceptualize a plan, he must register the sensory information and be able to formulate an idea. In Chapters 9 and 10, we addressed intervention strategies for children with ROA problems (registration, orientation, arousal). We discussed the fact that a child who fails to register and orient to sensory information fails to derive meaning from that information and is unable to develop the idea needed for motor planning.

When the child registers and orients to an object, he determines the significance of the object, at which time a neuronal model is formed. If the object has no significance to the child, he has no idea of the use of the object, a neuronal model will not be formed, and learning will not occur. Significance and meaning must be defined in the context of each child. What is meaningful to one child may have no meaning to another.

Ideational skill development is rooted in somatosensory processing and has a tremendous impact on the child's ability to learn. Problems with ideation are often connected to the child's knowledge of his body (body scheme), his ability to integrate the information and form normal engrams, and his ability to process feedback and feedforward. A child who has little idea of what to do with a toy or object will have difficulties with imitation, concept formation, initiation, and cognitive development.

Imitation, a foundation skill for learning, requires that the child have good somatosensory processing of sensory input and a good working knowledge of his body—how it is put together and the relationship between the parts (body scheme). This requires good tactile discrimination. It also requires that the child have good praxis. For the child to imitate the actions of another person, he must have the idea of what is expected, be able to organize the information, sequence it, and motorically be able to coordinate the movements.

Poor sensory processing has an adverse impact on concept formation. Concepts are tools of thought that are dependent in very large measures on sensory input, particularly feedback from movement. Concepts such as *over, under, between, through, fast,* and *slow* are learned normally in the context of movement during play and other ordinary activities (King 1991). A child with praxis difficulties often has problems processing sensory information, and in turn may have impaired body scheme and feedback from movement. Ideational skills necessary for concept development also may be impaired. Basic concepts such as *over* and *under* may not develop because the child has difficulty receiving adequate sensory information as well as organizing the sensory information once it comes in. Words that are associated with these movements may mean nothing to the child.

When a child demonstrates a lack of initiation, often he is viewed as being unable to organize sensory information to know what to do. The child may fail to register the information or develop the idea of what is expected or what he can do with the activity. If the child does have the idea, he may not be able to organize it sufficiently to act on it.

Cognition often is measured by the child's ability to form novel concepts (ideational skills), initiate and effectively interact in the environment, and effectively use language. Language requires praxis and motor planning. Effective language requires the child to register sensory information, formulate an idea, organize and sequence what he wants to say, and motorically speak. Cognition is dependent upon the development of concepts, which in turn is dependent upon a good body scheme and environmental interactions, which in turn is dependent upon good somatosensory processing and tactile discrimination.

Facilitating Concept Development

Sensory Registration and Ideation

Our goal is to help the child view the object or activity as significant, thereby facilitating sensory registration and orientation; and then enhance the significance of it by helping him develop the ideational skills by connecting the idea with the outcome. First, we must identify where the child is breaking down. Is he able to conceptualize the plan? If not, what is the primary problem? Is the child registering the sensory information? If registration is occurring, does the child have the idea?

Facilitating sensory registration and orientation is similar to the process described in chapter 10 on registration, orientation and arousal. The difference is that the child has an underlying tactile-proprioceptive problem, and often also a vestibular problem, that is the result of underresponsiveness to sensory input. Activities need enhanced sensory input to facilitate registration, ideation, and improved processing. See Figure 13.1.

A child who does not register sensory information as part of somatodyspraxia has a secondary problem of underresponsiveness to touch, proprioceptive input, and often vestibular input. By enhancing the sensory input of an activity sufficiently to cause a pleasurable feeling, the child will connect the pleasurable feeling with the activity, thus registering and orienting to the activity. As registration is obtained, work toward developing ideational skills.

Children may initially flip in and out of registering sensory information. They may be attending one minute, and staring off into space the next. Maintaining sensory registration is vital to engagement in any activity. Activities that provide enhanced sensory input often will hold a child's sensory registration throughout the activity. However, all activities may not enable enhanced sensory input, or the child may not realize the activity is capable of sensory feedback. In either case, sensory registration must be obtained throughout the activity to elicit active involvement. Intervention strategies may include enhancing sensory feedback through the activity, using a stronger sensory modality to elicit registration, or using an activity that is more meaningful to the child.

Use activities that are meaningful to the child to obtain registration for other activities, thus expanding the child's scope of interests. For example, if a child obsesses over trucks while simultaneously failing to register other information in

---

Sensory registration

To facilitate sensory registration and orientation, treatment strategies must

1. Promote an optimal level of arousal for the activity.
- If underaroused: Use the stronger modalities to increase arousal.
  - Use fast, regular, repetitive movement.
  - Use linear vestibular and deep-touch, proprioceptive input (if it is a stronger modality).
  - Modify the therapeutic environment and therapeutic use of self (voice inflections, high energy, enthusiasm, animation).
- If overaroused: Use inhibition techniques.
  - Lower anxiety; use environmental and organizational modifications.
  - Use slow, rhythmic, repetitive activities.
  - If calming, use deep-touch and deep proprioceptive input.
  - Modify the therapeutic environment and therapeutic use of self (lower voice, speak slowly and calmly, avoid animation and exaggerated movements).

2. Promote sensory registration and orientation as it relates to motor planning.
- Use a preferred meaningful activity. If necessary, couple the preferred activity with the weaker sensory modality or undesirable activity to get registration. Immediately make the intended activity meaningful to the child. Promote the child's active participation.
  - *Meaningful to the child* often requires that the child receive some form of sensory input from the activity, usually enhanced tactile, proprioceptive, or vestibular input.
  - Once the child learns the inherent satisfaction from the task, he will register the original activity without the need for the preferred toy or activity.
- Maintain sensory registration; keep the child interested and involved. If sensory registration begins to fade, a mismatch from the original stimulus must occur. Therefore, the input needs to be systematically changed in order to assure that the child continues to register and orient to the session.
- Couple a stronger sensory modality with a weaker modality to give the activity meaning and facilitate registration and orientation. Couple a pleasurable sensory experience with an undesirable task.

3. Promote orientation and the development of neuronal models (memories) through facilitating ideation.
- Develop neuronal models by linking the activity to a functional output. The child must link the activity with the idea. If necessary, complete the activity hand-over-hand to help the child receive the satisfaction from the output. The activity must have meaning to the child.

Ideation

To facilitate sensory registration and orientation, treatment strategies must:
- Work with tasks and activities that are familiar to the child.
- Connect the object with the outcome, thus formulating the idea.
- The outcome of the activity must have meaning to the child and, whenever possible, it must provide enhanced sensory feedback.
- Guarantee success!
- Grade assistance for success, and gradually fade out all assistance as the child masters the idea.
- Generalize the skills into all environments—home, school, and clinic.

Conceptualize the plan

FIGURE 13.2
Praxis: Conceptualizing the plan

ILLUSTRATION 13.1

The net swing provides linear vestibular input to increase his arousal level and enhance sensory registration. He receives proprioceptive input through sustained trunk extension and resistance applied to his arms as he climbs up the bars.

ILLUSTRATION 13.2

The child registers his favorite toy and begins to motor plan the sequence of movements needed.

the environment, use the trucks to expand the child's sensory registration and orientation. Be sure that the new activity has inherent sensory feedback and will be pleasurable to the child. As the child learns the inherent pleasure from the new activity, gradually fade the original activity.

Charlie loves bulldozers, cranes, and any form of construction truck. He is very difficult to engage in most activities. He acts shy, holds his head flexed, and must be firmly coaxed through activities that should be pleasurable. His motivation is poor, and most of the time he fails to register the tasks we are trying to engage him in. We decided to work with Charlie's obsession in order to improve his registration, ideation, and overall motor planning skills. We purchased several traction-driven toy construction trucks and magazines with pictures of trucks. Charlie quickly learned that we had a nice supply of his favorite toys. Equipment in our clinic that previously had meant nothing to Charlie soon became tools that enabled him to get his trucks. He ran into the clinic and raced to the net swing (registering and orienting to the swing). The swing, while a tool to get his trucks, also became a source of great sensory satisfaction, providing vestibular and proprioceptive input. Once in the swing, he could grab the bars nearby, climbing the rungs to get to the trucks. Eventually, he propelled himself in the swing in order to get the trucks that were placed high on a bolster. Outside the net, the trucks were hidden inside barrels and throughout obstacle courses, where Charlie propelled himself on a scooterboard. He enjoyed the physical challenges and began to throw the trucks into the barrel, jumping in after them. The trucks served as an avenue to help Charlie register and orient to activities that had no meaning to him. Eventually, he realized that he derived sensory pleasure from the activity itself and that he no longer needed the trucks.

The trucks also were effective in helping Charlie develop concepts. He quickly learned concepts such as *front, behind, in, on,* and *under* as they related to where the driver sat and where the wheels and doors were located. Generalizing the skills into other areas of his life followed.

A child who has poor ideation may not be capable of self-directed or self-initiated action because of the difficulty in knowing what to do with objects in the environment (Ayres 1979). Set up the therapeutic environment to provide structure, guidance, and assistance. Become part of the child's environment, generating enthusiasm and a playful attitude (when appropriate), in order to model the desired responses.

Success and inherent rewards are vital to the development of ideation. Without success, it is impossible for the child to connect the idea with the outcome. Physical assistance may be needed initially; then it can be reduced gradually as the child connects the idea to the outcome and initiation increases. Grade assistance from providing hand-over-hand physical assistance, to withdrawing physical guidance and modeling the activity, to providing verbal prompts (if verbal receptive skills are adequate) or visual prompts.

Use activities that are familiar to the child. For example, the playground may have more meaning to the child than SI therapy equipment. Always integrate something meaningful to the child into the therapy session. Just as we used Charlie's love for trucks to help him learn the play potential of barrels and hammock net swings, similarly, you may use familiar meaningful activities to help the child develop ideational skills when tasks are not familiar. Carryover of the idea to other activities in the child's environment is equally important. As Charlie learns the inherent satisfaction he obtains from the vestibular input on the hammock swing, it is important to teach him that swings on the playground can provide the same sensory input.

⊛ Planning, Sequencing, and Organizing the Information

Once the child registers the sensory information and formulates the idea, he then must organize the information into a plan. When he is able to effectively conceptualize the plan and organize the information, execution of the task will naturally follow. It is important not to concentrate therapy on the execution of the task because this will teach the child only splinter skills. He must learn how to organize and sequence multisensory information, learn how his body relates to the environment, develop normal motor engrams, and learn how to project actions into the future (feedforward).

A child may have difficulty organizing the information or plan if he:

- Is able to describe what he did but cannot organize or sequence what he would like to do

- Has an idea of what he would like to do, but cannot figure out how to do it

- May be able to tell you verbally what he is drawing or what he wants to do, but is unable motorically to do it

- Appears distractible or hyperactive; wants to do an activity, but quickly runs away from it and goes on to the next activity

- Plays with toys in the same way, over and over again

- Is unable to sequence an activity

- Is disorganized, forgetful, and either constantly late or obsessed with time

- Appears awkward and clumsy in his movements

- Has difficulty with tool usage such as crayons, pencils, scissors, spoon or fork.

- Has difficulty learning self-care tasks such as dressing and fastening buttons and snaps

- Has difficulty with any motor task that requires feedforward. This includes:
  - Kicking a rolling ball
  - Catching a thrown or bounced ball
  - Running and jumping over a bolster that is rolling toward him
  - Riding a bike through an obstacle course
  - Jumping rope
  - Playing hopscotch
  - Walking through a crowded room without bumping into anyone

Vestibular-Proprioceptive Deficits

It is the sequencing problem involved with praxis that first introduces the vestibular-proprioceptive system into this disorder. Deficits in bilateral integration are linked with deficits in sequencing (Ayres 1989), suggesting a possible neurobehavioral link between vestibular-proprioceptive functioning and bilateral integration and sequencing (Fisher, Murray, and Bundy 1991).

The vestibular system influences postural tone (especially extensor muscle tone) and balance reactions. It contributes to the child's awareness of his body position and movement through space, and to the child's ability to stabilize the eyes when the head is moving.

Proprioceptive processing is involved in the programming and planning of bilateral projected action sequences (feedforward) and in providing spatial information regarding the body and how it moves through space. It also provides us with sensory information that affects the rate and timing of our movements and how much muscle force is exerted. Together, the vestibular-proprioceptive system provides valuable information that affects the body's movement through space, coordination, timing and sequencing of movements, coordination of the two sides of the body, and general balance and muscle tone.

When a child has difficulty organizing the information for purposeful interaction within the environment (praxis), it is believed to be a disorder of processing vestibular, proprioceptive, and tactile sensory information that requires:

- Multisensory integration
- Organization of the plan
- Sequencing of the plan
- Good body scheme
- The development of normal neuronal models
- Feedback
- Feedforward

Postural-Ocular Movement Disorder

A postural-ocular movement disorder is the behavioral manifestation of a vestibular-proprioceptive processing disorder. It is hypothesized to be the basis for the bilateral integration and sequencing deficits.

Postural-ocular movement disorders are described in detail by Fisher, Murray, and Bundy (1991) and include:

- Hypotonia of the extensor muscles
- Poor postural stability
- Poor righting or equilibrium reactions
- Difficulty assuming and maintaining prone extension

In postural-ocular movement disorder, poor sensory processing of vestibular-proprioceptive input is believed to interfere with the development of posture. Intervention to improve postural-ocular control addresses improvement of:

- Tonic postural extension
- Tonic flexion

- Postural stability (balancing flexion and extension)
- Lateral flexion and rotation
- Righting and equilibrium reactions
- Ocular control

Bilateral Integration and Sequencing Deficits

Bilateral integration and sequencing deficits are indicated by a meaningful cluster of difficulties in the following areas (Fisher, Murray, and Bundy 1991):

- Depressed scores on the following tests of the SIPT:
  — Bilateral Motor Coordination
  — Sequencing Praxis
  — Graphesthesia
  — Oral Praxis
- Poor bilateral coordination
- Left-right confusion
- Avoidance of crossing the midline of the body
- Poor sequencing of projected movements, especially bilateral projected action sequences (feedforward)

Facilitating Sensory Integration

Planning, Sequencing, and Organizing Information

To organize, plan, and sequence information in order to transform the idea into the execution of a task requires complex intervention strategies. Our goal is not to teach task execution, but to provide the foundation skills the child needs to be able to organize and sequence this information independently. The complexity of this phase of intervention rests not in the areas we need to address, but in the ability to integrate all of these areas into the treatment session simultaneously and grade multiple factors within each category.

- Tactile discrimination problem. Address the underlying tactile discrimination problem that has an impact on the child's gross motor, fine motor, and oral motor skills and an adverse impact on the child's body scheme and development of normal neuronal models. Treatment must address enhanced tactile-proprioceptive input while facilitating adaptive responses from the child.

- Planning and sequencing disorder. Address the vestibular-proprioceptive problem underlying the sequencing problem, and grade intervention strategies to require greater amounts of projected action sequence (feedforward). Intervention strategies must take into account the postural-ocular movement disorder that is hypothesized to be the basis of the bilateral integration and sequencing problem.

- Use SI treatment principles to provide enhanced opportunities for tactile, proprioceptive, and vestibular input, and to promote integration of multiple sensory information and the ability to organize.

- Use SI treatment principles to provide enhanced opportunities for tactile, proprioceptive, and vestibular input; and promote integration of multiple sensory information and the ability to organize increasingly more difficult responses.

- Supine flexion difficulties correlate with this problem and often are associated with decreased chin tuck, which may result in instability throughout the muscles stabilizing the tongue and oral musculature.

- Facilitate carryover into multiple environments-home, school, and clinic.

Grading Feedback and Feedforward

SI treatment strategies require treatment activities to be graded to assure the just-right challenge and the child's continued internal motivation. We must grade the sensory input, the degree of difficulty required from the task, and the child's active involvement. We also must grade the degree of feedback and feedforward required from the task and from movement. The more feedforward required, the greater the degree of sequencing and timing required, and the greater the degree of difficulty.

Tasks may be made easier or more difficult by varying the speed of the movement of either the activity or the child, the timing of the movement, the size of the object or target, or the degree of accuracy required. For example:

- A child who is able to kick a large beach ball may find it more challenging when a smaller ball is used; or the child throwing a ball may be asked to throw it at a smaller target.

	Activity	Child	Sample Activity
Feedback	Stable	Stable	Kick a stationary ball Throw a ball
	Stable	Moving	Run to kick a stationary ball
	Moving	Stable	Kick a rolling ball Catch a thrown ball
Feedforward	Moving	Moving	Running to catch a thrown ball Jumping rope

FIGURE 13.3
Grading feedback and feedforward within an activity

- A child who can run and kick a ball may find it more difficult if the ball is smaller or if he has to run faster.

- A child who can kick a rolling ball may find it more difficult to kick a smaller ball or one that is rolling faster; or kick the ball at a target.

- A child who is able to catch a thrown ball may find it more difficult if the ball is thrown at different speeds or heights or distances.

- A child who is jumping rope may find it more challenging when the speed of the turning rope is increased; or when the way he jumps rope is varied, such as jumping while turning around or touching the floor every third turn.

Feedback and feedforward activities often require coordination between the two sides of the body—a task that is difficult for children with bilateral integration and sequencing difficulties. For these children, activities will need to be graded according to the amount and degree of bilateral integration required.

Children do not need to master one level before moving on to the next level; however, the information in Table 13.1 will help you grade activities within the child's capabilities. In general, bilateral upper-extremity activities are easier than activities involving the bilateral lower extremities, release of the hands is more

TABLE 13.1 General guidelines for grading the degree of bilateral integration and sequencing within an activity

Follow these general guidelines when analyzing the difficulty level of other aspects of an activity. Children do not need to master one level before progressing to the next.

Activities may be graded from bilateral:

1. Symmetrical upper-extremity activities	• Holding onto the ropes of a swing or platform swing as it propels forward and backward
2. Symmetrical lower-extremity movements	• Jumping with the feet together
3. Symmetrical release of the hands	• Letting go when swinging from a trapeze
4. Alternating upper-extremity activities	• Holding onto a glider swing and propelling side to side • Propelling a scooterboard while prone, with alternating hand movements
5. Asymmetrical upper-extremity activities	• Hold and do patterns, such as holding onto a tire swing while reaching with the other hand
6. Asymmetrical/alternating lower-extremity activities	• Running, skipping, pushing a scooterboard with the feet • Kicking a ball, standing on one leg, hopping on one foot
7. Symmetrical upper-extremity/ lower-extremity activities combined	• Jumping jacks, scissor jumps, breast stroke
8. Asymmetrical upper-extremity/ lower-extremity activities combined	• Propelling a tire swing with the feet while • holding on with one hand and reaching far with the other arm to secure an object • Bike riding, swimming

difficult than coordinating the two hands together, and activities that require the coordination of two extremities are easier than those that require coordinating four.

Sample Activities

While activities can be described that provide enhanced deep-touch, proprioceptive, or linear vestibular input, it is not the activity that creates the integration; it is the child's motivation, the grading of the activity to the child's functional level or just beyond, and the facilitation of his adaptive response. As the child masters an activity on one level, it must be modified for increased challenges at other levels. The process of grading activities for increased levels of difficulty is an ongoing process that is facilitated throughout the session. Grade the sensory input provided, the degree of difficulty required from the task, the child's active involvement, the degree of feedback and feedforward obtained, the degree of bilateral integration and sequencing required, and the progression of the therapy session.

Grade therapy sessions according to the three phases of treatment: preparation, facilitation, and function. Arousal levels, motivation, and self-esteem should gradually increase as the child progresses through the session into the facilitation phase. Because effective organization and planning of motor movements is dependent upon a good body scheme, the preparation phase of treatment should include resistive total-body activities and activities to improve tactile discrimination. See Chapter 12 for sample activities for the preparation phase. In the facilitation phase of treatment, include activities that provide linear vestibular, deep-touch, and proprioceptive input while promoting feedback and feedforward and bilateral integration and sequencing. Provide activities that require the child to plan, organize, and sequence just slightly beyond his level of ability. In the function phase of treatment, use activities that allow opportunities for the child to carry over the new level of integration into functional tasks that may be used at home, school, and play.

When using the sample activities provided here, there are several factors that must be kept in mind:

1. The goal of intervention is *not* to teach the child the activity or the end product of the activity, but the *process* that occurs as the child attempts to sequence, organize, and plan the activity and work on the adaptive responses.

2. It is crucial to grade the activity for the child's success, yet still provide challenge.

3. When grading the activity to the child's level, consider the sensory feedback provided by the activity, the developmental and postural requirements, the degree of bilateral integration, and the amount of feedforward required.

4. The process of grading activities for increased levels of difficulty is an ongoing process that is facilitated throughout the session. The activity must be changed, varied, and modified constantly, to prevent the child from "learning" the task. Once the task is learned, integration and motor planning are minimized.

5. Grade the activity to challenge the child while making it obtainable. Presenting activities too far beyond the child's abilities could place the child at risk for injury. Safety is a primary concern.

6. Other safety factors must be considered. Always assure that the area is padded, helmets are used when needed, children are closely guarded, and that hands-on facilitation is provided as needed.

Sample activities are presented according to the equipment used.

Scooterboard activities

Prone on the scooterboard

Pulling Game. (See Illustration 14.10.) Propel the child while he holds onto a pole or large ring. By having the child hold onto the bar or ring, he may obtain the proximal stability (shoulder control) needed to hold his arms up against gravity. Pull the child down the scooterboard ramp or in a linear direction. When the child is pulled, he receives traction to the shoulders, elbows, and hands, further facilitating extension. This is a bilateral symmetrical activity that provides feedback.

Block Knock. (See Illustration 14.15.) Have the child knock over blocks. He may actively propel himself down the ramp, holding his arms into forward extension as he pushes over blocks, secures rings suspended in extension, or plays other inventive games. He may carry a magic wand in both hands, parallel to the floor, to knock down a large foam block or wall. These are bilateral symmetrical activities that require some feedforward.

Ring Game. The child holds a ring in both hands, pushes forward from a wall or down a scooterboard ramp using only his feet, and places the ring on a cone at the end of the ramp. This is a symmetrical lower-extremity task requiring symmetrical upper-extremity control. It requires some feedforward processing.

Obstacle Course. Set up a scooterboard course. Lying prone on the board, the child propels through the course. Increase the difficulty by requiring more turns or by timing the child, who then tries to break his own time. For a variation, play a Policeman Game in which the child role-plays either a speeder or a policeman traveling the course to enforce the law. When the policeman catches the speeder, he may issue a ticket. Tickets are written up at the end of the game. This activity requires alternating upper-extremity control.

Therapist Pull. (See Illustration 14.31.) Sit on the scooterboard with the child lying prone on your lap. His legs will be on both sides of your body and extend behind you. The child then pulls you on the board. If necessary, provide assistance without the child noticing. This exercise provides resistive feedback to the alternating upper-extremity movement.

Variations

- The child can pull the therapist through the obstacle course.

- Two children can race to a goal, with therapists on the scooterboards.

- Two children, facing each other, take turns trying to pass each other to get to a goal. This requires the child to change directions in order to outmaneuver the other child.

Supine and sitting on the scooterboard

Supine scooterboard challenge. Anchor a rope from a doorknob across the room, and hold it securely. The child lies on his back on a scooterboard and propels himself along the rope with his hands, keeping his feet crossed above the rope. The child propels in the direction of his feet and focuses on where he is going. This will promote supine flexion and chin tuck.

Children enjoy playing games in which they are climbing a rope between two mountains trying to save people stranded on the mountain. The goal is to safely bring home the stranded people without falling off the mountain (the scooterboard). Balls serve as people, and the child holds the ball between his feet above the rope. This is a bilateral upper- and lower-extremity activity that is asymmetrical for the upper extremities and symmetrical for the lower extremities. It is feedback dependent and promotes head and trunk flexion.

Sitting scooterboard Thera-Band Game. Place a crash pad on either side of yourself. The child sits on a scooterboard facing you. Place the middle of a long strip of heavy, resistive exercise band (such as Thera-Band) behind the child's back. Hold onto the end of the resistive band while the child holds onto the

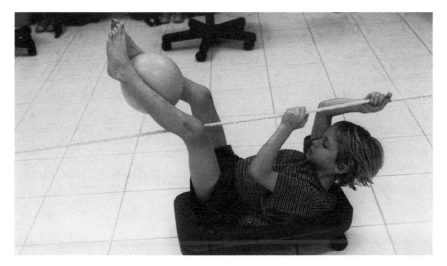

ILLUSTRATION 13.3
The supine scooterboard challenge promotes head and trunk flexion and bilateral control.

ILLUSTRATION 13.4
The child sustains trunk flexion as he shoots forward.

sides of the scooterboard. The child then pushes the scooterboard backward against the resistive band until you say, "Stop." Then cue the child, "Ready, set, go." The child leans back, raises his legs, and shoots forward on the scooterboard onto the crash pad. Be sure that the child is centered before allowing him to move forward. Also be sure that he complies with the command and does not move at random. This is a bilateral asymmetrical activity of the lower extremities with the upper extremities stabilized symmetrically. The activity promotes trunk flexion.

Net hammock swing activities

See Chapter 12 for precautions.

Ring Game. The child holds onto rings with each hand. Promote the child's gross grasp on the rings, and pull the child by using the rings. Encourage him to release the rings at a target as he swings forward. This is a bilateral symmetrical activity with feedback.

Symmetrical release on command. The child and the therapist hold onto the rings or a pole. The therapist pulls the child forward and gives the command, "Let go." The child releases and swings backward.

Reaching net activities. The child actively reaches and places objects while swinging in the net. Propel the child while he visually attends and focuses on the object he is asked to secure. Moving and reaching for a target requires motor planning (feedforward). Some children may not be able to comprehend the task while moving, or will be unable to time or sequence their reach to secure the object. In these cases, teach the task while the child is stationary. Progress to having the child swing forward, and stop him momentarily in midair so that he can reach for and obtain the object. As the child masters the timing and sequencing, decrease the assistance.

Variation

Swing the child forward, and have him grab rings from you and place them on cones as he swings forward again. This requires timing, spacial awareness, and feedforward (the child is moving and the object is stationary).

Bolster game. Position bolsters in front of the child, forcing him into end-range extension. The child swings forward and tries to push over the bolsters using both hands. This activity requires symmetrical upper-extremity work and feedforward (the child is moving and the object is stationary).

Basketball net games. The child flies forward in the net hammock swing, reaches into extension to secure a ball, then throws it through a target as he comes forward. This activity requires postural ocular control and timing, sequencing, and feedforward (the child is moving and the target is stationary). To increase the difficulty of feedforward, the child catches the ball as he flies forward, then throws the ball at the target (both the child and the ball are moving). If a large ball is used, symmetrical upper-extremity control is required. If a small ball is used, alternating control is required. Gradually increase the height of the target to facilitate greater extension. However, as the height is increased, the child's speed or excursion also must increase to allow the child to see the target.

Variation

The child throws balls at targets, reaches for objects positioned near the ceiling, or places slap bracelets on a bar positioned in extension. The child may propel himself, using a Bungee cord.

Tire swing activities

Riding the tire swing like a horse

Bolster game. Using his legs to propel the tire swing, the child knocks over bolsters positioned around him. This requires asymmetrical lower-extremity and symmetrical upper-extremity control and works toward feedforward (because the tire swing is moving).

Beanbag throw. Scatter beanbags across the floor. The child holds onto the tire with one arm and leans down to pick up the beanbags from the floor with the other. He then propels the tire toward the target and works to get the beanbag into a designated spot. This activity requires asymmetrical upper-extremity and lower-extremity control and some feedforward.

Sequencing game. Tape alphabet cards, pictures, or self-stick notes along the walls on all sides of the tire swing. Be sure that once the child is on the tire swing, he can physically reach the objects on the wall; however, he should have to physically reach beyond the tire swing. Using his feet to propel the tire, the child swings in the direction of the objects. As he comes near the wall, he will need to hold firmly with one arm and reach over the side of the tire swing to secure the object. This requires asymmetrical upper- and lower-extremity control and feedforward.

ILLUSTRATION 13.5

The child propels the tire forward as he reaches to retrieve the letters from the wall. This asymmetrical upper- or lower-extremity activity requires sequence, timing, and organizing motor movements.

Variations

- Have the child secure letters off alternating walls.

- Have the child remember and execute a sequence of letters

- Have the child secure self-stick notes off the walls without stopping and place them on the tire swing.

- Create games to accompany all of the activities.

Bumper cars. Secure two tire swings from the ceiling approximately six feet apart. Two children ride the tires (cars) with the goal of trying to bump the other child off the car. This requires feedforward and provides vestibular and proprioceptive input (both the tires and the children are moving and crashing).

Variation

- **Bumper-car soccer**. This game is similar to bumper cars, except the object is to get a ball into your goal in order to score points. Place a large, heavy therapy ball between two children. Assign each child a goal on either end of the mat. Using his legs, each child tries to maneuver the ball toward his goal.

- **Supine flexion wild horse game**. Prepare the area with heavy crash mats used under the tire swing. The child rides the swing like a horse, but is told to hold on tight with both hands and feet. Pull the bottom of the tire swing up against gravity and shake it. The child will start to "fall off the horse," requiring him to hold on harder. Verbally encourage the child to hold on tight. If the child uses chin jut versus chin tuck, cue the child to keep his head against the horse. Count to 10 while the child tries to hold on. The child wins the game if he holds on for 10 seconds. This activity requires symmetrical upper- and lower-extremity control, supine flexion, and provides deep-touch and proprioceptive input.

ILLUSTRATION 13.6

Playing bumper cars requires the children to time and sequence movements. Feedforward is required because both the children and the targets are moving.

Prone over the tire swing

Beanbag throw from the floor. Scatter beanbags across the floor, and place a target or bucket at one end of the room. The child balances his hips across the tire swing while placing his hands on the floor. Keeping legs straight and across the tire swing, the child walks on his arms to secure the beanbags and throw them at the target. This requires asymmetrical upper-extremity control and requires feedforward monitoring of the trunk and legs.

Variation

- Use a hammock net swing instead of a tire swing. Position the net at the child's hips or lower.

Wall pushes. This activity requires the child to closely monitor his center of gravity. *Do not do this activity if it is beyond the child's functional level or may endanger the child*. Pad the area and monitor closely for safety. The child balances across his stomach on the tire and holds onto your hands. On command, he lets go and flies back toward the wall, hitting the wall behind him with his feet. Verbally cue the child to push when he feels or hears his feet hit the wall. The child may either swing forward and grab your hands, or push forward and back using the wall behind him. This activity requires feedforward (sequencing and timing), movement backward into space, and nonvisual monitoring and sequencing of leg movements. It is a bilateral symmetrical activity of both the arms and legs.

Variations

- **Ball games**. Have the child push forward, secure a ball, then push forward again to throw it at a target.

ILLUSTRATION 13.7
The child stabilizes his trunk in extension while grading his arm movements to throw beanbags through the target.

- **Alternating wall pushes**. If you have two or three walls that the child can push off from, have him alternate pushing from one wall to the next wall to the next wall. The child will physically push himself in a circle by bouncing off each wall. This requires asymmetrical lower-extremity control, feedforward (sequencing and timing), and nonvisual monitoring of the legs.

Flexion with the tire swing

Target game. Lower the tire swing to one or two feet off the floor. Push a therapy ball into the center of the tire. The child lies on his back on the floor with his feet touching the ball and his head away from the tire. Lifting both feet together, he kicks the ball with both feet and tries to get it to fly out of the center of the tire. This game requires symmetrical lower-extremity control, feedforward, and sequencing and timing. The child must develop a strategy in order to kick the ball out rather than kick it further into the tire swing. Supine flexion also is required. If the child does not have sufficient flexion control for the game, use a wedge to raise his hips, physically facilitate his abdominal muscles, or place the child up on his elbows.

Variation

- Play the target game with two children opposite each other.

Platform swing activities

Jumping. Attach the platform swing to a vertical suspension device. The child stands on the platform and holds on securely to the ropes while you stabilize the base of the platform. He jumps up and down while you count to 10. A tire swing may be inserted on the platform to make the child feel more secure. This activity provides symmetrical upper- and lower-extremity coordination and requires some feedforward as the child sequences and times his movements.

ILLUSTRATION 13.8
The children use supine flexion (head, neck, and trunk flexion) as they time and sequence their movements to kick the ball out of the tire.

Variation

- The child falls when you count to a certain number. Let the child select the number. Falling on a number requires feedforward.

Rough water. The child stands on the platform swing (the boat) and holds on with both hands. The boat hits rough water, and the child must hold on and not fall into the water. He is required to use balance and equilibrium reactions to stay upright. This activity requires symmetrical and then alternating upper- and lower-extremity control.

Variation

- While the platform swings, the child grabs Mardi Gras necklaces from you and places them on the boat. This requires alternating upper-extremity control (a hold and do pattern) and feedforward (the child moves and the target is stationary).

Fishing. (See Illustration 14.28.) Secure a string between two ropes near the top of the swing. Scatter small clothespins (fish) under and around the platform swing. Using a fishing pole with a magnet on one end, the child stands on the platform swing and fishes. When he catches a fish, he removes it from the pole and places it on the string (that is, attaches the clothespin to the string).

Glider swing activities

Block game. Place a large foam block (for example, a Southpaw Monster Block) at the end of the glider swing. The child propels the glider to knock over the block. The position the child assumes when trying to knock over the block depends on your goals. He may stand facing the block (bilateral symmetrical), stand holding onto the ropes on either end (bilateral alternating), kneel or half-kneel facing the block, assume quadruped, or even sit facing the side of the block. The glider may be raised higher at one end, making the child change the required weight shift and therefore the motor plan. This activity requires bilateral integration depending on the task presented. It also requires feedforward because the child is moving and the activity is stationary.

Target game. The child assumes one of the positions described above on the glider swing. The goal is to throw an object at a target, through a hole, or into a bucket. By incorporating a throwing task, the activity moves from primarily symmetrical to asymmetrical and requires greater timing and sequencing.

Standing balance activities. The child stands with feet spread apart on the glider, hands holding onto the handles on either end. He *slowly* propels the glider from side to side. The child then lets go of the handles and picks up beads or objects from the platform, stands up, and strings them, all while keeping the glider moving slowly. This activity is an alternating lower-extremity and asymmetrical upper-extremity task.

Variation

- While keeping the glider moving, the child catches a ball that is thrown to him, and then throws it into a basket. This requires feedforward (both the child and the activity are moving). It also requires alternating lower-extremity and symmetrical upper-extremity control.

Flexion disc or flexion T-bar activities

Fishing game. Position the flexion disc one or two feet above the floor. Scatter beanbags (fish) over the floor. The child sits on the flexion disc and holds onto the center pole with one hand, reaches down with the other hand, scoops up the fish, and places them on the platform. The child's trunk and extremities are positioned into flexion. This activity promotes asymmetrical upper-extremity control while promoting flexion and feedforward (the child is moving and the activity is stationary).

For more feedforward, have the child save baby fish by scooping them up and throwing them into a larger pool (a barrel).

A. Flexion disc

B. Flexion T-bar

ILLUSTRATION 13.9
While holding onto the flexion disc or the flexion T-bar, the child develops symmetrical trunk and extremity flexion.

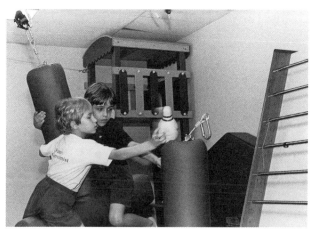

ILLUSTRATION 13.10
The children work to develop trunk rotation, asymmetrical control, and feedforward as they reach to secure objects.

Sky trolleys

Fun Ride™ Deluxe. A heavy-duty trolley is suspended on a wire from a structure. The child climbs up the structure, holds onto the trolley, and flies approximately 60 feet to the end. To integrate an obstacle course into the ride, require the child to fly over the house or drop balls into barrels or on specified targets. To integrate speech and language into the session, ask the child to describe the actions he is about to complete. This activity requires extensive feedforward (timing and sequencing), trunk and arm flexion, and bilateral symmetrical upper-extremity control and release.

Inflatable air-mat activities

(See Illustrations 12.8 and 14.19.)

A word of caution. When working with children on the air mats, monitor closely to prevent falls. Thickly pad the area, and stabilize the equipment to prevent extremes of movements.

These plastic inflatable air mats are excellent for balance activities that require bilateral upper- and lower-extremity control and feedforward from the dynamic nature of the activity. The activities provide enhanced proprioceptive input from the child's active muscle effort to balance. In addition, they promote graded arm control, shoulder and pelvic strengthening, and slow sustained midrange postural control. The moveable surface of the air mat enables the child to sustain developmental postures, such as standing, quadruped, kneeling, tall kneeling, and half-kneeling. To increase the difficulty, have the child raise a leg or an arm or perform a skilled task while in quadruped.

ILLUSTRATION 13.11
The child tucks into full body flexion as he flies across the room, timing and sequencing his movements.

Variation

- The child places objects on a rope suspended from the ceiling while balancing in various postures.

Trapeze activities

Alligator game. (See Illustration 14.18.) Raise the trapeze bar to be above the child's head. Place a chair or bench on either side of the trapeze bar. Place bolsters (alligators) in the space between the benches (the river). The child stands on one bench and swings across the river to the other bench, landing safely on the river's edge. This activity requires symmetrical upper- and lower-extremity control, hand release, and feedforward (sequencing and timing) (the child is moving but the chair is stationary).

Number game. Line up number cards on the floor under the trapeze. The child selects a number, stands on a chair, holds onto the trapeze, swings out over the numbers, and releases his grip to drop on the number. This activity requires symmetrical release and sequencing and timing (feedforward).

Building game. Construct a building of foam blocks under the trapeze bar. The child stands on the chair, holds onto the trapeze bar, swings over the building, and lands on the other side of it, making sure not to knock over the building. Gradually make the building taller, requiring the child to flex his body in order to clear the building. This activity requires symmetrical upper- and lower-extremity control and sequencing and timing of movements (feedforward).

Variation

- The child swings over the building and jumps into a barrel.

Backward somersault. Adjust the trapeze bar to enable the child to sit on the floor and hold onto it. The child places his feet on the bar, then slides the bar under his knees. Now he is hanging upside down. Holding on tightly, he brings his feet overhead into a backward somersault. Some children have difficulty coordinating both their arms and legs, and they may let go. *Take care to protect the child.* This is a complex sequencing task between the upper and lower extremities.

After the child is able to do the backward flips, he may alternate between a backward flip, then reverse it back to the original position.

Additional classroom, school-based, and recreational activities

Balance maze. The child stands on the balance maze or Southpaw Challenge Board and shifts weight from side to side or forward and backward to move the ball through the maze. This activity requires midline postural control and feedforward as the child plans and sequences his movements.

Variation

- The child places his hands on the balance maze and shifts his weight to move a marble through the maze. He is in either quadruped or with his legs supported on a chair.

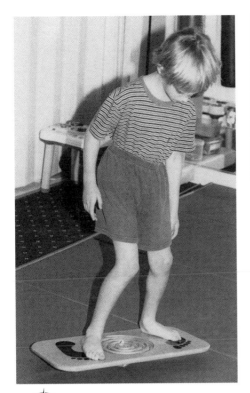

The goal of maneuvering the marble through the maze requires graded trunk and extremity control in either the upper or lower extremities.

Weight bearing on the arms. Weight-bearing activities in which the child supports his legs on a chair and places his hands on the floor may be adapted to incorporate bilateral control and feedforward (the child is stationary and the activity has movement). Games include travel basketball or other strategy games with movement incorporated into the game; or have several children bat a balloon back and forth while weight bearing on their arms.

Crab kickball. The child assumes the crab position and looks at you. Pass a balloon to him. He kicks it back to you.

Variation

● Have several children try to kick the balloon in a certain order. This activity requires asymmetrical lower-extremity control and feedforward.

Crab walk. This activity requires the child to use alternating upper- and lower-extremity movements. Vision is partially occluded due to the position of the body. Games may include crab races or obstacle course activities.

Monkey bars. Playground monkey bars provide opportunities for bilateral and feedforward and enhanced proprioceptive feedback. The child climbs the rungs of the monkey bars, holding with one hand and reaching with the next (asymmetrical upper-extremity control). If the child does not have the strength to do this, some of the body weight may be taken away by supporting him at the waist or ankles. Encourage him to try to land on a designated place (feedforward).

ILLUSTRATION 13.13

Crab kickball requires asymmetrical lower-extremity control, feedforward, and sensory awareness of the extremities (because the arms and legs cannot be visually monitored).

Parallel bars. Walking on the arms on parallel bars promotes asymmetrical upper-extremity control.

Trampolines. Use small trampolines to promote sensory feedback while having the child work on alternating or asymmetrical tasks. To enhance feedback, have the child wear arm or ankle weights or a weighted vest. He may hop on one foot, perform a sequence of hops (two right, three left, two right), alternate between hopping and jumping, perform sequences of feet together and then apart, or do scissors movements. To integrate upper-extremity activities, have him clap in rhythm or add overhead arm claps to jumping jacks. To increase feedforward, have the child bounce and catch a ball while jumping.

Use large trampolines for all of the previous activities; or use them to promote sequences of total-body activities (for example, jump, land on knees, then stand). *When working on a large trampoline, safety must be a primary concern.*

Sports. All sports-related activities require feedforward and bilateral motor control. To make the activities easier, look for ways to enhance sensory feedback by modifying or weighting either the equipment or the child.

- **Catching, throwing, or bouncing balls**. Use weighted balls, or slow down the action by using a beach ball.

- **Kickball**. Use weighted balls, enhance sensory feedback by using a beach ball, or weight the child's ankles.

- **Baseball**. Use a weighted bat, weight the child's extremities, or slow down the action by using a beach ball or balloon.

Bike riding. This activity requires bilateral asymmetrical lower-extremity control, dynamic midrange balance reactions, and feedforward as the child plans and sequences body movements to maneuver turns and changes in directions. The child may wear a weighted vest, a weighted belt, or arm weights.

Carrying Out the Sequence: Task Execution

In the function phase of treatment, concentrate on allowing opportunities for the child to carry over the new level of integration into functional tasks—the new sense of self-confidence and awareness obtained during the facilitation phase-into some functional tasks for home, school, or play activities.

Once the child is able to effectively conceptualize the plan and organize the information, the execution of the task will naturally follow. It is important that therapy not concentrate on the execution of the task or teach splinter skills, but provide the sensorimotor foundation skills that are needed in order to master tasks independently. Many children with autistic spectrum disorders, once provided with sensorimotor foundation skills, will automatically execute the task on their own. Once they have a sense of self, understand their body scheme and how it relates to the outside world, and have normal motor engrams from which to draw for future learning, they will automatically attempt new tasks at home and at school.

However, there are tasks that require teaching and demand motor planning until the task becomes automatic. These activities include tying shoes; tracing, writing, coloring, and many other school-related tasks; bike riding, ball activities, and most sports; and many activities of daily living and self-care skills. These tasks must not be approached in isolation. The same foundation skills are needed to master these skills as are required for full integration. Prepare the child for success by providing preparation and facilitation activities before any session that is designed to teach a skill.

School- and Home-Based Programs

School therapists and those who oversee home-based programs are involved in monitoring skill development and teaching tasks. They are responsible for assessing the child's current sensorimotor skills and functional levels and the demands of the task. This includes assessing sensory feedback provided from the task, the degree of bilateral integration and sequencing required, and the feedback or degree of feedforward required. The therapist then is responsible for grading the task for successful completion by the child. This may include modifying the task for enhanced sensory input.

Enhanced Sensory Feedback

Because the base problem of somatodyspraxia is poor tactile discrimination, an activity such as stacking blocks may be modified to stacking interlocking blocks to provide better sensory feedback and success.

Assess activities for their:

● Inherent sensory feedback

● Ability to be adapted for enhance sensory feedback through tactile, vestibular, proprioceptive, visual, or auditory input

Bilateral Integration and Sequencing

Tasks may need to be modified to decrease bilateral integration demands. Modifications may be needed to facilitate postural and ocular control. The child may:

- Use an easel or incline board for writing to decrease postural and ocular demands during classwork

- Sit on a cushioned wedge to enable some vestibular input and promote an upright posture

- Tape writing paper to the desk to reduce the bilateral demand of writing

Feedback and Feedforward

Any time a child is asked to take information from his mind and do something with it, the task will require feedforward and sequencing. School tasks can be analyzed according to the degree of feedforward required, and therefore the degree of difficulty. Most concrete tasks provide feedback, while abstract tasks require feedforward. When a child has difficulty with an abstract (feedforward) task, provide concrete prompts to help him process the task in a feedback mode. (See the following examples in "Writing a story from memory.") Some school-related tasks are:

- Tracing. Feedback is required.

- Copying. Feedback is provided, but the child must motor plan and sequence the movements with visual guidance.

- Writing the alphabet from dictation. Feedforward is required as the child motor plans and sequences the movements with auditory guidance.

- Writing the alphabet from memory. Feedforward and sequencing are required. The child must motor plan and sequence the movements and alphabet from memory.

- Writing a story from memory, Feedforward and sequencing are required. The child must organize his thoughts, sequence them, and then record them in writing. If the child cannot do this, the following strategies are often helpful:

  — Have the child physically perform a series of motor movements, then verbally tell you the sequence, then write the sequence as a story.

  — Provide concrete visual cues by having the child cut out pictures of the story, sequence them, then write the story.

  — Have the child write about a sequence of activities that he did that morning. Provide concrete cues. (For example, "After I got up, I . . . Then, I . . . ")

  — Give the child a list of important words that are needed for the story. The words will help him recall the events and sequence. He crosses out the words as they are used.

  — Have the child write about a sequence of events that is planned in the future.

Verbal Feedback

Providing verbal feedback is an art that often is necessary for task execution. Provide feedback at the child's level and in a manner that is not overwhelming. It must be task-specific and must point out exactly what was good. If you want to modify the child's response, direct the verbal feedback toward changing *only one aspect* of the task. In order to assure success, provide physical guidance.

Imagine that you are teaching a child to tie his shoes. As you observe the child's ability to sequence the task, you decide that he needs to change one strategy. Tell the child, "I liked how you crossed the laces and made the first tie. Now you need to bring the laces toward you—not away from you—when you wrap the lace." Then provide physical assistance to help the child successfully tie his shoes.

A word of caution. Do not provide too much verbal feedback. Physical cues and sensory feedback are more effective and work subcortically.

Carryover Into Other Environments

When working on task execution, do not expect the child to perform the task independently or automatically until the skill is totally mastered; that is, until he is able to practice it over and over again in an environment free of stress. Once the child is able to perform the task without conscious attention, he will need opportunities to generalize the skill in multiple environments. Never assume that a child will carry skills into other environments, even after he has appeared to master the skill within the therapy session.

For example, a child who has learned to tie laces on a Bunny Bow Tie® board should not be expected to generalize that skill to be able to tie his shoes. Similarly, a child who can tie his shoes off his feet cannot be expected to tie the shoes when his feet are in them; or a child who can tie his shoes in the clinic may not be able to tie them at home or at school. In each of these situations, the motor plan is different and may require practice and support. Generalizing skills learned across multiple environments is difficult. We must help both the child and the parents bridge that gap.

Facilitating Language and SI

We cannot overemphasize the importance of providing a holistic approach to intervention. Any one approach, in and of itself, will be ineffective in remediating the sensorimotor and functional problems encountered by the child with autism spectrum disorder. Remediating the communication deficits associated with this disorder is a perfect example of the need for an integrated approach. Occupational therapy, using a sensory integrative approach, prepares the child's nervous system for speech and language sessions. It is not coincidental that children do better in speech therapy when they are first treated by an occupational therapist. Speech and language are not isolated entities, but a complex, multifaceted process that requires sensory integration along multiple levels of the brain. Acquiring effective speech and language is more than just acquiring words or rote sentence use. It involves spontaneous communication with others—the ability to plan, sequence, and organize thoughts and words into meaningful expressions and integrate information throughout the brain on multiple levels.

Neurological and Sensory System Connections

There is a circular interaction between the development of the ability to communicate using language and the overall ability to organize and integrate sensory input for use. As children improve in sensory integrative functions, they improve in the course of speech and language acquisition. Similarly, as they are able to respond adaptively in the area of speech and language, there is a positive impact upon their sensory integrative processes (Windeck and Laure 1989).

The ability to use speech and language is not merely a cognitive function but is dependent upon central nervous system organization at all levels, from the brain stem to the cortex. Effective communication is described as a whole-brain function. The processing of language appears to be discretely located at both the cortical and thalamic levels of the brain (Ojemann 1983) and requires whole-brain function for communication. Auditory impulses travel to the brain stem where the auditory nuclei process auditory impulses. Auditory impulses travel to other brain-stem areas and to the cerebellum, where they mix with motor messages. Auditory information going to the cortical processing areas of the brain is not purely auditory, but is mixed with motor and sensory impulses. This convergence of information appears to be essential for auditory input to have meaning (Ayres 1978).

Windeck and Laure (1989) identified the importance of multisensory integration in auditory processing. Single-sensory channels process slower and less efficiently with a less organized response than polysensory neurons, which require intersensory information in order to fire. The neurons will fire when they receive information from three or more forms of input (vestibular, proprioceptive, tactile, auditory, visual). Auditory and visual systems must be continually verified by information from the vestibular, proprioceptive, or tactile systems. Therefore, auditory processing will be accomplished faster, more efficiently, and with a more organized response when it is combined with sensory information from the vestibular or somatosensory (tactile-proprioceptive) systems.

Processing of tactile and proprioceptive input is speculated to be related to the linguistic system through the trigeminothalamic tract (somatosensory system). Somatodyspraxia is a somatosensory processing disorder that is rooted in poor processing of tactile and proprioceptive sensory information. Oral motor problems, characteristic of the child with dyspraxia, are directly related to the inability to effectively perceive and process this sensory input. The lack of oral motor movements and motor control are related to sensory deficits. Secondary problems, such as difficulty with chin tuck, head and neck stability, trunk control, and breath control, are often related to postural control issues that have a direct impact on the ability to motorically produce speech.

Acquisition of Speech

Ayres (1978) states that early sensory motor experiences provide the basis for a person to learn about the boundaries and capabilities of his own body and about the environment. The effects of sensory motor experiences create the framework of understanding on which language is based. This framework enables meaningful experiences to be integrated and assimilated. The ability to use both expressive and receptive language requires that the brain have the capacity to organize sensory input.

Children need to attach meaning and words, to sensory motor experiences. Unless they can attach language to their experiences, needs, and wants, they will only be passive recipients of their environment, unable to verbally impact or control things around them. Occupational and physical therapists working in conjunction with speech therapists must help children connect words to their sensory motor experiences and movements. Children's ability to associate a word with an action is a form of sensory integration and requires interhemispheric integration (DeQuiros 1978).

Processing sensorimotor experiences with language, rather than without it, enables opportunities for children to understand, map out, and start to control the environment and the things that happen within it. Children will first acquire words that are meaningful to them and that help them impact their environments.

> Jason, 4-years-old, is nonverbal. He is underresponsive to somatosensory input and has a poor body scheme. He is driven to obtain sensory feedback. He always is running, crashing, and seeking opportunities for deep-touch and proprioceptive input. Safety is a major issue for Jason. He is hard to slow down, climbs to high places, and always jumps head first. During occupational therapy, he physically lashed out when his therapist tried to stop him. During sessions that provided deep-touch and proprioceptive input, Jason was guided through activities with the verbal cue, "Feet first." He soon realized that he could do any activity that he wanted as long as he went feet first. As he would start to climb head first into a tube standing on the floor, his therapist had only to approach him and he would change his motor plan, turn his body around, and proceed feet first. The first words Jason spoke were, "Feet first."

Basic communication is critical to the child's well-being and must be the first and primary goal for all professionals working with him. Establishing some form of communication, helping the child identify and communicate his desires and needs, must be integrated into all professional programs until a consistent method can be obtained. A child who cannot communicate will develop challenging, undesirable behaviors unless a system is established from the onset. However, first we must help the child register sensory information. He must understand that there is something to communicate. A child who is not processing or registering sensory information often is compliant. When he starts to process information, being able to identify his needs and wants but unable to effectively communicate those desires, disruptive behaviors begin to surface. Establishing an effective method of communication is critical to avoid disruptive and challenging behaviors.

Speech and Language as Related to Praxis

Effective speech and language requires that the child register sensory information (know that there is something to do or say), formulate the idea, plan and sequence his thoughts, and then speak. This is the same process that is required for motor planning and executing total-body activities. It is hypothesized that praxis and language share overlapping neural structures. It also is believed that when one area is impacted, it will overflow into related areas. A child who is unable to communicate due to dyspraxia will improve when his ability to motor plan total-body movements improves. Similarly, a child who improves in the ability to plan and sequence speech also will show improvements in his ability to plan and sequence total-body movements. Through integrating speech and language into motor planning tasks, language and motor planning skills will improve.

A child must register sensory information and formulate an idea in order to conceptualize what he is to say or what he wants. Concept formation is critical to the development of ideational skills. As the child acquires a repertoire of basic concepts, he develops the ability to organize and understand his experiences. Those experiences will enable him to think with language and formulate plans. During therapy, stop children before an activity and ask, "What do you want to do? Tell me first, and then we will do it."

When working to facilitate language acquisition, consider environmental factors. The amount of structure in the environment will have a direct impact on the child's ability to process language and follow verbal direction. Children give optimal attention when they are in small, enclosed areas and are given one-on-one instructions. Open environments with little structure are on the opposite end of the spectrum. Gradually integrate verbal instruction into open environments to facilitate the child's ability to process auditory information with background distractions (multisensory processing).

Grade verbal requests from the child to help him process using language. To think into the future-to describe what you plan to do-requires feedforward. To grade tasks, ask the child to:

- Describe what he is doing (present)

- Describe what he just did (past)

- Describe what he plans to do (future)

> Ben has difficulty with organizing and sequencing a plan. He was asked to plan out an obstacle course and write what he planned to do. He had a lot of ideas, but he was unable to organize them effectively. With assistance, he constructed the obstacle course, making it concrete. He went through the obstacle course, telling the therapist what he just did. Afterward, he wrote the sequence of activities he had completed, using the actual obstacle course as a visual prompt when he had difficulty recalling the sequence. If Ben had not been able to sequence the task after he went through the obstacle course, he could have described the activities as he went through them, connecting the action with the sequence.

Planning, organizing, and sequencing information for speech requires that the child organize what he wants to say or do, plan and sequence it, compare it to memories of previous experiences, and then produce speech. The sequencing of speech requires the child to organize, plan, and sequence a set of letters and words (project the sequence) into the future as feedforward. Sequencing difficulties may appear as the child having difficulty:

- Moving his lips and tongue to say a word

- Making inconsistent error patterns in articulation, such as saying *swi* for swing, while other times saying *gishw*

- Being unable to speak on demand. He may speak spontaneously, during play, or when he wants something, but be unable to speak when asked a question or asked to repeat what he said.

Speech is more than saying words. It is through planning, organizing, and sequencing information for speech that the child makes meaning of his world and is able to express his thoughts and perceptions. The child may use speech to:

- Map his world

- Describe his experiences, feelings, and thoughts

- Reflect a distance from the event (that is, describe events in the past or future)

- Change his perception of the world, abstractions, create new ideas, fantasize, change reality

Creative thinking is one of the goals of sensory integration. As the child can process multisensory information, organize and sequence information, and put concepts together in novel, unique ways, multisensory integration is occurring.

CHAPTER 14

Motor Control and Coordination Difficulties

Betty Paris

 Motor Control Theories

Motor control is the set of processes that organizes and coordinates functional movements. Neural maturation alone does not guarantee the development of motor control. Current theories on motor control have two basic, but competing, views of how the brain organizes movement. One is a hierarchal view, and the other is a dynamic systems view.

Hierarchal View

In a hierarchal view, the nervous system is viewed as having several levels of functional units within the central nervous system (CNS), with each unit or level having discrete functions. Reflex responses are assigned as functions of lower levels, and volitional movements or inhibitory actions are assigned to higher levels. Inherent in the hierarchal view is the idea that the properties of the system are the properties of the various functional units. If a unit is damaged, there is little chance that other functional units can take over to subserve a function.

Systems View

A systems model for motor control looks at the functions of the CNS in a distributed fashion. Each of the functional units within the system shares responsibility, and the properties of the system emerge through the interaction between the units. Information is handled in a reciprocal fashion, enabling greater flexibility and control. The system view of motor control holds that the system can vary its response according to the context of the task, or environment. Various functional units have the potential to assume control, based upon the context and the goal. Implied is that if one functional unit cannot adequately do the job, there are potentials for other functional units to accomplish the task.

TABLE 14.1 Basic assumptions in a dynamic systems view

- Movement is dependent upon the laws of physics and nature.
- The system is self-organizing.
- At times it is stable, and at other times unstable.
- The subsystems are interactive.
- The system is adaptable to change.
- There is no super-controller; no one system has a higher priority or power.
- The system is very sensitive to small changes.

 Motor Learning Concepts

Feedback Versus Feedforward

Feedback as a form of motor control is one in which the motor response may be in response to a change in the environment or the result of a stimulus. Our head and body righting reactions, protective extension responses, and balance and equilibrium reactions are forms of feedback motor control. However, feedback also is the mechanism used for initial acquisition of a skill. Feedback involves making use of the sensory input resulting from a motor act or stimulus to alter future responses. It enables us to judge whether our initial responses are adequate and what, if any, adaptations to make in subsequent motor responses. It implies a degree of learning that occurs as a result of our movement experiences. Feedback is paramount in a dynamic systems view of motor control.

Feedforward motor control is one in which the motor act does not rely on sensory information to be generated. It happens in advance of a motor act as preparation. For example, when a child prepares to hit a pitched ball, he is able to posturally set his body in advance of hitting and can adjust where he swings the bat to strike a pitched ball. With repetition, the movement pattern becomes more hard-wired into the circuitry of the brain and more automatic. It becomes a motor program. The more motor programs you have, the more automatic, skilled, and efficient you are and the more freedom you have during function. In treatment, feedforward forms of motor control enable us to perform action sequences, such as kicking a rolling or bounced ball.

Plans or Engrams

Motor learning is a process in which the capacity for motor performance is changed permanently. It is the end product of experience and practice of a motor

task that has had the benefit of feedback—not changes in motor performance that are the result of developmental or aging processes (Schmidt 1988). Fitts (1964) described three stages of motor learning:

- A cognitive phase in which all sensory systems are used to gather and validate information

- An associative phase in which the task is practiced and feedback used to alter performance

- An autonomous phase in which the task is performed with skill on a subconscious level (Cech and Martin 1995)

Lashley (1951) proposed the idea of motor programs within our memory, or engrams. These engrams provide a set of instructions that have been stored based upon our experiences. They become hard-wired in, if you will. Motor engrams can be called up and implemented for learned motor responses so that the CNS does not have to reinvent a motor sequence every time it is called. Features in a motor plan that do not vary include the order, timing, and relative force of the movements. Variable qualities include overall duration and intensity of the muscle contractions. Shoe tying is an example of a motor engram. At first, it is a cognitive process, but with practice the typical child can tie his shoes without looking or giving it a conscious effort.

Alterations in Neuromotor Status

Motor control can be influenced and affected by a number of factors, including:

- Impairments within the central nervous system

- Impairments within the musculoskeletal system

- Impairments within the peripheral nervous system

- Impaired ability to motor plan an action

- Impaired sensory processing

If there is damage within the CNS, such as that because of a cerebral artery hemorrhage or cerebral palsy, there will be somewhat predictable primary and secondary impairments in motor control (Bierman 1998). That is, the impairment in motor function is because of damage within the CNS and its ability to send appropriate signals to the musculoskeletal system for the smooth and coordinated control of movement. Therefore, there is impairment in the neuromotor control. Motor control can be affected by a change in the neuromotor status in which spasticity, rigidity, or ataxia hinders the quality of motor control.

Impairments in the musculoskeletal system may be because of changes in joint alignment, soft-tissue constriction, and in the range of motion available to perform activities with motor control. Children with arthrogryposis, in which there are malformed joints, lack good motor control because they will not be able to move throughout the normal range of motion or with the normal flexibility. Motor control will be affected by the lack of that flexibility, creating the need for compensatory motor strategies. Joint contractures, often seen as secondary effects of a variety of disorders, also will have deleterious affects on motor control by restriction of the normal movement patterns and the muscle actions that control them.

Peripheral nerve impairments such as that found in children with spina bifida also will impair motor control. The damage here lies within the spinal cord and affects the peripheral nervous system. The muscles of the affected nerve roots cannot function properly. They may function partially or not at all, thereby affecting motor control.

Motor planning involves several steps, both cognitive and motoric. Motor planning is knowing what to do and how to do it. It is the ability to conceptualize, organize, and direct purposeful interaction with the physical world. It involves:

- Registering sensory information or knowing that there is something there to interact with

- Formulating the idea-realizing the play potential of the toy or object

- Generating the plan and knowing how to organize and sequence the task

The first step is to recognize an object separate from everything else in the surrounding environment or registration. Next is to appreciate the potential for interaction with that object. A motor plan involves the idea of how to use the object or what to do with it. ("Will I sit on a scooterboard, or lie on it?") In order to be successful in my interaction with that scooterboard, I need to sequence my actions. ("What do I need to do in order to get onto the scooterboard and not fall off? Then, how will I propel it?") Finally, I need the motor control—the sensory processing, strength, flexibility, and coordination-to execute the planned action successfully.

Effects of Sensory Input on Motor Control

The role of sensory input and the effect of the sensory systems are crucial to motor control. In the infant, sensory input is what typically stimulates or motivates the initiation of motor behaviors. As the baby sees an object, he may swipe out at it. If he is successful in grasping it, he is driven to mouth it. If he drops that object, the sound it makes as it hits the surface reinforces to the baby that he has indeed dropped it. If he hears an adult's voice, he will turn toward it. He may begin to roll or to pivot in prone to follow the sounds and sights he perceives. Visual input is compared to and confirmed by the other sensory systems.

The sensory systems guide and organize motor activity. In feedback forms of motor control, it is the sensory information that is used to detect whether the result is as expected. It is used to correct subsequent motor responses. It also is sensory input that formulates the building blocks for feedforward motor control.

If you ascribe to a dynamic systems approach, you can see that motor control can be impacted by the quality of sensory information and processing within the system. Nashner's model of postural control is a good example of a systems theory (Cech and Martin 1995). Nashner (1977, 1990) studied the effects of the sensory systems on standing balance, that is, the visual, vestibular, somatosensory (tactile or cutaneous), and proprioceptive systems. The support surfaces were varied as well as the visual field surrounding the subjects. He found that when the visual field moved in concert with the subject's postural sway, the visual system could not be relied upon for balance in standing. Consequently, the vestibular system took control.

Nashner took his studies one step further. He blocked the person's ability to use an ankle strategy for balance. Typically, when the support surface is perturbed, a person's first strategy is to call upon the muscles of the calf (which control movement at the ankle) to maintain balance. When this action was blocked, Nashner found that the hips and knees were used as an alternate functional unit to maintain balance. Nashner's work proved that multiple sensory systems can be called upon to interpret and influence standing balance depending upon the context or the environment. He further demonstrated the flexibility of the dynamic systems theory in that if one strategy is not available to the individual, another may be called upon to do the job.

As a result of Nashner and others studying the effects of sensory input and its impact on standing balance, we know that the motor control strategies are affected and altered by impaired sensory processing. Because motor reactions are the product of input from a variety of interdependent subsystems, a dysfunction in sensory processing directly affects the type, quality, and success of the motor response.

 ## Motor Control in Children With Autism

The pathophysiology of autism is yet unknown and currently is being investigated. We know that there are not impairments in the joint structures inherent in autism, as there are in conditions such as arthrogryposis. We also know that the peripheral nervous systems are intact. Indeed, there are those who believe that because there are no consistent demonstrable pathophysiology and predictable motor impairments in autism, motor control is not an issue.

Children with autism often are cited as being clumsy, uncoordinated, having a lack of attention, and being hyperactive, all of which may be due in part to a deficiency in motor control. Impairments in motor control within this population do not follow a predictable course; they may be present in some children and not readily identified in others. Yet a number of motor abnormalities have been noted in these children, with relatively little clinical significance assigned to them.

Jones and Prior (1985) reported that children with autism are universally dyspraxic; and Vilensky and colleagues (1981) reported that they manifest disturbances of gait. Hallett and colleagues (1993) felt that many continue to manifest gait disturbances into adulthood. Adrien (1992) found that blind raters were able to differentiate children with autism from normal children based upon their motor skills and other factors from home movies taken before autism was diagnosed. Sears and colleagues (1994) cited the classical eyeblink conditioning, a hallmark characteristic of cerebellar functions, as being abnormal in children with autism. Haas and associates (1996) found that patients with autism showed abnormalities that they felt were indicative of cerebellar and parietal lobe dysfunctions, based upon standard neurological exams (Belmonte and Carper 1998).

The first suggested neuropathological bases for these types of functional impairments found in autism occurred when Williams and associates (1980) detected a low Purkinje cell count in the cerebellum of four autistic brains. Ritvo and associates (1986) confirmed this by reporting 41% loss of Purkinje cells within the vermis portion of the cerebellum and a 35% loss in the hemispheres of four autistic brains, compared to normal counterparts. Multiple nuclear magnetic resonance

imaging studies since the late 1980s have confirmed the depletion of cells manifested as a deficit in size of the cerebellar vermis and the cerebellar hemispheres (Courchesne et al. 1987, 1988; Gaffney et al. 1987; Murakami et al. 1989; Hashimoto et al. 1995).

In 1991, Margaret Bauman, M.D., found a depletion of Purkinje and granule cells in autopsy studies of other autistic brains, but no evidence of the gliosis that would occur if the neurons had degenerated after infancy. Bauman and her colleagues also found abnormally enlarged cells in the cerebellar deep nuclei, which are the destinations of the Purkinje fibers. Bauman also found small cell bodies in the lateral portion of the inferior olive, the source of climbing-fiber input to Purkinje cells, again without evidence of retrograde cell death. This, like the absence of gliosis in the cerebellar cortex, indicates onset of abnormalities early in fetal life. Bauman and Kemper (1993) speculated that the olivary and deep nuclear abnormalities might be a consequence of the retention of fetal neuronal circuitry in which climbing fibers do not send the major branches of their axons into the cerebellar cortex. Bauman put this in layman's terms when she stated that the brain of a child with autism, while not damaged, may be neurologically wired in a dysfunctional or inefficient manner. These postulations would account for a pattern of short-circuiting that would sabotage the regular topography of the cerebellar cortical map (Belmonte and Carper 1998).

The cerebellum is known to have a main function in coordinating complex movements. It is essential for balance, fine motor control, and muscle coordination. The cerebellar vermis is connected to brain regions that govern attention, arousal level, and the assimilation of sensory information. Many researchers believe that the failure of development within the cerebellum occurs either in the first few months after conception or during the first and second years of life. Thus, it would affect the way the entire system interconnects, interacts, and develops.

Other areas of the brain have been cited as having abnormalities. The causes are yet unclear and may be due to the same process that damages the cerebellar vermis. Another possibility is that damage to the cerebellum alters the development of associated brain areas. The result may be underdevelopment of the cerebellum and other areas of the brain.

Also prevalent in the research, and gaining increasing acceptance, is the observation that the effect of a lesion in a developing brain is thought to be more severe than the effect of a similar lesion in a mature brain that has undergone normal development. This is because the brain systems are dependent upon correct input for their proper maturation. Improper input leads to inadequate maturation, faulty performance, and functional impairments. This increasingly popular observation among researchers today was a basic tenet in A. J. Ayres' theory of sensory integration.

Sensory Processing and Motor Control Problems

Abnormal sensory processing is a problem of those with autism. Many children with autism cannot rely on the information from their tactile, proprioceptive, vestibular, visual, and auditory systems. The observation that a lesion or problems within a developing brain will lead to more severe and global deficits or impairments because of the interdependencies of brain systems upon correct information for maturation coincides with Ayres' theories on SI and Bobath's theories of postural and motor control. Both theories are based upon the belief that improper input leads to inadequate maturation, faulty performance, and functional impairments.

As a result of Ayres' factor-analytic studies, several discrete dysfunctions have been linked to specific systems.

Problems That May Be Tactile-Based

Tactile discrimination

Problems with the ability to discriminate tactile information will cause a variety of impairments in motor control.

Gross motor control will be impacted and be characterized by

- Decreased body scheme
- Impaired balance reactions
- Postural insecurity
- Motor clumsiness

Hand control will be affected as evidenced by

- Impairments in grasp and prehension patterns
- Lack of isolated finger control
- Poor in-hand manipulation skills
- Impaired skilled tool usage
- Shortening of the intrinsic muscles of the thenar eminence (thumb)
- Shortening of the hand intrinsic musculature

Oral motor control will be impacted and be characterized by

- Decreased isolated tongue movements
- Poor lip closure
- Instability of the jaw
- Articulation difficulties

Poor tactile discrimination also will cause impairments in overall coordination, gross motor skills, standing and walking balance, activities of daily living, fine motor skills, and even in the oral motor functions for speech and feeding.

Infants use tactile exploration of the body within the first few months of life to discern their body maps. They play with their own hands, pull at their legs, and tug on their feet, thereby establishing a mental knowledge of the configuration of their bodies. Tactile perception also is a motivator to young infants. Babies are driven to touch, mouth, and explore objects they encounter. They begin to push against the floor to move toward objects, getting sensory feedback through the hands, feet, and trunk. As they develop further, they begin to transition to various postures, all the while learning more about the body scheme. As they learn to creep, stand, and walk, they discern various tactile cues and how to use their hands and later their feet to balance. As they learn dressing skills, they maneuver their arms through the armholes of shirts and legs through pants. They learn to wiggle into and out of socks and shoes.

As they interact with toys, they develop a variety of grasp and prehension patterns. They begin to isolate the fingers. They reinforce eye-hand coordination in learning to feed themselves. They learn first about textures during finger-feeding experiences, and later about how to manipulate forks and spoons. They begin to scoop or stab at food and bring it to their mouths successfully. With a variety of food textures, they learn to move the food within the mouth while they chew. They play with tongue movements as they spit food out, blow raspberries, and experience food textures.

Hand control and skill acquisition continues through the early school years in the acquisition of activities of daily living as they learn to feed and dress themselves, to maneuver buttons, zippers, and other fasteners, and later as they perform paper-and-pencil tasks. They learn to use scissors, pencils, and finally pens with control to make discrete and skilled movements for writing. Bimanual coordination develops with interest in sports-related activities.

As language develops, children continue to refine skills within the oral motor systems. They play with pitch, volume, tone, and differing rates of movement required for sound production. Language streams increase, as do endurance and respiratory control.

The inability to discriminate tactile information is a major limiting factor toward the development of a reliable body percept and skill acquisition. Children with autism often miss the sensory experiences that teach typical children about their bodies and about the world around them. This leads to impairments in body scheme and the ability to move the body reliably for gross motor skills, hand use, and oral motor functions.

A lack of tactile discrimination leads not only to impairment in body percept, but an inability to perceive objects and changes within the environment. Feedback derived from sensory experiences is faulty because of faulty tactile discrimination. The result is often a clumsy and uncoordinated child who bumps into people, drops objects, and trips over his own feet. Feet that don't discriminate the type of surface they are on can't adjust well for balance. Foot placement may be irregular and unreliable. This child may exhibit postural insecurity stemming from a lack of balance skills, an uncertainty of where his legs and feet are, and what type of surface he is on. He has difficulty walking on carpet, gravel, and grass. He may be overly cautious or fearful, with good reason.

Hands that cannot discriminate tactile information don't perceive the shapes or size of the objects in them. They don't discern when an object is in the hands or how to orient it for use. The hands don't discriminate textures and don't know how to grasp or use a pincer movement for finer tasks. Children with poor or impaired tactile discrimination miss developing isolated finger control and skilled manipulation or interaction with toys and other objects.

Oral motor control also suffers. Children who lack tactile discrimination have a poor sensory awareness of the mouth and face. They may drool because they don't perceive the presence of saliva or lack the ability for lip closure. These children do not perceive where the tongue is in their mouths, what textures the foods are, and how to move food in the mouth in order to chew or to swallow. They may develop a strict preference for certain foods because those are the foods that they have learned to manage. New foods present new threats of choking and new challenges to eating. Vocalizations may lack variety simply because these children are unaware of where to place the tongue in the mouth for sound production. Speech is delayed and intelligibility; and once it begins to emerge, its quality is poor.

Simple dressing skills also are impacted. Arms that don't perceive tactile stimulation have difficulty pulling on clothing. Legs and feet that don't perceive tactile information may not go into pants or socks easily. Putting shoes on feet that don't perceive tactile information is difficult. Toes curl instead of extending, and the child can't wiggle his heels into shoes. Buttons, zippers, and other fasteners may be beyond the child's abilities.

Somatodyspraxia

The term *dyspraxia* often is used by neurologists and therapists to describe the situation in which a person has difficulty learning a new motor skill or performing a specific skill or task on demand. When it is seen in an adult, there is the assumption that the person was able to perform the skills and that whatever insult occurred to the CNS caused the difficulties in performance. However, in a child, we must consider the possibility that the neuronal circuitry is variable, and therefore performance is variable. We must consider that development was abnormal and that limitations in performance are the result of that development.

Somatodyspraxia is a more pervasive impairment than a tactile discrimination problem. It involves the central processing within the brain, and it limits not only motor control, but motor planning. Fundamental in this condition is the system's ability to recognize objects within the environment, recognize what is to be done, establish a plan of action, and execute that plan in an effective sequence to accomplish the task. Persons with a somatodyspraxia have severe tactile discrimination, proprioception, and vestibular components to the dysfunction. Motor control develops with many secondary problems and compensations.

Motor learning and subsequent task performance in children with somatodyspraxia are not automatic; they require tremendous cognitive effort. Tasks must be broken into components and taught separately in order to foster motor engrams needed to accomplish the task. Furthermore, these children learn the components of a particular skill in a particular setting, but may fail to alter those engrams when environmental conditions are altered. A lack of variety in movement patterns and strategies is characteristic. These children must be taught to generalize the information under a variety of environmental and situational conditions.

Limitations in motor control stemming from a somatodyspraxia include:

- All problems listed under tactile discrimination
- Impaired gross motor control stemming from
  - Decreased body scheme
  - Impaired balance reactions with postural insecurity

- Motor clumsiness secondary to impaired proprioception and vestibular functioning
- Impaired motor planning for gross motor skills

- Limited hand control
  - Impaired grasp and prehension patterns
  - Poor isolated finger control
  - Poor in-hand manipulation
  - Lack of skilled tool usage
  - Impaired motor planning for skilled hand use

- Oral motor impairments
  - Decreased isolated tongue movement
  - Poor lip closure
  - Instability of the jaw
  - Impaired motor planning for speech production
  - Articulation difficulties

- Weakness throughout the cervical musculature as evidenced by:
  - Decreased ability to right the head against gravity in any direction

ILLUSTRATION 14.1
Impaired grasp and prehension patterns

- Diminished flexion in the neck (as evidenced by poor performance on supine flexion tests) may result in

  — Possible decrease in downward gaze (ocular motor control)

  — Poor jaw stability

  — Impaired internal stability to the base of the tongue for oral motor skills

  — Impaired static balance skills

  — Lack of midline orientation

- Muscle and tendon shortening throughout the trunk and extremities. This develops as a result of atypical patterns of development and limited movement experiences. As a compensatory strategy, the child assumes postures that allow adaptive shortening of muscles in order to provide passive stability for function. This in turn results in

  — Poor spinal mobility

  — Impaired thoracolumbar control

  — Impaired pelvic control

  — Shortened muscles throughout the trunk and extremities

- Decreased internal stability secondary to the use of the lack of variety of motor patterns

  — Impaired slow, sustained muscular control throughout the trunk

  — Poor proximal stability in the scapulae, shoulders, pelvis, and hips

  — Poor internal stability elbow, wrist, hand, knee, ankle, and foot

- Impaired activities of daily living (for example, feeding and dressing)

- Problems with feedback and feedforward forms of motor control

Tactile defensiveness and avoidance

Problems arise from the fact that sensory perceptions are distorted, painful, or unpleasant, and thus are avoided. A child may seek to avoid weight-bearing patterns and activities that involve objects contacting the palm of the hands. Consequently, grasp patterns, body movements, and foot placements are altered in order to control and avoid touch sensations that are loathsome. The ability to use the hands for resistive or heavy work activities is not developed.

Motor control issues seen in children with tactile defensiveness or avoidance include muscle shortening, muscle weakness and joint instabilities secondary to the lack of weight-bearing experiences, a lack of resistive activities and a lack of hand use. Internal stability fails to develop because of a lack of variety of movement patterns and an intolerance of weight-bearing postures.

Upper extremity

- Shortening is noted in the lateral rotator muscles of the shoulder because of a lack of inferior and medial scapular stabilization.

- The interosseous membrane between the radius and ulna is shortened as the child functions with forearm pronation.

- Shortening throughout the extrinsic and intrinsic muscles of the thumb results in thumb to midfinger opposition or other prehension patterns.

- Overstretching of the metacarpal phalangeal (MCP) joint ligaments develops secondary to use of the tripod posture in weight bearing.

- Weakness throughout the proximal segments of the upper extremity leads to impaired function distally.

ILLUSTRATION 14.3
Tripod weight bearing causes ligamentous instabilities in the MCP joints.

- The child fails to develop the muscles on the medial and inferior border of the scapulae to render scapular stability.

- The child lacks strength in the muscles that control the shoulder, particularly the rotator cuff muscles required for shoulder stability in weight-bearing positions as well as for positioning the upper extremity for hand function.

- The child fails to develop midrange, graded elbow control.

- The wrist remains unstable and often functions in wrist flexion rather than the more functional position of near neutral or extended position.

- The child uses the tips of his fingers to grasp objects and manipulate them, and therefore fails to develop internal stability within the hand. The result is poor hand strength and a lack of a powerful grip. However, the child will exhibit skilled fingertip usage.

Lower extremity

- Shortening often occurs in the hip flexor muscles.

- Also shortened are the lateral hip rotator muscles.

- There may be tightness in the hip abductors muscles.

- The child must be screened for capsular tightness in the hip joint.

- There may be shortening in the heel cords and long toe flexor muscles.

- Graded knee and ankle control fails to develop in midranges. Rather, the knee functions in full flexion or in hyperextension, while the ankle functions in plantarflexion or in inversion in order to avoid tactile input to the plantar aspect of the foot. If the child is unable to assume plantarflexion or inversion, the ankle and foot will fall medially.

- Weakness throughout the proximal segments of the lower extremity leads to impaired function in distal segments.

- Ligaments at the knee, ankle, and within the foot may be overstretched as avoidance postures are used.

- The normal arching of the foot fails to develop.

- Balance reactions may fail to develop.

- Medial-lateral dissociation of the foot will fail to develop.

Problems That May Be Vestibular- and Proprioceptive-Based

High tolerance of movement

A high tolerance for movement disorder is caused by a hyporeactive response to movement. The child will persist in one type of vestibular input (for example, rocking back and forth or spinning) without seeming to benefit from the input. Proponents of SI theory often interpret the child as seeking that particular type of vestibular input. There are less autonomic responses (such as dizziness and nausea) associated with the movements. Often these children will be impulsive, explosive, and use poor judgment or safety awareness as they move within the environment. They must be screened for difficulties with postural reactions and poor sustained muscular control.

Intolerance of movement (vestibular input)

This dysfunction constitutes a low tolerance for or a hyperreactive response to movement. The person experiences nausea, vomiting, dizziness, and other autonomic nervous system reactions to very low levels of vestibular input. There may be flushing of the skin, irritability, and feelings of malaise or generalized discomfort. These children frequently have problems tolerating postures out of upright. They will avoid spending time in quadruped, in prone, or on moveable equipment. Frequently they fail to develop sufficient balance and equilibrium in postures other than in upright, but may have weaknesses throughout the scapular and shoulder girdles, pelvis, and hip musculature.

Postural insecurity

This condition is a fear of movement that stems from an underlying impairment in postural control and balance mechanisms. The child distrusts his own ability to make adequate postural and balance responses to prevent loss of balance. He is an overly cautious child who is not steady on his feet when crossing various terrains. He may have great difficulty stepping up or down a curb; may be overly clingy or adverse to movement; or he may take a fast approach to movement, thereby making use of momentum to quickly avoid a task, but never developing slow, sustained control. Motor control may be adequately developed for normal walking, but often is lacking for higher-level skills such as rough-and-tumble play, climbing, or sports-related activities.

Gravitational insecurity

The child with gravitational insecurity has a problem with the perception or processing of vestibular input and a primal fear reaction to movement. Displacements of the body create a reaction that is out of proportion with the perturbation. The child's vestibular system triggers primal reactions of fight-or-flight when he is moved out of the upright posture, and particularly into backward space. It is believed that this dysfunction stems from inadequate macular functioning in which the information from the utricle and saccule is inadequate or inappropriate. Balance reactions and pelvic and scapular stability may be lacking.

Bilateral integration and sequencing

This disorder is characterized by poor bilateral coordination, or inability to use the two sides of the body together in a well-coordinated fashion. Children with this disorder have difficulty crossing midline of body and poor ability to sequence or perform projected action sequences such as catching a bounced ball, kicking a rolling ball, or performing a jumping pattern such as hopscotch.

Postural-ocular movement disorder

This disorder is characterized by poor ability to right the head against gravity (prone and supine positions), low tone or hypotonicity of extensor muscles, poor proximal joint stability, and a lack of or deficiency in postural adjustments or automatic background adjustments. Background adjustments include postural adjustments to perturbations in the center of gravity, to shift as muscle groups fatigue, or to posturally set in advance of a task. In postural-ocular movement disorder, there also may be poor equilibrium and support reactions as evidenced by poor performance on standing and walking balance tests, poor kinesthetic awareness, and depressed postrotatory nystagmus scores. Problems typically seen include:

- Low muscle tone characterized by
  - Hyperextension of middle joints
  - Lordotic posturing
- Decreased ability to sustain prone extension
- Decreased performance of supine flexion with an inability to right the head against gravity and sustain the position
- Adaptive shortening of muscles and tendons

Somatodyspraxia also is a problem stemming from faulty proprioceptive and vestibular input, which must be addressed in treatment.

Effect of the Visual System on Motor Control

The child's first perceptions of his world develop primarily from tactile, kinesthetic, and vestibular input. Vision and auditory input is later matched against the other senses and integrated into the child's perception of his world.

Because visual perception is believed to be the end product of normal sensory integration, many motor control issues with a visual-motor and visual-perceptual basis are considered as dysfunctions within the realm of sensory integration. Motor control problems may be based in faulty ocular-motor control or visual-perception even when visual acuities fall within normal limits. The result may be motor clumsiness because of a number of problems.

Children may experience discrete visual-motor control difficulties, including:

- Decreased eye-head dissociation (isolated ocular-motor control)
- Decreased downward gaze
- Decreased central acuity with a reliance on peripheral vision
- Problems with visual perception
  - Visual closure
  - Figure-ground
  - Form constancy
  - Visual memory
- Decreased sustained visual attention
- Decreased visual scanning and convergence

Eye-head dissociation is the ability to separate the eye gaze from the direction in which the face is pointing. Voluntary control of eye movements that enable the eyes to remain fixed on a stationary object while the head and body move is a vestibular-ocular function. Problems with eye-head dissociation often stem from a lack of cervical strength and are seen when a child has difficulty in extending and/or flexing his neck against gravity. The child lacks the internal stability needed to hold the head steady while moving the eyes in a separate direction for

Exploring the Spectrum of Autism and Pervasive Developmental Disorders

visual tracking or visual fixation as the child is moving through space. Treatment is directed at developing the required internal stability.

Poor downward gaze often is a by-product of decreased development of flexion throughout the neck and trunk. Typically, infants develop downward gaze as they strive to raise the head and later to sit up against gravity. The gaze is directed downward during babies' efforts to overcome gravity. If downward gaze does not develop sufficiently, a child may not use the lower visual field functionally. This may cause him to miss changes in the support surface, such as stairs or curbs or objects in his path, resulting in the child tripping and falling frequently. Poor downward gaze also may affect school-related skills such as reading, pencil-and-paper tasks, and use of scissors.

Use of peripheral vision is common in an estimated 25% of the children with autism. The child will appear to be looking in another direction while walking or playing with toys; however, he is using the outer portions of his visual field for vision. Depth perception is affected, and objects that are centrally located may be missed and become obstacles to performance. Acuity may be reported as normal or correctable with lenses in all of the above cases, causing confusion in parents who wonder why, if the problem is within the visual system, optometrists or ophthalmologists may not perceive or report a problem.

Poor visual-spatial relationships may be the result of poor sensory processing during development, resulting in a misperception of the size, shape, and distance of surfaces or objects. Spatial relations are learned first in relationship to the child's body. As he reaches for an object and secures it, he learns the position of the object, its height, size, and other attributes. This information forms the basis for visual perception. If the child's sensory awareness of his arms or body is not accurate, the child may misperceive the distance his hand is from an object, its size, or its shape. Secondary visual-perceptual inaccuracies and difficulties develop.

If you have ever experienced changes in your visual perception due to medication, anesthesia, or use of magnification lenses or prism glasses, you will appreciate how clumsy you can be when your perception is skewed. It is difficult to see how large an object may be or how near or far away it is. Eye-hand and eye-foot coordination also are greatly impacted. A child with a visual perception problem cannot perform fine motor tasks such as writing, or participate in skilled sports such as hitting or kicking a moving ball. The child also may not be able to perceive the differences in the shapes of letters in learning to read or write. Treatment must address the underlying sensory systems including tactile, proprioceptive, and vestibular input combined with visual-motor activities.

Tests of visual perception often are administered by occupational therapists. Poor performance in one or more areas is considered to indicate problems within the visual processing system and may impact the child's ability to function.

Visual closure is the ability to identify objects from incomplete representations. The person must be able to mentally match the object with previously stored information. It enables the child to recognize an object or to avoid obstacles in his path even if part of that object is obscured or hidden from sight.

Figure-ground is the differentiation of foreground from background. It enables the child to select a toy from a roomful of toys. It necessitates the ability to separate essential visual information from the surrounding distracting information.

Visual memory is the ability to recall objects after they have been removed from sight. For many people, visual memory contributes to the ability to find our way around familiar surroundings when the lights are out.

Binocularity is the ability to coordinate and work together in all visual activities. Poor binocular control requires compensatory efforts to sustain visual attention. Poor binocular function also affects spatial judgements such as depth perception. Symptoms can include head turn, tilting of the head, closing or covering one eye, poor depth perception, headache after concentrating on something close, and double vision. Decreased depth perception may cause a child not to recognize when the surface he is walking on changes. He may miss steps, trip over thresholds, or fail to adjust for inclines or ramps.

Decreased sustained visual attention may stem from a lack of registration, the inability to choose relevant visual information from irrelevant information, or a lack of endurance. Endurance is needed for head stability, ocular-motor control (binocularity), and compensatory strategies in the presence of faulty sensory perception leading to visual-spatial problems. Excessive compensatory efforts are fatiguing and difficult to sustain. A lack of the ability to sustain visual attention often is associated with an inability to sustain other postures. Fixating inaccuracy is usually related to losing the place while reading, skipping words or lines, or misreading of words that are read correctly when presented in isolation.

Decreased visual scanning or tracking skills are related to smooth eye movements used to follow a line of sight in drawing or writing. Convergence is the ability to use the eyes together quickly and accurately as an object comes nearer or further away. Visual convergence, fixation, and tracking are involved in copying activities. These require and represent the skilled, precise fine motor control of the muscles involved in controlling eye movements.

Visual perception has an impact on:

- Eye-hand coordination
- Eye-hand and eye-foot dissociation
- Impaired reading, spelling, math, and handwriting skills
- Impaired organizational skills

Visual perception has a direct impact on eye-hand and eye-foot coordination. The ability to use the two eyes together in a coordinated fashion to fixate, track, and discriminate changes within the environment will affect how well we are able to use our hands for functional tasks and how well we move through our environment. Accurate visual perception integrates with other sensory input to validate our orientation in space and spatial relationships with objects in our environment; and also to reinforce body scheme. Inaccurate visual perceptions serve to confuse our orientation in space, lead to mistargeting of objects and poor body scheme. They also have an adverse impact on motor planning.

Eye-hand dissociation is the ability to use the hands without the benefit of visually monitoring what the hands are doing. It enables us to direct our gaze in a direction separate from the work our hands are doing. Many of the tasks we perform every day are examples of eye-hand dissociation. For example, tying our shoes, once learned, can be done without the benefit of visual monitoring. Typing, for some, is another example. Eye-hand dissociation necessitates an accurate processing of the sensory information from our hands on an unconscious level in order to function; and visual perception contributes to the formation of motor engrams required for the performance of the tasks. The same concepts apply to eye-foot dissociation. Accurate visual perception can contribute to the formation of the body scheme to allow us to place a foot accurately on a step or lift it over an obstacle without having to visually direct our foot placements.

Visual perception contributes to the performance of school-related tasks. Copying, reading, spelling, math, and art skills require intact visual perceptual skills. The child's ability to succeed in performing the motor aspects of those tasks will be directly impacted by the integration of visual input into the sensorimotor attempts to write, color, cut, or paste.

Finally, visual perception contributes to the overall ability to organize information. Visual perception is used to validate other sensory and motor information coming into the system and subserves motor coordination and performance. A child who has sensory processing problems will have problems in visual perception and will appear disorganized and scattered in his motor function.

SI Techniques to Increase Motor Control

Intervention from a sensory integrative perspective requires the therapist to have a very basic understanding of the receptors within the systems believed to be the root of the particular dysfunction. By understanding where the receptors are located and how they are triggered, we can better design programs geared at facilitating the integration of input.

Vestibular Components in Motor Control

The receptors for the vestibular system are located in the inner ear. The receptors include semicircular canals and the otoliths, the uticles and saccules.

Semicircular canals are each oriented in a specific plane and triggered only by specific movement patterns within that plane. They are comprised of fluid-filled canals. When movement of the head occurs, the fluid in the canals begins to move, thereby bending hair cells which send impulses to the CNS. Depending on which set of hair cells is fired, the CNS is apprised of what plane of movement the head is experiencing. The bent hair cells maintain that position until the movement of the fluid within the canal ceases. When a child starts to spin, fluid in one of the semicircular canals sends information to the CNS at the onset of the spinning. However, the child's system is not stimulated again until the movement stops or changes direction. This is why many of the children we treat will spin endlessly, but never appear to register or benefit from that input. They have accommodated to the spinning in the one plane that they perform and often do not vary the direction of the head movement or the plane of the head; nor do they stop and start the spinning to give themselves the needed vestibular input.

Within the macular region of the vestibular receptors are located other receptors called the utricle and saccule. These are small otoliths, or stone-like structures, that are filled with calcium carbonate crystals. They are responsible for sensing our position with respect to gravity. These gravity stones or gravity sensors act in conjunction with the semicircular canals to provide our systems with a compass, if you will. As these crystal-filled stones tilt, the movement of the crystals inside them triggers impulses to tell the CNS in which plane the movement of the head occurred. The crystals within the utricle shift to yield perception in a horizontal plane, and those within the saccule are oriented to detect movement in the vertical plane (Fisher and Bundy 1989).

Problems in vestibular processing are typified by:

- Decreased head righting

- Decreased balance and equilibrium reactions

- Decreased protective reactions to a loss of balance

- Decreased postural reactions or postural adjustments that are the automatic, unconscious movements used to prepare for an activity

- Poor anti-gravity muscle tone (in the postural extensor groups), which can contribute to poor sustained postures

- Inability to co-contract or stabilize a joint for weight bearing

- Poor performance on standing and walking balance tests

- A lack of head stability for ocular-motor control, which can directly affect visual attention

Proprioceptive Components in Motor Control

The receptors for the proprioceptive system are located within the muscles, tendons, and joint spaces. They are, very simply, responsible for our position sense. Some receptors are triggered by static positions, other by changes in muscle force, tension, and joint angle.

Although the receptors for the vestibular system are located within the head and therefore denote its positions with response to gravity, our proprioceptive system is tied to our vestibular responses, contributing to total-body control and awareness of where we are in space. To oversimplify, we receive information about where our head is in space through the vestibular receptors, and where our body is in relation to our head from the proprioceptive system. Indeed, the results of the work done by Jean Ayres in the area of sensory integration point to the fact that the dysfunctions are often ascribed to processing failures in both the vestibular and proprioceptive systems; and that the functions of one system cannot be separated from the functions of the second.

Problems in proprioceptive processing include:

- Over- or undershooting of movements

- Poor grading of muscular efforts

- Hyperextension of middle joints

- Poor automatic background activity (for example, position sense, postural tone)

- Poor conscious and unconscious awareness of body position in space

- Poor performance of standing and walking balance tests (poor extremity placements for weight bearing)

- Insecurity in moving in space

- Poor performance on graphesthesia tests

See Table 14.2 for motor control issues specifically related to SI dysfunctions.

TABLE 14.2 Motor control issues in sensory integrative dysfunction

Hyporesponsive Systems				Hyperresponsive Systems		
Postural-Ocular Movement Disorder	**Bilateral Integration and Sequencing Disorder**	**Postural Insecurity**	**Somatodyspraxia**	**Gravitational Insecurity**	**Intolerance to Movement**	**Tactile Defensiveness**
Poor head righting	Lack of head righting	Poor righting reactions (head and body on body)	Global impaired central processing: • Poor registration • Poor motor planning • Poor sequencing • Poor execution	Impaired vestibular-proprioceptive perceptions	Low tolerance to vestibular displacements such as riding in a car, carnival rides, and so on	Impaired sensory perceptions making light touch aversive and intolerable
Lack of head stability	Poor proximal stability	Poor thoraco-lumbar control	Impaired righting reactions (head and body)	Primal fear reactions that are out of proportion to the perturbation	Reactions include dizziness, nausea, headache, vomiting, and irritability	Behaviors include avoidance of touch, rubbing the area after it is touched, and intolerance of certain types of textures, possibly evidenced by: • Decreased manipulation skills with awkwardness • Toe walking
Lack of upper-trunk control	Poor midline orientation	Poor pelvic stability (anterior, posterior, and lateral)	Poor thoracolumbar control	Fear of movement into backward space		
Poor lumbo-pelvic control	Poor use of both sides of the body	Lack of graded lower-extremity control	Impaired pelvic control (anterior, posterior, and lateral)			Bizarre or abnormal body postures or movements in avoidance of touch
Lack of eye-head dissociation	Trouble with feed-forward	Poor ankle strategies for balance	Poor balance strategies			
Lack of visual fixation	Impaired body scheme	Impaired tactile discrimination in the feet	Poor oral motor control			
Lack of visual tracking		Impaired body scheme	Trouble with both feedforward and feedback			
Poor form and space skills			Impaired body scheme			
Impaired eye-hand coordination						
Impaired body scheme						

Intervention Strategies for SI Dysfunctions

Intolerance of Movement and Gravitational Insecurity

Intervention in these cases involves use of slow, quiet vestibular input interspersed or combined with the proprioceptive input that will aid in calming the child's system and reinforcing the sensory information he must reset his internal compass. In each of these dysfunctions, the system is easily overstimulated and hyperresponsive to vestibular input. Precisely and carefully grade the use of vestibular input to avoid triggering a counterproductive result. You may choose to position the child initially in a static position off midline, perhaps in prone or inclined position, while you distract him with an activity. Head and neck joint compressions can be used as proprioceptive input to calm the anxiety caused by the vestibular input. Gradually introduce unstable surfaces or slowly moving equipment to increase the child's tolerance for movement.

Postural Insecurity

Use of vestibular input in treating postural insecurity must be geared at facilitating equilibrium and protective reactions that are fast enough and reliable enough for the child to count upon in order to function. Balance and equilibrium reactions must be present throughout the developmental sequence for the postural insecurity to be ameliorated. Reinforce position awareness through the use of proprioceptive input to give the child the awareness of his body position at all times. NDT therapy ball techniques are good for this, as are the use of platform swing activities, scooterboard activities, and balance and weight-shifting exercises in general.

High Tolerance to Vestibular Stimulation

Vestibular input here must be varied. Start with the child's preferred vestibular input; that type of input is not threatening. For example, say the child prefers spinning. Remember that spinning triggers the vestibular receptors only at the onset and at the end of the spinning. Once the fluid in the semicircular canals starts to move, the hair cells are not triggered again until the fluid in them comes to a stop. Therefore, to give the child the input needed to reset the compass, interrupt the spinning. Provide the stops and starts required to stimulate the child's system. Allow time for the fluid to stop traveling in the semicircular canals and time for the child's system to process the information. Also vary the direction of the movement in order to stimulate the other vestibular receptors. Horizontal, vertical, and bouncing movements stimulate the utricles, saccules and otoliths. For the child who rocks or jumps, intersperse vestibular input in body positions other than upright. You may find that the child you thought had a high tolerance to vestibular stimulation has a very low tolerance to positions or movement in other planes. The child may be adverse to lying horizontal or to the inverted prone position. Start with firmer, more predictable equipment. Use prone extension on a 45-degree incline, and gradually move toward horizontal. Choose a scooterboard or therapy ball or bolster before you try the net swing. Grade input until the child becomes more comfortable in the new positions. Add proprioception in the form of head and joint compression when introducing a new body position in a different plane of reference.

Bilateral Integration and Sequencing

In this dysfunction, there is a lack of or inadequate head righting on the body in both flexion and extension, a lack of proximal stability within the scapular and the pelvic and hip girdles, poor midline orientation, and poor use of both sides of the body together.

Treatment must incorporate the use of strategies and activities to address each of these issues. Emphasis must be on the use of proprioceptive and linear vestibular input that will foster anti-gravity extensor muscles to increase proximal stability and head stability. Tonic postural control or holding postures must be incorporated into treatment so that postural control and proprioception are increased. Use a variety of head positions in linear vestibular activities to increase sustained head stability. Use phasic, angular vestibular input to encourage quick reciprocal postural and head stabilization. Work in neck flexion to increase midline orientation while working two hands together at midline. Initiate bilateral activities in the form of two-extremity coordination, and progress to four-extremity activities. As the child is ready, add sequencing and crossing of midline.

These children have trouble with feedforward activities such as catching a ball, kicking a rolling ball, and participating in sports activities. They also have difficulty learning to ride a bicycle, which is a four-extremity coordination activity. Rhythmic activities such as clapping, reciprocal arm or leg patterns as in marching, and jogging will help them develop sequencing and timing. Enlist rhythmic nursery rhymes, counting, and sounds to assist the child in learning the timing of the motor task. Start with feedback activities before expecting success in feedforward. If you want the child to learn to hit a ball, begin by using a T-ball stand before you expect him to be able to hit a thrown ball. This enables feedback to occur for learning the motor act before you expect a feedforward performance. Add resistance through the use of wraparound weights, heavier equipment, or increased muscular efforts to any and all activities to increase body scheme, reinforce feedback, and assist the child in completing an activity successfully.

Postural-Ocular Movement Disorder

This dysfunction includes poor head righting in both supine and prone positions, a lack of head stability resulting in poor ocular motor control, and a lack of proximal stability. There is poor lumbar-pelvic control (anterior-posterior control) as well as poor lateral pelvic and hip stability. There is a lack of eye-head dissociation, lack of sustained visual fixation, poor visual tracking, poor form and space skills, and poor eye-hand coordination. Body image also is impaired.

To treat this condition, facilitate and develop prone extension, strengthen cervical flexion, and improve the ability to sustain these positions. This will develop the head stability necessary to develop the ocular motor control. Incorporate visual-motor and visual perceptual activities that require the child to fixate on objects while adding vestibular input. Incorporate activities such as fishing games with the child on a platform swing, throwing bean bags at a target from the net swing, or ring placements with the child on a moving scooterboard. These work well to enable the child to visually shift between and distinguish foreground from background, visually track moving targets, dissociate the eyes from the head, and facilitate sustained visual fixation. Also include visual discrimination activities while applying phasic and sustained vestibular input. Facilitate postural

TABLE 14.3 Intervention strategies for motor control issues in SI dysfunctions: Hyporesponsive systems

Postural-ocular movement disorder

Facilitate head righting in prone and supine
Facilitate and strengthen extensor muscles through the use of linear vestibular inputs
Increase proximal stability
Improve postural adjustments and equilibrium reactions through the use of phasic or angular vestibular inputs
Incorporate proprioceptive/kinesthetic activities
Incorporate visual scanning, fixation, tracking, and discrimination exercises

Bilateral integration and sequencing disorder

Facilitate and strengthen tonic postural control with sustained and linear vestibular input
Use a variety of head positions in linear vestibular input
Emphasize proprioceptive efforts
Once postural concerns have been addressed, add sequencing and crossing of midline
Start with two-extremity activities in feedback, and progress to four-extremity activities
Move to feedforward two-extremity activities, and then to feedforward four-extremity activities

Postural insecurity

Facilitate and strengthen head righting on body using angular, phasic vestibular inputs
Progress to body-on-body righting using angular, phasic vestibular inputs
Progress to sustained postural control with increased proprioceptive activities
Develop proximal stability in scapular and pelvic girdles
Work on graded extremity control
Include tactile discrimination activities for the feet
Facilitate ankle and hip balance strategies

Somatodyspraxia

Tactile discrimination

TABLE 14.4 Intervention strategies for motor control issues in SI dysfunctions: Hyperresponsive systems

Gravitational insecurity

Reset the compass
Facilitate head righting on a stable body and progress to body-on-body righting
Use sustained linear vestibular in holding postures
Grade vestibular input combined with proprioceptive inputs to ground the child and calm the system
Add phasic or angular displacements only after the child is comfortable in the new postures or positions

Intolerance to movement

Use sustained linear vestibular with graded amounts of movement
Reinforce body position in space through the application of proprioceptive input
Combine the use of vision to enable the child to visually monitor where he is in space

Tacile defensiveness

Use deep-touch pressure and proprioceptive input
Brushing program may be indicated. Refer to Deep Pressure and Proprioceptive Technique (DPPT) in Chapter 10.
Calming techniques may include linear vestibular input in the form of slow rocking
Use a minimum of changes in hand placements when touching the child (predictable touch is more easily tolerated)

equilibrium reactions and automatic postural adjustments during visual activities. Provide proprioceptive feedback to reinforce body position, body scheme, and feedback in whatever activity the child is engaged.

Important Considerations in Treatment

In attempting to address vestibular and proprioceptive processing, we must remember to incorporate several components within the scope of our treatments. Those treatments must incorporate vestibular input that triggers the receptors in a manner that will register and send important sensory information into the system. Treatment must include vestibular input that is of strong enough intensity to register and yet not overwhelm the child, triggering an adverse reaction to it. Vestibular input must include movement in all planes for which there are vestibular receptors, stops and starts, changes in head position, and variations in direction. Proprioceptive input must be applied in such a manner that it reinforces the body percept and body position in space.

Both semicircular canal and otolith input in a well-functioning system will elicit compensatory head, trunk, and limb movements aimed at opposing head perturbations by increasing head stabilizations in response to the perturbations, opposing postural sway by increasing truncal stabilizations, and opposing tilt through righting and equilibrium reactions.

Transient tilts or rotational head movements that stimulate semicircular canals elicit phasic reactions. Sustained tilt or holding of head positions against gravity yield more sustained forms of motor and postural control. The degree of response is dependent upon the strength and endurance levels available to the child. Proprioceptive input must involve changes in rate, speed, direction, muscle force, and tension and both phasic and sustained muscular efforts. The combination of the two types of input will aid in building and reinforcing the correct body map for the child to use for improved motor planning and motor control.

Postural Control

Postural control, for our purposes, is the control of the head, neck, and trunk. It includes motor control issues as related to the scapulae and pelvis.

The clinical observations typically cited as indicators of poor postural control include:

- Standing posture: Forward-tipped shoulders, anterior pelvic tilt with a pot-belly appearance, hyperextension of the knees, or increased distal fixing patterns

- Delayed or absent balance and equilibrium reactions

- Inability to sustain postures. Typically, the child slouches when sitting or standing or cannot sit or stand still. The child simply lacks the sustained muscular control to do so.

However, the issues of impaired postural control are much more complex. To simply address motor control issues from a strengthening perspective is to address only part of the problem; we must take a holistic approach. Neurodevelopmental treatment (NDT) techniques offer a view of motor control issues and a variety of hands-on treatments to address the issues of muscle activation, biomechanical malalignments, and muscle and tendon shortening that are secondary effects of the underlying hypotonia and its sequelae. SI techniques address the inefficiencies in sensory systems that also subserve motor control, body awareness, and body scheme. The tactile, proprioceptive, and vestibular systems must be addressed in treatment.

The NDT Perspective

The characteristic posture illustrated here is indicative of:

- Poor proximal stability of the scapular-related muscles

- Inability or limited ability to co-contract or sustain weightbearing on the upper extremities

- Poor proximal stability of the pelvis with anterior and posterior tilting of the pelvis and an inability or limited ability to hold the pelvis stable at midline (a lack of anterior-posterior control)

- Poor proximal stability of the hip-related muscles with inability or limited ability to hold the pelvis stable in a lateral plane (a lack of lateral pelvic/hip control)

The SI Perspective

The characteristic posture illustrated here is indicative of:

- Impaired or insufficient vestibular processing, resulting

    — Diminished head righting on body

    — Diminished anti-gravity muscle tonus

- Impaired proprioceptive processing resulting in poor awareness of body in space or of body postures

Problems with postural control may result in:

- Postures that are typical in the hypotonic child:

- Forward head posture

- Forward-tipped shoulders; rounded-shoulder appearance

- Pot-bellied or lordotic posture

- Hyperextension at the elbows and knees

- A clumsy or uncoordinated appearance

- Impediments in limb use and skilled hand function

- Attentional deficits

- Poor eye contact (inability to stabilize the head for ocular motor control)

- Hyperactivity (inability to sustain postures or positions)

- Bizarre posturing (distal fixing patterns)

- Disturbances in gait (either clumsy or stiff-legged, toe walking, and so on)

- Seeking of vestibular input (total-body rocking, poor postural responses)

Tests for Postural Control
Prone extension

ILLUSTRATION 14.4
Prone extension test for postural control

Lying prone, the child lifts the head, arms, and legs up off the surface.

Children 5 years of age should be able to:

- Assume and maintain the head steady and within 45 degrees of vertical
- Lift the shoulders, chest, and arms off the surface
- Raise the distal one-third of both thighs off the floor
- Maintain the knees in less than 30 degrees of flexion
- Do so quickly and nonsegmentally, and while talking aloud

Children 6 years of age or older should be able to assume a full prone extension position and hold it for 30 seconds (Fisher and Bundy 1989).

Supine flexion

ILLUSTRATION 14.5
Supine flexion test for postural control

Lying supine with arms crossed over his chest, the child lifts his head and legs and rolls into a ball.

- The goal is to raise the head to between 70 and 90 degrees, remain stable on the surface, and sustain the posture for 15 seconds.
- A tendency to lead with the chin or the presence of a head lag may indicate diminished vestibular-proprioceptive processing, and may link with a somatodyspraxia and clusters with problems of static balance control.

Other tests of postural control

- Upper-extremity weight-bearing
- Postrotary Nystagmus Test (SIPT)

Tests of standing and walking balance

- Balance on an object (SIPT)
- Single-limb stance
- Romberg test, both sharpened and nonsharpened
- Walk a line

Poor Head Control and Stability

Clinical observations

- Delays in head righting in all positions
- Use of chin jut in supine flexion, sit-up maneuvers
- Inability to sustain erect head postures
- Impaired visual-perceptual, visual-spatial skills
- Lack of or impaired downward gaze
- Delays in speech and language
- Feeding issues
- May have poor use of hands at midline
- Difficulty with static balance skills

Intervention strategies

Begin with head righting skills.

- Center initial efforts around phasic, or short, concentric muscle efforts to right the head in flexion, extension, and lateral planes.
- NDT ball techniques, transitions from supine to sit, and from prone to sit are excellent methods to increase head righting on body.

Once head righting has been gained, work on the ability to stabilize the head during perturbations in sway.

- NDT ball techniques can be used to cause the child to hold the head stable as the surface he is resting on is moved.
- Work on the platform swing also offers an excellent way to develop head stability. Perturbations and postural sway can be introduced in both anterior-posterior and lateral directions.
- Include activities that require visual fixation on objects to enable the child to hold the desired head position.
- Prone extension in the net swing offers sustained cervical extension.

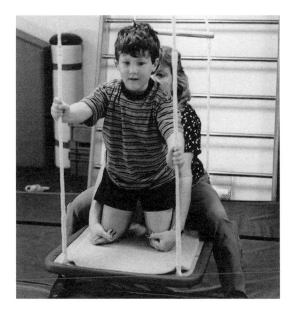

ILLUSTRATION 14.6
Swinging activities de-
velop head control and stability
throughout movement

- The scooterboard offers use of prone extension and several methods to de-velop sustained cervical flexion.

- Place the child in heel-sitting or in kneeling on the scooterboard, and ask him to lean forward and pull the scooterboard along. This offers a method of strengthening the abdominal muscles needed for trunk flexor control.

- To gain cervical flexor control, place a small balloon, ball, or other object under the child's chin and ask him to hold the object while propelling the scooterboard.

- Later, have the child lie in the supine position on the scooterboard and try to raise his head to see where he is going.

- Place a ball or other object under the child's chin to gain a chin tuck pos-ture and offer a distal point of stability for the chin while working the flexor muscles in a sustained postural-control effort.

ILLUSTRATION 14.7
Abdominal and cervical
flexor strengthening through
scooterboard exercises

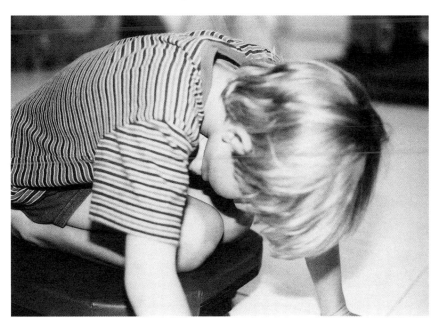

Poor Scapular Stability

Clinical observations

Posture will include:

- Forward head posture
- Winging of scapulae or shoulder blades
- Rounded shoulder posture
- Excessive lateral migration of the scapulae (shoulder blades) on the rib cage wall
- Inability to sustain weight-bearing over the upper extremities

Intervention strategies

Proximal stability for scapular-related muscles

NDT professes that alignment dictates function. It is here that we start in our intervention strategies.

- Thoracic flexion will cause the scapulae to migrate upward and laterally on the posterior rib cage wall.
- Use spinal mobility activities to reinforce extension as a precursor to working on scapular stability to gain the alignment needed to activate and strengthen the muscles for that stability.
- Passively draw the scapulae back into a normal resting position.
- Realize that you may well need to elongate various muscle groups if they have undergone adaptive shortening, or you will lose the scapular placements the moment the child moves an arm.

**ILLUSTRATION
14.8**

Lateral rotators of the humerus

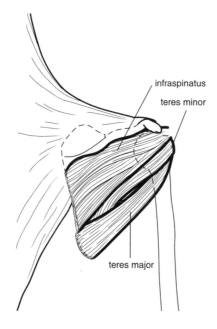

infraspinatus

teres minor

teres major

- The muscle groups to address include:
  — Pectoralis major and minor
  — Lateral rotator muscles of the humerus (teres major, teres minor, and infraspinatus)
  — Upper trapezius
  — Levator scapulae muscle
- Once alignment has been gained, the next step in the process is to facilitate or activate and strengthen the muscles that will offer medial and inferior stabilization to the scapulae.
  — Those muscles include lower trapezius and abdominal muscles that act in synergy to fixate and stabilize the scapulae inferiorally and depress the scapula onto the rib cage wall in order for glenohumeral function to occur.
  — The rhomboids major and minor and middle trapezius are required for scapular retraction and resist lateral migration of the scapulae.
  — The spinal erector muscles are required to stabilize the spinal extension needed for the scapulae to work properly.
- Activities include:
  — Net swing to develop sustained work throughout the back extensors. Include pull-push efforts to work the larger back muscles such as trapezius, latissimus dorsi, and the scapular-related muscles.

ILLUSTRATION 14.9
Push-pull activities work the larger back muscles

- Scooterboard pulls elongate latissimus dorsi and lower trapezius muscles if the arms are extended. This activity offers:

  — Proprioceptive input through traction of the upper body

  — Biomechanical advantage to the back extensor and, eventually, the gluteal muscles by passively extending the spine

  — Linear vestibular input to facilitate activation of anti-gravity postural extensor muscles

ILLUSTRATION 14.10

Scooterboard pulls

Propelling a scooterboard in prone also can work the muscle groups mentioned previously, provided there is sufficient postural and head extension while the child is propelling the scooterboard.

Extension work on the platform swing also can be beneficial. For additional specific activities, see Chapters 10 through 13.

ILLUSTRATION 14.11

Thoracic extension must support the work of the scapular muscles

Scapular winging

The next scapular function to address is the issue of scapular stability in weight-bearing positions. Because the characteristic of proximal instability in the scapular muscles is scapular winging off the rib cage, the actions to be reinforced and developed are those that maintain scapular depression and thoracic extension in weight-bearing positions.

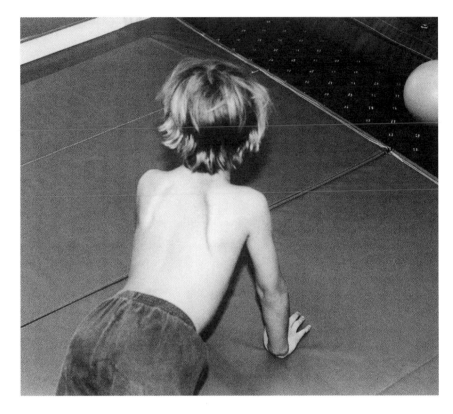

ILLUSTRATION 14.12
Scapular winging is a hallmark of scapular instability

Typically, therapists are taught that weight bearing develops scapular stability; and consequently they place the child immediately in prone weight-bearing postures. There are two problems that often work against all efforts to develop scapular stability.

- **Head position**. The activity or child's attention encourages the child to look down at the surface, facilitating or negating efforts at the thoracic extension required for scapular seating and stability, at least in the early phases of developing scapular stability.

- **Poor trunk control**. Often the child's body weight is unable to be supported by his scapular strength. Because a child with poor scapular stability also has poor pelvic stability and control, when the therapist encourages the head-up position to encourage thoracic extension, often the child's abdomen will sag, the weight of which will cause the medial border scapular muscles to lose their hold and winging will occur.

To combat the common errors in prone weight bearing, it may be beneficial to initiate weight-bearing on a vertical or inclined surface versus a horizontal surface, or by supporting the child more proximally in horizontal prone position.

**ILLUSTRATION
14.13**

Collapse of weight bearing and winging

**ILLUSTRATION
14.14**

Support the child proximally to facilitate scapular stability

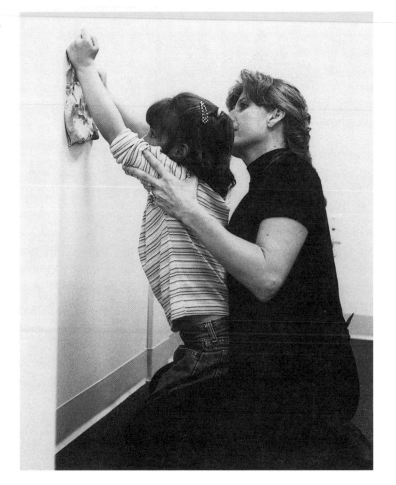

- Strengthen extensor muscles. Use lumbar extension exercises, first in phasic or short duration repetitions such as single-limb lifts in prone or quadruped positions; and later in a more sustained method through airplane exercises, prone extension in the net swing, on a bolster, ball, or scooterboard.

- Progress to pelvic control exercises aimed at increasing the ability to sustain postural control throughout the developmental framework. Use positions such as kneeling, half-kneeling, and step-standing exercises that encourage and should require neutral hip extension.

- More phasic type of control involves balance and equilibrium reactions. Use seated positions on a narrowed or unstable surface to encourage equilibrium reactions. Do not allow the child to collapse against a table, into an anterior tilted posture or a flat back posture.

- Use forward-back propulsion on a glider or platform swing with the child in heel-sit, quadruped, or tall-kneel to assist and teach anterior-posterior pelvic tilting.

- Use of a glider is an excellent method to teach midline pelvic control for postural sway, balance, and equilibrium reactions and automatic postural adjustments.

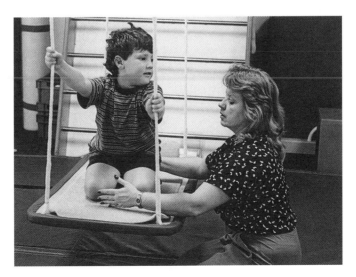

ILLUSTRATION 14.21

Use NDT hands-on facilitation to teach the motor strategies and help develop motor engrams.

ILLUSTRATION 14.22

Add vestibular input to gain midrange control during postural sway and perturbations in balance.

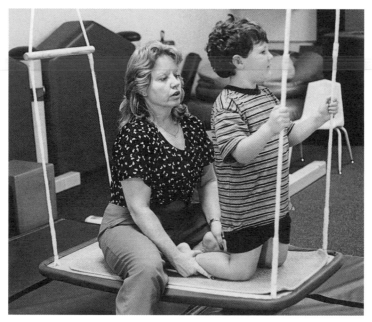

- Use sit-to-stand transitions with freeze and hold at various points of pelvic tilt to assist in developing sustained midrange control.

- Use a wedge or tilt bench during seated activities to develop sustained forms of pelvic postural control.

Pelvic control in a lateral plane

In an adequately functioning hip with good lateral proximal stability, the hip abductor muscles contract over the weight-bearing femur (lower extremity) to elevate the opposite pelvis. This is sustained during activities such as single-limb stance, hopping activities, stair climbing, and stepping over obstacles.

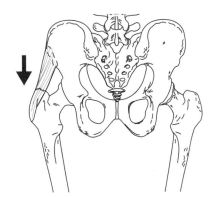

ILLUSTRATION 14.23

Hip abductor mechanism

In cases of poor proximal (lateral) pelvic or hip stability, problems arise in the ability to stabilize the pelvis over the femur. The opposite side of the pelvis will drop.

- The child will be unable to stand on one foot.

- Pelvis opposite the weight-bearing leg will drop (Trendelenberg).

- The child will stabilize with the nonweight-bearing leg against the weight-bearing leg.

- The child will have difficulty stepping over obstacles.

Alignment is important in the activation of the muscles needed for lateral pelvic control.

- For activation of the hip abductor mechanism, the femur needs to be in a neutral or near-neutral position with regard to both extension and internal and external rotation initially.

- For phasic control, use assisted hip abduction exercises in which the child stands on one leg and abducts or lifts the opposite lower extremity from the floor, elevating the pelvis on the side being raised.

  — Initially, you may need to assist in controlling the pelvis to lift. If this does not occur, the hip abductor mechanism may not be activated.

  — Common substitutions involve maneuvering the body or the position to kick with hip flexion rather than abduction.

  — Leg abduction kicks with slight hip extension are better than when abduction is performed with hip flexion.

- Progress to stepping over obstacles in a side-step approach. This also will act to activate the hip abductor mechanism.

  — As the child attempts to lift the foot over an obstacle, the extended lift often will involve activation of the hip abductor mechanism on the weight-bearing side.

  — As the weight is then shifted to the opposite foot, there is development of graded control for controlling body weight and weight shift in a lateral plane.

ILLUSTRATION 14.24

Walking on an elevated surface, on which the supports can be separated, increases the level of graded hip control required.

- Concentric-eccentric control in a lateral plane then can be practiced with side-stepping activities as on a line, progressing to performance on a balance beam.

  — Side-stepping or walking on an elevated surface increases the difficulty, as does separating the supports.

  — Have the child perform an obstacle course activity, such as stepping from one cube chair to another. This increases concentric-eccentric or graded control in the lateral plane.

- Sustained lateral pelvic control can be developed in:

  — Tall and half-kneel on an inflatable surface

  — Step-standing postures with the child performing an activity in free space (for example, ball activities, a constructional activity)

  — Having the child stand with a single leg up is one way of strengthening. It is best used in testing because it is an inherently boring activity that most children will not invest in readily.

Integrating NDT and SI in Treatment for Postural Control

Poor postural control can arise from a number of deficiencies, all of which may be or may not be present. By analyzing the different components of postural control, we are better able to identify specific target strategies for treatment. By using an NDT perspective in looking at the issues of postural control and an SI perspective in addressing possible areas of insufficient sensory processing, we are able to target both the muscular issues of activation, strength, and endurance, and the central processing (sensory integrative) components of postural control.

It is important to incorporate the sensory processing aspects within the program aimed to improve postural control. To take a purely strengthening approach to motor control is to teach splinter skills without addressing the underlying root of the problem.

From a sensory integrative standpoint, consider a few basic tenets as you design the program.

1. The more sustained the muscular effort, the more difficult the task, but the greater the proprioceptive input that later will be used for the development of sustained and graded control and to reinforce body scheme development.

2. Linear vestibular input in horizontal reinforces extensor-muscle activity. This is required to develop the internal stability to maintain an erect head, to position the scapulae on the rib cage wall, and to aid in facilitating the muscles needed to maintain the position. It also is necessary to aid in developing anterior-posterior pelvic control (back extensors and hip extensor muscles).

3. Linear vestibular input in vertical planes reinforces extensor tone through facilitating a supporting reaction provided that the postural and lower-extremity muscle control is sufficient to stabilize against the tendency to collapse to the surface.

4. Angular vestibular input produces or facilitates phasic responses that are short in duration. These:

   — Are the types of reactions required for balance and equilibrium

   — Provide us the intermittent or phasic postural stabilizations against the perturbations of balance due to changes in direction

   — Are the types of input that may be used to facilitate transitional movements

5. Both linear and angular input may be used to raise or lower our arousal and attentional levels, depending upon speed and variability of input.

6. Motor planning an activity, incorporating the muscles or movements you want, reinforces motivation, sensory processing, sensory integration, and the central processing components while working on motor control. For example, performing climbing activities or negotiating an obstacle course are much more intrinsically motivating and involve far more integration of sensory information than performance of an exercise program. Be sure to provide the just-right challenge (Koomar and Bundy 1991) to engage and motivate the child. Motor learning and sensory integration will occur much more dramatically.

7. Once the child is able to perform activities with visual monitoring, progress to activities with his vision partially or fully occluded. With vision occluded, the child will learn to rely on kinesthetic awareness to control his body, and body scheme will be enhanced.

**ILLUSTRATION
14.25**
The just-right challenge

Motor Control in the Extremities

Motor control includes not only postural but also extremity control. Extremities must be strong enough to support body weight in weight-bearing positions while allowing controlled weight shifts throughout varying ranges without collapse. They also must have the internal stability to allow the distal extremity to function with skill and precision. Movements must be graded with strength and pressure that is appropriate to the task and yet able to accurately target placements of the extremity without over- or undershooting.

These functions demand:

- Co-activation for weight bearing, which is defined as contraction in agonist-antagonist muscle combinations around a joint to support that joint during weight shifts and sways or throughout the range of motion

- Concentric control, or the ability to control an extremity by shortening contractions of the muscles

- Eccentric control, or the ability to control an extremity or the body through lengthening contractions for weight shifts or graded muscular control (for example, lowering of body weight)

- Strength and pressure appropriate to the task

- Skilled, precise control

Inability to Co-Activate for Weight Bearing

Clinical observations

Shoulder or hip

- Avoidance of task
- Collapse of the extremity during weight-bearing efforts
- Rapid transitions over the extremity
- Use of internal or external rotation at the shoulder or the hip

ILLUSTRATION 14.26
Internal rotation and adduction at the hip and collapse of the knees indicate inability to co-activate for weight bearing.

ILLUSTRATION 14.27
External rotation at the shoulder may be due in part to proximal instability.

- Rolling or pushing on one extremity only; avoidance of use of one side as opposed to the other side

- Hyperextension of middle joints

Elbow or knee

- Avoidance of task

- Collapse

- Hyperextension or locking of middle joints

- For the elbow, the child may function only in pronation; for the knee, the child may stand with excessive ankle pronation or supination

Wrist

- Avoidance of task

- Weight bearing on dorsal aspect of the hand

- Weight bearing on tripod: hyperextension of metacarpal phalangeal (MP) joints with thumb posted in abduction

- Weight bearing on fisted hand

ILLUSTRATION 14.28

Medial collapse at the ankles

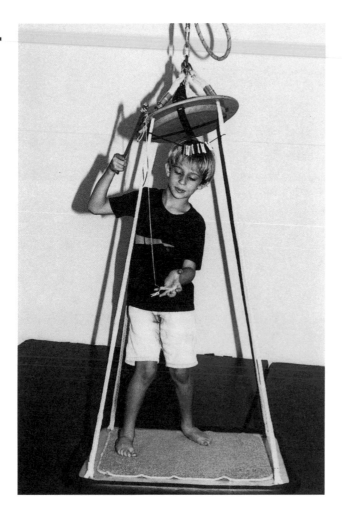

Ankle

- Avoidance of task

- Use of toe walking

- Medial-lateral shifting of the joint

Intervention strategies

At first, co-activation is facilitated through supported or partial weight-bearing experiences. Infants phasically push or lift from a surface. They begin to develop sustained co-activation through supported or partial weight-bearing patterns, assisted by their caretakers. These are methods to use in treatment.

ILLUSTRATION 14.29

Encourage both phasic and sustained co-activation, which are proprioceptive in nature, by using an inflatable surface.

- Use developmental progression.

- Start with phasic weight-bearing efforts and supported weight bearing, and grade the time spent in weight bearing and the amount of support given.

- As support of body weight emerges, begin to add very graded, gradually increasing arcs in weight-shifting exercises.

- Transient tilts and angular or rotational movements promote balance reactions and phasic co-activation through protective extension responses. Sustained tilt postures foster a more sustained reaction.

Concentric-Eccentric Control

Clinical observations

- Use the previous strategies.

- There will be an inability to sustain weight shifts.

- There will be an inability to dissociate the extremity from the trunk (that is, for extended reach or an inability to take large steps).

- The child may be able to raise his body weight for prone push-ups or stepping onto a curb, but may not perform eccentric or lengthening contractions to control lowering of body weight.

Intervention strategies

- Use weight shifts progressing to transitions. This is an excellent method of increasing concentric-eccentric control in a closed kinetic chain.

ILLUSTRATION 14.30
Weight shifts and open-chain training for concentric-eccentric control

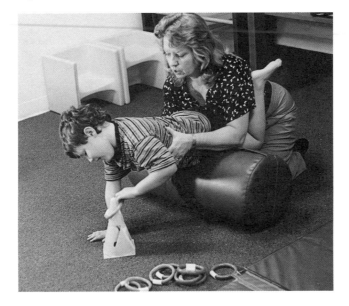

- Open-chain training for concentric-eccentric control includes arm lifts or reaching activities or leg lifts in middle ranges.

- Build more sustained motor control into the program by slowing down the child's efforts or asking him to hold positions.

- The use of SI principles includes:

  — The application of transient head movements to stimulate the semicircular canals for phasic extension of the limbs on the side of rotation or tilt (downhill side) and phasic flexion of the uphill limbs

  — Sustained tilt or movement to promote maintained extension on the downhill limbs and sustained flexion on the uphill limbs with sustained head-righting efforts

Graded Control

Clinical observations

- The child will work in the end ranges with phasic, quick bursts of movement and will be unable to slow down his efforts.

- Often, the child will require the fixing of an extremity or the trunk against the body or against the work surface.

- He will exhibit overshooting or mistargeting.

- He will use too much or too little pressure to accomplish the task.

> Sara tried to string beads, but lacked the graded control at the elbow and wrist to do the task. She needed to adduct her upper extremities against her trunk and rest her wrists on the table to stabilize her elbow and wrist for hand use.

Jared could not stabilize his pelvis and hip for lateral stability on the weight-bearing side in order to perform a single-limb stance. His pelvis on the opposite side would drop, and he would press his knee on the nonweight-bearing side against the weight-bearing lower extremity to increase his ability to perform.

Alex could not control his pelvis in an anterior-posterior plane, and therefore could not perform tall-kneel activities with graded pelvic control. Instead, he would either lean on the surface for support or revert to a heel-sit position.

Rachel, who lacks graded muscular control, also over- or under-shoots or misses the targeted object. She seems to reach past her targeted point, often knocking over her cup or missing the step or the curb she is attempting to climb.

Many children also exhibit the use of too much or too little pressure for the task. In writing tasks, children who press too hard often break the tips of their pencils or tear their paper. They may break their toys while attempting to play with them, crush paper cups while trying to drink, or walk with heavy, noisy steps. They appear rough in their play attempts, and they are clumsy in their social interactions. Children who use too little pressure make pencil marks that are too light to see. They often drop items because they inherently misjudge the pressure or strength required to hold objects. These may be signs of impaired tactile discrimination, proprioception, and/or vestibular functioning.

Intervention strategies

Midrange control is often lacking in children with autism. They operate with phasic bursts between end ranges and are unable to control or hold and sustain in midrange.

- Control is developed through transitions over a weight-bearing extremity and work within the middle range of movement at each major joint

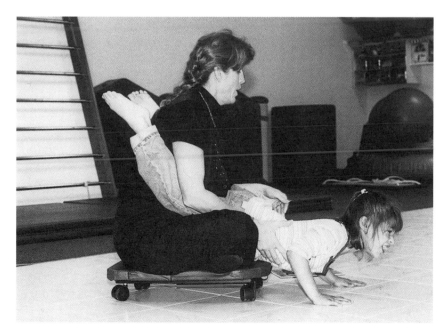

ILLUSTRATION 14.31

Work in midrange control, and add assistance or support as needed. Resistance adds proprioception to contribute to body scheme.

- Efforts must include slowing those transitional efforts to the point of being able to freeze and hold a position in midrange.

- From the SI perspective, deep proprioceptive input combined with heavy work and resistive activities, joint compression and traction, changes in joint angle, muscle length, and timing all contribute to the body image and body awareness needed for graded control throughout the extremities.

Skilled, Precise Control

Clinical observations

Hand

Tactile processing may be impaired and consist of one of the following:

- The child may exhibit evidence of tactile defensiveness, in that he will avoid touching the palmar aspect of the hand. The child may be reported to have good fine motor skills, when in actuality he substitutes tip-to-tip manipulation to the exclusion of in-hand manipulation.

- Tactile discrimination may be the underlying issue. If this is the case, the child will lack the ability to manipulate objects within the hand, and therefore tactile tests for stereognosis will be impeded or low.

Other Clinical Observations

The child:

- Uses wrist flexion with finger flaring during scissor skills

- Uses total-arm movements when coloring or writing, rather than isolating wrist and finger control of the writing implement

- Uses a fisted grasp on pencils, tools, with or without a pronated approach to tasks

- Is unable to perform or has difficulty with performance of stereognosis tests due to a lack of in-hand manipulation skills

- Is unable to use the second and third fingers in opposition to the thumb secondary to:

  — Inability to stabilize the lateral or ulnar portion of the hand for radial or medial isolation

  — Collapse of the thumb web space or thumb instability

Foot

The child will have tactile processing problems consisting of one of the following:

- Tactile defensiveness, if it exists, may cause the child to avoid walking on various surfaces or revert to toe-walking postures.

- Tactile discrimination contributes to tripping and delayed balance and equilibrium reactions on variable surfaces. Feet that do not discriminate the surface they are on do not react to changes in surface texture, grading, and elevations.

Other clinical observations

The child:

- May lack balance on variable surfaces such as grass or gravel simply because of delayed balance and equilibrium responses

- May use pronated or supinated foot postures

- Will be unable to stabilize either the medial or lateral aspect of the feet on a surface while raising the toes on the opposite border

- Will not be able to isolate toe flexion and extension to pick up marbles or wiggle the toes.

Intervention strategies

- Tactile issues may include either a tactile defensiveness or a problem with tactile discrimination, previously described. A problem in sensory modulation will further complicate the picture. The appropriate intervention for the particular tactile dysfunction must be implemented before skilled, precise control will occur in either the hand or the foot.

- Also required is the combining of somatosensory (tactile with proprioceptive) and proprioceptive-vestibular components and visual and auditory input. When we are learning a new skill, we use all of the sensory systems in the first stage of learning. Intervention needs to include somatosensory input that prepares the sensory system and also provides proprioceptive input to reinforce the sensory information gained through the work opportunities that are provided by treatment.

- A hyperresponsive problem or tactile defensiveness requires that you treat to decrease and calm the system with proprioceptive input of deep-touch, deep pressure into the palm of the hands and fingers or on the plantar surface of the feet and toes.

- Use deep-touch massage with only enough lotion on your hands to decrease skin dryness and avoid the sensation of skin tearing for the child.

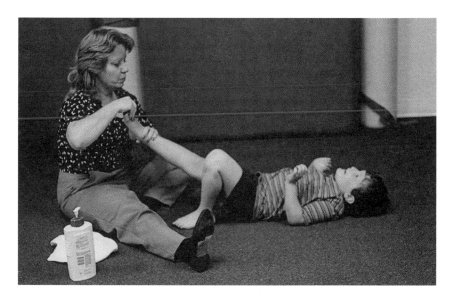

ILLUSTRATION 14.32

Intersperse massage with deep-touch pressure with joint compression and traction in the hyper-responsive child.

- Use vibratory stimulation, weight bearing, tapping, or joint compression without many changes in your hand placements.

- Remember that each time you change your hand placements on the child, you are triggering the defensiveness and making it necessary for the child to accommodate and calm his system before he is open to learning.

- For a hyporesponsive system where tactile discrimination is an issue, use sensory stimulation to wake up the system. Tactile discrimination activities include:

  — Tasks that require the child to find objects buried in rice or other mediums

ILLUSTRATION 14.33

Rice, shaving cream, and other mediums offer sensory stimulation. Add tactile discrimination by having the child find objects hidden in the medium.

  — Brisk rubbing of the hands

  — Work in finger paint or shaving cream

  — Adding proprioception into the equation to have the child work against resistance, thereby reinforcing body scheme and position awareness while addressing the issues of concentric-eccentric control, graded muscle control, and strength and endurance within the hand.

A word of caution

- Fluctuating sensory modulation difficulties include periods of both hyper- and hyporesponsiveness in relation to tactile processing with a volatility that cannot be predicted. Strong sensory stimulation or facilitating techniques are ill advised. Use those applications that have a proprioceptive component in order to modulate the central nervous system's ability to process and allow learning to occur.

- Besides tactile and somatosensory (tactile combined with proprioceptive) issues, a major cause of a lack of skilled, precise hand movement is a lack of internal stability across the wrist and within the hand itself. Any skilled movement requires both postural control and the strength for internal stability throughout the midranges of the joint (or joints) proximal to where the work is occurring.

  — The fingers will not isolate if the wrist and carpal-metacarpal joints are weak and unstable.

  — The radial functions of the hand will not develop without the ability to stabilize the ulnar aspect (third and fourth digits) into the palm. Radial functions will not develop if the wrist cannot attain and sustain wrist extension to post the hand for function.

- Wrist stability is a key component to hand skills. The child must be able to stabilize the wrist in neutral or extended position. Due to improper weight-bearing experiences throughout development, many children never fully elongate the flexor carpii ulnaris muscle, which places the extensor carpii ulnaris at a biomechanical disadvantage for posting the wrist in extension. The extensor carpii ulnaris muscle is a key component in the ability to stabilize ulnarly and isolate the thumb and first and second fingers for precise radial prehension, pencil grasp, and other positions.

- Therapeutic efforts must address for any shortening in the flexor carpii ulnaris muscle, thereby providing full range of motion into wrist extension.

- Weight bearing on the hands can provide elongation to the necessary muscles if the proximal palmar surface is in contact with the floor.

This is the method used during normal development to prepare and strengthen the necessary wrist components for skilled function. Take care to assess whether the child has the available range of motion to bear weight on the palm. If not, address range-of-motion issues at the wrist and throughout the fingers before using this position in treatment.

ILLUSTRATION 14.34

Weight bearing must be with the palm in contact with the floor in order to elongate the wrist flexors so that the extensor carpii ulnaris will activate during radial prehension tasks.

Elongation occurs naturally during weight shifts in anterior-posterior, medial-lateral, and diagonal patterns over the hand. We then must provide activation and strengthening activities for wrist extension. Through weight shifting, the child gains alignment, eccentric-concentric, and graded muscular control throughout the wrist in a closed kinetic chain. Open-chain wrist activities include phasic wrist flexion-extension efforts such as occur in yo-yo exercises, tearing paper, and tweezer activities.

- Perform isolated finger exercises with the wrist posted in neutral or extended positions. Activities such as paper crumpling, finger pointing, and poking call for isolated finger control.

- To encourage radial-ulnar separation, place a small amount of therapy putty in the ulnar portion of the palm with the third and fourth digits pressed into it for added stabilization.

  — Have the child perform activities that include radial functions, such as scissors skills, writing, or tool use.

  — Add proprioceptive components by using tools that offer a resistance, such as olive or pickle pickers, tweezers, escargot clamps, and resistive clothespins.

- School-related paper tasks of writing, coloring, and cutting are not replete with sensory feedback in and of themselves, and therefore are not inherently motivating or interesting to a child who does not perceive the feedback that is offered.

  — To enhance tactile components, build in somatosensory aspects to writing activities. Photocopy written worksheets onto heavier paper stock and place various grades of sandpaper under the worksheets, thereby offering resistance and texture to the activity.

  — Use hand and wrist weights.

  — Use a pencil grip, rubber band, or pipe cleaner to provide a cue for where to hold on the pencil.

  — For a visually challenged or hyporesponsive child, use paper with raised lines that offer cues for where the pencil mark should stop and end in a vertical plane.

  — Vibrating pens and thick pencils or pens offer increased tactile and proprioceptive information. Try several to determine what may work best with the child, based on the child's preference and what is appropriate within the particular setting.

- The same issues seen in problems with isolated control in the hand cause problems of skilled, precise motor control within the ankle and foot. A foot will not develop the skilled balance movements and isolated toe flexion and extension if the ankle and tarsal area lacks internal strength for internal stability. The child will lack the dissociation of the great toe from the lateral four toes needed for adequate push-off in gait and for medial-lateral balance and weight shift over the plantar surface. Overcompensations include plantar flexion such as toe walking, pronation or medial collapse of the foot, or supination in which the medial border is sustained off the surface.

- Appropriate interventions for any tactile dysfunctions must be implemented.

- For defensiveness, use activities to trigger the dorsal column medial lemniscus; that is, deep-touch, pressure, and proprioceptive input including:

  — Increased resistance

  — Changes in joint effort

  — Increased muscular effort

- For tactile discrimination, use sensory stimulation activities to awaken the ankle and foot. Add proprioceptive input here as well to reinforce body scheme.

- The next step is to combine somatosensory (tactile-proprioceptive) with visual and perhaps auditory input to reinforce motor learning.

  — Use rhythmic activities for the lower extremities, and particularly the ankle and foot.

  — Progress to isolation of toe flexion and extension, which will build the intrinsic muscles of the foot and internal stability.

  — Traditionally, therapists use the activities of balancing rings or other objects on the top of the foot or picking up objects with the toes.

  — Older children may be able to wrinkle a cloth by using their toes.

  — Wriggling feet in sand or rice buckets is also effective.

  — Progress to balance activities after activating the intrinsics of the feet. In this way, the balance skills will develop for functional tasks.

A Final Word

Whether you ascribe to a belief in the hierarchal form of motor control or a dynamic systems approach, motor control issues are typically developed in a sequential format through the developmental framework. Sensory and motor issues contribute to the act of motor learning. Children with autism have documented problems or issues with both sensory processing and motor control.

There have been certain clustering of symptoms through the data gathered by use of the SIPT that help describe some conditions that may apply to children with autism. The treatment strategies outlined to address those issues can offer tools to use in designing treatment strategies for not only the children with autism, but other children that you see.

The treatment techniques offered through a neurodevelopmental treatment approach can be used to follow a treatment progression of preparation, facilitation, strengthening, and carryover into function. NDT offers a systematic approach to gaining the components required for postural control in the head and trunk and motor control in the extremities.

There are other ideas, theories, and treatment strategies that are helpful in the treatment of motor control issues. However, it is the characteristics of autism and PDD that compound the challenges and confuse us. We must be adept at observation, and we must constantly analyze the behaviors of the child with autism so that we may tease out the components that are delayed or lacking. Our efforts must be guided by an understanding of how the child with autism interprets input and information during treatment. In addition to all of the sensory and motor control strategies, we must simultaneously manage sensory registration, sensory regulation, gain the child's interest, and make the learning of motor control inherently motivating.

CHAPTER 15

Improving the Child's Ability to Communicate

Robin Parker and Betty Paris

All people have a need to function. In order to function, they must be able to communicate their wants and needs. They must know how to relate to people they come into contact with in the environment. Human interaction necessitates a shared method of understanding what is being communicated. Most people think of verbal methods when they think of communication, but there are many forms of very effective nonverbal communication. Consider the nonverbal skills used by infants—grimaces, smiles, frowns, crying, laughter. Think of the tantrums of typical 2-year-olds who lack the verbal skills to negotiate or verbalize their desires, excitement, frustration, or displeasure, and therefore use crying, screaming, kicking, and other total-body language to communicate. Young children communicate by pointing, waving, and using total-body gestures that remind us of mime efforts. Other forms of nonverbal communication include sign language, picture systems, and written or mechanized communication systems (VOCAS).

Communication Impairments in Children With Autism

As described in *The Diagnostic and Statistical Manual of Mental Disorders* (American Psychological Association 1994), the lack of communicative and social skills is a core problem in autism. We know that children with autism often either fail to develop or are delayed in developing functional speech and language skills. Autism seems to affect their basic intuitive sense of how to communicate. These children lack the ability to spontaneously use nonverbal strategies typically used by nonverbal persons who do not have autism. Often they have deficits in the ability to use sustained eye contact, facial expressions, body language, and gestures or mime spontaneously. These deficits in social interaction skills are different from those deficits seen in other language-delayed youngsters. Children with autism often learn to take an adult's hand, using the adult as a tool to get simple tasks performed. They do not gesture as to what is to be done, but rely on the adult to deduce what is needed and to comply. Their methods of communication may be atypical and unconventional. These children may use screaming as their only form of verbal communication. They may use hand flapping, tooth grinding, total-body rocking, or self-abusive types of behavior such as head slapping or hand biting to communicate excitement, escalating stress, frustration, or anger. They may use flight behaviors as a method to communicate, "I don't want to do this"; or they may revert to aggressive behavior, striking out in order to convey their messages.

The reasons for impairments in their communicative skills are not fully understood. Indeed, communication impairments are complex in these children. Some are postulated to be caused by differences in brain-tissue structure, some by sensory-processing problems, others by motor control issues, and still others by yet unexplained causes. It generally is believed that multiple etiologies may result in the symptoms of autism and related disorders. Children with autism are a heterogeneous group with many possible reasons for their socio-communicative deficits.

Researchers have demonstrated differences in the structure of certain areas of the brain and have pointed to the possibility of differences in the circuitry or wiring of the brain. There is ever-increasing evidence that these differences in structure set the stage for atypical processing of information. Impairment in development of all of the brain functions may cause limitations in learning to occur.

 # Sensory- and Motor-Based Problems

Dyspraxia

Neurologists and therapists often use the term *dyspraxia* in conjunction with autism and other disorders to describe a person who has difficulty learning a new motor skill or performing a specific skill or task on demand.

The terms *verbal dyspraxia* or *developmental apraxia* are often used by speech-language pathologists to refer to a specific speech impairment commonly seen in autism. Verbal or developmental apraxia refers to a condition in which there is difficulty planning the motor movements for volitional speech. Apraxia involves difficulty in sequencing. The child has problems in timing and sequencing the articulators for speech production. This apraxia within autism impedes the articulation of words and sentences. A child will appear to be trying to form the words, but has difficulty moving his lips and tongue to accomplish the task. This difficulty, or groping, is one indicator of apraxia. Another indicator is inconsistent error patterns in articulation; for example, a child might first say *pi* for *pig*, but another time say *gi* for *pig*. The difficulties resulting from apraxia do not include problems of weakness or paralysis of the speech muscles, but those with difficulty sequencing the movements of the articulators for purposeful speech movements.

However, this does not go far enough to explain the pervasive nature of the dyspraxia. Ayres (1979) described developmental dyspraxia as a brain dysfunction that begins early in the child's life and affects his development as he grows. She described dyspraxia as a sensory integrative dysfunction that results in the inability to use sensory information from the proprioceptive, vestibular, and tactile systems effectively, not only for motor planning, but for learning. Ayres described motor planning as one of the most complex functions demanded of children. It involves conscious attention, is closely linked to mental and intellectual functions, and depends upon complex sensory integration throughout the brain. The brain commands the muscles what to do, but the sensations from the body enable the brain to perform this function. Motor planning is the bridge between the sensorimotor and intellectual aspects of brain function. This definition describes a central processing dysfunction that includes sensory processing, mental formulation of an idea from abstraction, and the motor production of a response called communication, whether verbal or nonverbal. The terms *dyspraxia* or *developmental apraxia* used in regard to speech impairments reflect difficulty learning (new motor skill), initiating, and performing a specific skill or task on demand, and difficulty sequencing the performance due to the impairments of whole-brain functions.

Limitations in performance in children with autism are the result of atypical development, a lack of the ability to interpret sensory information for use, and the innate inability to process what it is, what is to be done, and how to do it. Treatment must attach on all fronts to enhance the child's level of performance.

The Motor Planning of Communication

Ideation

Communication, whether verbal or nonverbal, is a complex motor planning process. The child must register things, people, and changes in the environment, formulate an intellectual concept of what he wishes to communicate, and then sequence, time, and execute the communication. That communication may be as simple as a gesture or use of a picture symbol, or as complex as dissertation on what he wants to communicate, why it is of importance, and the sequence of events to occur.

At the root of the communication disorders are the problems with registration, attention, and arousal that hinder the developing infant's and young child's ability to respond to people and changes within the environment. If the child fails to register people in the environment, there most certainly will be no motivation for communicative efforts. If he fails to register or understand the intended communication from those around him, he cannot respond appropriately to them.

If he registers people, but fails to attend to interactions and events, communicative efforts will be nonemergent, delayed, or shortened. If he fails to attend, he will not absorb the prerequisite information from verbal interactions before verbal attempts at communication, as occurs with typical children. The young child who is able to attend has shared many communication sequences as a nonverbal participant long before those first utterances ever occur. If the child has limited ability to attend, his communication will be functional for the first part of a communicative sequence, but may rapidly deteriorate as his ability to attend deteriorates.

If the child's arousal level is too low, he may lack the ability to spontaneously attempt communication. If his level of arousal is too high, the child cannot process events or cannot accurately analyze his needs or formulate verbal or nonverbal attempts at communication.

Verbal skills may be delayed further because of a number of other of problems encountered in autism. These include:

- Problems in registration, orientation, attention, and arousal
- Motor planning problems
- Sensory processing problems of tactile, vestibular, and proprioceptive input
- Auditory processing issues
- Motor problems
- Social interaction problems

Sensory processing problems set the stage for delays in speech and language. The ability to use speech and language is dependent upon CNS organization at all levels, from the brain stem to the cortex.

Auditory impulses travel through the brain stem to the cerebellum, where the impulses are matched to motor messages. Impulses travel throughout the cortex to processing areas. Poor auditory registration, faulty auditory processing, and difficulties filtering out pertinent from nonpertinent sounds make auditory discrimination poor. The acquisition of sounds is delayed by the lack of the ability to discern and discriminate sounds in the environment. The child may not discern his name being called by a parent, and therefore will not respond. He may fail to attach meaning to the sounds he hears. He may fail to decode the auditory messages appropriately for function. He may fail to begin to label objects for the lack of auditory discrimination. The infant attaches no meaning to the words, *mama*, *dada*, or *baba*. Early vocalizations may be delayed by the fact that the child cannot discern vocalizations from other noises in the environment. When random vocal efforts do occur, the lack of auditory registration and discrimination or processing may make feedback ineffectual. Therefore, learning is delayed.

Auditory hyperresponsiveness, on the contrary, may cause the child to avoid people, have an aversion to voices and laughter, and be unable to discriminate between sounds due to the aversive nature of the input. The child then unconsciously learns that people cause discomfort simply because of the noise they make. Contact and communicative efforts may be avoided. Communication, nonverbal and verbal, therefore is atypical.

Motor Components

Defazio (1986) described some of the motor components involved in beginning speech efforts. They include:

- Normal postural tone to reinforce the motor control and respiratory base required for speech

- Normal movement patterns in order to coordinate the articulators (tongue, lips, and cheeks) for sound production

- Appropriate timing of movements to sequence and execute language

- Coordination of respiration and phonation required for sound production to occur

- Precise motor control of the soft palate, tongue, lips, and jaw in order to articulate intelligibly

- The ability to select and appropriately use these muscles for intelligible speech

- The timing, sequencing, and duration of effort necessary for correct and intelligible production of speech

Hypotonia compounds the effort by adding low tone in the muscles that stabilize the jaw and move the tongue and cheeks for sound production. Timing, strength of effort, and coordination with respiration may be lacking. The lack of tactile and proprioceptive awareness, combined with the hypotonic muscle tone, results in a lack of facial expression and an inability to formulate normal patterns of movements needed for articulation. Intelligibility may be less than optimal when it does occur.

Concomitantly, there is often poor truncal tone and poor respiratory capacity for sound production. Strength within the postural flexors (the abdominal muscles) contributes to poor postural mechanisms and diminished respiratory support for language attempts. Endurance is poor. The net result may be low volume, omission of final consonants (*cu* for *cup*), a lack of sustained vocalizations, limited numbers of words produced, or use of single-word utterances and poor intelligibility.

Hyporesponsive systems in which tactile and proprioceptive feedback is poor and unreliable affect the motor components of speech and language production. It is difficult for the child to know where the tongue is in his mouth and how to move the tongue, soft palate, lips, and jaw. This limits the child's ability to place the tongue and move the oral-facial musculature appropriately for sound production. The selection and use of muscles may not be accurate, and the timing may be sluggish. The sequencing of muscular efforts and their duration (endurance) also will be affected.

Execution

For whatever reasons, motor learning, and therefore motoric performance, in a child with dyspraxia is not automatic. Rather, the child must exert tremendous cognitive effort to learn and perform a task. If inherent in that task is an inability to visually monitor the child's efforts, as in speech attempts, the act of motor learning and output is made even more difficult, contributing to delays. Motor performance of communication is an *on demand* type of task. Further impeding the individual with autism is the difficulty with initiating any motoric act, especially on demand. Speech may occur spontaneously in response to a stimulus or object, but often it cannot be reproduced consistently on demand in a conversation or human interaction.

When Speech Emerges

There are a profusion of other problems that occur as speech does emerge. These deficits can range from very limited word use and comprehension to complex speech with errors. Problems with registration, attention, and arousal can continue to limit the emerging acquisition of appropriate language, as can all of the sensory processing issues. Respiratory endurance and the ability to sustain vocalizations can remain limited, thereby limiting the number of words that can be produced in a phrase or sentence. Auditory discrimination and auditory hypersensitivities can lead to inaccurate and unreliable self-monitoring due to faulty feedback mechanisms and the avoidance of communicative efforts altogether. The child may not discern the differences between words and cannot possibly be expected to self-correct for errors in articulation or production. The monotone speaking voice that often is a characteristic in the child with autism may be the result of impaired auditory processing and discrimination and faulty self-monitoring systems. Faulty somatosensory (tactile and proprioceptive) mechanisms compound the difficulty of speech production.

Motor engrams for speech may be formulated, but are restricted in number and variety. The child may stay on a particular topic too long (perseveration) or repeat words or phrases over and over simply because that is the motor engram that has become hard-wired into his system. A robotic quality may be the result of a learned motoric pattern or engram.

We also know that children with autism have impaired ability to discern inferred information. They have difficulty registering, recognizing and interpreting body language, gestures, expressions and intonation of others. Because of this, they do not develop the skill of learning and adjusting to changing social situations. They may not know when to use a particular form of language such as a greeting, may not comprehend when a slang term is used, and may not glean the correct meaning of the words they hear. Once again, sensory processing difficulties contribute to poor receptive skills and development of comprehension. Often we see children who use terms that may be advanced for their age, but are incorrect or out of context to the conversation.

Descriptive language is often missing in the language skills of the child with autism. Many descriptive terms are sensory-based in what they describe—a feeling, a texture, a quality. Again, this may be the result of a underlying lack of the ability to process, personalize, analyze, and constructively use sensory information. The child simply may not be able to connect the feeling with the words to label descriptions. He may have an easier time labeling colors or sizes (big or small), which are easier and more concrete descriptive concepts to learn.

Pragmatics refers to the social way language is used. It is the language we use in making our needs met and socially using words and gestures to interact. A child with autism often lacks the pragmatic language skills needed to communicate effectively. This impairment of pragmatics prevents the child from being able to describe how or what he feels, make requests, ask questions to clarify a topic, or even to realize that he has a question or a reaction. The child may have difficulty taking turns in a conversation, using eye contact or vocal tone to emphasize a point, and using personal pronouns such as *I* and *me*. Often he will use his name when referring to himself. Pragmatic language problems can make the child sound different even if speech intelligibility and frequency of language are good.

Children with autism have been cited as not understanding or reacting or showing emotions appropriately. We cannot be certain that they comprehend the information the way it was intended and understand the implied meaning of a situation; and if they voice a reaction, that reaction may not be phrased accurately. The child's facial expressions may not correlate with either his verbal messages or his responses.

Unreliable receptive language skills, limited and atypical nonverbal communication skills in the form of facial expressions, emotionally labile responses, and difficulties in pragmatic expressive language set the stage for miscommunication, errors, misunderstanding, and wrongful assumptions on both parties. Communicative efforts may be confusing and offer unpredictable conclusions, leading to impaired learning of communication skills. These children can't pose questions for validation or clarification. Therefore, labeling of objects may be impaired, and information gained from descriptive language may be faulty or even meaningless.

Impact of Impaired Play Skills on Communication

Typical children learn through play. Early play experiences emphasize use of the whole body in environmental interactions. These total-body play experiences serve as primary ways to enhance the child's ability to organize sensations for use in creating more complex adaptive behaviors.

The quality of sensorimotor experiences creates the framework of understanding on which language is later based. As children become more organized in their ability to perform, learn to manipulate objects, and move through the environment, they acquire concepts such as direction, spatial relationships, and motor skills through the manipulation of their bodies and of objects within their environment.

As they increase their capacity for and control over movement, they develop the motor control required for postural mechanisms and the anti-gravity flexor control required for an adequate respiratory base and internal jaw and tongue stability for language efforts. As motor control develops, initially crude interactions become refined and adaptive responses to objects and people grow in number and complexity, setting the stage for the ability to attend and imitate.

Imitative play begins with mimicking facial gestures, vocalizations, and motor sequences from older children and adults with whom they interact. Children typically progress to a cause-effect type of play in which some action causes a reaction from a toy. At approximately the first birthday, babies begin to replicate situations encountered in real life. They will brush a doll's hair, give the doll a bath, or pretend to offer the doll a drink. As imaginary play develops, they create new opportunities for problem solving and new physical challenges. Their ability to attend increases. They learn to replicate the words they've heard over and over again, and they begin to label objects.

Verbal skills begin to expand and language develops. Children learn about descriptive language and pragmatics, the language needed for social interactions and asking questions. As concepts and relationships increase, their play sequences become longer and more complex. They learn role delineation, social interaction, recognize and label their emotions, and develop coping strategies to deal with these emotions. They learn to request, demand, negotiate, and voice displeasure.

In children with autism, play is limited by decreased initiation, decreased eye contact, a lack of imitation, reduced symbolic or pretend play, and perseveration of the learned play repertoires. Perseveration is the repetition of a motor act or vocalization, and it is neurological in nature; it is not a willful behavior. These children are unable to stop or change the behavior. Their play is limited to actions that they have learned, but it lacks the flexibility and creativity needed to master their environments, expand their capabilities, and generalize data.

The sensory feedback that they experience in play is characterized by mixed messages and unpredictable performances. Children with autism do not easily and readily learn to or from their play experiences. Often their early play experiences are disorganized, unpredictable, and unsuccessful. They lack opportunities to organize the sensation into creating more complex adaptive responses, and they lack the inherent ability to initiate play or the ability to play creatively. They also have difficulty imitating others.

Children with autism have difficulty acquiring the basic concepts afforded children in typical development. They fail to develop the idea of how to interact with objects and persons in their environments, and therefore they don't develop the neuronal models necessary for analyzing new situations. They fail to acquire language for labeling, requesting, or describing play. They are ill-prepared for interactive play. They can't identify or explain their confusion, disorganization, and emotional reactions. They don't negotiate with peers because they lack the language and social skills to do so. Concept formation, role delineation, social interaction, and emotional development all suffer.

Remember that there are anatomical changes within the areas of the brain that analyze, combine, filter, and store information. The *data banks* of children with autism contain the spatial, temporal, and sensory components of their experiences just as yours and mine do. The difference may be that theirs are based upon perceptions and conclusions that may be faulty. Therefore, the components in their data banks also are faulty. The ability to accurately perceive the physical environment and to act upon it are the basic materials required for organization of more complex behaviors (Ayres 1979).

It is the job of clinicians, teachers, and parents to aid in the perception and analysis of the components within the child's environment and to teach strategies to act effectively upon that environment. We must provide the basic materials for organizing more complex behavior. We also must provide methods of communication in order to avoid frustration and behavioral issues that may stem from the child's inability to communicate effectively and functionally even the most basic needs or wants.

Intervention Strategies

For the child with autism who has verbal or nonverbal communication disorders, intervention should occur in natural, functional activities. Play is a natural environment for children. Through the sensorimotor experiences provided by development, the child learns about his world and how to move and act upon it. The internal body map that is the by-product of those sensorimotor experiences gives the child a frame of reference as he formulates concepts and attaches meaning to his experiences. The receptive and expressive language that develops allows him the ability to define, organize, store, and effect changes in his experiences. Language is the cement that holds the matrix of concepts, emotions, and ideas in a cohesive, usable format. It is through play experiences that we give the language-delayed child the opportunities to practice the requisites of communication and language.

Normal infants and children begin to communicate well in advance of verbal development, and so do children with autism. We must provide the sensorimotor experiences they need to formulate comprehension of the meaning of communication; and we must provide opportunities for communication even before verbal skills begin to develop. Shaping and directing the child's method of communication as communicative strategies emerge is a much easier process than attempting to correct or alter undesirable behaviors or strategies once they have been established.

Registration, Orientation, and Arousal

Problems with registration, orientation, attention, and arousal must be addressed before communication will begin to develop. The child must be in a calm-alert state in order to process, organize, plan, and produce communicative strategies. If he is underresponsive, we may need to use vestibular and proprioceptive input to increase his level of arousal to within the optimum window for learning. If the child is overresponsive, we must use calming strategies to remove extraneous stimuli from the immediate environment and assist the child in calming himself. See Chapter 10 for discussion and techniques.

Environmental Considerations

The most important aspect of empowering children to communicate at home and at school is to provide frequent opportunities across all activities. Initially, you may need to use environmental set-up and control to help the child register relevant information and remain within or regain his calm, optimal level of participation. As the child is able, you can begin to increase the amount of environmental distractions in his surroundings while continuing to assist him in registering and orienting to that which is relevant.

- Remove distractions by limiting the number of people and items in the area in which you are working. By controlling the number and variety of objects in the child's environment, we are better able to increase the likelihood of successful registration and orientation. This may include the decreased use of fluorescent lights, because many children with autism perceive the flickering of fluorescent lights that others are unaware of.

- Reduce noise levels. The child may be hyperalert and aware of air as it whistles through the air-conditioning system, the sounds of cars or trucks outside, vacuum cleaners up the hallway, and other noises that others routinely block out. He also may be disorganized by your own verbal prompts. Your voice volume, pitch, resonance, and laugh may be aversive to him. He may be distracted and confused by the number of sentences you use. In the absence of verbalizations from the child, or in response to his verbalizations, many of us attempt to fill the void with banter. Carefully monitor the effects of your own communication style on the child. Do not disorganize, irritate, or distract him. For the overreactive child, you may need to lower your voice and limit the number of verbalizations you give. For the underresponsive child, you may need to raise your voice or pitch to gain registration.

- Limit the amount of light touch or tactile input in your physical prompts or assistance. If the child requires assistance, place your hands in a position to assist and do not remove them until you are finished with the task. Constantly placing your hands on the child and taking them away during his work efforts may be distracting. The child may have a difficult time adjusting to the touch stimulus every time it changes. Whenever you remove your hands and need to introduce a new touch stimulus, give the child warning verbally ("Let me help," or "Help me"). Enabling the child to visualize your approach will help him anticipate it.

- Set up communication temptations. Offer frequent opportunities to request desired items, to protest or comment on changes or disruptions within the environment, and to enjoy being the center of attention.

- Develop a systematic prompting hierarchy. Verbal prompts are more intrusive than nonverbal prompts. Visual strategies can be effective in improving both receptive and expressive communication. As soon as a prompt is provided, try to fade it in order to increase the child's spontaneous language. Use a most-to-least prompting hierarchy so the child knows what to expect, and then switch to a least-to-most hierarchy.

ILLUSTRATION 15.1

Add visual prompts to schoolwork routines. The child knows where he is expected to be and what he is expected to do.

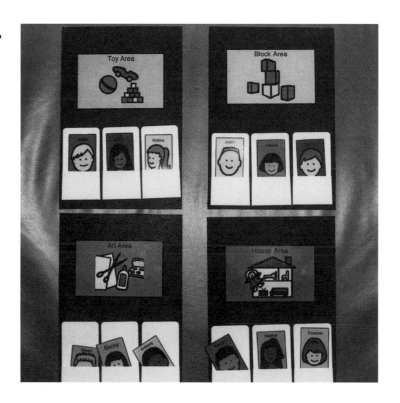

- Set up verbal routines at home and at school. Once a routine is established, omit a part of the routine and wait. The child will be likely to fill in the omission. Routines help provide structure to language and provide opportunities for the child to participate. Establish discussions on a daily activity such as preparing a meal or getting ready for school. Visual systems may help the child become organized within those routines.

Behaviors, both desirable and undesirable, are triggered by events or needs, and then are sustained by either the sensory benefits (pleasure) or the effectiveness that the behaviors provide. Use this fact in your treatments. We need to assist the child with registering appropriate, relevant stimuli from irrelevant stimuli. To do this, we must help him attach meaning to objects and persons. Then we must attach verbal or nonverbal communicative strategies to those objects and persons. If we engage the child in play with a swing, give him the pleasurable experience of enjoying the swing, and then attach the use of a picture for requesting the swing or a verbal attempt at requesting the swing. Thus, the child will learn to register, orient to, and request the swing. The child must learn that if he points to an object, the request will be recognized and addressed. If he uses a picture to communicate, it will be acknowledged. He will quickly learn that these methods of communication are empowering and effective with those in his world who are attentive and open to forms of communication. He also will quickly revert to other less desirable strategies that quickly get him the attention he seeks with persons who are not alert, attentive, and adept at deciphering his attempts at communication.

Provide Feedback and Develop Motor Engrams

Feedback is used for the initial acquisition of a skill. It also is used in the cognitive phase of learning in which all sensory systems are used to gather and validate information (Fitts 1964). It is therefore of utmost importance that we assist in providing feedback. It may be in the form of sensory (tactile, proprioceptive, vestibular, visual, auditory), verbal, or any form of task validation. We must help the child register and orient to his success as he demonstrates emerging attempts at communication. We must be wary not to overstimulate or excite him to the point of overarousal, but the feedback must sufficiently emphasize the behavior so that there is no mistaking that this is the behavior or communicative attempt that will be rewarded.

A hyporesponsive system in which tactile and proprioceptive feedback is poor and unreliable will affect the motor components of speech and language production. Sounds are produced when the tongue is placed in a variety of positions within the mouth. Lips may be pressed together as the *mmm* sound or other bilabial sounds (*mama, baba*). The *d* sound requires that the tongue be elevated and pressed against the palate. The child can't make raspberries unless he can protract his tongue forward. If he has no tactile and position in space awareness, he will not be able to place his tongue or operate his lips and cheek muscles for intelligible sound production. Speech production is laboriously and minimally effective.

Tactile and proprioceptive input is important in order to awaken the system in a hyporesponsive system.

- Use brushing techniques to increase the child's awareness within his mouth. The Nuk brush techniques are well documented. Infa-Dents are a softer version of a brush that slip over a finger and can be used to brush the tongue, palate, gums, and inner cheeks of the very young child who does not bite.

- Vibrating or musical toothbrushes offer the ability for the older child to do his own brushing or sensory stimulation to awaken the system. Vibrators, facial massages, and facial toweling also are effective for increasing awareness of the muscles of the face.

- Manual stroking or tractioning through the muscles of the cheek and around the lips is an effective method of adding proprioceptive awareness to those areas.

- Toweling of the oral-facial musculature increases awareness by the tactile input.

- Touching where the tongue is to be placed assists the child in knowing where the targeted area is.

- Resisting tongue movements also increases awareness of the position and location of the tongue.

- Use of a mirror reinforces these techniques by making use of polymodal neurons for learning.

Motor engrams are affected by the underlying muscle tone and the muscle's ability to perform or execute the plan. Hypotonia compounds the effort of verbal communication by the added complication of low muscle tone in the muscles that stabilize the jaw and move the tongue and cheeks for sound production. Children with low muscle tone often have not developed strength in the cervical or neck muscles. Therefore, intervention must address this.

Supine Flexion

- We use the supine flexion test to identify the children who are unable to pull the head up against gravity from supine.

  — A baby at 5 to 6 months of age typically is able to raise his head from a surface to initiate a sit-up maneuver. By 5 years of age, a child in supine or back-lying position should be able to flex his neck, raising his head up from the surface, without using a chin jut; and hold the chin tuck with his arms across his chest and knees held in a tuck position for 15 seconds.

  — A lack of flexor strength leads to a lack of jaw stability. Because the base of the tongue originates from and is dependent upon the jaw, the ability to control and direct the tongue is affected in the child who has poor cervical flexor strength.

- Flexion activities that include head righting against gravity and chin tuck are a must in treatment. Refer to Chapter 14 for methods or activities.

Hypotonia also contributes to poor trunk tone. Poor tone, and therefore overall strength of the muscles of respiration, leads to poor respiratory capacity. The child's ability to take in sufficient air and his ability to control exhalation in combination with sound production is affected. Initially, there may not be the sustained control present to utter more than a single word. Volume is affected. Often, respiratory endurance is a contributing factor to rapid fatigue in a child with hypotonia. The child simply doesn't have the respiratory capacity to sustain activity

and/or sound production. He must be taught to increase his inspiratory efforts and sustain the muscle control required for more prolonged exhalation efforts.

- Initially, get the child to imitate humming or chanting hmmmm.

- Manual vibration techniques on the rib cage and abdomen can change the sound as the child vocalizes. Often the child will begin to giggle as he feels the changes within his trunk and hears the sounds being produced.

- Blowing bubbles and performing other blowing activities will strengthen the intercostal muscles, diaphragm, and abdominal muscles required to increase respiratory capacity.

- Add resistance by having the child blow larger objects such as confetti, craft puffballs, and, later, blow up beach balls and balloons and use whistles. Resistive activities are proprioceptive in nature. The child will gain better awareness of the muscles involved in the blowing activities, including his mouth, cheeks, diaphragm, and abdominal muscles.

Dyspraxia, or the inability to conceptualize a motor plan, has a direct impact on speech and language.

- The child must accurately process sensory impulses in order to register objects and persons within the environment. If he fails to register, that is where to start in treatment. The child must attach meaning to the things in his environment and be able to formulate a plan of action. If this is where the breakdown is occurring, then this is where to begin. (See Chapters 10 and 12.)

- If the child has difficulty sequencing, use modeling, verbal, visual, and tactile cues for prompting and begin to fade those prompts as soon as the child begins to sequence the plan himself.

- If the problem is in the motor execution, direct the intervention toward giving the needed postural and motor control, the body scheme, and the assistance to complete the motor task or tasks.

- For motor learning to occur, we need to take a multisensory or multimodal approach to learning by providing enhanced sensory experiences and assistance in interpreting the feedback offered by those experiences.

  — There are polysensory neurons that require intersensory information (that is, vestibular, proprioceptive, and auditory stimuli) before they will fire.

  — Auditory and visual information must be validated by a comparison of information from somatosensory, vestibular, and proprioceptive systems. It is important to combine modalities that will produce an impact on the sensory processing, and therefore the learning.

The ability to visually monitor the tongue, teeth, mouth, cheeks, and neck or throat is an important component in teaching the child about his body. Use of a mirror is a must for feedback to occur. Do not worry that the child will self-stim. Direct his attention through the application of sensory, auditory, and visual input. Visual monitoring is critical and allows for self-monitoring until the child has a good body awareness of his face and mouth and a knowledge of how speech is produced.

Effective visual monitoring incorporates several methodologies:

- A mirror enables the child to have a better awareness of the articulators (lips, tongue, cheeks).

- For additional visual and tactile cues, use blocks to teach the child about the syllables in a word. This will help the child learn to sequence syllables correctly. For example, place two blocks with raised letters in front of the child. Have him say and touch the blocks as he says "Bubble" (or any two-syllable word). This exercise provides multimodality (visual and tactile) cues to help in all areas of motor planning.

- Other tactile cues include touching the child to indicate how a sound is produced. For example, running a finger on the child's arm when a consonant sound is produced will help him learn the rule that some sounds keep going (for example, /s/, /f/, /sh/).

- For developmental apraxia of speech, teach sounds through a systematic approach based on developmental norms, increasing overall speech intelligibility and sound stimulability.

- To teach strings of syllables, have the child repeat syllables while you hold up a finger as each syllable is repeated. The visual cues will help the child replicate two, three, or more syllables. The same technique can be used for stringing words together.

Clearly, with all types of dyspraxia, it is important to use a multimodality approach that combines general body awareness and specific speech techniques.

- A multisensory approach may well entail the use of different flavors and textures of foods to increase the awareness in and around the mouth and to provide resistive exercise and proprioceptive input to the muscles therein.

- Chewing provides resistance to the muscle of mastication and to the tongue as it moves the food around within the mouth. Gum, candies, and other hard textures can be therapeutic in addressing the sensory and motor control issues in a child with autism or PDD.

Difficulty producing a motor act on demand is a component of dyspraxia. In treatment, encourage spontaneous speech and language, and then help the child generalize the abilities to be produced in demand situations.

Formulate motor engrams through practice and feedback. As engrams form, the child no longer has to motor plan the activity. Once those engrams are formed, begin to generalize their use into a variety of settings and under a variety of conditions.

Teach Communication Skills

Children with autistic spectrum disorders have a variety of communication and language difficulties. They can have little or no functional speech. Even those with speech can have obvious deficits that can interfere with communications. Therefore, communication may be taught in nonverbal as well as verbal forms. Because the development of speech and language skills is an ongoing process, it is necessary to challenge children to the next language level as each language milestone is achieved.

ILLUSTRATION 15.2

A picture system offers a nonverbal method of communication that can be recognized universally.

Language is a system of symbols people use to communicate. It is a way to give and receive information. *Expressive language* involves output, which encompasses the modalities of talking and writing. Echolalia (the parroting of words the child hears), pronoun reversals (for example, substituting *he* for *she*), prosody (intonation) deficits, and atypical social use of language all have an impact on linguistic functioning and must be addressed. *Receptive language* involves input, which is the understanding or comprehension of language. It is demonstrated in the modalities of listening and reading. Spontaneous language learning is easier when it is whole, sensible, interesting, relevant, part of a real event, and has a purpose for the learner.

A variety of techniques may be used to teach communication, language, and interactional skills. These techniques are derived from typical parent-child interactions and from professionals working with children who have specific communication and language deficits. They can be incorporated into all therapeutic and everyday activities.

Gestural Communication

Teach gestural communication. Pointing is a key natural gesture. Gestures are a form of universal communication and are used by verbal people in everyday situations to punctuate, clarify, and reinforce verbal communicative efforts. Gestures will assist in ingraining concepts and in improving the child's communicative success. They can help the child communicate basic wants and needs before he is able to say words.

Picture Cues

Pictures will help a child express concepts and wants, and can be paired with a verbal attempt. Fade the picture to increase spontaneous verbalizations and as intelligibility enables the child to be understood.

Speech and Language

Promoting speech and language skills is very important in intervention programs for children with autistic-spectrum disorders. Because the core symptoms of autism include impairments in speech, language and communication (American Psychiatric Association 1994), it is important to focus on these deficit areas as often as possible, and from many different directions. Incorporate a language focus into all environments and activities. Language cannot be taught through isolated exercises and homework, but must be integrated into all interactions throughout the child's daily life. Language drills that are strictly cortical in nature may not help the child generalize the skills, because the drills may lack the just-right challenge, may not be intrinsically motivating for the child, and may not provide the feedback mechanisms required for learning.

- Vocalizations and auditory processing can be facilitated best through the use of vestibular input during play experiences. Many of the auditory receptors are polyneuron receptors and are best triggered by combinations of vestibular and auditory input. Add movement to the program in order to facilitate decoding of sounds, auditory processing, and auditory memory for imitation of sounds. Vocalizations often will begin to occur spontaneously and effortlessly through the use of movement. Those vocalizations can be shaped through modeling.

- Language most often is facilitated through play. It is the behavior most reported to be observed in research on play. Through play, children develop the ability to organize and direct themselves and their interactions with people and objects in the environment. They use early sensorimotor play to establish an internal map that is incorporated into their body schemes, and later into external maps of their bodies in relationship to the environment.

- Language development is a whole-brain process. The brainstem organizes sensory information. Postural control is regulated by the cerebellum and brainstem levels. The right hemisphere forms internal maps, and the left hemisphere attaches appropriate language to them (DeQuiros 1978). Children use those maps to formulate and understand concepts, describe experiences, and form perceptions of the world. They begin to think with language and to formulate ever-increasing levels of complexity. Therefore, play can be considered one of the most effective methods of facilitating children's development and language.

Teach Play Skills

Teaching imitative and then symbolic play skills is very important, because imitation is a primary teaching strategy and a powerful mode of learning. Symbolism, or the attachment of meaning to objects, is highly related to language. The ability to use symbolism in play enables children to maximize their creative language skills.

Presymbolic play skills include:

- **Means-end comprehension**. A child recognizes that pushing a button makes a toy pop up, a tool may be used to pry open an object, or by pulling a string a toy may be obtained.

- **Imitation.** This is commonly taught through banging objects together or on a surface, playing with toy figurines, dolls or trucks.

Primary or basic symbolic play includes:

- Pretend play on oneself (for example, pretending to eat or brush hair)

- Extending that pretend play to others (for example, pretending to feed a doll)

Imitation often is used to teach beginning appropriate use of toys and beginning symbolic play. Initially, familiar events are represented in play sequences. These are events or actions that children see often (for example, talking on the telephone).

In later stages of play, use less familiar and more complex play sequences (for example, going to the doctor or making dinner).

Teach Pragmatic Skills

Turn-taking, nonverbal communication, polite forms, and eye contact are examples of pragmatic skills. Greetings are an example of a pragmatic communicative function. In teaching pragmatics, it is important to know the sequential development of pragmatic skills. Then focus on a skill that is difficult for the child.

- Teach pragmatic skills through modeling and practice. Model specific pragmatic concepts, and then set up multiple activities for the child to practice.

- Provide multiple opportunities for practice. For example, model waving and saying "Hi" or "Bye" to all people who enter or leave the house, school room, or therapeutic room.

- Teach spontaneous greetings via a prompting hierarchy, from a full physical prompt to a wait-and-signal prompt.

- Be sure that all people who interact with the child know the goals and incorporate them into activities whenever possible.

- Teach pragmatics in natural situations to ensure spontaneous use of the skills.

Use Communication Temptations

Communicative temptations are structured situations designed to entice communication. These temptations are a key to facilitating spontaneous language.

- A communication temptation centers on what a child wants or is interested in, and requires him to get someone's attention and comment on his desire. For example, if the child likes to swing, he is required to indicate *push* before he is permitted to swing. He can express this by touching a picture of push, looking at the person pushing the swing, saying "Swing," or saying, "Please swing me."

- Structure all communication temptations at or just above a child's level.

Expansions and Extensions

Expansions and extensions are the adult's verbal response to the child's spontaneous verbal or nonverbal communicative behavior. For example, when a child says, "Push," the adult pushes and at the same time says, "More push."

A good formula to use when employing this technique is:

- If a child uses nonverbal communication, expand with one word.

- If the child uses one word, then expand with two words.

- If the child uses two words, then expand with three words, and then with four words.

- If a child is spontaneously and consistently using more than four words, focus the expansions on a new concept or a more complex grammatical structure.

This technique helps children learn the next language level.

Modeling

Modeling is a demonstration of a behavior you want the child to use. It shows what is expected. For example, pointing to the sky and saying "Bird" is a model of a social comment.

- It is important to model and then immediately tempt the child to use the modeled language or communication in a similar situation.

Follow the Child's Lead

- Talk about and play with toys that the child is interested in.

- Let the child have choices when deciding what to play with or work with. The more control given to the child, the more likely he will be to participate.

- Incorporate goals into the activity.

Wait-and-Signal

This refers to waiting, with eyebrows raised, thus indicating to the child that you expect him to communicate. Wait no more than one or two seconds, because this is a long communicative pause and you do not want to lose the child's interest.

Limited Questions

A question represents a demand to talk, and many children tend to talk less spontaneously when specific demands are made. Also, a question tends to serve as a prompt and may lead to prompt dependence, or a child waiting for a question before talking.

- Try to insert a comment rather than a question, and then set up the situation so that the child has an immediate chance to practice what was modeled. For example, the child pulls you toward a jar of candy. Instead of asking, "What do you want?" model "Want candy" and eat a small piece. Then look at the child expectantly, with eyebrows raised, and wait for him to communicate.

Scaffolding

Scaffolding is the technique of using language that is based upon previous and relevant experiences. It involves building on consistent and predictable language behavior.

- Base problem-solving strategies on past experiences and situations.

Chains

Use consistent routines, and then change one aspect of the routine. This encourages a child to notice the difference and either request the correct chain or comment on your mistake. For example, ask a child to "Roll ball" without a ball present.

Have Fun!

Language is most easily learned when both the teacher and the learner are spontaneous and enjoy themselves. This creates a positive language environment that encourages participation.

Strategies for Promoting Receptive Language Skills

Gestural Cues

Natural gestures facilitate comprehension. Pointing facilitates identification of specific objects and obtaining wants and needs. Waving may be a greeting or parting gesture, or it may be used to indicate that an object or activity is not desired. Children with autism must be taught to use gestures and to interpret gestures as part of communication strategies.

Picture Cues

Pictures will help a child understand a command or concept when paired with the verbal sentence. Fade the picture over time to increase spontaneous comprehension. Also use pictures to help children transition or choose activities. For a full review of using visual communication to enhance learning, see Hodgson 1995.

Written Cues

A written cue helps the older child hold on to what is being said longer than speech allows.

- It is better to write only key words rather than an exact transcription.

- Later, written step-by-step instructions help the child succeed in school- or work-related tasks by enhancing the use of visual comprehension if auditory cues are not the child's strongest modality.

ILLUSTRATION 15.3

Use picture cues to prompt step-by-step instructions for schoolwork.

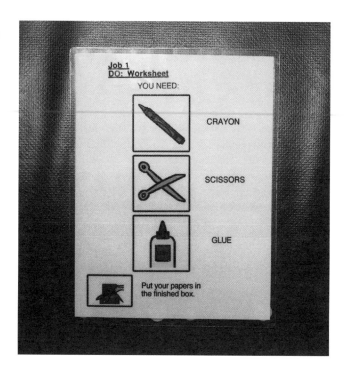

Voice Inflection

Emphasize a key word in a phrase or use a slightly louder volume. Use this strategy when a child typically follows the first part of a command, but not the second. For example, if the command is, "Throw it in the garbage and then get the blocks," use a slightly louder voice when you say the words "then get the blocks."

Physical Prompts

This refers to physically manipulating the child to complete a direction or command. For example, if you say, "Put the blocks away" and the child does not respond, put your hand on the child's hand to help him pick up a block and put it in the container.

Repeating Commands

Do not repeat commands more than two or three times. The more frequently you repeat a command without a correct response, the more you are teaching an incorrect response.

● It is essential that once a command is given, it is followed by a correct response, either spontaneously or with prompts. For example, when there is no response to the command, "Get the ball," give a gestural cue by pointing to the ball and repeating the command. If the child still does not get the ball, provide a physical prompt.

Routines

Consistently pair verbal language with particular routines. This will help a child understand the language used.

Attention

Before you give a command or ask a question, make sure the child is looking at you and paying attention. It is easier to understand when you are focused to the relevant stimuli.

Sentence Length

- Use short sentences to increase understanding.

- Use sentences that are just above the child's expressive language level.

- Use concrete words in sentences if understanding is a major issue.

 A Final Word

Communication typically develops very early in life. Long before infants begin to speak, they communicate with facial expressions, body language, and gestural communication strategies. Individuals with autism also should do so. Communication both depends upon and is affected by development and learning. It is at the very core of a person's ability to function and must be included in all aspects of daily life.

Overall, both receptive and expressive skills can be facilitated in a variety of ways. Use techniques that are relevant and appropriate. Apply these strategies to children with a wide range of communication skills, from nonverbal to those speaking in long sentences. Be creative in incorporating them into all therapeutic activities. By coordinating and integrating therapeutic techniques from a variety of disciplines, children truly will have a comprehensive program of learning.

Monitor the child's reactions and associations. Be constantly vigilant against wrongful associations. We must read behaviors, gestures, and responses within the child to discern what associations or rules may be developing or are being re-inforced. In children who are verbal, word use may be advanced while word comprehension may be lagging. Sensory perceptions probably are different from your own, and therefore the child's sensory interpretations may be faulty and may contribute to faulty learning that must be corrected.

CHAPTER 16

Augmentative and Alternative Communication

Carole Zangari

Augmentative and alternative communication (AAC) refers to the strategies, techniques, and tools used to enhance communication for individuals who have little or no functional speech. AAC was first used in the 1950s, but became a more widely accepted intervention option in the 1980s. It now is used frequently in teaching children with autism to communicate more effectively. It also is used with children and adults who have severe communication disorders because of other developmental or medical conditions.

The term *augmentative communication* is used in discussing tools and strategies to supplement an individual's existing communicative repertoire. For example, 3-year-old LaShawna knows the words *Mama* and *Barney* and uses them appropriately along with sounds that she uses to express pleasure or unhappiness. She also communicates by leading her parents to certain areas of the house (for example, the refrigerator, VCR cabinet, bathroom) by tugging on their arms and by pointing to things she wants. AAC strategies may be used to teach LaShawna additional ways of communicating, perhaps by pointing to pictures of places where she goes during the week. The intent is to help LaShawna expand the array of communicative tools she has at her disposal. While speech development is our primary goal, the use of AAC can help LaShawna express herself in other ways as well. This is the goal for most children learning AAC strategies.

In some instances, *alternative communication* is used to replace the communication skills a person has lost due to accident, injury, or illness. For example, a child in the intensive care unit of a hospital after a car accident may be unable to move or speak due to a serious medical condition. Alternative communication may be used to help the child communicate despite his physical limitations.

AAC services are provided by professionals from a variety of disciplines. Speech-language pathologists are almost always part of an AAC team. Occupational therapists may provide AAC services if the child has fine motor, sensory, or visual-spatial difficulties that impact functional use of AAC skills. Educators also are involved in AAC services and play a critical role in ensuring that new or emerging communication skills become functional communicational tools throughout the school day. Physical therapists, occupational therapists, physiatrists, and psychologists also may be members of an AAC team if the needs of the individual child require the expertise of these professionals. At the center of the AAC team is the child and his family, who should be major players in the assessment, intervention, and decision-making processes.

Why Use AAC Strategies With Individuals With Autism?

Although more research is needed, it is estimated that approximately 50% of individuals with autism are unable to communicate effectively through speech (Wing and Atwood 1987). AAC strategies have been used as a way to enhance functional communication and language learning by children and adults with a variety of physical and learning difficulties. Studies of AAC intervention have documented successful outcomes with individuals with autism, cerebral palsy, developmental delay, mental retardation, and motor speech disorders in addition to conditions acquired through injury or illness. See Table 16.1 for selected research studies of successful AAC use involving persons with autism and related disorders.

There are several reasons for teaching AAC strategies to children with autism. Perhaps the most important rationale is that AAC tends to have a positive affect on speech development. In many of the studies listed in Table 16.1, vocal behavior or speech improved during the course of AAC intervention. A second reason relates to the notion that many children with autism who can speak clearly do not use their speech skills in a meaningful or functional way. For example, Danielle can clearly repeat common phrases from popular TV shows and commercials. Her echolalic behavior occurs most frequently when she is anxious, upset, or if her daily routine is altered. Her spoken language, while clear and easy to understand, is not being used as tool to express her personal desires or ideas. Children like Danielle sometimes find that AAC strategies enable them to communicate in a more meaningful way.

Another important rationale for using AAC is that functional speech may take a while to develop in some children with autism. Teaching other ways of communicating enables children to develop improved communication and language skills even when their ability to communicate orally is severely limited.

TABLE 16.1   Selected studies of ACC use by individuals with autism and related disorders

Researchers	Individuals Studied	Type of AAC Used	Results
Bird et al. (1989)	2 adults with autism and mental retardation (1 also had self-inflicted blindness)	Tangible symbols; manual signs	Increased AAC skills Decreased self-injurious behaviors
Campbell and Lutzker (1993)	1 child with autism	Manual signs and gestures	Increased AAC skills Decreased challenging behaviors
Day et al. (1994)	1 child with autism, 2 children with mental retardation	Manual signs, speech, and card with printed words	Increased AAC skills Decreased challenging behaviors
Fulwiler and Fouts (1976)	1 child with autism	Manual signs (ASL)	Increased sign use and natural speech Increased social interaction and attentiveness
Horner and Budd (1985)	1 child with autism and and mental retardation	Manual signs	Increased AAC skills Decreased challenging behaviors
Konstantareas et al. (1975)	5 children with autism	Manual signs	Improved AAC skills Improved social skills
Miller and Miller (1973)	19 children with autism	Manual signs and pictures	Improved AAC skills 2 improved speech, 17 did not improve speech
Offir (1976)	30 children with autism	Manual signs	Improved AAC skills 20 improved speech, 10 did not improve speech
Schaeffer et al. (1976)	3 children with autism	Manual signs	Improved AAC skills All speech improved speech
Sigafoos and Meikle (1996)	1 child with autism	Gesture and pictures	Increased AAC skills Decreased challenging behaviors
Wacker et al. (1990)	1 child with autism, mental retardation, and seizure disorder	Gesture	Increased AAC skills Decreased challenging behaviors

Children can succeed in school, at home, and in the community without *speech*, but without *language* their life options are extremely reduced. A third reason for teaching augmentative means of communicating deals with the frustration that children experience when they are unable to communicate effectively. Ryan, a 6-year-old child with autism, often screamed and lashed out at his teacher when presented with a task that was new or difficult. When he was taught a more socially appropriate way of communicating, (pressing an adapted tape recorder that said "Break. I need a break, please"), he became less disruptive. The teacher would allow him a short break (one or two minutes), then redirect him to the difficult task. Ryan's ability to use augmentative means to communicate made it more pleasant to work with him, thus increasing the amount of time that others spent interacting with him. It also enabled him to have a measure of control over his environment. With this increased control, Ryan was able to tolerate longer, more complex tasks without resorting to challenging behaviors. There is an abundant literature documenting the effectiveness of AAC strategies at reducing difficult behaviors demonstrated by individuals with developmental disabilities; Schlosser (1998) provides an excellent discussion of this literature.

AAC and Children at Different Stages of Communicative Development

Growing children communicate at one of three levels. Typically developing children pass through each of these levels in the first 18 months of life. For children with autism, the process may take much longer. AAC can be helpful for children at all three levels, although the focus of intervention would be quite different at each level.

Pre-Intentional Level

Some children with autism communicate at the pre-intentional level, meaning that they are not purposefully sending communicative signals. Two-year-old Theo, for example, fusses and whines when he sees something that he wants but cannot reach (such as a favorite video on a high shelf). Because he fusses and whines whether or not anyone else is in the room, we have a pretty good idea that Theo exhibits that behavior as an instinctive emotional response. At this level, he is not fully aware that his behavior sends a signal to people that can cause them to respond in a certain way. Nevertheless, adults who observe Theo's signals infer meaning from them even though they were not produced in order to get the adult to respond in any particular way. Thus, when his grandmother hears Theo whine, she responds as though he had asked for help in getting the video. ("Oh, Theo, you want your kitty tape? Okay! Gramma get it for you.") The focus of AAC intervention for children at this level is to teach them the power of communication. Specifically, children learn that behaviors they exhibit in the presence of an attentive partner will cause the partner to respond in a particular way.

Intentional, Pre-Symbolic Level

Once children learn that their behaviors can communicate a need or idea to others, they enter the intentional, pre-symbolic level of communication. At this stage, children have learned that exhibiting a certain behavior can help them achieve the desired outcome. However, the signals they use are quite basic in nature. By age three, Lemuel had learned to get help from his family by communicating with them. If he wanted a bowl of cereal, he might pull his older sister into the kitchen. If he couldn't open the door, he might take his dad's hand and put it on the doorknob. To get more milk, Lemuel might give his mother his empty cup. Using these and other presymbolic signals, Lemuel can effectively communicate concrete concepts related to things and people in his immediate environment. Goals at this level would focus on:

- Increasing the frequency and consistency of communicative acts

- Making the child's signals more overt

- Transitioning to more conventional symbolic communication

Symbolic Level

To express abstract thoughts or concepts outside the here and now, children must learn to communicate by using symbols. At this level, children learn that one thing—a symbol of some sort-can be used to represent something else—an object, event, or idea. Symbols, such as spoken or printed words, manual signs, or pictures, allow children to communicate about a much larger array of topics. Using photographs of playground equipment, Joshua can tell his mother what he did during recess. By age seven, Tamara had learned the meaning of a wide variety of picture symbols. She was able to create picture sentences, such as "See color rainbow in car mom" to tell her teacher that she saw a very colorful rainbow in the car with mom earlier today. Symbolic communication is the highest level of communication. Children with autism can progress through this stage, beginning with simple single-symbol messages (like Joshua's) to longer, more complex sentences (like Tamara's). Once they are effective symbolic communicators, children can learn to use more conventional symbolic forms. In Tamara's case, spoken and/or printed words eventually may take the place of pictures.

Symbolic AAC approaches taught to children with autism use aided or unaided means of communication. Unaided strategies, like gestures and manual signs, require nothing external to one's own body. Aided strategies use pictures, words,

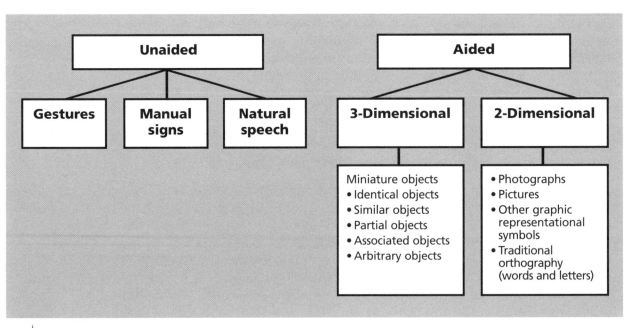

FIGURE 16.1
Types of symbols used in AAC intervention

Exploring the Spectrum of Autism and Pervasive Developmental Disorders

and/or objects on some sort of communication aid or device. See Figure 16.1 for a list of both aided and unaided symbol types. In most cases, a multimodal approach is used, with children learning to use both aided and unaided symbols. Lemuel's therapy program, for example, may include teaching him to say approximations of certain words and use gestures and pictures to communicate.

Types of AAC Systems

The term *AAC systems* refers to the constellation of communication modes and tools that an individual uses. Danielle uses an electronic communication device that speaks and can be connected to a computer. Her AAC system includes that device along with her natural speech (primarily echolalic), manual signs, gestures, and nonelectronic communication aids. The various parts of her multimodal AAC system work together to form a menu of communicative options. Although some of the specific strategies Danielle uses are different from how other children communicate, we all use multiple modes of communication. Danielle's teacher uses her facial expression and tone of voice to convey messages. She gestures as she speaks, and she writes on the chalkboard. Like her teacher, Danielle has learned that specific communication strategies are more useful in some situations and less useful in others.

Advantages of AAC Strategies That Use Picture Symbols

One frequent use of AAC with children who have autism is to teach the use of picture symbols for communicative purposes. For example, in Corrina's kindergarten classroom, children select jobs to do as classroom helpers. Corrina points to the pictures *me* and *line leader* on a Circle Time communication board to tell her teacher that she would like to be the line leader that day. This AAC strategy has several advantages over speech-language therapy that focuses exclusively on the development of spoken communication.

One advantage is that the picture symbols used in AAC intervention are more concrete than the symbols we typically use in conversation (that is, spoken words). Children with learning difficulties often benefit from that concreteness and appreciate the strong relationship between a picture and the thing it represents. A picture of a chair generally looks like the chairs children see and sit in every day. By contrast, the word *chair* is an arbitrary representation of the object; there is nothing in the auditory signal *ch-air* that in any way resembles the furniture on which we sit. This rationale breaks down with concepts for which we do not easily form a mental representation, such as the words *please, Thursday, is,* and *uncomfortable.* In general, however, pictographic symbols are more concrete than spoken words.

The second advantage of picture-based AAC systems is that the symbols are, for the most part, static and do not disappear. A spoken or signed word vanishes immediately after it is uttered. Pictures, whether in a book, on a card, or on a communication device that speaks, remain available for the child to look at and refer to later. This is an important benefit to children with autism, who may be slow in processing language and require additional time to refer to the symbol again.

Another important feature of picture-based AAC systems relates to our ability to teach children new skills. Children with autism touch, press, point to, or pick up the pictures that they use for communicative purposes. Those who are just learning to do so can be physically guided to do this even at the earliest stages of AAC intervention. Thus, the interventionist can be certain that the child responds correctly (although not independently) right from the beginning of the intervention program. In contrast, the speech-language pathologist using a speech-only approach can tempt the child to speak and model the desired word, but cannot physically guide a correct response. In other words, there is nothing the educator or therapist can do to ensure that the child leaves the teaching trial having spoken the correct word or sentence in a speech-only approach. Working with the same child using a picture-based AAC approach, the educator or therapist can use skillful prompting to help the child communicate the desired object by touching or pointing to the picture. As the adult responds to the child's message (for example, by providing the item that was requested), a spoken response can be facilitated ("Puzzle. Danielle wants puzzle"). As the child gains knowledge of what each picture symbol means, prompts are systematically faded.

 ## Developing AAC Intervention Programs

All AAC intervention programs should be built on information gleaned from a comprehensive assessment conducted by a team of professionals who can look at the individual's abilities and needs. For a thorough description of the AAC assessment process and the principles that guide it, see Beukelman and Mirenda (1998) and Wasson, Arvidson, and Lloyd (1998). Formal tests and informal protocols will be used to identify current abilities and potential for developing new skills. The team will observe the individual in his natural environment and conduct interviews with significant others. The AAC assessment should result in answers to two important questions:

1. What communication skills does this person currently have?

2. What communication skills does this person need in order to successfully participate in the various educational, social, and daily living activities that are part of his regular routine?

The answers to these two questions will serve as a starting point for the therapeutic process and will be instrumental in identifying initial goals and objectives.

AAC intervention programs for children with autism typically involve the teaching of multiple modes of communication. In her AAC program, Alyssa, age 14, used speech, manual signs, and a communication book. With much training, Alyssa learned to say 25 words that could be easily understood by familiar and unfamiliar communication partners. She also learned manual signs for frequently used concepts such as *more, want, give me, and finished* (although Alyssa's signs were approximations of the standard form of the signs). She used a communication book with more than 100 pictures and printed words to communicate additional messages in school and in the community.

Picture Symbols

Picture symbols are used frequently to enhance the production and understanding of language. They have benefits for many children with autism. There are many commercially available picture sets and systems; see Fuller, Lloyd, and Stratton (1998) for a review of AAC symbols.

Determining which set or system is most appropriate for a given child is an important part of the AAC assessment process. A child who does not learn quickly with color photographs may do better with other symbol types, such as line drawings or black-and-white photographs. Picture symbols vary widely in the amount of information they contain and how that information is conveyed. The speech-language pathologist can help determine what kinds of symbols are most appropriate for each child. Once the appropriate picture type is selected, pictures can be used for many different purposes. In almost all cases, the written label is printed above or below each picture used for receptive or expressive communication.

There may be several ways in which pictures symbols are used, but the primary distinction is between receptive communication and expressive communication. It is impossible to understate the importance of providing individuals who use AAC with experiences that allow them to see AAC symbols being used for a variety of purposes. Receptive exposure to any form of communication generally enhances expressive production of that form of communication. Typically developing babies, for example, hear language for at least a year before we expect them to begin talking. Children with autism, on the other hand, may have no prior receptive experiences with AAC symbols before being expected to use that form of communication in a functional expressive way. Receptive AAC experiences can take many forms. See Table 16.2 for different aspects of picture use for receptive communication purposes.

Pictures often are used to help children with autism express their needs, thoughts, and feelings. Once a decision has been made to use a picture-based approach, several questions must be answered, including:

- What type of picture should be used? Photographs? Line drawings? Color or black-and-white?

- What messages should the pictures represent?

- How many pictures should there be? One on a page? Four? Sixteen?

- Should the pictures represent single words (*cookie, want*) or whole sentences ("I want a cookie")?

- How will the pictures be arranged? On a single card? In a wallet? In a communication book? In categories (for example, foods, toys, clothes)? By activity (circle time, snack, playground)?

- How will the child use the pictures? By looking at them? By handing them to someone? By pointing to them?

Common ways of using pictures to facilitate expressive communication include putting them in a communication book, board, or wallet. Children point to symbols representing desired messages to make requests ("more"), get assistance ("help"), answer questions ("Today Tuesday"), make choices ("me line leader"), express feelings ("I'm bored."), and given directions to others ("Pay attention to me, please"). Picture-based communication aids must consist of vocabulary and messages that help children become active participants in their typical daily routines and facilitate interaction with others. Tamara, for example, has a communication board used only when her parents read her favorite stories. The communication board contains messages that invite interaction and allow Tamara to be an active partner in the process ("What's that?" "Turn the page," "Use a funny voice," "Read it again").

TABLE 16.2   Using pictures for receptive communication

Specific purpose	What messages the pictures might represent	How the pictures are used	Example
Helping children to understand what is said to them	Messages represented by pictures correspond to the things that the adult is saying to the child.	Pictures are displayed on a communication board. The adult points to the corresponding to key words that are said	Tia is looking at a book. Mom is trying to engage Tia in interaction. Mom labels the things she sees and simultaneously points to picture symbols on a communication board. (Here, boldface is used to indicate which words are pointed to.) " Tia, **look. Lion.** That **lion** is **hungry. Turn page.** Tia **turn**ed the **page.** . . **Uh-oh!** The **lion** is **eat**ing **cookies.** Yum!
Helping children to manage transitions by facilitating their understanding of the routine of daily life Often, children tolerate transitions better when they know what to expect.	Messages are chosen to represent activities that occur regularly in the child's routine	Pictures are displayed in a common area, such as a bulletin board or in the child's personal communication aid (for example, communication wallet or book).	Teacher is helping the children clean up from their final activity and prepare to go home. As the last supplies are put away, she takes Theo to an area of the classroom where each major activity in his day is represented on a picture schedule. "Theo, look. Finished with **art.** Time to go **home.**" As Theo's skills progress, the teacher may use the picture schedule to review the day's events. "We did a lot today. First we had **free play.** Then we had **book circle.** Then we had **snack.** Now it's time to go **home.**"
Helping children to manage their own behavior	Messages that remind children how they are supposed to act (for example, hands quiet, sit down, wait)	Pictures are displayed in an area that is very visible to the children when they are engaged in a particular activity.	Jason frequently unbuckles his seat belt while riding in the car. Laminated pictures representing the message *seat belt on* are affixed to the back of the seat in front of him to remind him not to unbuckle. For the first two days, the family took several short trips around the neighborhood with his mother sitting next to him in the back seat. She directed him to the *seat belt on* picture whenever he started to unbuckle his seat belt.
Helping children to learn and/or remember the steps of a task.	Step-by-step picture instructions for how to complete a task, such as hand washing, making a sandwich, or starting the computer to playing a computer game. The steps that are represented through pictures and words are specific to the task that the child is trying to learn.	Picture instructions for a simple tasks are mounted on a laminated card. More complex sets of instructions require multiple pages and are organized on a small small flip chart.	Micah, age 7, is learning to complete self-care routines independently. On the bathroom wall, his mother posted a chart with pictures (and words) showing the steps involved in tooth brushing. In the beginning, she points to the picture representing each step as Micah is doing that step. Shawniese, age 17, is using the same approach to learn to do her laundry. She carries a small wallet with her to the laundry room. Each page of the wallet illustrates a step in the process. Her teacher points out each step as she and Shawniese do it.

The Picture Exchange Communication System (PECS) (Frost and Bondy 1994) is a specific way of using pictures for expressive communication. Because the PECS approach initially requires the child to give the picture symbol to another person, it is especially helpful for children who are learning that interaction requires a communication partner. It also is used to facilitate eye contact with others. PECS is a specific way of using picture symbols. Parents and professionals helping children communicate with PECS should be familiar with the full curriculum and methodology associated with this approach.

Voice-Output Communication Aids

Many children with autism benefit from AAC systems that include voice-output communication aids (VOCAs). These devices speak novel or preprogrammed messages when the child activates the desired symbol. They range from small, simple pieces of assistive technology that say only one word or sentence, to those that are complex and powerful. VOCAs are indicated when:

- The child is *or is learning to* become an intentional communicator,

- An auditory model (that is, the spoken word or sentence) is desired,

- The child shows interest in the auditory output, and/or

- The addition of speech output would enable the child to be a more active or independent participant in home, school, or community activities.

Selecting an appropriate VOCA is part of a comprehensive assessment process that involves identifying the device features that the child needs and structuring opportunities for the child to try one or more appropriate devices. When high-tech VOCAs are indicated, a period of trial use is generally included in the assessment process. The trial period enables children and their families to sample one or more VOCAs over a period of weeks or months in order to determine which, if any, device is most appropriate.

Manual Signs

Manual signs have been used to enhance communication by children with autism and cognitive impairments for more than two decades. When using signs with autistic children, it is important to distinguish between sign languages and other ways of using manual signs. Sign languages, like all other languages, evolved over time to meet the communication needs of individuals in a particular community. Each sign language has a unique structure that differs from the spoken language in that community. American Sign Language (ASL), for example, has a different word order than spoken English. If an ASL signer simultaneously spoke and signed the sentence, "Tomorrow we have to go to the doctor's office," there would not be a one-to-one correspondence between the words that were signed and the words that were spoken. This can be very confusing for a child with autism who is struggling to learn language for the first time. To avoid this confusion, most interventionists avoid using sign languages with children with autism in favor of using manual signs in a way that corresponds more directly with spoken English. That way, children hear and see the same message. In key word signing, the speaker signs only the content-laden words within a longer sentence. Using the previous example, a key word signer might sign only the words *tomorrow*, *go*, and *doctor*, and would sign those words at the same time they were spoken in the sentence, "**Tomorrow** we have to **go** to the **doctor's** office." Formal sign systems that have been developed to maximize the similarities between spoken and signed forms of a language (for example, Signing Exact English, Signing Essential English, Linguistics of Visual English) also can be useful for children with autism. In general, forms of visually coded English, like key word signing or formal sign systems, are preferred over natural sign languages for children with autism. These children who learn to sign as a primary expressive communication strategy also should learn some form of graphic symbol communication so that they can communicate effectively with nonsigners.

Frequently Asked Questions About AAC

Parents, educators, and other stakeholders who are considering the use of AAC for a particular child raise valid and important concerns that must be addressed in order for them to make informed decisions. Some of the more frequently asked questions are discussed below.

I understand what my child is trying to tell me. Why should we use AAC?

Most children with autism communicate best with familiar partners and in settings in which the routine is predictable and familiar. Under these circumstances, even children with very limited communication skills can make their needs and desires known. AAC strategies still may be useful in helping the child communicate longer, more abstract concepts and for helping children communicate more effectively in less familiar settings. Lemuel, who gives his mother his empty cup to ask for more milk, may not use that strategy in school with his teacher. The goal of using AAC with Lemuel may not center on improving communication at home, but rather on teaching him ways of communicating that make it more likely that others will understand him. In some situations, the child's method of communicating is subtle or unconventional, making it likely that less familiar communication partners will miss or misinterpret the message. AAC strategies may give the child a clearer, less ambiguous means of communicating with others.

What about talking? If I use an AAC approach, won't it take longer for my child's speech to improve?

While this is certainly a common and valid concern, it is not likely that AAC will negatively affect speech development. Research and anecdotal experience both suggest that if AAC approaches have an affect on speech, it is a positive, facilitating affect. AAC approaches have been demonstrated to *enhance* speech and language development and do not inhibit it in any way. There are several possible reasons for this.

The focus of intervention using AAC approaches is *communication*; that is, getting one's needs, preferences, and ideas across in a meaningful and functional way. In AAC intervention, individuals are provided with experiences in being effective communicators using many different methods. The more successful one is as a communicator, the easier it is to learn *other* ways of communicating, such as talking.

Some AAC approaches have advantages that spoken language does not. For example, some pictures are more concrete than words, enabling a person with learning problems the ability to grasp concepts more quickly and easily.

Spoken language is fleeting. Speech vanishes the moment it leaves your mouth. This can make language learning hard for some individuals with severe communication difficulties. Picture symbols, whether on plain paper or on an electronic communication device, are stationary. Because they don't disappear, the language learner can refer to them as often as needed.

In many instances, AAC intervention works on the *simultaneous* development of speech and other means of communicating. For example, a child with autism may be learning how to ask for "more bubbles" with both pictures and spoken words.

Isn't it too soon to consider an augmentative approach? What's the harm in just waiting to see how my child's speech develops?

For some individuals, delaying the use of AAC can cause additional problems. Consider the following points.

Speech—the physical act of saying words—and language—the use of a rule-governed system of sounds and words—may develop at different rates. For individuals who learn the physical act of speaking quite slowly, delaying AAC approaches can mean holding back on language development. Early use of AAC approaches enables these individuals to continue to develop their language skills even though their ability to speak still may be quite limited.

Individuals who cannot speak effectively may become increasingly frustrated at their inability to communicate with others. In some cases, this frustration is demonstrated through crying, temper tantrums, and aggression. AAC approaches offer individuals a more socially appropriate way of expressing their needs and thoughts, which reduces overall frustration.

My child has been receiving therapy for years. Why didn't anyone start us on AAC before now?

AAC is a relatively new field that has emerged over the past few decades. It is important to realize that most professionals in speech-language pathology and other disciplines had little or no AAC training or experience in their professional preparation programs. While many professionals may have gained information on AAC from workshops or conferences, they may not feel comfortable providing AAC intervention. In some cases, the professionals may not know enough about AAC to determine whether it is an appropriate option for a given child. Finding a speech-language pathologist with experience in AAC is an important step.

How do I find the best person to provide AAC services to my family member (or client)?

- Ask questions. (For sample questions see the following "Interviewing the Potential Speech-Language Pathologist.")

- Check the person's credentials.

- Ask to see a copy of the person's ASHA Certificate of Clinical Competency (CCC). A professional who holds the CCC in speech-language pathology has successfully completed a master's level training program in communication disorders, participated in a 10-month Clinical Fellowship Year under the supervision of a more experienced clinician, and passed a national exam. Contact ASHA (For the address see the following "Resources") to find out whether the person is a current ASHA member.

- Ask to see a copy of the person's state license.

- Ask to observe an AAC evaluation or treatment session. Does this person seem like someone who would work well with your family member? Is the evaluation/treatment situation to your liking?

- Ask for references.

- Talk with individuals and families who have received services from this individual. Questions to ask include the following:
  - What was the best thing about working with this professional?
  - What was the most difficult thing?
  - How well/poorly did this person meet your expectations?
  - How has the child's (or adult's) communication changed since working with this professional?
  - Would you consult this professional again?

- Find out about charges and billing procedures. Also, if an AAC device is recommended, can this person help you find funding for that device?

Interviewing the Potential Speech-Language Pathologist

Questions to ask include the following.

AAC Training and Experience

What kind of training have you had in AAC?

Look for: Courses at the graduate level or attendance at multiple AAC conferences, workshops, and so on. A few university programs offer majors or minors or other specializations in AAC.

What do you do to stay current in the field of AAC? (As with all fields that involve technology, the AAC field changes quickly.)

Look for

- Memberships in organizations dealing with AAC, such as USSAAC or divisions within larger organizations, such as ASHA's Division on AAC (#12). (See Resources.)

- Recent attendance at workshops or conference presentations

- Reading AAC journals and periodicals

- Networking with colleagues

What kind of hands-on AAC work do you do on a regular basis?

Look for

- Regular involvement with individuals who need and use AAC

- Experience with individuals who are somewhat similar to your family member (for example, similar age, type of disability, level of severity)

What kind of AAC devices and equipment do you feel comfortable in using?

Look for

- A range of devices, including those that do and do not use technology
- Experience in programming and using these devices

Where do your referrals come from?

Look for: Referrals from individuals and/or agencies who are respected members of the medical, educational, or disability community

AAC Resources and Equipment

What AAC materials and equipment do you have?

Look for

- A wide range of devices, from the very simple to the very sophisticated
- Devices that are most applicable for the individual being assessed
- Evidence that the equipment is current
- Evidence that the professionals involved know how to program, use, and teach use of the various pieces of equipment

What would happen if you needed a piece of AAC equipment that you did not have?

Look for: Evidence of a plan to access some collaborative relationship where equipment could be borrowed or rented, or referral to an agency where that equipment can be tried.

The Actual AAC Evaluation or Intervention Program

What is the purpose of the AAC assessment (or intervention) program?

Look for: A purpose that matches your own. For example, you may want to see what technology may be appropriate for your family member, or you may want to know what course or courses of treatment will advance the communication skills of your family member.

Can you explain how the assessment (or intervention) will be carried out?

Look for:

- At least some of the evaluation to occur in natural environments (the home, school, daycare, work place)
- Evidence that the speech-language pathologist has a specific plan in mind
- Evidence that the speech-language pathologist will work with or consult professionals from other disciplines

What is my role in the assessment (or intervention)?

Look for

- A specific plan for involving significant others

- A level of involvement that you feel comfortable with

- Expectations that are consistent with your own (for example, a particular treatment approach that requires a significant amount of family involvement, time, and/or training may work for some families, but be impossible for others)

- Respect for family priorities and perspectives

What, if any, financial gain would you experience as a result of this assessment (or intervention)?

Look for

- Objectivity

- Individuals who are not overly influenced by the income they may generate as a result of making specific recommendations (for example, do they receive commission or other financial compensation for AAC devices recommended and purchased?)

What should I expect to happen as a result of this evaluation (or intervention)?

Look for

- Specifics that meet your needs and expectations (for example, develop and implement an individualized program, trial use of an AAC device, follow-up visit)

- Written documentation

- Opportunity for follow-up

What might come up during the evaluation (or intervention) that would be outside your area of expertise? How would you handle that?

Look for

- Evidence that the professional knows what is outside his or her ability to assess/treat. Everyone has limitations; the danger is when those limitations are not recognized or acknowledged.

- Referral to appropriate sources

Funding for AAC Devices and Services

Funding available for AAC devices and services varies according to the age of the individual and several other factors. Many children with autism are eligible for an AAC evaluation through the public education system via the Individuals with Disabilities Education Act. That law requires that each child's assistive technology needs be addressed during the individualized education plan (IEP) process. If the IEP team determines that the child requires an AAC device to achieve his educational objectives, then the school system must provide that child with access to an appropriate device. If the team determines that the child needs the AAC device to communicate at home or in the community, individual schools or professionals cannot restrict access to the school grounds. Other sources of funding include public health insurance (for example, Medicaid) and private health insurance. Disability groups and service and charitable organizations also have assisted in funding devices for specific children. When seeking funding, it is important to ascertain that monies also are available for therapy and training. Years of experience with AAC devices have taught us that this is a critical issue. Appropriate training will enhance the likelihood of successful communication.

Resources

Parent and professional organizations can provide the interested reader with additional information on AAC. Sources for additional information include the following.

American Speech-Language Hearing Association (ASHA)
10801 Rockville Pike
Rockville, MD 20852-3279
301-897-5700

The major professional organization for speech-language pathologists, ASHA has a separate division (Division 12) specifically for AAC. To identify a speech-language pathologist with AAC experience, obtain a list of Division 12 affiliates in your state. ASHA also publishes Preferred Practice Parameters, standards that guide speech-language pathologists in planning and implementing AAC services.

United States Society for Augmentative and Alternative Communication (USSAAC)
PO Box 5271
Evanston, IL 60204-5271
847-869-2122
e-mail: ussaac@northshore.net
USSAAC involves professionals from various backgrounds and AAC users/consumers.

CHAPTER 17

The Importance of Play In Learning and Development

Mary Murray and Betty Paris

Play is the work of childhood. Much of children's early learning is achieved through play, and their physical, socioemotional, and intellectual development is dependent upon the quality of their play experiences. By touching, manipulating, exploring, and testing, children find out about the world around them, and through interacting with other children and adults, they find out about themselves and their relationships to others. They imitate adults and experiment with what it means to be a caregiver, a doctor, a police officer. Through play, they learn how to solve problems and work cooperatively with others. They develop many skills including the creation of voluntary intentions and the formation of real-life plans and volitional motives from play.

According to Piaget (1948, 1962), it is through play that children construct a sense of order and meaning from their environment. They are constantly organizing and reorganizing new information and experiences. This process of altering previously established patterns of organization is what Piaget calls learning. It is not the same kind of learning as simple recall of names or facts. Experience has an effect upon children's play. Some children may not know how to play constructively and imaginatively. Children who are accustomed to more passive activities, such as watching television, may not have developed their natural tendencies to investigate and ask questions. Very physical children may be used to running, climbing, or swinging, but may not develop the ability to concentrate long enough to develop an idea to completion through several levels of play. Although an environment in which toys are an important component is more conducive to learning, it may not be sufficient to provide interesting and suitable play materials. These children most likely will need a model to assume the child's role and enter into the play. Modeling by adult and typical peers is a very effective tool in developing play skills in developmentally disabled children.

Play offers a practical vehicle to enlist a child's attention, to practice specific motor and functional skills, and to promote sensory processing, perceptual abilities, and cognitive development (Rast 1986). Children have an innate drive to develop physically as well as mentally. They use play to master each new level of development and to foster further development and maturation of the CNS. As they endeavor to respond to ever greater challenges, they force integration of increasingly complex sensory experiences and adaptive responses. Concomitantly, the CNS must develop the capability to analyze, organize, and store information that is greater in both quantity and complexity (Lindquist 1982).

For example, a child will work at climbing stairs until the skill is mastered. A child who can climb well then will want to play on the stairs. Each child, as he masters a new level of development, will incorporate that new developmental skill into more intricate play strategies. To the casual observer, both behaviors—climbing the stairs and playing on the stairs—are play; but to the trained observer, playing on the stairs represents an increase in movement and play strategies and a higher level of learning.

ILLUSTRATION 17.1
As children master a new developmental level, they incorporate it into more intricate play strategies.

Children use play to promote neuronal organization and growth as they challenge their nervous systems to deal with ever-increasingly difficult challenges. Children force development through exploration, imitation, variations, additions, and alterations in the play process and repetition of novel behaviors. Schaaf and Burke (1992) cite a child playing with blocks. Initially, the child might demonstrate simple interactions such as stacking or aligning the blocks; but with mastery of basic stacking skills will come the emergence of larger structures, use of irregular shapes, and increasingly complex designs. The child challenges his nervous system to respond to increasingly complex experiences through increasingly complex adaptive responses. The higher level of adaptive behavior is partly due to the maturation and organization of the CNS that occurred during the first interactions.

Children engage in different types of play depending upon their circumstances and particular needs. Types of play range from inactive observation to participation in group play requiring planning and cooperation. It is important to know how typical children develop play skills and how they interact with peers during play periods. This information can be used to compare how children with autism differ from typical children in this area and to provide a framework of normally occurring social skills that then may be used in intervention efforts with children with autism (Stone and LaGreca 1986).

Typical Development of Early Play Skills

During a child's first year of life, one purpose of play is to develop knowledge about himself and significant others in his environment. From birth to around 6 months, infants are typically passive interactors in the play process. They may show appreciation towards the play activities initiated by parent or others by smiling and cooing; however, usually they do not initiate the activities themselves, nor do they have the manipulative skills to play with toys. They combine sensory information with their developing control of movement to develop exploratory and play behavior. From 6 months to 1 year, babies begin to share interest with familiar people in their surroundings. Imitative play begins with mimicking facial gestures, vocalizations, and motor sequences from older children and adults with whom they interact. They also may begin to initiate familiar play routines, smile and coo to get attention, and tentatively begin the sharing process with toys (Wolfberg 1995). Early play experiences emphasize use of the whole body in environmental interactions. These total-body play experiences serve as primary ways to enhance infants' ability to organize sensations for use in creating more complex adaptive behaviors. They begin exploring and manipulating objects and enjoy mouthing, grasping, waving, banging, and throwing, but do not attach any symbolic meaning to the toy or object. Babies will interact with varying schemas and strategies. Each effort is slightly different from the previous one. Feedback is obtained, integrated, and incorporated into subsequent efforts.

Another purpose of play the first year is to begin to work with objects and simple problem-solving skills. As babies become more organized in their ability to perform, learn to manipulate objects and move through the environment, they acquire concepts such as direction, spatial relationships, and motor skills through the manipulation of their bodies and objects. Basic concepts begin to be formulated. The concept of causality begins to develop as they poke at objects, shake them, throw containers, and empty them. They use trial and error to enable learning and to perfect new combinations of movements and interactions. They learn to press a button and have a toy pop up or pull a top and have a container open. Eventually, they come to realize that they don't have to act directly on an object to make something happen. They may pull a string to obtain a toy, or operate a light switch to turn the lights on and off across the room. Object permanence develops as they learn that objects obscured from sight still exist. Object permanence is the prerequisite for requesting a drink or a toy not already within sight. Means-end concepts develop as they begin to work to move toward attainment of a desired object. Children build motor sequences in order to obtain a desired object or outcome. Gradually they build on those strategies in order to string chains of sequences together. Spatial relationships begin to solidify as they begin to fill and stack objects. There is no symbolic meaning attached to the objects, but early concepts of relationships are developed. Size, shapes, and form constancy begin to emerge.

Around the child's first birthday, pretend play begins to emerge. Pretend play is the ability to imitate adult behaviors in different contexts (Wallach and Miller 1988). Children begin to demonstrate an increasing understanding of the use of familiar objects. They first relate familiar objects to their bodies, as in use of a cup or hairbrush. As functional use of objects becomes ingrained, representational play begins. They learn to combine and interrelate objects, place objects in a container, sort by similarities, and begin to act out familiar activities. Toward the second year, children use nonrealistic objects in pretend-play situations. A block becomes a car or truck, a box becomes a castle.

Between the ages of one and four, children play *mommy* or *daddy* or imitate the play behaviors of older siblings and other children. At this stage, they spend time watching how other children play, imitate the actions of other children, and engage in parallel play with other children (Wolfberg 1995). Piaget (1962) suggested the importance of imitation as a major factor in typical children's development of social and cognitive skills. Because children with autism do not spontaneously imitate, the development of social and cognitive skills may well be impaired. Munoz (1986) found that developmentally disabled children could be trained and reinforced to imitate the free play of normal children at a similar developmental level. This is a concept that must be incorporated in our treatment strategies.

Several social behaviors that develop in the preschool years facilitate positive play interactions between children. Some of these positive behaviors include "the frequency of smiling and laughing, sharing, and co-operative acts, good eye contact, and physical proximity" (Stone and LaGreca 1986). Typically, cooperative play begins to develop around the age of four. Cooperative play (that is, sustained play between two or more children) is a complex process termed *metaplay* by Wallach and Miller (1988). Children must understand the concept of taking on different roles, they may adapt their movements and voices to fit the play situation; and they have to be able to talk about how to play with each other. They also must understand rules regarding turn taking. For example, children typically give each other directions about what action will happen and when to change play scenarios.

Again, children with autism are hindered. Their lack of social relatedness impedes interactions with others. They don't often initiate sharing, cooperative acts, or eye contact, and they may not tolerate the physical proximity of others. For these children to be competent in cooperative play, they must be able to receive sensory input (appropriate in amount, kind, and at the correct time). They must be able to process that input effectively. Shared joint attention is difficult for children with autism because they have difficulty with sensory processing and filtering out the nonpertinent goings-on and directing their attention to pertinent aspects of the play situation.

They may have issues stemming from poor postural control (see Chapter 14), which can interfere with the ability to visually attend and maintain that attention. Learning about the function of objects and about basic daily life is influenced by the opportunities to observe and is a prerequisite for imitative and representational play (Rast 1986). Impairments in eye contact may stem from a lack of postural and oculomotor control, and sensory issues may not afford them the ability to tolerate the proximity of others. The result is that they develop very limited play strategies and often lack the ability to adapt to a variety of play scenarios.

Later in the Development of Play

The nature of play changes over time (Vygotsky 1978). It starts out as a representation of real life; young children simply remember a sequence of events and act them out. Then play begins to become more abstract; they are able to separate the meaning from the object. Children with autism have difficulty attaching meaning to objects and then varying play with that object. They must be helped to attach correct meaning to objects and taught how to vary their play with use of the object.

Children in elementary school display quite sophisticated play skills. The sharing and cooperation skills that they learned in early childhood continue to develop and are important for successful peer relationships. School-age children learn new play and social skills such as how to enter ongoing peer activities and to extend invitations to peers (Stone and LaGreca 1986). Children at this age also become more responsive to their play partner's needs and are more likely to change the play situation to suit their partner's desires. Vygotsky (1978) believed that play was not as serious for school-age children, primarily because school occupies so much of their time. However, others do not agree with this sentiment. According to Wolfberg (1995), games and sports are the dominant play activities formally available to children in school and through recreation programs, while occasions for make-believe play activities are rare. Nevertheless, the impulse to pretend continues into middle childhood, particularly when opportunities for imaginative activities are made available.

Children with autism are not responsive to their play partners and have difficulty altering the situation to meet the needs of others. Their view of object use is too constrained and restricted, and they have a difficult time understanding that others may have a perception or need that differs from their own. Often they will express an interest in establishing peer relationships, but they do not know intuitively how to go about doing this. They have to cognitively strategize how to make friends, extend invitations to peers, and share interests.

Adolescence

Play changes again as children reach adolescence (Vygotsky 1978). Their more mature play helps them develop abstract thought. Ideas and concepts that had not been considered important before now become dominant. Play prepares them for the adult roles they will assume. Social play allows them to develop social, communications, and complex interactive skills needed for dating, mate selection, and interactions within the family unit. Play also enables them to develop the complex social skills they will need in the work force and coping strategies for economic survival.

Parten (1932) described the stages of social attributes of play:

1. **Unoccupied**. Children observe interesting action and play with their own bodies, but do not engage in interactions with others.

2. **Solitary play**. Children play alone with toys that are different than those of others in their proximity.

3. **Parallel play**. Children play alongside others with the same or related toys, but do not play interactively.

4. **Associated play**. Children play in a group, performing a common activity, but no roles are taken.

5. **Cooperative play**. Children participate in organized activities for achieving the same goals.

It is important in intervention to take into account what stage of social attributes the child has acquired in order to set realistic goals for teaching and facilitating the next step.

Play At Any Age

Play contains several components that can be found in various play situations and across age groups. These characteristics include the descriptions that "play is pleasurable, involves active engagement in a freely chosen activity, is intrinsically motivating, includes flexibility, and has a nonliteral quality" (Wolfberg 1995). Bettelhaeim (1987) believes that play enables people to process events in their past, deal with the present, and prepare for the future. Play provides the release of frustrations, energy and emotion. Florey (1981) stated that play has an organizing effect on human behavior. It provides feedback from the process of play, and that feedback aids organization and maturation within the central nervous system.

Children with autism have much different play routines and play characteristics than those of typical children. All children with autism are different. and each child will display his or her own individual play habits (or lack of play habits). However, there are some common features of the play of children with autism. Wolfberg (1995) summarizes the characteristics in this way:

Overall, these children lack the spontaneous and flexible qualities characteristic of play. When left to their own devices, they commonly impose rigid and perseverative play routines. Once established, many children with autism express considerable resistance to a play routine being disrupted. They tend to exhibit less time and diversity in advanced play skills, fewer functional play sequences, and fewer symbolic play acts related to dolls and others. Language, gestures, and sound effects that are indicative of imagination are rarely spontaneously incorporated. They may repeatedly construct and reconstruct the same intricate layout of buildings and roadways, but never incorporate novel elements into constructions.

Intervention Strategies

Ayres and Tickle (1980) declared that learning depends upon the registering of information, filtering out of extraneous input, and having an optimal state of arousal to attend to a task. Bruner (1972) emphasized the importance of control against gravity and emerging flexible patterns of interaction with the environment in the development of self-initiated intentional behavior, sustained attention, and adequate social support. Piaget (1962) called learning the process of altering previously established patterns of organization.

Children with autism often cannot construct a sense of order and meaning from their environment. They may fail to register, filter, attend to, or organize new information and experiences. The autistic child's play is limited by decreased initiation, decreased eye contact, a lack of imitation, reduced symbolic play, a lack of the ability to pretend play, and by perseveration of the learned play repertoires. The sensory feedback that they experience in play may be characterized by mixed messages and unpredictable performance. Their levels of arousal may be less than optimal. They do not easily and readily learn to play, nor do they learn from their play experiences. Often their early play experiences are disorganized, unpredictable, and unsuccessful. They lack opportunities to organize the sensations into creating more complex adaptive responses. The process that Piaget called learning and others describe as a method of driving neuronal development and maturation therefore is impeded.

Children with autism tend to remain on the fringes of their peer groups, although they do occasionally attempt to interact with peers. This contact is generally very limited and negative in nature. The reasons for this may be found in our understanding of normal play and social skills development. Children with autism seem to lack these skills right from the beginning of life (Stone and La-Greca 1986). They fail to develop the idea of how to interact with objects and people, and therefore don't develop the neuronal models necessary for analyzing new situations. They do not acquire language for labeling, requesting, or describing play. They can't identify or explain their confusion, disorganization, or their emotional reactions. They don't negotiate with peers because they lack the language and social skills to do so. Concept formation, role delineation, social interaction, and emotional development all suffer. They fail to spontaneously develop the skills for play interactions. They very often lack the communication skills to understand and guide their play.

Intervention must take into account how typical children use and develop through play. We must identify where the child with autism is failing and employ polymodal approaches to teach him how to play, how to interact, and therefore how to learn.

We know that in unstructured or free-play situations, children with autism produce significantly less pretend and less functional play, compared with chronological or mental-age matched comparison groups. Sustained attention and joint attention are problematic in these children. Knowing that children with autism have various degrees of difficulty with social skills and play skills, it is apparent that they will need to be taught how to play in structured settings and methodologies.

Basic Strategies for Promoting Play

Provide the Just-Right Challenge

(For discussion of the just-right challenge, see Koomar and Bundy 1991.) The following is adapted from Lindquist et al (1982).

- The activity should be sufficiently novel to tap the child's inner drive to interact with the toy or environment.

- An environment that includes toys can be arranged to reduce maladaptive behaviors and to reinforce desired behaviors by including toys that the child prefers (Tebo 1986).

- The task should arouse the child's curiosity and affective involvement.

- New tasks are threatening. Expect avoidance or increased anxiety levels and stress when a new task is presented initially. (See Chapter 6 for information on identifying and dealing with these issues.)

- Do not overwhelm the child with a task so large or complex that failure is perceived as inevitable.

- Do not bore the child with overly simple activities that have no meaning to him.

- Enable problem solving. Challenge the child with the task, but do not enable him to fail.

- Use imitation and modeling to get the child to engage.

- Assist him to register, attach meaning to the object, organize, and sequence his motor actions and to execute the task as needed.

- Catch the child doing something good and give positive reinforcement.

Parten's levels of play (previously described in this chapter) also may provide an indicator of the child's level of development and a methodology to use in moving the child's capabilities along the continuum of development.

There are other problems and interventions identified in the autistic population.

- Failure or impairments in sensory registration, orientation, and arousal. See Chapter 9.

- Impairments in sensory processing and therefore interventions to promote sensorimotor exploration. See Chapters 9–13. At this stage, vary movement and sensorimotor experiences.

- Failure or impairment in the ability to imitate in play. From a Sensory Integrative theory, imitation requires:

  — Tactile discrimination

  — An intact body scheme

- — Adequate orientation of body in space

- — Motor and postural control

- — A method of communication

Children who lack these foundation skills also lack the tools needed for play and learning. These are the children who are in need of occupational, physical, and speech therapy services in order to build the foundation needed for learning. See Chapters 9–17.

Once imitation skills begin to emerge, we can use them to build the skills needed for higher levels of development, play, and learning.

- Select two to four items or skills to work on at a time.

- Demonstrate and explain to the child how to play with a toy.

- Hand the toy to the child.

- If necessary, repeat the instruction, demonstration, and role-playing steps again and again until the child learns purposeful play.

- Gradually increase the variety of responses the child makes with the toy, and increase the amount of time the child stays with the activity.

- Once the critical steps are learned, encourage the child to practice and continue to develop skills in the most natural environment possible.

Do not be limited to only those activities you think the child might enjoy. The purpose of the lesson is to expand the child's range of interests, and that will take time to develop. Initially it will be very important to provide huge quantities of reinforcement for engaging in an activity for even a brief duration. At first, keep the practice sessions brief so that the child does not find the activity aversive. Increase the duration and fade the reinforcement as the activities become intrinsically reinforcing.

In the beginning, provide guidance, demonstration, verbal prompts, or any combination. Gradually fade these physical prompts so that the child is performing independently.

Develop Communication

For the child with speech and language delays as occur in autism, an environment of play is the therapeutic treatment of choice. Language, the behavior most often reported to be observed in play, provides a natural environment for the development of communication skills. Ogura (1991) reported the correspondence between the onset of language landmarks; that is, emergence of first words, naming words, vocabulary spurts, and word chains and play categories. She also found that both language and play reflect the development of the child's underlying symbolic abilities.

Children with autism show poor coordination of affective responses. They are less likely to combine smiles with eye contact and to smile in response to smiles; and they are impaired in their empathic responses toward others. However, they do attempt to communicate. It is important to provide constructive and effective methods for that communication to avoid frustration and undesirable behaviors while promoting successful interactions with adults and peers.

Initiate Varied Play

For children who have impairments in the ability to initiate variety in their play, we must engineer the environment and play scenarios to introduce increasing adaptive responses. Make changes in small increments and one at a time.

Form Concepts

For those with impairments in concept formation, teach:

- Causality

- Object permanence

- Means-end

- Spatial relationships

- Early concepts of how objects relate

Concepts often are learned on the body or in relation to the child's body first and then applied to object relatedness. Cause and effect actions in which the child pushes over a stack of blocks or presses a pop-up toy teach the child about how his body relates to the world and the impact he can have on it. Teach object permanence first on the child's body. Covering a foot and then uncovering it teaches the child that his foot exists even when it is covered. Spatial relationships are first developed through gross motor interactions. Foster concepts of distance, size, and dimension by taking the child through gross motor activities such as climbing over a bolster, into a box, under a table, or through a tunnel. Teach object relatedness by having the child relate objects to his body and then to other objects. Having the baby pull rings off an arm or leg may be a prerequisite to stacking those same rings on a cone or dowel. Banging blocks together with two hands may be a foundation for stacking those blocks later.

Pretend Play

- Teach how to relate objects to the body (use of a hairbrush or cup).

- Then teach how objects relate to each other (blocks, puzzles, sorting).

- Use modeling by teacher, therapists, parents, or peers.

Role Play

- Modeling and imitation are the most commonly used strategies.

- Clarkson (1986) recommends use of specially fabricated costumes to facilitate imaginative games through dress up activities. A cowboy hat and boots, a Superman costume, or other items of a favorite character can assist in promoting role play and imitative play.

- Social stories provide an effective method of teaching the child what to expect and how to respond in a variety of social contexts.

Shared Joint Attention

Shared joint attention is needed in order to play successfully with others. Teach skills such as:

- Mutual visual regard, which requires
  - Sensory registration
  - Orientation
  - Optimal levels of arousal
  - Postural control
  - Ocular-motor control for sustained visual attention
- Mutual object manipulation, which requires
  - Shared interest in the object
  - Tactile discrimination
  - Intact body scheme
  - Postural and extremity motor control
  - Sensory processing to tolerate close physical proximity with others
- Personal interaction skills, which may include
  - Establishing and maintaining eye contact
  - A method of shared communication
  - An ability to tolerate variance in play sequences
  - An ability to produce a variety of adaptive responses
  - An understanding of turn-taking or cooperation

ILLUSTRATION 17.2
Shared joint attention requires mutual visual regard, mutual object manipulation, and personal interaction skills.

Cooperative Play

Cooperative play requires that two or more children have a shared communication method.

- Mediate the communication between the children so that each derives the intentions of the other in order to cooperate in their play efforts. Engineer the environment to facilitate the process of goal establishment and the communication of intended play activities. It may be necessary to remove other toys or distractions.

- At first, facilitate peer play by setting up an enticement. Use a strong motivator that can be obtained only by interacting with a peer. Then mediate how the child will request his turn, and monitor the interaction.

- For truly cooperative peer play to occur, each child must understand the play activity. Assist the children in initiating the activity, and mediate conflicts as they arise. Enable the child to formulate motor plans, initiate an intended interaction, and (provided that it will not injure anyone) perform the intended interaction. If needed, help the child benefit from the learning experience by providing extra feedback, either by increasing the sensory input to enhance body scheme or awareness, giving verbal feedback, or helping the child visually monitor the success or failure of the interaction. Increase the level of physical challenge as skills develop. Add complexity to the rules as the child's comprehension improves, and foster the child's ability to negotiate with others.

Because children with autism must cognitively plan how to make friends, extend invitations to peers, and share interests, it is important to incorporate these strategies as you facilitate cooperative play.

Abstract Play

- Teach the child to use objects in the environment to represent other things in play. For example, use a cardboard box or a scooterboard as a car that the child gets in to drive.

ILLUSTRATION 17.3
Facilitate abstract play through games and picture boards.

- Modeling is a typical strategy. Mimic using a block as a car or truck, pretend to brush the doll's hair by stroking the hair without having a hairbrush in your hand, or sing "Pat-a-cake" and pretend to roll it as the song progresses.

- Use picture boards and games.

Combine Strategies

Pull It All Together

Combining the use of imitation, role play, and abstract, symbolic play is extremely useful in assisting individuals from the toddler stage to adulthood in learning to deal with real-life encounters and learn coping skills that will last them a lifetime. In these forms of play, the individual's readiness to take risk and responsibility, cooperate in, and complete short projects is increased. Use this to expand the skills of the child with autism.

Toddlers can build entire scenarios around a set of cardboard boxes made to represent a train. Teach spatial concepts such as *front* and *back*, *inside* and *outside* as the children board the train. Teach early math concepts by counting the passengers. Give each child a ticket, and have the children hand them to the ticket taker, thus teaching sequencing of behaviors and social and communicative skills.

Use the same combinations of strategies to teach living, community-entry, and work-related skills to adolescent and teenage populations. For example, direct the class in planning a trip to the food market. Have the students read newspaper ads and make lists of food and toiletry items. Then have them add the prices and prepare to pay for their purchases. If they haven't enough money, help them select the items to go back. Use both play money and real money to replicate the exchange. Show pictures of the store, and talk about how the aisles are set up and how to find the articles that they intend to purchase. Encourage family members to reinforce the new skills. The culmination of this process is an actual trip to a local food market.

Replicate trips to local restaurants as well. Collect menus from various restaurants. Direct the students in role-playing going into the restaurant and waiting to be seated. Seat them at tables that are set with salt and pepper shakers, a table tent advertisement, and flatware wrapped in a napkin. Menus are distributed, and each child reads a menu and makes a lunch selection. After several practice sessions of the role-play situation, the class participates in a field trip to a restaurant. Many parents report that after that training, they experienced the first truly pleasant trip to a restaurant with their child with autism.

Work skills may be fostered in the same venue. Some schools have established partner relationships with clothing retail chains and independent boutiques. Students are instructed in hanging clothing items on hangers, attaching price tags, and hanging clothing items on racks. They go in groups of two or three to the nearby stores for 30 minutes before the store opens to return clothing from the dressing rooms to the racks, hang sales signs, and participate in other work-related tasks. The same structure is used to teach office skills, with students assisting in volunteer jobs at local police stations and small offices.

The goal is that the child acquire age-appropriate play skills that will help him learn about himself and life concepts and skills in general. The objectives for the educational play experience are based on the needs of the individual child. Typical objectives are to:

- Develop skills to reduce self-stimulatory behaviors
- Develop skills that are critical in facilitating social interaction
- Develop age-appropriate interests
- Improve quality of life
- Develop specific daily-life skills

In general, strategies include these:

- Select the target play skill
- Divide the skill into teachable parts
- Teach one step at a time
- Make the time requirements brief, then gradually expand
- Provide abundant reinforcement
- Use body language, voice, and affect to communicate to the child that he is performing in a desirable fashion
- Fade the assistance and supervision while encouraging and reinforcing the child for appropriate play
- Look at the nature of self-stimulatory behaviors, and identify play activities that include this aspect (see Chapter 6)
- Provide structure; children with autism do not perform well in unstructured settings
- Keep waiting to a minimum. During down times, give the child with autism strategies or tasks to complete, such as counting, doing push-ups, or reciting or singing the ABC song.

Repeat this process for every play activity; that is, explain the play activity, demonstrate and role-play, and encourage practice with a gradual increase in time playing and variety of responses. Provide the necessary input and assistance for feedback, the repetitions required for learning, and the generalization of skills across activities and settings.

A Final Word

Schaaf and Burke (1992) define the contribution of play to human development as an active, open-ended process that, by its nature, continually challenges and perpetuates the growth, development, and competence of the individual. Play challenges the individual to go beyond his present skill level to higher levels of abilities and behaviors.

It is the job of clinicians, teachers, and parents to help the child perceive and analyze the components within his environment and to teach strategies to act effectively upon that environment. We must provide the basic materials for organizing more complex behavior and provide methods of communication so that the child can avoid frustration and behavioral issues that may stem from his inability to communicate even the most basic needs or wants effectively and functionally. By increasing the child's ability to play, we can increase his ability to communicate, to formulate concepts, and expand his cognitive abilities, thus helping him grow, mature, and cope within his environment.

Additional Reading

Allison, M. 1992. New research in the neurobiology of learning. *Headlines* 3(3) (May/June): 2–11.

Attwood, T. 1998. *Asperger's syndrome, A guide for parents and professionals.* New York: Athenaeum Press.

Ayres, A. J., and Z. Mailloux. 1981. Influence of sensory integration procedures on language development. *American Journal of Occupational Therapy* 35: 383–390.

Bailer, D. 1991. Occupational therapy approaches to treating Fragile X syndrome. *Fragile X Exchange, The Newsletter of the Fragile X Association of New York.* Spring: 1–2.

Ballinger, B. 1995. Visual influences in the learning process. *Sensory Integration Quarterly* 33(1) (Summer): 1–4.

Baranek, G. T., L. G. Foster, and G. Berkson. 1997. Tactile defensiveness and stereotyped behavior. *American Journal of Occupational Therapy* 51(2) (February): 91–95.

Bauer, B. 1977. Tactile-sensitive behaviors in hyperactive and nonhyperactive children. *American Journal of Occupational Therapy* 31(8) (August): 447–450.

Bauman, M. L., and T. Kemper, editors. *The neurobiology of autism.* Baltimore: Johns Hopkins University Press, 119–145.

Benbow, M., B. Hanft, and D. March. 1992. *Handwriting in the classroom: Improving written communication.* Tucson, AZ: Therapy Skill Builders.

Bennett, J. W., and C. Q. Peterson. 1995. The touch inventory for elementary-school aged children: Test-retest reliability and mother-child correlation. *American Journal of Occupation Therapy* 49(9) (September): 795–801.

Blanche, E., T. Botticelli, and M. Hallway. 1995. *Combining neuro-developmental treatment and sensory integration principles: An approach to pediatric therapy.* Tucson, AZ: Therapy Skill Builders.

Bly, L. 1983. *The components of normal development during the first year of life and abnormal development.* Oak Park, IL: Neuro-Developmental Treatment Association.

Boehme, R. 1998. *Treatment of the forearm in central nervous system dysfunction.* Oak Park, IL: Neuro-Developmental Treatment Association.

Bonadona, P. 1981. Effects of a vestibular stimulation program on stereotypic rocking behavior. *American Journal of Occupational Therapy* 35(12) (December): 775–789.

Bright, T., K. Biottick, and B. Fleerman. 1981. Reduction of self-injurious behavior using sensory integration techniques. *American Journal of Occupational Therapy* 35(3) (March): 167–172.

Cammisa, K. 1991. Testing difficult children for sensory integration dysfunction. *AOTA Sensory Integration Special Interest Section Newsletter* 14 (2) (June).

Carlucci, D. 1999. Brain wiring in autism. *ADVANCE for Speech-Language Pathologists and Audiologists.* January 4: 7–9.

————. 1999. AAC and Autism. *ADVANCE for Speech-Language Pathologists and Audiologists*. January 4: 13–15.

Carrasco, R. C., and C. E. Lee. 1993. Development of a teacher questionnaire on sensorimotor behavior. *Sensory Integration Special Interest Section Newsletter* 16(2) (June): 5–6.

Case-Smith, J. 1991. The effects of tactile defensiveness and tactile discrimination on in-hand manipulation", *American Journal of Occupational Therapy* 45(9) (September): 811–818.

Case-Smith, J., A. S. Allen, and P. N. Pratt. 1996. *Occupational therapy for children*. 3d ed. St. Louis: Mosby.

Case-Smith, J., and C. Pehoski. 1992. *The development of hand skills in the child*. American Occupational Therapy Association: Rockville, MD.

Cermak, S. 1988. The relationship between attention deficit and sensory integration disorders. *Sensory Integration Special Interest Section Newsletter* (February/March) 11(2/3): 1–5.

Cermak, S., and S. A. Goodgold-Edwards. 1990. Integrating motor control and motor learning concepts with neuropsychology perspectives on apraxia and developmental dyspraxia. *American Journal of Occupational Therapy* 44(5) (May): 431–438.

Cermak, S., and A. Henderson. 1988. The efficacy of sensory integration research. *Sensory Integration News* 16(3): 3–9.

————. 1989. The efficacy of sensory integration procedures: Part 1. *Sensory Integration Quarterly*. Sensory Integration International. 17(4) (December): 1–5.

————. 1990. The efficacy of sensory integration procedures: Part 2. *Sensory Integration Quarterly*. 18(1). Sensory Integration International. 18(1) (March): 1–5, 17.

Chandler, B. E. 1997. *The essence of play, a child's occupation*. Bethesda, MD: American Occupational Therapy Association.

Chu, S. 1991. Sensory integration and autism: A review of the literature. *Sensory Integration Newsletter* (September): 3–6.

Clark, F., Z. Mailloux, and D. Parham. 1989. Sensory integration and children with learning disabilities. In P. N. Pratt and A. S. Allen, editors. *Occupational therapy for children*. St. Louis: Mosby, 457–507.

Clark, F., and D. Pierce. 1988. Synopsis of pediatric occupational therapy effectiveness. *Sensory Integration News* 16(2): 1–14.

Clark, P. 1982. Research on neuropathophysiology of autism and its implications for occupation therapy. *Occupational Journal of Research* 3: 3–22.

Clark, R. G. 1975. *Essentials of clinical neuroanatomy and neurophysiology*. Philadelphia: F. A. Davis.

Clark, R. P. M. 1993. A theory of general impairment of gene expression manifesting as autism. *Individual Differences* 14: 465–482.

Cohen, H., and E. A. Keshner. 1989. Current concepts of the vestibular system reviewed. 1: The role of the vestibulospinal system in postural control. *American Journal of Occupational Therapy* 43(5) (May): 320–330.

————. 1989. Current concepts of the vestibular system reviewed. 2: Visual/vestibular interaction and spatial orientation. *American Journal of Occupational Therapy* 43(5) (May): 331–338.

Coling, M.C. 1991. *Developing integrated programs: A transdisciplinary approach for early intervention.* Tucson, AZ: Therapy Skill Builders.

Connolly, B., and P. Montgomery. 1987. *Therapeutic exercise in developmental disabilities,* Chattanooga. TN: Chattanooga Corporation.

Connor, F. 1990. Physical education for children with autism. *Teaching Exceptional Children* (Fall).

Cool, S. 1995. Does sensory integration work? *Sensory Integration Quarterly* 23 (1): 1, 5–9.

Courtney-Tupper, L., and K. Kosterman-Miesner. 1995. *School hardening: Sensory integration strategies for classroom and home.* Tucson, AZ: Therapy Skill Builders.

DeGangi, G. 1990. Perspective on the integration of neurodevelopmental treatment and sensory integrative therapy: Part 1. *NDTA Newsletter* (January).

———. 1990. Perspective on the integration of neurodevelopmental treatment and sensory integrative therapy: Part 2. *NDTA Newsletter* (March).

———. 1990. Perspective on the integration of neurodevelopmental treatment and sensory integrative therapy: Part 3. *NDTA Newsletter* (May).

DeMauro, G. 1992. The use of an NDT approach for a child with hyperkinesis. *NDT Network* (September).

DeRenne-Stephan, C. 1980. Imitation: A mechanism of play behavior. *American Journal of Occupational Therapy* 34 (2) (February): 95–102.

Dunn, W., and G. DeGangi. 1992. Sensory integration and neuro-developmental treatment for educational programming. *AOTA Self-Study Series: Classroom Applications for School Based Practice.* Rockville, MD: American Occupational Therapy Association.

Dunn, W., and A. G. Fisher. 1983. Sensory registration, autism and tactile defensiveness. *AOTA Sensory Integration Special Interest Section Newsletter* 6(2): 1–4.

Edelson, S. 1995. *Landau-Kleffner syndrome.* Salem, OR: Center for the Study of Autism.

Eller-Miller, E. 1997. Expanding the realities of children with autism and pervasive developmental disorder. *ADVANCE for Speech-Language Pathologists and Audiologists.* April 21: 17.

Embrey, D. G. 1987. A developmental program for the minimally involved child. *Clinical Management* 7(3) (May/June): 20–25.

Exner, C. E. 1992. In-hand manipulation skills. In J. Case-Smith and C. Pehoski, editors. *Development of hand skills in the child.* Rockville, MD: American Occupational Therapy Association.

———. 1993. Content validity of the in-hand manipulation test. *American Journal of Occupational Therapy* 47(6): 506–512.

Fewell, R., and M. Glick. 1993. Observing play: An application process for learning and assessment. *Infants and Young Children* 5 (4) (April): 35–43.

Fisher, A., and W. Dunn. 1983. Tactile defensiveness: Historical perspectives, new research − a theory grows. *Sensory Integration Special Interest Section Newsletter* 6(2).

Florey, L. 1971. An approach to play and play development. *American Journal of Occupational Therapy* 25: 275–280.

Freeman, B. J. 1993. The syndrome of autism: Update and guidelines for diagnosis. *Infants and Young Children* 6: 1–11.

Freeman, B. J., and E. R. Ritvo. The syndrome of autism: Establishing the diagnosis and principles of management. *Pediatric Annals* 13(4) (April): 284–305.

Freeman, S., and L. Dake. 1997. *Teach me language: A language manual for children with autism, Asperger's syndrome, and related developmental disorders.* Langley, BC: SKF Books

Frick, S., and N. Lawton-Shirley. 1994. Auditory integrative training from a sensory integrative perspective. *AOTA Sensory Integration Special Interest Section Newsletter* 17(4) (December): 1–3.

Gellhorne, E. 1964. Motion and emotion: The role of proprioception in the physiology and pathology of emotions. *Psychological Review* 1(3): 57–72.

Gilfoyle,E., A. Grady, and J. Moore. 1990. *Children adapt.* 2d ed. Thorofare, NJ: Slack.

Gillingham, G. 1996. *Autism: Handle with care. Understanding and managing behavior of children and adults with autism.* Arlington, TX: Future Education, Inc.

Grandin, T. 1992. An inside view of autism. In E. Schopler and G. B. Mesibov, editors. *High functioning individuals with autism.* New York: Plenum Press.

Greenspan, S. 1992. *Infancy and early childhood.* Chapter 22: Regulatory disorders. Madison, CT: International University Press.

Haron, M., and A. Henderson. 1985. Active and passive touch in developmentally dyspraxic and normal boys. *Occupational Therapy Journal of Research* 5: 102–112.

Herbert, J. 1992. Guarding against sensory overload in autism treatment. *ADVANCE for Speech and Language Pathologists and Audiologists.* April 6.

———. 1992. Stepping into the world of autism. *ADVANCE for Occupational Therapists.* March 9.

Heydorn, B. L. 1985. A psychometric study of developmental changes in stereognostic abilities. *Perceptual and Motor Skills* 61: 1206.

Holmes, D. 1989. The years ahead: Adults with autism. In M. Powers, editor. *Children with autism.* Bethesda, MD: Woodbine House, 253–276.

Hoop, N. H. 1971. Haptic perception in preschool children. Part 1. Object recognition. *American Journal of Occupational Therapy* 25: 415–419.

Hutchinson, K. 1995. Interview with Lorna Jean King. *The Advocate: Newsletter of the Autism Society of America, Inc.* (September-October).

Inamura, K. N., T. Wiss, and D. Parham. 1990. The effects of the hug machine usage on the behavioral organization of children with autism and autistic-like characteristics. *Sensory Integration Quarterly* 17(3): 1–3, 5, 20–21.

Iskowiz, M. 1999. Grading autism. *ADVANCE for Speech-Language Pathologists and Audiologists.* January 4: 10–12.

———. 1999. Visual support for language. *ADVANCE for Speech-Language Pathologists and Audiologists.* January 4: 16–17.

Kaler, S. 1995. The syndrome of autism: A social communication approach to intervention. *School System Special Interest Section Newsletter* 2(4) (December): 2–3.

Kanner, L. 1943. Autistic disturbances of affective contact. *Nervous Child* 2: 217–250.

Kantar, R., B. Kantar, and P. Clark. 1982. Vestibular stimulation effect on language behavior in mentally retarded children. *American Journal of Occupational Therapy* 36 (1) (January): 36–41.

Karsteadt, K. 1983. The effect of vestibular stimulation on visualization and attending behaviors of the autistic child. *AOTA Sensory Integration and Special Interest Section Newsletter* 6(1): 1–4.

Koomar, J. 1996. Vestibular dysfunction and dyspraxia associated with anxiety rather than behavioral inhibition. *AOTA Sensory Integration Special Interest Section Newsletter* 19(3) (September): 1–4.

Larkin, M. 1992. The tools of cognitive therapy: Three case studies. *Headlines* 3(3) (May/June): 17–20.

Lauerman, J. 1992. Neurologic impairment: Understanding the effect on learning. *Headlines* 3(3) (May/June): 12–15.

Lowrey, G. H. 1986. Growth and development of children. In *Mosby Yearbook,* 8th ed. Chicago: Mosby.

Magrum, W., K. Ottenbacher, S. McCue, and R. Keefe. 1981. Effects of vestibular stimulation on spontaneous use of verbal language in developmentally delayed children. *American Journal of Occupational Therapy* 35(2) (February): 101–104.

Margolis, N. Undated. *Vision and autism.* Unpublished work.

Martin, S. 1995. *Functional movement development across the life span.* Philadelphia: W. B. Saunders.

Maurice, C., G. Green, and S. C. Luce. 1996. *Behavioral intervention for young children with wutism.* Austin, TX: PRO-ED.

McClannahan, C. 1990. Sensory integration and hand function: A clinical perspective. *Sensory Integration Special Interest Section Newsletter* 13 (1).

Miller, A., and E. Eller-Miller. 1989. *A new way with autistic and other children with pervasive developmental disorder.* Boston: The Language and Cognitive Development Center.

Miller, L., and D. McIntosh. 1998. The diagnosis, treatments and etiology of sensory modulation disorder. *Sensory Integration Special Interest Section Quarterly* 21(1) (March): 1–3.

Missiuna, C., and H. Polatajko. 1995. Developmental dyspraxia by any other name: Are they all just clumsy children? *American Journal of Occupational Therapy* 49(7) (July/August): 619–627.

Montagu, A. 1978. *Touching: The human significance of the skin.* New York: Harper & Row.

Moore, J. 1994. The functional components of the nervous system: Part l. *Sensory Integration Quarterly* 12(3) (Fall): 1–7.

Oetter, P. A. 1986. sensory integrative approach to the treatment of attention deficit disorders. *Sensory Integration Special Interest Section Newsletter* 9(2): 1–2.

Parham, D. 1987. Coping with dyspraxia in preschoolers. *OT Week* (June 11): 5–8.

Peele, T. L. 1977. *The neuroanatomic basis for clinical neurology.* 3rd ed. New York: McGraw-Hill, 436–455.

Pehoski, C., A. Henderson, and I. Tickle-Degnen. 1997. In-hand manipulation in young children: Rotation of an object in the fingers. *American Journal of Occupational Therapy* 51: 544–552.

Petit, K. 1980. Treatment of the autistic child: A demanding challenge. *Sensory Integration Special Interest Section Newsletter* 4(1).

Powers, M. 1989. What Is Autism? In M. Powers, editor. *Children with autism*. Bethesda, MD: Woodbine House, 1–29.

Reichelt, K. L. 1990. Gluten, milk proteins, and autism: Dietary intervention effects on behavior and peptide secretion. Abstract. *Journal of Applied Nutrition* 42(1).

Reisman, J., and B. Hanschu. 1992. *Sensory integration inventory-Revised: For individuals with developmental disabilities*. Hugo, MN: PDP Press.

Richter, E., and P. Montgomery. 1988. *The sensorimotor performance analysis*. Hugo, MN: PDP Press.

Rimland, B. 1987. Holding therapy: Maternal bonding or cerebellar stimulation? *Autism Research Review International* 1(3): 3.

———1988. Physical exercise and autism. *Autism Research Review International* 2(4): 3.

Royeen, C. 1986. The development of a touch scale for measuring tactile defensiveness in children. *American Journal of Occupational Therapy* 46(2): 414–419.

———. 1989. Tactile defensiveness: An overview of the construct. Paper presented to the International Society for Social Pediatrics, Brixen, Italy.

Royeen, C., and J. C. Fortune. 1990. Touch inventory for elementary-school-aged children. *American Journal of Occupational Therapy* 44(2): 155–160.

Ruff, H. A. 1989. The infant's use of visual and haptic information in the perception and recognition of objects. *Canadian Journal of Psychology* 43: 302–319.

Sanders, D. 1993. Selected literature and case studies supporting the effectiveness of a sensorimotor and behavior modification approach to autism. *Sensory Integration Special Interest Section Newletter* 16(1): 3–6.

Scheerer, C. 1992. Perspectives on an oral motor activity: The use of rubber tubing as a "chewy." *American Journal of Occupational Therapy* 46(4) (April): 344–352.

Schlosser, R. W. 1998. Communication-based approaches to problem behavior. In L. Lloyd, D. Fuller, and H. Arvidson, editors. *Augmentative and alternative communication: A handbook of principles and practices*. Boston: Allyn and Bacon, 445–473,

Shoemaker, A. 1997. Ambient senses can improve attention, posture. *ADVANCE for Occupational Therapists*. March 24.

Sinclair, K., and V. Hawley. 1992. Sensory integrative therapy and the dyspraxic child: A single case study. *Sensory Integration Special Interest Section Newletter* 15(4): 1–2, 7–8.

Smilansky, S. 1968. *The effects of social dramatic play on disadvantaged children: Preschool children*. New York: John Wiley and Sons.

Stancliff, B. 1996. Autism: Defining the OT's role in treating this confusing disorder. *OT Practice* (July): 18–19.

Swenson-Miller, K. 1979. Sensory integration theory applied to infant intervention during the first three years of life. *Sensory Integration Special Interest Section Newsletter* 2(4): 2

———. 1979. Affective development and sensory responsiveness. *Sensory Integration Special Interest Section Newsletter* 2(4): 3.

Trott, M. C., M. K. Laurel, and S. L. Windeck. 1993. *SenseAbilities: Understanding Sensory Integration*. Tucson, AZ: Therapy Skill Builders.

Tubiana, R. 1981. *The hand*. Vol. 1. Philadelphia: W. B. Saunders.

Weeks, Z. 1979. Effects of the vestibular system on human development: Part 2. *American Journal of Occupational Therapy* 33(7) (July): 450–457.

Wilbarger, P., editor. 1971. *The identification, diagnosis, and remediation of sensorimotor dysfunction in primary school children.* Title 111 EAEA Project Report 5127. Goleta Union School District, California State Department of Education.

Williams, M., and S. Shellenberger. 1994. The Alert program for self-regulation. *Sensory Integration Special Interest Section Newsletter* 17(3) (September): 1–3.

Willoughby, C., and H. Polatajko. 1995. Motor problems in children with developmental coordination disorder: Review of the literature. *American Journal of Occupational Therapy* 49(8) (September): 787–794.

Wilson, J. 1996. *A parent's introduction to behavior modification.* Arlington, TX: Future Horizons.

Wolkowicz, R., J. Fish, and R. Schaffer. 1977. Sensory integration with autistic children. *Canadian Journal of Occupational Therapy* 44: 171–175.

Internet Resources

Asperger's syndrome. A support network. http://www.vicnet.net.au. . .community/Asperger

Autism Society of America. http://www.autism-society.org

Autistic disorder. American description. *Internet Mental Health.* http://www.mentalhealth.com/disl/p21-ho6

Goldberg, M. J. Autism and the immune connection. http://web.syr.edu/-jmwo. . .m/immune-connection

Long, P. 1988. Autistic disorder: Autism and the brain. *The Harvard Medical School Mental Health Letter* (October), page 1. http://www.mentalhealth.com\magl\p5h-aut1

———. 1990. Autism in the family. *The Harvard Medical School Mental Health Letter* (December), page 1. Copyright © 1995, 1997 by Philip Long. http:\\www.mentalhealth.com\magl\p5h-aut3

Lovaas, I. 1989. Autism: A new behavioral treatment. *The Harvard Medical School Mental Health Letter* (June), pages 1–4. http:\\www.mentalhealth.com\magl\p5h-aut2

Research study on low levels of sulphate in autism at Birmingham University, UK. AIA Home Page. http:\\www.demon.co.uk/charities/AlA/aia2.htm

Research at Yale in high-functioning autism and Asperger's syndrome. The Yale-LDA Social Learning Disabilities Project: Program Description and Summary http:\\info.med.yale.edu. . .ism/asp-description

Society for the Autistically Handicapped. 1997. *Breaking news.* Updated May 15, 1997. http:\\www.mplc.co.uk\e.11courses\prog.htm\#1.v

———. 1997. *TEACCH program.* Updated April 3, 1997. http:\\www.mplc.co.uk\e.11courses\prog.htm\#1.v

———. 1997. *Treatment and approaches.* Updated March 14, 1997. http:\\www.mplc.co.uk\e.11courses\prog.htm\#1.v

———. 1997. *Welcome to the World of Autism.* Updated April 29, 1997. http:\\www.mplc.co.ul\e.11courses\prog.htm\#1.v

Vaccines and viruses as a possible trigger for autism. JABS and the Encephalitis Support Group, AIA Home Page. http:\\www.demon.co.uk/charities/AIA/aia5

Vitamin/mineral supplementation. AIA Home Page. http:\\www.demon.co.uk/charities/AIA/aia5

References

Adrien, J. L., A. Perot, D. Sauvage, E. Ledder, C. Larmande, L. Hameury, and C. Barthelemy. 1992. Early symptoms in autism from family home movies: Evaluation and comparison between first and second year of life using I.B.S.E. scale. *Acta Paedopsychiatrica* 55(2):71–75.

American Psychiatric Association (APA). 1994. *The diagnostic and statistical manual of mental disorders*. 4th ed. *(DSM-IV.)* Washington, DC: The American Psychiatric Association.

Ashton, J. 1987. *Brain disorders and psychotropic drugs*. New York: Oxford University Press.

Autism Society of America, Home Page: http://www.autism-society.org 8/16/99

Ayres, A. J. 1961. The development of body scheme in children. *American Journal of Occupational Therapy* 15(3):99–102, 128.

———. 1964. Tactile functions: Their relations to hyperactive and perceptual motor dysfunction in children. *American Journal of Occupational Therapy* 18:6–11.

———. 1968. *Southern California perceptual-motor tests*. Los Angeles: Western Psychological Services.

———. 1969. Deficits in sensory integration in educationally handicapped children. *Journal of Learning Disabilities* 2:44–52.

———. 1972a. Improving academic scores through sensory integration. *Journal of Learning Disabilities* 5:338–343.

———. 1972b. *Southern California sensory integration tests*. Los Angeles: Western Psychological Services.

———. 1972c. Types of sensory integrative dysfunction among disabled learners. *American Journal of Occupational Therapy* 26:13–18.

———. 1973. *Sensory integration and learning disorders*. Los Angeles: Western Psychological Services.

———. 1974. *The development of sensory integrative theory and practice*. Dubuque, IA: Kendall/Hunt.

———. 1975a. Sensory integrative dysfunctions in autism. *Proceedings of the Seventh Annual Conference of the National Society for Autistic Children*. New York: National Society for Autistic Children.

———. 1975b. *Southern California postrotary nystagmus test manual*. Los Angeles: Western Psychological Services.

———. 1977. Cluster analyses of measures of sensory integration. *American Journal of Occupational Therapy* 31:362–366.

———. 1978. Learning disabilities and the vestibular system. *Journal of Learning Disabilities* 11:30–40.

————. 1979. *Sensory integration and the child.* Los Angeles: Western Psychological Services.

————. 1980. *Southern California sensory integration test manual.* Revised ed. Los Angeles: Western Psychological Services.

————. 1985. *Developmental dyspraxia and adult onset apraxia.* Torrence, CA: Sensory Integration International.

————. 1989. *Sensory integration and praxis test manual.* Los Angeles: Western Psychological Services.

Ayres, A. J., and L. S. Tickle. 1980. Hyper-responsivity to touch and vestibular stimulation as a predictor of responsivity to sensory integrative procedures by autistic children. *American Journal of Occupational Therapy* 34(6):375–381.

Baron-Cohen, S., J. Allen, and C. Gillberg. 1992. Can autism be detected at 18 months? The needle, the haystack, and the CHAT (Checklist for Autism in Toddlers). *British Journal of* Psychiatry 161 (December):839–843.

Bauman, M. L. 1991. Microscopic neuroanatomic abnormalities in autism. *Pediatrics* 87(5):791–796.

Bauman, M. L., and T. L. Kemper. 1993. The contribution of neuropathologic studies to the understanding of autism. *Neurologic Clinics* 11(1):175–187.

Becker, M. 1980. Autism: A neurological model. *Sensory Integration Special Interest Section Newsletter,* 3(1):220–221.

Belmonte, M., and R. Carper. 1998. Neuroanatomical and neurophysiological clues to the nature of autism. In B. Garreau, editor. *Neuroimaging in child neuropsychiatric disorders.* New York: Springer-Verlag.

Bettelhaeim, B. 1987. The importance of play. *Atlantic Monthly* (March):37–46.

Beukelman, D. R., and P. Mirenda. 1998. *Augmentative and alternative communication: Management of severe communication disorders in children and adults.* Baltimore: Paul H. Brookes.

Bierman, J. 1998. NDT theoretical overview. *NDTA Network.* (A bimonthly publication of the Neuro-Developmental Treatment Association) July-August:10.

Bird, F., P. Dores, D. Moniz, and J. Robinson. 1989. Reducing severe aggressive and self-injurious behavior with functional communication training. *American Journal of Mental Retardation* 94:37–48.

Bobath, B. 1970. *Sensory motor development.* Unpublished paper.

————. 1972. *Sensori-motor development.* Unpublished paper.

Boehme, Regi. 1988. *Improving upper body control.* Tucson, AZ: Therapy Skill Builders.

Brooks, V. B. *The neural basis of motor control.* New York: Oxford University Press.

Bruner, J. 1972. Nature and uses of immaturity. *American Psychologist* 27(8):687–708.

Bruner, J. S., A. Jolly, and K. Sylva, editors. 1976. *Play: Its role in development and evolution.* New York: Basic Books.

Campbell, R., and J. Lutzker. 1993. Using functional equivalence training to reduce severe challenging behavior: A case study. *Journal of Developmental and Physical Disabilities* 6:203–216.

Cech, D., and S. Martin. 1995. *Functional movement development across the life span.* Philadelphia: W. B. Saunders.

Chess, S. 1971. Autism in children with congenital rubella. *Journal of Autism and Childhood Schizophrenia* 1:33–47.

———. 1977. Followup report on autism in congenital rubella. *Journal of Autism and Developmental Disorders* 7:69–81.

Chusid, J. G. 1979. *Correlative neuroanatomy and functional neurology.* 17th ed. Los Altos, CA: Lange Medical Publishers.

Clarkson, J. D. 1986. Who do you want to be today? The use of costumes as dressing training in occupational therapy. *Play: A skill for life.* Bethesda, MD: American Occupational Therapy Association.

Courchesne, E., J. R. Hesselink, T. L. Jernigan, and R. Yeung-Courchesne. Abnormal neuroanatomy in a nonretarded person with autism: Unusual findings with Magnetic Resonance Imaging. *Archives of Neurology* 44(3):335–341.

Courchesne, E., R. Yeung-Courchesne, G. Press, J. R. Hesselink, and T. L. Jernigan. Hypoplasia of cerebellar vermal lobules VI and VII in autism. *New England Journal of Medicine* 318(21):1349–1354.

Criteria for *DSM-IV* Classifications Autism and Asperger's Syndrome: http://www.netlink.com.au/'ashker/page1.html

Day, H. M., R. Horner, and R. O'Neill. 1994. Multiple functions of challenging behaviors: Assessment and intervention. *Journal of Applied Behavior analysis* 27:279–290.

Defazio. J. L. 1986. *Intervention in oral motor skills.* Office of Education Report. Akron, OH: Children's Hospital Medical Center.

DeQuiros, J. 1978. *Neuropsychological fundamentals in learning disabilities.* Novato, CA: Academic Therapy Publications.

Exner, C. E. 1989. Development of hand function. In P. N. Pratt and A. S. Allen, editors. *Occupational therapy for children.* St. Louis: Mosby.

———. 1990. In-hand manipulation skills in normal young children: A pilot study. *Occupational Therapy Practice* 1:63–72.

Fisher, A. G. 1989. Objective assessment of the quality of response during two equilibrium tests. *Physical Therapy and Occupational Therapy in Pediatrics* 9(3):57–78.

Fisher, A. G., and A. C. Bundy. 1989. Vestibular stimulation in the treatment of postural and related disorders. In O. D. Payton, R. P. DeFabio, S. V. Paris, E. J. Protas, and A. F. VanSant, editors. *Manual of physical therapy techniques.* New York: Churchill Livingstone.

Fisher, A. G., E. A. Murray, and A. C. Bundy. 1991. *Sensory integration theory and practice.* Philadelphia: F. A. Davis.

Fitts, P. M. 1964. Perceptual motor skills learning. In A. W. Melton, editor. *Categories of human learning.* New York: Academic Press, 265–292.

Florey, L. 1981. Studies of play: Implications for growth, development, and for clinical practice. *American Journal of Occupational Therapy* 35:519–524.

Frost, L., and A. Bondy. 1994. *The picture exchange communication system training manual.* Cherry Hill, NJ: Pyramid Educational Consultants.

Fuller, D. R., L. L. Lloyd, and M. M. Stratton. 1998. Aided AAC symbols. In L. Lloyd, D., Fuller, and H. Arvidson, editors. *Augmentative and alternative communication: A handbook of principles and practices.* Boston: Allyn and Bacon, 48–79.

Fulwiler, R. L., and R. S. Fouts. 1976. Acquisition of American Sign Language by a noncommunicating autistic child. *Journal of Autism and Childhood Schizophrenia* 6:43–51.

Gaffney, G. R., L. Y. Tsai, S. Kuperman, and S. Minchin. 1987. Cerebellar structure in autism. *American Journal of Diseases of Children* 141(12):1330–1332.

Ganong, W. 1975. *Review of medical psysiology*. Los Altos: Lange Medical Publishers.

Gardner, E. P. 1988. Somatosensory cortical mechanisms of feature detection in tactile and kinesthetic discrimination. *Canadian Journal of Physiology and Pharmacology* 66:439–454.

Gerlach, E. 1996. *Autism treatment guide*. Eugene, OR: Four Leaf Press.

Getman, G. N. 1985. Hand-eye coordination. *Academic Therapy* 20:261–275.

Gibson, J. J. 1962. Observations of active touch. *Psychological Review* 69:477–491.

Gillberg, C. 1986. Brief report: Onset at age 14 of typical autistic syndroms. A case report of a girl with herpes simplex encephalitis. *Journal of Autism and Developmental Disorders* 16:369–375.

Gilliam, J. E. 1981. *Autism, diagnosis, instruction, management, and research*. Springfield, IL: Thomas.

———. 1995. *Gilliam autism rating scale* (GARS). Austin, TX: PRO-ED.

Gold, M., and J. Gold. 1975. Autism and attention: Theoretical considerations and a pilot study using reaction time. *Child Psychiatry and Human Development* 6:68–80.

Gottfried, W. W. 1984. Touch as an organizer for learning and development. In C. C. Brown, editor. *The many facets of touch*. Skillman, NJ: Johnson and Johnson Baby Products, 114–122.

Gray, J. A. 1982. *The neuropsychology of anxiety*. New York: Claredon Press.

———. 1991. *The psychology of fear and stress*. Cambridge, England: Cambridge University Press.

Greer, M., M. Lyons-Crews, L. B. Mauldin, and F. R. Brown, III. 1989. A case study of the cognitive and behavioral deficits of temporal lobe damage in herpes simplex encephalitis. *Journal of Autism and Developmental Disorders* 19:317–326.

Gubbay, S. S. 1975. *The clumsy child*. Philadelphia: W. B. Saunders.

———. 1979. The clumsy child. In F. C. Rose, editor. *Pediatric neurology*. London: Blackwell.

———. 1985. Clumsiness. In P. J. Vinken, G. W. Bruyn, and H. L. Klawans, editors. *Handbook of clinical neurology*. Revised. New York: Elsevier.

Haas, R. H., J. Townsend, E. Courchesne, A. J. Lincoln, L. Schreibman, and R. Yeung-Courchesne. Neurologic abnormalities in infantile autism. *Journal of Child Neurology* 11:84–92.

Hallett, M., M. K. Lebiedowska, L. L. Thomas, S. J. Stanhope, M. B. Denckla, and J. Rumsey. 1993. Locomotion of autistic adults. *Archives of Neurology* 50(12):1304–1308.

Hashimoto, T., M. Tayama, K. Murakawa, T. Yoshimoto, M. Miyazaki, M. Harad, and Y. Kuroda. 1995. Development of the brainstem and cerebellum in autistic patients. *Journal of Autism and Developmental Disorders* 25(1):1–18.

Henderson, A., and C. Pehoski. 1995. Hand function in the child. *Mosby yearbook*. Chicago: Mosby.

Hodgson, L. A. 1995. *Visual strategies for improving communication*. Vol. 1: Practical supports for school and home. Troy, MI: Quirk Roberts Publishing.

Hollins, M., and A. K. Goble. 1988. Perception of length of voluntary movements. *Somatosensory Research* 5:335–348.

Horner, R., and C. Budd. 1985. Acquisition of manual sign use: Collateral reduction of maladaptive behavior and factors limiting generalization. *Education and Training of the Mentally Retarded* 20:39–47.

Janzen, Janice E. 1996. *Understanding the Nature of Autism: A Practical Guide*. San Antonio: Therapy Skill Builders.

Johansson, R. S., and G. Westling. 1990. Tactile afferent signals in the control of precision grip. In M. Jeannerod, editor. *Attention and performance*. Vol. 13: Motor representation and control. Hillsdale: Lawrence Erlbaum Associates.

Johnson, K. O., and S. S. Hsiao. 1992. Neural mechanisms of tactile form and texture perception. *Annual Review of Neuroscience* 15:227–250.

Jones, V., and M. Prior. 1985. Motor imitation abilities and neurological signs in autistic children. *Journal of Autism and Developmental Disorders* 15(1):37–46.

Kandel, E. R., J. H. Schwartz, and T. M. Jessel. 1995. *Essentials of neural essence and behavior*. Norwalk, CT: Appleton and Lange.

King, L. J. 1992. Sensory integration: An effective approach to therapy and education. *Sensory Integration Quarterly* (March):3–5.

Knickerbocker, B. M. 1980. *A holistic approach to learning disabilities*. Thorofare, NJ: C. B. Slack.

Konstantareas, M. M., J. Oxman, C. D. Webster, H. Fischer, and K. Miller. 1975. *A five-week simultaneous communication programme for severely dysfunctional children: Outcome and implications for future research*. Toronto: Clarke Institute of Psychiatry.

Koomar, J. A., and A. C. Bundy. 1991. The art and science of creating direct intervention from theory. In A. G. Fisher, E. A. Murray, and A. C. Bundy, editors. *Sensory integration theory and practice*.Philadelphia: F. A. Davis, 25–114.

Kravitz, H., D. Goldenberg, and A. Neyhaus. Tactile exploration by normal infants. *Developmental Medicine and Child Neurology* 20:720–726.

Lashley, K. S. 1951. The problem of serial order in behavior. In L. A. Jeffress, editor. *Cerebral mechanisms in behavior*. New York: John Wiley & Sons.

Ledoux, J. 1996. *The emotional brain*. New York: Simon and Schuster.

Lindquist, J. E., W. Mach, and L. D. Parham. 1982. A synthesis of occupational behavior and sensory integrative concepts in theory and practice. Part 2, Clinical Application. *American Journal of Occupational Therapy* (July) 36(7):433–437.

Lovaas, O. I., L. Schreibman, R. Koegel, and R. Rehm. 1971. Selective responding by autistic children to multiple sensory input. *Journal of Abnormal Psychology* 77(3):211–222.

Markowitz, P. I. 1983. Autism in a child with congenital cytomegalovirus infection. *Journal of Autism and Developmental Disorders* 13(3):249–253.

Matthews, P. B. C. 1988. Proprioceptors and their contribution to somatosensory mapping: Complex messages require complex processing. *Canadian Journal of Physiological Pharmacology* 66:430–438.

Melzack, R., and J. Southmayd. Dorsal column contributions to anticipatory motor behavior. *Experimental Neurology* 42:274–281.

Melzack, R., and P. D. Wall. 1965. Pain mechanism: A new theory. *Science* 150:971–979.

Merck and Co., Inc. 1996–97. *Merck manual*. Whitehouse Station, NJ: Author.

Miller, A., and E. E. Miller. 1973. Cognitive-developmental training with elevated boards and sign language. *Journal of Autism and Childhood Schizophrenia* 3:65–85.

Miller, L. J. 1982. *Miller assessment of preschoolers (MAP)*. San Antonio: The Psychological Corporation.

Mountcastle, V. B., J. C. Lynch, A. Georgopoulos, H. Sakata, and C. Acuna. 1975. Posterior parietal association cortex of the monkey: Command functions for operations within extra-personal space. *Journal of Neurophysiology* 38:871–908.

Munoz, J. P. 1986. The significance of fostering play development in handicapped children. *Play: A skill for life*. Bethesda, MD: American Occupational Therapy Association.

Murakami, J., E. Courchesne, G. Press, R. Yeung-Courchesne, and J. Hesselink. 1989. Reduced cerebellar hemisphere size and its relationship to vermal hypoplasia in autism. *Archives of Neurology* 46(6):689–694.

Nashner, L. M. 1977. Fixed patterns of rapid postural responses among leg muscles during stance. *Experiential Brain Research* 30:12–24.

———. 1990. Sensory, neuromuscular, and biomechanical contributions to human balance. In P. Duncan, editor. *Balance: Proceedings of the APTA Forum*. Alexandria, VA: American Physical Therapy Association, 5–12.

Oetter, P., E. Richter, and S. Frick. 1995. *M.O.R.E.: Integrating the mouth with sensory and postural functions*. 2d ed. Hugo, MN: PDP Press.

Offir, C. W. 1976. Visual speech: Their fingers do the talking. *Psychology Today* 10(1):72–78.

Ogura, T. A. 1991. A longitudinal study of the relationship between early language development and play development. *Journal of Child Language* 18:273–294.

Ojemann, G. 1983. Brain organization of language from the perspective of electrical stimulation mapping. *Behavior and Brain Sciences* 6(2):189–230.

Ornitz, E. M. 1974. The modulation of sensory input and motor output in autistic children. *Journal of Autism and Childhood Schizophrenia* 4:197–214.

Parten, M. B. 1932. Social participation among preschool children. *Journal of Abnormal Social Psychology* 27:243–269.

Pediatric Database (PEDBASE) 10/21/94: http;//www./condata.com/dbase/files/RETTSYND.htm

Piaget, J. 1962. *Play, dreams, and imitation in childhood*. New York: Norton Press.

Piaget, J., and B. Inhelder. 1948. *The child's conception of space*. New York: Norton Press.

Pribram, K. 1991. *Brain and perception*. Hillsdale, NJ: Erlbaum.

Pribram, K., and D. McGuinness. 1975. Arousal, activation, and effort in the control of attention. *Psychological Review* 82:116–149.

Rast, M. 1986. Play and therapy, play or therapy. *Play: A skill for life*. Bethesda, MD: American Occupational Therapy Association.

Reeves, G. 1998. From cell to system: The neural regulation of emotion and behavior. *Sensory Integration Special Interest Section Newsletter* 21(3):1–4.

Rimland, B. 1965. *Infantile autism: The syndrome and its implications for a neural theory of behavior*. New York: Appleton-Century-Crofts.

Ritvo, E. R., B. J. Freeman, A. B. Scheibel, T. Duong, H. Robinson, D. Guthrie, and A. Ritvo. 1986. Lower Purkinje cell counts in the cerebella of four autistic subjects: Initial findings of the UCLA-NSAC autopsy research report. *American Journal of Psychiatry* 143(7):862–866.

Ritvo, E. R., C. Pingree, P. B. Peterson, W. R. Jenson, W. M. McMahon, B. J. Freeman, L. B. Jorde, M. J. Spencer. 1990. The UCLA-University of Utah epedemiologic survey of autism: Prenatal, perinatal, and postnatal factors. *Pediatrics* 86(4):514–519.

Rose, S., A. Gottfried, and W. Bridger. 1978. Cross-modal transfer in infants: Relationship to prematurity and socioeconomic background. *Developmental Psychology* 12:311–320.

Rosenbloom, L., and M. E. Horton. 1971. The maturation of fine prehension in young children. *Developmental Medicine and Child Neurology* 13:3–8.

Royeen, C. B. 1989. Commentary on tactile functions in learning-disabled and normal children: Reliability and validity considerations. *Occupational Therapy Journal of Research* 9:16–23.

Schaaf, R., and J. Burke. 1992. Clinical reflections on play and sensory integration. *Sensory Integration Special Interest Section Newsletter* 15(1):1–2.

Schaeffer, B., P. McDowell, P. Musil, and G. Kollinzas. 1976. *Spontaneous verbal language for autistic children through signed speech.* Research Relating to Children (ERIC Clearinghouse for Early Childhood Education). Bulletin 37:98–99.

Schlosser, R. W. 1998. Communication-based approaches to problem behavior. In L. Lloyd, D. Fuller, and H. Arvidson, editors. *Augmentative and alternative communication: A handbook of principles and practices.* Boston: Allyn and Bacon, 445–473.

Schmidt, R. A. 1988. *Motor control and learning.* 2d ed. Champaign, IL: Human Kinetics.

Schopler, E., R. J. Reichler, R. F. DeVellis, and K. Daly. 1980. Toward objective classification of childhood autism: Childhood Autism Rating Scale (CARS). *Journal of Autism and Developmental Disorder* 10:91–97.

Sears, L. L., P. R. Finn, and J. E. Steinmetz. 1994. Abnormal classical eye-blink conditioning in autism. *Journal of Autism and Developmental Disorders* 24(6):737–751.

Sigafoos, J., and B. Meikle. 1996. Functional communication training for the treatment of multiply determined challenging behavior in two boys with autism. *Behavior Modification* 20:60–84.

Sinclare, D. 1981. *Mechanism of cutaneous sensation.* New York: Oxford University Press.

Stancliff, B. 1998. Play with a purpose: Sensory integration treatment and developmental disabilities. *OT Practice* (October):34–54.

Stone, W. L., and A. M. LaGreca. 1986. The development of social skills in children. In E. Schopler and G. B. Mesibov, editors. *Social behavior in autism.* New York: Plenum Press, 35–60.

Stubbs, E. G. 1978. Autistic symptoms in a child with congenital cytomegalovirus infection. *Journal of Autism and Childhood Schizophrenia* 8:37–43.

Stubbs, E. G., E. Ash, and C. P. Williams. 1984. Autism and congenital cytomegalovirus. *Journal of Autism and Developmental Disorders* 14(2): 183–189.

Stutsman, R. 1948. *Guide for administering the Merrill-Palmer scales of mental tests.* New York: Harcourt, Brace & World.

Tebo, S. E. 1986. Evaluating toy selection. *Play: A skill for life.* Bethesda, MD: American Occupational Therapy Association.

Vilensky, J. A., A. R. Damasi, and R. G. Maurer. 1981. Gait disturbances in patients with autistic behavior: A preliminary study. *Archives of Neurology* 38(10):646–649.

Vinogradova, O. 1970. Registration of information and the limbic system. In G. Horn and R. A. Hinds, editors. *Short-term changes in neural activity and behavior.* Cambridge, England: Cambridge University Press.

Vygotsky, L. S. 1978. *Mind in society: The development of higher psychological processes.* Cambridge, MA: Harvard University Press.

Wacker, D., M. Steege, J. Northrop, G. Sasso, W. Berg, T. Reimers, A. Cooper, K. Cigrand, and L. Donn. 1990. A component analysis of functional communication training across three topographies of severe behavior problems. *Journal of Applied Behavior Analysis* 23:417–429.

Wall, P. D. Sensory role of impulses traveling in the dorsal column. *Brain* 93:505–524.

Wallach, G. P., and L. Miller. 1988. *Language intervention and academic success.* Austin, TX: PRO-ED.

Wasson, C., H. Arvidson, and L. L. Lloyd. 1998. AAC assessment process. In L. Lloyd, D. Fuller, and H. Arvidson, editors. *Augmentative and alternative communication: A handbook of principles and practices.* Boston: Allyn and Bacon, 169–198.

Wilbarger, P. 1984. Planning an adequate sensory diet: Application of sensory processing theory during the first year of life. *Zero to three* 5(1):7–12.

———. 1995. The sensory diet: Activity programs based on sensory processing theory. *Sensory Integration Special Interest Section Newsletter* 18(2):1–4.

Wilbarger, P., and J. Wilbarger. 1991. *Sensory defensiveness in children aged 2–12.* Santa Barbara, CA: Avanti Educational Programs.

Williams, R. S., S. L. Hauser, D. P. Purpura, G. R. DeLong, and C. N. Swisher. 1980. Autism and mental retardation: Neuropathologic studies performed in four retarded persons with autistic behavior. *Archives of Neurology* 37(12):749–753.

Windeck, S., and M. Laure. 1989. A theoretical framework combining speech-language therapy with sensory integration treatment. *Sensory Integration, Special Interest Section Newsletter* 12(1) (March):1–5.

Wing, L. 1981. Asperger's syndrome: A clinical account. *Psychological Medicine* 11:115–129.

———. 1991. Asperger's syndrome and Kanner's autism. In U. Frith, editor. *Autism and Asperger's syndrome.* Cambridge, England: Cambridge University Press.

Wing, L., and T. Atwood. 1987. Syndromes of autism and atypical development. In D. Cohen and A. Donnellan, editors. *Handbook of autism and pervasive developmental disorders.* New York: John Wiley & Sons, 3–19.

Wolfberg, P. J. 1995. Enhancing children's play. In K. Quill, editor. *Teaching children with autism: Strategies to enhance communication and socialization.* New York: Delmar, 193–216.

Index

Crab walk in facilitating sensory integration, 269
Creative thinking, 277
Cueing, 54
Cushioned grips in tactile discrimination, 223
Cutting tasks in tactile discrimination, 222

D

Data banks of children with autism, 16, 340
DCML. See Dorsal column medial lemniscus (DCML) system
Deep pressure
to cheeks, 228–30
into jaw, 227
Deep-touch input
in facilitating sensory integration, 159
and tactile discrimination, 227
Deep-touch massage, 327
Deep-touch pressure, 120
as intervention strategy for sensory modulation disorders, 152–55, 157
Deep-touch pressure and proprioceptive technique (DPPT), 146, 162–63
Defensive behaviors, 110, 118–19
Defensive sensory modulation disorders, 110, 112–13, 113t, 117–19
arousal problems, 118–19
orientation problems, 118
registration problems, 118
working theories for intervention, 122–24
Defined boundaries for autistic children, 39
Defined rules for autistic children, 44
Delayed gratification, 50–51, 62
Delayed reinforcement techniques, 45
Demonstration, 55
Descriptive language in autism, 338
Desired behaviors, approximating, 58
Development
impact of sensory integrative disfunction on, 95–96
importance of play in, 370–84

normal, of tactile system, 173–78
sensory integration and normal, 90–93
Developmental apraxia, 334–35
Developmental dyspraxia, 335
Developmental sequence, 81–82
Diagnostic and Statistical Manual of Mental Disorders, Fourth Edition (DSM-IV)
asperger's syndrome in, 3
autism in, 1, 2, 3, 7–8
pervasive development disorder not otherwise specified in, 3
Diminished sensory registration, 109
Disruptive behavior, association of, with somatosensory or tactile discrimination disorders, 187t
Distance receivers, 83
Dorsal column medial lemniscus (DCML) system, 87, 88, 120–21, 121t, 178
impairment of, 178–79
and sensory stimulation, 192
Down time for autistic children, 43
Drinking-straw games, 154
Dyspraxia, 334–35, 345
characteristics of, 237
criteria for diagnosing, 238
defined, 237
types of, 238–39
verbal, 334

E

Early infantile autism, 1–2
Eating as functional activity in tactile discrimination, 230–32
Eccentric control, 318, 320, 323–24
Echolalia, 5, 347
Effort, facilitating normal levels of, 143–46, 145t
Elbow, inability to co-activate for weight bearing, 322
Emotion, disorders in, 84–85
Emotional crisis, foreseeing, in anxiety management, 138
Emotional environment for autistic children, 41–45
Empowering child
to communicate at home, 341–43

to maintain calm-alert state, 146–51
Enhanced sensory activities, in facilitating sensory integration, 157–63, 223–24
Environment for autistic children
clutter-free, 40
creating, for optimal functioning, 38–45, 39t, 40t, 42t
emotional, 41
in promoting challenging behaviors, 29–30
sensory, 40–41
Escape behaviors
in autism, 34–36
intervention strategies for, 64–74
Escargot clamps in tactile discrimination, 216
Events, avoidance of, 35, 64–68
Executive functions, 91–92
Expansions in communication, 350
Expressive language, 18, 347
Extensions in communication, 350
External resistance to body movements, 199–200
Exteroceptors, 83
Extracurricular activities in facilitating sensory integration, 163
Extraneous verbalizations for autistic children, 44
Extremities, motor control in, 320–31
Eye flexion in tactile discrimination, 202
Eye-foot coordination, 293
Eye-hand coordination, 293
Eye-hand dissociation, 294–95
Eye-head dissociation, 292–93

F

Face, deep-touch pressure technique for, 152
Facial expressions, 18
Facial massages in tactile discrimination, 225
Facilitating input, 107
Facilitation techniques, 47. See also Intervention strategies
Factor-analytic studies, 80–81
Faulty sensory modulation, theory of, 15

Impulses, inhibiting, 107–8
Incline boards in tactile discrimination, 219–20
Infa-Dents, 343
Inflatable airmat activities
in facilitating sensory integration, 267–68
and tactile discrimination, 203
Information
learning of, in autism, 18–19
processing and decoding, in sensory integration, 83–84
storage of, in autism, 16–17
In-hand manipulation skills in tactile discrimination, 217–19
Inhibiting impulses, 107–8
Input, facilitating, 107
Integration. See Neuro-developmental treatment (NDT); Sensory integration (SI); Sensory modulation
Intentional, pre-symbolic level, of augmentative and alternative communication (AAC), 357–58
Interesting tasks in autism, 45
Intermittent reinforcement, 50
Internal resistance in tactile discrimination, 198–99
Internal/systemic, sensory-based avoidance reactions, 72–73
Internal/systemic obtaining behaviors in autism, 33–34
Internal/systemic responses in autism, 36–37
Internal/systemic visceral-based avoidance reactions, 73–74
Interoceptors, 83–84
Intervention. See also Neuro-developmental treatment (NDT); Sensory Integration (SI)
defined, 125
goal of, 47
timing of, 47–48, 48t
Intervention strategies
for auditory defensiveness, 130, 135t
augmentative and alternative communication as, 360–64
manual signs, 363–64
picture symbols, 360–61, 362t, 363
voice-output communication aids, 363

for avoidance or escape behaviors, 64–74
for communication impairments
environmental considerations, 341–43
providing feedback and developing motor engrams, 343–46
registration, orientation, and arousal, 341
teaching play skills, 348–49
teaching pragmatic skills, 349
teaching skills of, 346–48
temptations in, 349–51
for gravitational insecurity, 130, 134t
involving play, 376–83
just-right challenge, 377–78
for obtaining behaviors, 61–64
for sensory modulation disorders, 125–71, 126
anxiety and its impact on calm-alert state, 136–43, 140–41t
empowering child to maintain calm-alert state, 146–51
facilitating integration, 156–71
facilitating normal levels of attention, arousal, and effort, 143–46, 145t
fluctuating or defensive, and calm-alert state, 129–30, 131–34t
obtaining calm-alert state, 127–29, 128t
oral motor programs in, 151–56
for somatodyspraxia, 237–77
conceptualizing plan, 246–51
facilitating language and sensory integration, 273–77
facilitating sensory integration, 254–72, 256t
planning, sequencing and organizing information, 252–71
school- and -home-based programs, 271–73
sensory registration and ideation in, 248, 249, 250–51
task execution in, 271–73

for vestibular proprioceptive deficits, 252–54
for tactile defensiveness, 130, 131–34t
for tactile discrimination disorders, 94, 94t, 130, 191–236
body scheme in, 193–207
characteristics of, 183, 183–89, 184, 185, 186, 187t
defined, 191
eliminating sensory-seeking behavior associated with, 233–36, 236t
identification of, 179
intervention strategies for food in, 155–56, 155t
and somatosensory processing, 239
teamwork in, 78
Intolerance of movement
sensory Integration for, 291
as vestibular- and procioceptive-based, 291
Isolated exploration in tactile discrimination, 212–15

J
Jaw, deep-touch pressure technique for, 153, 227
Just-right challenge, 97, 377–78

K
Kanner, Leo, 1
Knee, inability to co-activate for weight bearing, 322
Knee-jerk reflex, 84

L
Landau-Kleffner syndrome, 5
Language, 92. See also Speech
in autism, 8–9
body, 19
deficits of, in autism, 17–18
delays of, in autism, 378–79
descriptive, in autism, 338
expressive, 18, 347
facilitating sensory integration and, 273–77
pragmatic, 8–9
promoting skills in, 348
receptive, 347, 351–53
as related to praxis, 275–77
spontaneous learning of, 347
strategies for promoting receptive, 351–53

intervention strategies involving, 376–83

just-right challenge in, 377–78

in learning and development, 22–23, 370–84

presymbolic skills in, 348–49

in school-age children, 374

shared joint attention in, 380

and somatodyspraxia, 242

symbolic, 22

teaching, 348–49

Pons, 84, 85

Positive atmosphere, creating, in anxiety management, 138–39

Positive attention, 32

intervention strategies for, 61–62

Postural control, 301–18

head control and stability in, 304–5

improving slow, sustained, 200–203

integrating sensory integration and neuro-development treatment, 318–19

neuro-developmental treatment for, 318–19

poor head control and stability in, 304–5

poor pelvic stability in, 313–18

poor scapular stability in, 306–12

sensory integration for, 318–19

slow, sustained, 209

tests for, 303–4

Postural insecurity, 21

sensory integration for, 298

and tactile discrimination, 193

as vestibular- and procioceptive-based, 291

Postural-ocular movement disorder, 253–54, 299, 301

as vestibular- and procioceptive-based, 291–92

Postural praxis, testing for, 244

Posture in autism, 21

Pragmatic language, 8–9

Pragmatics, 18

in autism, 338–39

teaching skills in, 349

Praxis, 239–41

fundamental concepts of, 245

problems with, 244–45

speech and language as related to, 275–77

on verbal command, 238

Predictable sensory ROA (registration, orientation and arousal) difficulties, 110, 111–12, 113*t*

predictable problems

with arousal, 115–17

with orientation, 115

with registration, 114–15

working theories for intervention, 122–24

Pre-intentional level of augmentative and alternative communication (AAC), 357

Presymbolic play skills, 348–49

Pretend play

in autistic child, 379

early development of, 373

Primary reinforcers, 49

Proactive approach, 47–48

Productive sensory behaviors in autism, 33–34

Prompting, 53, 77

demonstration and modeling, 55–56

physical, 53

shaping behaviors, 57–58

verbal, 56–57

visual, 54–55

Prone extension

and postural control, 303

and tactile discrimination, 200

Proprioception, 88–89

impulses in, 89

input in, 12, 49, 120

in motor control, 296, 297*t*

processing in, 253

receptors in, 90

Proprioceptive-based problems

bilateral integration and sequencing as, 291

gravitational insecurity as, 291

high tolerance for movement disorder as, 290

intolerance of movement as, 291

postural insecurity as, 291

postural-ocular movement disorder as, 291–92

Proprioceptive input in providing feedback, 343–44

Proprioceptive systems, 80, 91, 172–73

normal development of, 173–78

Proprioceptors, 84

Proximal stability for scapular-related muscles, 306–8

Pulling game in facilitating sensory integration, 258

Purkinje cell count in autism, 282–83

Push-pull games in facilitating sensory integration, 161

Q

Qualitative impairments in social interaction, 7–8

Quantified tasks in autism, 45

R

Reaching net activities

in facilitating sensory integration, 260

and tactile discrimination, 200

Receptive language skills, 347

strategies for promoting, in autistic children, 351–53

Reflexes

optic, 90

vestibular, 90

Reflex responses, 278

Registration. See ROA (registration, orientation, or arousal) disorders; Sensory registration

Regulation, disorders in, 84–85

Reinforcement

delayed, 45

intermittent, 50

Reinforcers

and delayed gratification, 50–51

grading, 49–50

primary, 49

secondary, 49, 59

negative attention, 46–47

Remediation for behavior in autism, 25–28, 30

Repetitive motor movements in autism, 9

Resistive clothespins in tactile discrimination, 216

Resistive equipment in facilitating sensory integration, 161

Resistive mediums in tactile discrimination, 213

Resistive upper-extremity activities in facilitating sensory integration, 159–60
Respiratory control, deep touch pressure technique for, 154–55
Reticular activating system, 120
Reticular formation, 84–85
Rett's syndrome, 2, 3
Rewards, 50
Rhythmic activities
    in managing anxiety, 138
    in teaching social interaction, 65
Rhythmic movements, 72
Rhythmic songs, 65
Rib mobilizations in tactile discrimination, 228
Rice box activities in tactile discrimination, 195
Ring game in facilitating sensory integration, 258, 260
Rituals, 18–19
ROA (registration, orientation, or arousal) disorders, 114–19, 335–36
    fluctuating or defensive responses, 110, 112–13, 113t
        arousal problems, 118–19
        orientation problems, 118
        registration problems, 118
    intervention for, 341
    predictable sensory, 110, 111–12, 113t
        arousal problems, 115–17
        orientation problems, 115
        registration problems, 114–15
    working theories for intervention, 122–24
Role delineation, 22
Role play in autistic child, 379
Rotational head movements, 301
Rough water in facilitating sensory integration, 265
Routines
    change in, 71
    in communication, 352

S
Saccule, 90
Sand box activities in tactile discrimination, 195, 209
Sbling studies, 6
Scaffolding in communication, 351

Scapular control, graded, 312
Scapular-related muscles, proximal stability for, 306–8
Scapular stability, poor, 306–12
Scapular winging, 309, 311–12
Schedules for autistic children, 41–43, 42t
Schizophrenia, 3, 6
Schizotypal personality disorder, 3
School-age children, play skills in, 374
School-based programs, task execution in, 271–73
School-related tasks and somatodyspraxia, 242
Scissors in tactile discrimination, 222
Scooterboard activities
    in facilitating sensory integration, 161, 258–60
    static supine flexion on, 203
    in tactile discrimination, 202, 204
Secondary behavioral problems, 25
Secondary reinforcers, 49
    and autistic behavior, 25–28, 30, 59
    negative attention as, 46–47
Seizures, 4
    in sensory modulation disorders, 119–20
Self-abusive behaviors, 72
Self-aggressive behaviors, 9
Self-regulation, teaching, in empowering child to maintain calm-alert state, 147–51
Self-stimulating behaviors, 53, 64
Self-stimulation patterns, 144
    and sensory-seeking behaviors, 232–36, 236t
Semicircular canals, 295
Sensorimotor experience, importance of, in neuro-development, 100–101
Sensory awareness in tactile discrimination, 193
Sensory-based activities, 73, 195–97
    avoidance of, in autism, 36–37
    in improving fine motor control, 209
Sensory-based intervention strategies, 124
Sensory-based oral motor program, establishing, 229–30

Sensory-based problems in autistic children, 334–39
Sensory boxers in tactile discrimination, 213–14
Sensory defensiveness, 122
Sensory deprivation, 15
Sensory diets, in empowering child to maintain calm-alert state, 146–47
Sensory environment for autistic children, 40–41
Sensory experience, food as, 155–56, 155t
Sensory feedback in task execution, 271–72
Sensory histories, obtaining, in identifying tactile discrimination disorders, 187–88
Sensory impairments, 10
Sensory information, 83
    integration of, 86–87
    processing and decoding, 83–84
Sensory input
    effects of, on motor control, 281–82
    enhancing, through active physical involvement, 198–200
Sensory Integration and Praxis Test (SIPT), 238, 244, 304
Sensory integration (SI), 80–97
    assumptions in, 81–82
    brain stem and midbrain in, 84–85
    cerebellum in, 85
    cerebral cortex in, 86–87
    child's inner drive in, 97
    components of, 96
        adaptive response, 96–97
        child's inner drive, 97
    definition of, 82–83
    facilitating, 156–71, 254–72, 256t
        language in, 273–77
    goal of, 96, 165
    in increasing motor control, 295, 297t, 303
    and normal development, 90–93
    principles of, 163–69
    processing and decoding information in, 83–84
    proprioception in, 88–89
    senses in, 83
    spinal cord in, 84
    tactile system in, 87–88

theory on, 82–83
  evolution of, 100
  integrating, with neuro-developmental treatment (NDT), 106
  in treating postural control, 302, 318–19
  vestibular system in, 90
Sensory integrative disorders, 21–22, 82, 93–96, 94t
  impact on development, 95–96
Sensory modulation, 107–24
  arousal in, 110
  defined, 108
  habituation in, 108–9
  orientation in, 109–10
  phases in normal, 108
  registration, 109
  theories of, 120–22, 121t
Sensory modulation disorders, 110, 111, 113t
  fluctuating or defensive responses in, 110, 112–13, 113t
  arousal problems, 118–19
  and calm-alert state, 129–30, 131–34t
  orientation problems, 118
  intervention strategies for, 125–71, 126
  anxiety and its impact on calm-alert state, 136–43, 140–41t
  empowering child to maintain calm-alert state, 146–51
  facilitating integration, 156–71
  facilitating normal levels of attention, arousal, and effort, 143–46, 145t
  obtaining calm-alert state, 127–29, 128t
  oral motor programs, 151–56
  working theories for, 122–24
  predictable registration, orientation, or arousal (ROA) difficulties in, 111–12, 113t
  arousal problems, 115–17
  orientation problems, 115
  registration problems, 114–15
  seizures in, 119–20
  theories of, 120–22, 121t
Sensory overload, 37, 73

Sensory processing in autism, 12–14, 100, 101, 283–92, 334–39
Sensory registration, 12, 114. See also ROA (registration, orientation, or arousal) disorders
  and concept development, 248, 249, 250–51
  defined, 109
  diminished, 109
  facilitating, 139, 140–41t, 141–43
  and orientation problems, 118
  in sensory modulation disorders, 109, 111–12, 114–15
Sensory-seeking behaviors, 63–64
  and self-stimulation patterns, 232–36, 236t
Sensory stimulation and dorsal column medial lemniscus (DCML) system, 192
Sensory system
  anterolateral, 87–88
  connection with neurological system, 274
  dorsal column medial lemniscus (DCML), 88
  proprioception, 88–89
  tactile, 87–88
  vestibular, 90
Sensory testing in identifying tactile discrimination disorders, 188
Sentence length in communication, 353
Sequencing deficits and bilateral integration, 254
Sequencing game in facilitating sensory integration, 261
Serotonin activity, 6
Shaping behaviors in achieving desired behavior, 57–58
Shared joint attention in autistic child, 380
Shift in tactile discrimination, 217
Sholder, inability to co-activate for weight bearing, 321–22
Shoulder stability
  and graded arm control, 210–12
  improving slow, sustained, 203–4
SI. See Sensory integration (SI)
Simon Says in tactile discrimination, 200

Simple rotation in tactile discrimination, 217
Sitting scooterboard thera-band game in facilitating sensory integration, 259–60
Sit-ups in tactile discrimination, 202
Skill analysis, 68–69
Skilled, precise control, 326
Skilled tool usage and adaptive equipment, 219–24
Sky trolleys in facilitating sensory integration, 267
Slant-top (pizza box) writing board in tactile discrimination, 220–22
Social-communicative obtaining behaviors, 31–33, 61–63
  positive attention, 61–62
Social interaction, 22
Social relatedness, 19
Somatodyspraxia, 237–77
  behavioral characteristics, 243–44
  characteristics of, 239–44
  clinical history of child with, 242–43
  conceptualize plan, 246–51
  defined, 238–39
  evaluation findings, 244–45
  intervention strategies for
    conceptualizing plan, 246–51
    facilitating language and sensory integration, 273–77
    facilitating sensory integration, 254–72, 256t
    planning, sequencing and organizing information, 252–71
    school- and -home-based programs, 271–73
    sensory registration and ideation in, 248, 249, 250–51
    task execution in, 271–73
    for vestibular proprioceptive deficits, 252–54
  and motor control, 286–88
  and types of dyspraxis, 238–39
Somatodyspraxis, and supine flexion, 244–45
Somatosensory processing
  neurological pathways for, 178–79
  and tactile discrimination, 239

Touch receptors, 90
Tourette syndrome, 6
Toweling in tactile discrimination, 194
Trampoline activities
    in facilitating sensory integration, 157–58, 270
    in tactile discrimination, 196–97, 209
Transient tilts, 301
Transitions for autistic children, 43–44
Trapeze activities in facilitating sensory integration, 268
Treatment strategies in facilitating positive outcomes, 46–54
Tuberous sclerosis, 4
Twin studies, 6

U

Underarousal, 16, 127–28, 128*t*
United States Society of Augmentative and Alternative Communication (USSAAC), 369
Utricles, 90

V

Velocity receptors, 89
Verbal apraxia, 334–35
Verbal command, praxis on, 238
Verbal dyspraxia, 334
Verbal feedback, 273
Verbal prompts, 56–57, 342
Vestibular components in motor control, 295–96

Vestibular defensiveness and aversion to movement, 118
Vestibular input, 12
    and motor planning, 240–41
Vestibular processing impairment, 21
Vestibular-proprioceptive deficits, 252–54
Vestibular stimulation, sensory integration for high tolerance to, 299
Vestibular system, 80, 90, 91, 122
    reflexes in, 90
Vestiobular-based problems
    bilateral integration and sequencing as, 291
    gravitational insecurity as, 291
    high tolerance for movement disorder as, 290
    intolerance of movement as, 291
    postural insecurity as, 291
    postural-ocular movement disorder as, 291–92
Vibration in tactile discrimination, 226–27
Visual closure, 293
Visual memory, 294
Visual perception, 294
Visual prompts, 54–55
Visual receptors, 91
Visual scanning, 294
Visual space perception, 175
Visual systems, 80, 91, 122
    effect of, on motor control, 292–95

Visuodyspraxia, 238
Visuopraxis test scores, 245
Voice inflection
    teaching skills of, 352
    in verbal prompts, 56–57
Voice-output communication aids
    in augmentative and alternative communication (AAC) intervention programs, 363
Volume in verbal prompts, 56–57

W

Wait-and-signal in communication, 350
Wall pushes in facilitating sensory integration, 263
Wall push-ups in facilitating sensory integration, 159
Wants
    in intervention strategies, 62–63
    obtaining, 32–33
Weight-bearing activities
    co-activation for, 320, 321–23
    in facilitating sensory integration, 159–60, 269
Weighted vests in facilitating sensory integration, 161–62, 195
Wilbarger protocol, 146, 162
Williams syndrome, 6
Wing, Lorna, 3
Wrist, inability to co-activate for weight bearing, 322
Wrist stability, 329
Written cues, teaching, 351